The World's Classics

478

THE PLAYS OF
CHRISTOPHER MARLOWE

Oxford University Press, Amen House, London E.C.4

GLASGOW NEW YORK TORONTO MELBOURNE WELLINGTON
BOMBAY CALCUTTA MADRAS CAPE TOWN

Geoffrey Cumberlege, Publisher to the University

THE PLAYS OF
CHRISTOPHER
MARLOWE

Geoffrey Cumberlege
OXFORD UNIVERSITY PRESS
London New York Toronto

CHRISTOPHER MARLOWE

Born, Canterbury   ·   ·   ·   ·   1564
Died, Deptford   ·   ·   ·   ·   1593

The Plays were first published in The World's Classics *in 1939 and reprinted in 1946 and 1950.*

PRINTED IN GREAT BRITAIN

CONTENTS

CONTENTS

Tamburlaine

the Great.

Who, from a Scythian Shephearde,
by his rare and woonderfull Conquests,
became a most puissant and migh-
tye Monarque.

And (for his tyranny, and terrour in
Warre)was tearmed,

The Scourge of God.

Deuided into two Tragicall Dis-
courses, as they were sundrie times
shewed vpon Stages in the Citie
of London.

By the right honorable the Lord
Admyrall, his seruantes.

Benj Ayl̄o

Now first, and newlie published.

LONDON.

Printed by Richard Ihones: at the signe
of the Rose and Crowne neere Hol-
borne Bridge. 1590.

The Prologue

FROM jigging veins of rhyming mother-wits,
And such conceits as clownage keeps in pay,
We'll lead you to the stately tent of war,
Where you shall hear the Scythian Tamburlaine
Threatening the world with high astounding terms,
And scourging kingdoms with his conquering sword.
View but his picture in this tragic glass,
And then applaud his fortunes as you please.

Dramatis Personæ

Mycetes, *King of Persia.*

Cosroe, *his brother.*

Meander,
Theridamas,
Ortygius, } *Persian lords.*
Ceneus,
Menaphon,

Tamburlaine, *a Scythian shepherd.*

Techelles,
Usumcasane, } *his followers.*

Bajazeth, *Emperor of the Turks.*

King of Fez.

King of Morocco.

King of Argier.

King of Arabia.

Soldan of Egypt.

Governor of Damascus.

Agydas,
Magnetes, } *Median lords.*

Capolin, *an Egyptian.*

Philemus, Bassoes, Lords, Citizens, Moors, Soldiers, and Attendants.

Zenocrate, *daughter to the Soldan of Egypt.*

Anippe, *her maid.*

Zabina, *wife to* Bajazeth.

Ebea, *her maid.*

Virgins of Damascus.

The Two Tragical Discourses of Mighty Tamburlaine, the Scythian Shepherd.

The First Part of

TAMBURLAINE THE GREAT

Act I. Scene I.

Enter Mycetes, Cosroe, Meander, Theridamas, Ortygius, Ceneus, Menaphon, *with others.*

Myc. Brother Cosroe, I find myself agriev'd,
Yet insufficient to express the same,
For it requires a great and thundering speech:
Good brother, tell the cause unto my lords;
I know you have a better wit than I.
  Cos. Unhappy Persia, that in former age
Hast been the seat of mighty conquerors,
That, in their prowess and their policies,
Have triumph'd over Afric, and the bounds
Of Europe, where the sun dares scarce appear   10
For freezing meteors and congealed cold,
Now to be rul'd and govern'd by a man
At whose birthday Cynthia with Saturn join'd,
And Jove, the Sun, and Mercury denied
To shed their influence in his fickle brain!
Now Turks and Tartars shake their swords at thee,
Meaning to mangle all thy provinces.
  Myc. Brother, I see your meaning well enough;
And through your planets I perceive you think
I am not wise enough to be a king: 20
But I refer me to my noblemen,

That know my wit, and can be witnesses.
I might command you to be slain for this:
Meander, might I not?
   Mean. Not for so small a fault, my sovereign lord.
   Myc. I mean it not, but yet I know I might;
Yet live; yea, live; Mycetes wills it so.
Meander, thou, my faithful counsellor,
Declare the cause of my conceived grief,
Which is (God knows) about that Tamburlaine   30
That, like a fox in midst of harvest-time,
Doth prey upon my flocks of passengers;
And, as I hear, doth mean to pull my plumes:
Therefore 'tis good and meet for to be wise.
   Mean. Oft have I heard your majesty complain
Of Tamburlaine, that sturdy Scythian thief,
That robs your merchants of Persepolis
Trading by land unto the Western Isles,
And in your confines with his lawless train
Daily commits incivil outrages,   40
Hoping (misled by dreaming prophecies)
To reign in Asia, and with barbarous arms
To make himself the monarch of the East:
But, ere he march in Asia, or display
His vagrant ensign in the Persian fields,
Your grace hath taken order by Theridamas,
Charg'd with a thousand horse, to apprehend
And bring him captive to your highness' throne.
   Myc. Full true thou speak'st, and like thyself, my
      lord,
Whom I may term a Damon for thy love: 50
Therefore 'tis best, if so it like you all,
To send my thousand horse incontinent
To apprehend that paltry Scythian.
How like you this, my honourable lords?
Is it not a kingly resolution?
   Cos. It cannot choose, because it comes from you.
   Myc. Then hear thy charge, valiant Theridamas,

32 passengers] travellers   52 incontinent] at once

The chiefest captain of Mycetes' host,
The hope of Persia, and the very legs
Whereon our state doth lean, as on a staff   60
That holds us up and foils our neighbour foes:
Thou shalt be leader of this thousand horse,
Whose foaming gall with rage and high disdain
Have sworn the death of wicked Tamburlaine.
Go frowning forth; but come thou smiling home,
As did Sir Paris with the Grecian dame:
Return with speed, time passeth swift away;
Our life is frail, and we may die to-day.
     Ther. Before the moon renew her borrowed light,
Doubt not, my lord and gracious sovereign,   70
But Tamburlaine and that Tartarian rout
Shall either perish by our warlike hands
Or plead for mercy at your highness' feet.
     Myc. Go, stout Theridamas; thy words are swords,
And with thy looks thou conquerest all thy foes.
I long to see thee back return from thence,
That I may view these milk-white steeds of mine
All loaden with the heads of killed men,
And, from their knees even to their hoofs below,
Besmear'd with blood that makes a dainty show.   80
     Ther. Then now, my lord, I humbly take my leave.
     Myc. Theridamas,—farewell ten thousand times.
                              [*Exit Theridamas.*
Ah, Menaphon, why stay'st thou thus behind,
When other men press forward for renown?
Go, Menaphon, go into Scythia,
And foot by foot follow Theridamas.
     Cos. Nay, pray you, let him stay; a greater [task]
Fits Menaphon than warring with a thief:
Create him pro-rex of Africa,
That he may win the Babylonians' hearts,   90
Which will revolt from Persian government,
Unless they have a wiser king than you.
     Myc. Unless they have a wiser king than you!
These are his words; Meander, set them down.

Cos. And add this to them,—that all Asia
Lament to see the folly of their king.
    Myc. Well, here I swear by this my royal seat—
    Cos. You may do well to kiss it, then.
    Myc. Emboss'd with silk as best beseems my state,   100
To be reveng'd for these contemptuous words.
O where is duty and allegiance now?
Fled to the Caspian or the Ocean main?
What, shall I call thee brother? no, a foe,
Monster of nature, shame unto thy stock,
That dar'st presume thy sovereign for to mock!
Meander, come: I am abus'd, Meander.
                [*Exeunt all except Cosroe and Menaphon.*
    Men. How now, my lord! what, mated and amaz'd
To hear the king thus threaten like himself?
    Cos. Ah, Menaphon, I pass not for his threats;   110
The plot is laid by Persian noblemen
And captains of the Median garrisons
To crown me emperor of Asia:
But this it is that doth excruciate
The very substance of my vexed soul,
To see our neighbours, that were wont to quake
And tremble at the Persian monarch's name,
Now sits and laughs our regiment to scorn;
And, that which might resolve me into tears,
Men from the farthest equinoctial line
Have swarm'd in troops into the Eastern India,   120
Lading their ships with gold and precious stones,
And made their spoils from all our provinces.
    Men. This should entreat your highness to rejoice,
Since Fortune gives you opportunity
To gain the title of a conqueror
By curing of this maimed empery.
Afric and Europe bordering on your land,
And continent to your dominions,
How easily may you, with a mighty host,

107 mated] confounded   109 pass not] care not
                117 regiment] rule

Pass into Græcia, as did Cyrus once,   130
And cause them to withdraw their forces home,
Lest you subdue the pride of Christendom!

                             [Trumpet within.

    Cos. But, Menaphon, what means this trumpet's
      sound?
    Men. Behold, my lord, Ortygius and the rest
Bringing the crown to make you emperor!

Re-enter Ortygius *and* Ceneus, *with others, bearing a
crown.*

    Orty. Magnificent and mighty prince Cosroe,
We, in the name of other Persian states
And commons of this mighty monarchy,
Present thee with th' imperial diadem.
    Cen. The warlike soldiers and the gentlemen,   140
That heretofore have fill'd Persepolis
With Afric captains taken in the field,
Whose ransom made them march in coats of gold,
With costly jewels hanging at their ears,
And shining stones upon their lofty crests,
Now living idle in the walled towns,
Wanting both pay and martial discipline,
Begin in troops to threaten civil war,
And openly exclaim against the king:
Therefore, to stay all sudden mutinies,   150
We will invest your highness emperor;
Whereat the soldiers will conceive more joy
Than did the Macedonians at the spoil
Of great Darius and his wealthy host.
    Cos. Well, since I see the state of Persia droop
And languish in my brother's government,
I willingly receive th' imperial crown,
And vow to wear it for my country's good,
In spite of them shall malice my estate.
    Orty. And, in assurance of desir'd success,   160
We here do crown thee monarch of the East,
Emperor of Asia and of Persia,

Great lord of Media and Armenia,
Duke of Africa and Albania,
Mesopotamia and of Parthia,
East India and the late-discovered isles,
Chief lord of all the wide vast Euxine Sea,
And of the ever-raging Caspian Lake.
Long live Cosroe, mighty emperor!

    Cos. And Jove may never let me longer live   170
Than I may seek to gratify your love,
And cause the soldiers that thus honour me
To triumph over many provinces!
By whose desires of discipline in arms
I doubt not shortly but to reign sole king,
And with the army of Theridamas
(Whither we presently will fly, my lords,)
To rest secure against my brother's force.

    Orty. We knew, my lord, before we brought the crown,
Intending your investion so near   180
The residence of your despised brother,
The lords would not be too exasperate
To injure or suppress your worthy title;
Or, if they would, there are in readiness
Ten thousand horse to carry you from hence,
In spite of all suspected enemies.

    Cos. I know it well, my lord, and thank you all.

    Orty. Sound up the trumpets, then. God save the king!   [*Trumpets sounded.*
                                             [*Exeunt.*

Scene II.

Enter Tamburlaine *leading* Zenocrate; Techelles, Usumcasane, Agydas, Magnetes, Lords, *and* Soldiers *loaden with treasure.*

    Tamb. Come, lady, let not this appal your thoughts;
The jewels and the treasure we have ta'en
Shall be reserv'd, and you in better state

Than if you were arriv'd in Syria,
Even in the circle of your father's arms,
The mighty Soldan of Egyptia.

   Zeno. Ah, shepherd, pity my distressed plight,
(If, as thou seem'st, thou art so mean a man,)
And seek not to enrich thy followers
By lawless rapine from a silly maid,   10
Who, travelling with these Median lords
To Memphis, from my uncle's country of Media,
Where all my youth I have been governed,
Have pass'd the army of the mighty Turk,
Bearing his privy signet and his hand
To safe conduct us thorough Africa.

   Mag. And, since we have arrived in Scythia,
Besides rich presents from the puissant Cham,
We have his highness' letters to command
Aid and assistance, if we stand in need.   20

   Tamb. But now you see these letters and commands
Are countermanded by a greater man;
And through my provinces you must expect
Letters of conduct from my mightiness,
If you intend to keep your treasure safe.
But, since I love to live at liberty
As easily may you get the Soldan's crown
As any prizes out of my precinct;
For they are friends that help to wean my state
Till men and kingdoms help to strengthen it,   30
And must maintain my life exempt from servitude—
But, tell me, madam, is your grace betroth'd?

   Zeno. I am, my lord,—for so you do import.

   Tamb. I am a lord, for so my deeds shall prove;
And yet a shepherd by my parentage.
But, lady, this fair face and heavenly hue
Must grace his bed that conquers Asia,
And means to be a terror to the world,
Measuring the limits of his empery
By east and west, as Phœbus doth his course.   40
Lie here, ye weeds, that I disdain to wear!

This complete armour and this curtle-axe
Are adjuncts more beseeming Tamburlaine.
And, madam, whatsoever you esteem
Of this success, and loss unvalued,
Both may invest you empress of the East;
And these that seem but silly country swains
May have the leading of so great an host
As with their weight shall make the mountains quake,
Even as when windy exhalations,   50
Fighting for passage, tilt within the earth.

    Tech. As princely lions, when they rouse themselves,
Stretching their paws, and threatening herds of beasts,
So in his armour looketh Tamburlaine.
Methinks I see kings kneeling at his feet,
And he with frowning brows and fiery looks
Spurning their crowns from off their captive heads.

    Usum. And making thee and me, Techelles, kings,
That even to death will follow Tamburlaine.

    Tamb. Nobly resolv'd, sweet friends and followers!
These noble lords perhaps do scorn our estimates,   61
And think we prattle with distemper'd spirits:
But, since they measure our deserts so mean,
That in conceit bear empires on our spears,
Affecting thoughts coequal with the clouds,
They shall be kept our forced followers
Till with their eyes they view us emperors.

    Zeno. The gods, defenders of the innocent,
Will never prosper your intended drifts,
That thus oppress poor friendless passengers.   70
Therefore at least admit us liberty,
Even as thou hops't to be eternized
By living Asia's mighty emperor.

    Agyd. I hope our lady's treasure and our own
May serve for ransom to our liberties:
Return our mules and empty camels back,
That we may travel into Syria,
Where her betrothed lord, Alcidamus,
Expects th' arrival of her highness' person.

Mag. And wheresoever we repose ourselves,   80
We will report but well of Tamburlaine.

Tamb. Disdains Zenocrate to live with me?
Or you, my lords, to be my followers?
Think you I weigh this treasure more than you?
Not all the gold in India's wealthy arms
Shall buy the meanest soldier in my train.
Zenocrate, lovelier than the love of Jove,
Brighter than is the silver Rhodope,
Fairer than whitest snow on Scythian hills,
Thy person is more worth to Tamburlaine   90
Than the possession of the Persian crown,
Which gracious stars have promis'd at my birth.
A hundred Tartars shall attend on thee,
Mounted on steeds swifter than Pegasus;
Thy garments shall be made of Median silk,
Enchas'd with precious jewels of mine own,
More rich and valurous than Zenocrate's;
With milk-white harts upon an ivory sled
Thou shalt be drawn amidst the frozen pools,
And scale the icy mountains' lofty tops,   100
Which with thy beauty will be soon resolv'd:
My martial prizes, with five hundred men
Won on the fifty-headed Volga's waves,
Shall all we offer to Zenocrate,
And then myself to fair Zenocrate.

Tech. What now! in love?

Tamb. Techelles, women must be flattered:
But this is she with whom I am in love.

Enter a Soldier.

Sold. News, news!

Tamb. How now, what's the matter?   110

Sold. A thousand Persian horsemen are at hand,
Sent from the king to overcome us all.

Tamb. How now, my lords of Egypt and Zenocrate!
Now must your jewels be restor'd again,

97 valurous] valuable

And I, that triumph'd so, be overcome?
How say you, lordings? is not this your hope?

Agyd. We hope yourself will willingly restore them.

Tamb. Such hope, such fortune, have the thousand
Soft ye, my lords, and sweet Zenocrate!   [horse.
You must be forced from me ere you go.   120
A thousand horsemen? we five hundred foot?
An odds too great for us to stand against.
But are they rich? and is their armour good?

Sold. Their plumed helms are wrought with beaten
        gold,
Their swords enamell'd, and about their necks
Hangs massy chains of gold down to the waist;
In every part exceeding brave and rich.

Tamb. Then shall we fight courageously with them?
Or look you I should play the orator?

Tech. No; cowards and faint-hearted runaways 130
Look for orations when the foe is near:
Our swords shall play the orators for us.

Usum. Come, let us meet them at the mountain foot,
And with a sudden and an hot alarm
Drive all their horses headlong down the hill.

Tech. Come, let us march.

Tamb. Stay, Techelles; ask a parley first.

The Soldiers *enter.*

Open the mails, yet guard the treasure sure:
Lay out our golden wedges to the view,
That their reflections may amaze the Persians; 140
And look we friendly on them when they come:
But, if they offer word or violence,
We'll fight, five hundred men-at-arms to one,
Before we part with our possession;
And 'gainst the general we will lift our swords,
And either lance his greedy thirsting throat,
Or take him prisoner, and his chain shall serve
For manacles till he be ransom'd home.

138 mails] trunks

    Tech. I hear them come: shall we encounter them?

    Tamb. Keep all your standings, and not stir a
       foot:

Myself will bide the danger of the brunt.   151

         Enter Theridamas, *with others.*

    Ther. Where is this Scythian Tamburlaine?

    Tamb. Whom seek'st thou, Persian? I am Tambur-
       laine.

    Ther. Tamburlaine? A Scythian shepherd so em-
       bellished

With nature's pride, and richest furniture!

His looks do menace heaven and dare the gods;

His fiery eyes are fix'd upon the earth,

As if he now devis'd some stratagem,

Or meant to pierce Avernus' darksome vaults

To pull the triple-headed dog from hell.   160

    Tamb. Noble and mild this Persian seems to be,

If outward habit judge the inward man.

    Tech. His deep affections make him passionate.

    Tamb. With what a majesty he rears his looks!—

In thee, thou valiant man of Persia,

I see the folly of thy emperor.

Art thou but captain of a thousand horse,

That by characters graven in thy brows,

And by thy martial face and stout aspect,

Deserv'st to have the leading of an host?   170

Forsake thy king, and do but join with me,

And we will triumph over all the world:

I hold the Fates bound fast in iron chains,

And with my hand turn Fortune's wheel about;

And sooner shall the sun fall from his sphere

Than Tamburlaine be slain or overcome.

Draw forth thy sword thou mighty man-at-arms,

Intending but to raze my charmed skin,

And Jove himself will stretch his hand from heaven

To ward the blow, and shield me safe from harm. 180

See, how he rains down heaps of gold in showers,

As if he meant to give my soldiers pay!
And, as a sure and grounded argument
That I shall be the monarch of the East,
He sends this Soldan's daughter, rich and brave,
To be my queen and portly emperess.
If thou wilt stay with me, renowned man,
And lead thy thousand horse with my conduct,
Besides thy share of this Egyptian prize,
Those thousand horse shall sweat with martial spoil 190
Of conquer'd kingdoms and of cities sack'd:
Both we will walk upon the lofty clifts,
And Christian merchants, that with Russian stems
Plough up huge furrows in the Caspian Sea,
Shall vail to us as lords of all the lake;
Both we will reign as consuls of the earth,
And mighty kings shall be our senators.
Jove sometime masked in a shepherd's weed;
And by those steps that he hath scal'd the heavens
May we become immortal like the gods.   200
Join with me now in this my mean estate,
(I call it mean, because, being yet obscure,
The nations far-remov'd admire me not,)
And when my name and honour shall be spread
As far as Boreas claps his brazen wings,
Or fair Boötes sends his cheerful light,
Then shalt thou be competitor with me,
And sit with Tamburlaine in all his majesty.
    Ther. Not Hermes, prolocutor to the gods,
Could use persuasions more pathetical.   210
    Tamb. Nor are Apollo's oracles more true
Than thou shalt find my vaunts substantial.
    Tech. We are his friends; and if the Persian king
Should offer present dukedoms to our state,
We think it loss to make exchange for that
We are assur'd of by our friend's success.
    Usum. And kingdoms at the least we all expect,

195 vail] lower their flags   207 competitor] associate
210 pathetical] stirring

Besides the honour in assured conquests,
Where kings shall crouch unto our conquering swords,
And hosts of soldiers stand amaz'd at us, 220
When with their fearful tongues they shall confess
These are the men that all the world admires.

Ther. What strong enchantments 'tice my yielding soul!
Ah, these resolved noble Scythians!
But shall I prove a traitor to my king?

Tamb. No, but the trusty friend of Tamburlaine.

Ther. Won with thy words, and conquer'd with thy
I yield myself, my men, and horse to thee,   [looks,
To be partaker of thy good or ill,
As long as life maintains Theridamas.   230

Tamb. Theridamas, my friend, take here my hand,
Which is as much as if I swore by heaven,
And call'd the gods to witness of my vow.
Thus shall my heart be still combin'd with thine
Until our bodies turn to elements,
And both our souls aspire celestial thrones.
Techelles and Casane, welcome him.

Tech. Welcome, renowned Persian, to us all!

Usum. Long may Theridamas remain with us!

Tamb. These are my friends, in whom I more rejoice
Than doth the king of Persia in his crown;   241
And, by the love of Pylades and Orestes,
Whose statues we adore in Scythia,
Thyself and them shall never part from me
Before I crown you kings in Asia.
Make much of them, gentle Theridamas,
And they will never leave thee till the death.

Ther. Nor thee, nor them, thrice noble Tamburlaine,
Shall want my heart to be with gladness pierc'd,
To do you honour and security.   250

Tamb. A thousand thanks, worthy Theridamas.
And now, fair madam, and my noble lords,
If you will willingly remain with me,
You shall have honours as your merits be;
Or else you shall be forc'd with slavery.

Agyd. We yield unto thee, happy Tamburlaine.
Tamb. For you, then, madam, I am out of doubt.
Zeno. I must be pleas'd perforce,—wretched Zeno-
    crate!   [*Exeunt.*

Act II.   Scene I.

Enter Cosroe, Menaphon, Ortygius, *and* Ceneus, *with*
Soldiers.

Cos. Thus far are we towards Theridamas,
And valiant Tamburlaine, the man of fame,
The man that in the forehead of his fortune
Bears figures of renown and miracle.
But tell me, that hast seen him, Menaphon,
What stature wields he, and what personage?
Men. Of stature tall, and straightly fashioned
Like his desire, lift upwards and divine;
So large of limbs, his joints so strongly knit,
Such breadth of shoulders as might mainly bear   10
Old Atlas' burthen; 'twixt his manly pitch,
A pearl more worth than all the world is plac'd,
Wherein by curious sovereignty of art
Are fix'd his piercing instruments of sight,
Whose fiery circles bear encompassed
A heaven of heavenly bodies in their spheres,
That guides his steps and actions to the throne
Where honour sits invested royally;
Pale of complexion, wrought in him with passion,
Thirsting with sovereignty, with love of arms;   20
His lofty brows in folds do figure death,
And in their smoothness amity and life;
About them hangs a knot of amber hair,
Wrapped in curls, as fierce Achilles' was,
On which the breath of heaven delights to play
Making it dance with wanton majesty;
His arms and fingers long and sinewy,

11 pitch] shoulders

Betokening valour and excess of strength:
In every part proportioned like the man
Should make the world subdu'd to Tamburlaine. 30
   Cos. Well hast thou portray'd in thy terms of life
The face and personage of a wondrous man:
Nature doth strive with Fortune and his stars
To make him famous in accomplish'd worth;
And well his merits shew him to be made
His fortune's master and the king of men,
That could persuade, at such a sudden pinch,
With reasons of his valour and his life,
A thousand sworn and overmatching foes.
Then, when our powers in points of swords are join'd,
And clos'd in compass of the killing bullet,   [40
Though strait the passage and the port be made
That leads to palace of my brother's life,
Proud is his fortune if we pierce it not;
And, when the princely Persian diadem
Shall overweigh his weary witless head,
And fall, like mellow'd fruit, with shakes of death
In fair Persia noble Tamburlaine
Shall be my regent, and remain as king.
   Orty. In happy hower we have set the crown   50
Upon your kingly head, that seeks our honour
In joining with the man ordain'd by heaven
To further every action to the best.
   Cen. He that with shepherds and a little spoil
Durst, in disdain of wrong and tyranny,
Defend his freedom 'gainst a monarchy,
What will he do supported by a king,
Leading a troop of gentlemen and lords,
And stuff'd with treasure for his highest thoughts!
   Cos. And such shall wait on worthy Tamburlaine. 60
Our army will be forty thousand strong,
When Tamburlaine and brave Theridamas
Have met us by the river Araris;
And all conjoin'd to meet the witless king,

   42 port] gate   50 hower] hour

That now is marching near to Parthia,
And, with unwilling soldiers faintly arm'd,
To seek revenge on me and Tamburlaine;
To whom, sweet Menaphon, direct me straight.

 Men. I will, my lord.   [*Exeunt.*

Scene II.

Enter Mycetes, Meander, *with other* Lords; *and* Soldiers.

 Myc. Come, my Meander, let us to this gear.
I tell you true, my heart is swoln with wrath
On this same thievish villain Tamburlaine,
And of that false Cosroe, my traitorous brother.
Would it not grieve a king to be so abus'd,
And have a thousand horsemen ta'en away?
And, which is worst, to have his diadem
Sought for by such scald knaves as love him not?
I think it would: well then, by heavens I swear,
Aurora shall not peep out of her doors,   10
But I will have Cosroe by the head,
And kill proud Tamburlaine with point of sword.
Tell you the rest, Meander: I have said.

 Mean. Then, having pass'd Armenian deserts now,
And pitch'd our tents under the Georgian hills,
Whose tops are covered with Tartarian thieves,
That lie in ambush, waiting for a prey,
What should we do but bid them battle straight,
And rid the world of those detested troops?
Lest, if we let them linger here a while,   20
They gather strength by power of fresh supplies.
This country swarms with vile outragious men
That live by rapine and by lawless spoil,
Fit soldiers for the wicked Tamburlaine:
And he that could with gifts and promises
Inveigle him that led a thousand horse,
And make him false his faith unto his king,
Will quickly win such as are like himself.

       8 scald] scurvy

Therefore cheer up your minds; prepare to fight:
He that can take or slaughter Tamburlaine,   30
Shall rule the province of Albania;
Who brings that traitor's head, Theridamas,
Shall have a government in Media,
Beside the spoil of him and all his train:
But, if Cosroe (as our spials say,
And as we know) remains with Tamburlaine,
His highness' pleasure is that he should live,
And be reclaim'd with princely lenity.

Enter a Spy.

  Spy. An hundred horsemen of my company,
Scouting abroad upon these champion plains,   40
Have view'd the army of the Scythians;
Which make reports it far exceeds the king's.
  Mean. Suppose they be in number infinite,
Yet being void of martial discipline,
All running headlong, after greedy spoils,
And more regarding gain than victory,
Like to the cruel brothers of the earth,
Sprung of the teeth of dragons venomous,
Their careless swords shall lance their fellows' throats
And make us triumph in their overthrow.   50
  Myc. Was there such brethren, sweet Meander, say,
That sprung of teeth of dragons venomous?
  Mean. So poets say, my lord.
  Myc. And 'tis a pretty toy to be a poet.
Well, well, Meander, thou art deeply read;
And having thee, I have a jewel sure.
Go on, my lord, and give your charge, I say;
Thy wit will make us conquerors to-day.
  Mean. Then, noble soldiers, to entrap these thieves
That live confounded in disorder'd troops,   60
If wealth or riches may prevail with them,
We have our camels laden all with gold,
Which you that be but common soldiers

  35 spials] spies   **40** champion] champaign

Shall fling in every corner of the field;
And, while the base-born Tartars take it up,
You, fighting more for honour than for gold,
Shall massacre those greedy-minded slaves;
And, when their scatter'd army is subdu'd,
And you march on their slaughter'd carcasses,
Share equally the gold that bought their lives,   70
And live like gentlemen in Persia.
Strike up the drum, and march courageously:
Fortune herself doth sit upon our crests.

Myc. He tells you true, my masters; so he does.—
Drums, why sound ye not when Meander speaks?

                     [Exeunt, drums sounding.

Scene III.

Enter Cosroe, Tamburlaine, Theridamas, Techelles,
    Usumcasane, *and* Ortygius, *with others.*

  Cos. Now, worthy Tamburlaine, have I repos'd
In thy approved fortunes all my hope.
What think'st thou, man, shall come of our attempts?
For, even as from assured oracle,
I take thy doom for satisfaction.

  Tamb. And so mistake you not a whit, my lord;
For fates and oracles [of] heaven have sworn
To royalise the deeds of Tamburlaine,
And make them blest that share in his attempts.
And doubt you not but, if you favour me,   10
And let my fortunes and my valour sway
To some direction in your martial deeds,
The world will strive with hosts of men-at-arms
To swarm unto the ensign I support.
The host of Xerxes, which by fame is said
To drink the mighty Parthian Araris,
Was but a handful to that we will have:
Our quivering lances, shaking in the air,
And bullets, like Jove's dreadful thunderbolts,
Enroll'd in flames and fiery smouldering mists,   20

Shall threat the gods more than Cyclopian wars;
And with our sun-bright armour, as we march,
We'll chase the stars from heaven, and dim their eyes
That stand and muse at our admired arms.

 Ther. You see, my lord, what working words he
  hath;
But, when you see his actions top his speech,
Your speech will stay, or so extol his worth
As I shall be commended and excus'd
For turning my poor charge to his direction:
And these his two renowned friends, my lord, 30
Would make one thrust and strive to be retain'd
In such a great degree of amity.

 Tech. With duty and with amity we yield
Our utmost service to the fair Cosroe.

 Cos. Which I esteem as portion of my crown.
Usumcasane and Techelles both,
When she that rules in Rhamnus' golden gates,
And makes a passage for all prosperous arms,
Shall make me solely emperor of Asia,
Then shall your meeds and valours be advanc'd 40
To rooms of honour and nobility.

 Tamb. Then haste, Cosroe, to be king alone,
That I with these my friends and all my men
May triumph in our long-expected fate.
The king your brother is now hard at hand:
Meet with the fool, and rid your royal shoulders
Of such a burthen as outweighs the sands
And all the craggy rocks of Caspia.

Enter a Messenger.

 Mes. My lord, we have discovered the enemy
Ready to charge you with a mighty army. 50

 Cos. Come, Tamburlaine, now whet thy winged
  sword,
And lift thy lofty arm into the clouds,
That it may reach the king of Persia's crown,

<hr>

37 Rhamnus] Nemesis

And set it safe on my victorious head.

   Tamb. See where it is, the keenest curtle-axe
That e'er made passage thorough Persian arms!
These are the wings shall make it fly as swift
As doth the lightning or the breath of heaven,
And kill as sure as it swiftly flies.

   Cos. Thy words assure me of kind success: 60
Go, valiant soldier, go before, and charge
The fainting army of that foolish king.

   Tamb. Usumcasane and Techelles, come:
We are enough to scare the enemy,
And more than needs to make an emperor.

                  [*Exeunt to the battle.*

Scene IV.

Enter Mycetes, *with his crown in his hand, trying to hide it.*

   Myc. Accurs'd be he that first invented war!
They knew not, ah, they knew not, simple men,
How those were hit by pelting cannon-shot
Stand staggering like a quivering aspen-leaf,
Fearing the force of Boreas' boisterous blasts.
In what a lamentable case were I,
If nature had not given me wisdom's lore!
For kings are clouts that every man shoots at,
Our crown the pin that thousands seek to cleave:
Therefore in policy I think it good   10
To hide it close; a goodly stratagem,
And far from any man that is a fool:
So shall not I be known; or if I be,
They cannot take away my crown from me.
Here will I hide it in this simple hole.

          Enter Tamburlaine.

   Tamb. What, fearful coward! straggling from the
     camp,
When kings themselves are present in the field?

   Myc. Thou liest.

Tamb. Base villain, dar'st thou give the lie?

Myc. Away, I am the king; go, touch me not. 20
Thou break'st the law of arms, unless thou kneel,
And cry me 'mercy, noble king!'

Tamb. Are you the witty king of Persia?

Myc. Ay, marry, am I: have you any suit to me?

Tamb. I would entreat you to speak but three wise
words.

Myc. So I can when I see my time.

Tamb. Is this your crown?

Myc. Ay: didst thou ever see a fairer?

Tamb. You will not sell it, will ye?

Myc. Such another word, and I will have thee exe-
cuted. Come, give it me. 30

Tamb. No; I took it prisoner.

Myc. You lie; I gave it you.

Tamb. Then 'tis mine.

Myc. No; I mean I let you keep it.

Tamb. Well, I mean you shall have it again.
Here, take it for a while: I lend it thee,
Till I may see thee hemm'd with armed men;
Then shalt thou see me pull it from thy head:
Thou art no match for mighty Tamburlaine.   [*Exit.*

Myc. O gods, is this Tamburlaine the thief? 40
I marvel much he stole it not away.
[*Trumpets within sound to the battle*: *he runs out.*

Scene V.

Enter Cosroe, Tamburlaine, Menaphon, Meander,
Ortygius, Theridamas, Techelles, Usumcasane, *with
others.*

Tamb. Hold thee, Cosroe; wear two imperial
crowns;
Think thee invested now as royally,
Even by the mighty hand of Tamburlaine,
As if as many kings as could encompass thee
With greatest pomp had crown'd thee emperor.

Cos. So do I, thrice-renowned man-at-arms;
And none shall keep the crown but Tamburlaine:
Thee do I make my regent of Persia,
And general lieutenant of my armies.
Meander, you that were our brother's guide,   10
And chiefest counsellor in all his acts,
Since he is yielded to the stroke of war,
On your submission we with thanks excuse,
And give you equal place in our affairs.

Mean. Most happy emperor, in humblest terms
I vow my service to your majesty,
With utmost virtue of my faith and duty.

Cos. Thanks, good Meander. Then, Cosroe, reign,
And govern Persia in her former pomp.
Now send embassage to thy neighbour kings,   20
And let them know the Persian king is chang'd,
From one that knew not what a king should do,
To one that can command what 'longs thereto.
And now we will to fair Persepolis
With twenty thousand expert soldiers.
The lords and captains of my brother's camp
With little slaughter take Meander's course,
And gladly yield them to my gracious rule.
Ortygius and Menaphon, my trusty friends,
Now will I gratify your former good,   30
And grace your calling with a greater sway.

Orty. And as we ever aim'd at your behoof,
And sought your state all honour it deserv'd,
So will we with our powers and our lives
Endeavour to preserve and prosper it.

Cos. I will not thank thee, sweet Ortygius;
Better replies shall prove my purposes.
And now, Lord Tamburlaine, my brother's camp
I leave to thee and to Theridamas,
To follow me to fair Persepolis;   40
Then will we march to all those Indian mines
My witless brother to the Christians lost,
And ransom them with fame and usury;

And, till thou overtake me, Tamburlaine,
(Staying to order all the scatter'd troops,)
Farewell, lord regent and his happy friends.
I long to sit upon my brother's throne.

Mean. Your majesty shall shortly have your wish,
And ride in triumph through Persepolis.

[*Exeunt all except* Tamb., Ther., Tech., *and* Usum.

Tamb. And ride in triumph through Persepolis? 50
Is it not brave to be a king, Techelles?
Usumcasane and Theridamas,
Is it not passing brave to be a king,
And ride in triumph through Persepolis?

Tech. Oh, my lord, 'tis sweet and full of pomp.

Usum. To be a king, is half to be a god.

Ther. A god is not so glorious as a king:
I think the pleasure they enjoy in heaven
Cannot compare with kingly joys in earth;
To wear a crown enchas'd with pearl and gold, 60
Whose virtues carry with it life and death;
To ask and have, command and be obey'd;
When looks breed love, with looks to gain the prize;
Such power attractive shines in princes' eyes.

Tamb. Why, say, Theridamas, wilt thou be a king?

Ther. Nay, though I praise it, I can live without it.

Tamb. What says my other friends? will you be
kings?

Tech. Ay, if I could, with all my heart, my lord.

Tamb. Why, that 's well said, Techelles; so would I:
And so would you, my masters, would you not? 70

Usum. What then, my lord?

Tamb. Why then, Casane, shall we wish for aught
The world affords in greatest novelty,
And rest attemptless, faint, and destitute?
Methinks we should not. I am strongly mov'd,
That if I should desire the Persian crown,
I could attain it with a wondrous ease:
And would not all our soldiers soon consent,
If we should aim at such a dignity?

Ther. I know they would with our persuasions.   80
Tamb. Why, then, Theridamas, I'll first assay
To get the Persian kingdom to myself;
Then thou for Parthia; they for Scythia and Media;
And, if I prosper, all shall be as sure
As if the Turk, the Pope, Afric, and Greece,
Came creeping to us with their crowns apiece.
Tech. Then shall we send to this triumphing king,
And bid him battle for his novel crown?
Usum. Nay, quickly then, before his room be hot.
Tamb. 'Twill prove a pretty jest, in faith, my
  friends.   90
Ther. A jest to charge on twenty thousand men?
I judge the purchase more important far.
Tamb. Judge by thyself, Theridamas, not me;
For presently Techelles here shall haste
To bid him battle ere he pass too far,
And lose more labour than the gain will 'quite:
Then shalt thou see the Scythian Tamburlaine
Make but a jest to win the Persian crown.
Techelles, take a thousand horse with thee,
And bid him turn his back to war with us,   100
That only made him king to make us sport:
We will not steal upon him cowardly,
But give him warning and more warriors.
Haste thee, Techelles; we will follow thee.
                              [*Exit* Techelles.
What saith Theridamas?
Ther. Go on, for me.   [*Exeunt.*

Scene VI

Enter Cosroe, Meander, Ortygius, *and* Menaphon,
              with Soldiers.

Cos. What means this devilish shepherd, to aspire
With such a giantly presumption,
To cast up hills against the face of heaven,

92 purchase] plunder   96 quite] requite

And dare the force of angry Jupiter?
But as he thrust them underneath the hills,
And press'd out fire from their burning jaws,
So will I send this monstrous slave to hell,
Where flames shall ever feed upon his soul.

   Mean. Some powers divine, or else infernal, mix'd
Their angry seeds at his conception;   10
For he was never sprung of human race,
Since with the spirit of his fearful pride,
He dares so doubtlessly resolve of rule,
And by profession be ambitious.

   Orty. What god, or fiend, or spirit of the earth,
Or monster turned to a manly shape,
Or of what mould or mettle he be made,
What star or state soever govern him,
Let us put on our meet encountering minds;
And in detesting such a devilish thief,   20
In love of honour and defence of right,
Be arm'd against the hate of such a foe,
Whether from earth, or hell, or heaven he grow.

   Cos. Nobly resolv'd, my good Ortygius;
And since we all have suck'd one wholesome air,
And with the same proportion of elements
Resolve, I hope we are resembled,
Vowing our loves to equal death and life.
Let 's cheer our soldiers to encounter him,
That grievous image of ingratitude,   30
That fiery thirster after sovereignty,
And burn him in the fury of that flame
That none can quench but blood and empery.
Resolve, my lords and loving soldiers, now
To save your king and country from decay.
Then strike up, drum; and all the stars that make
The loathsome circle of my dated life,
Direct my weapon to his barbarous heart,
That thus opposeth him against the gods,
And scorns the powers that govern Persia!   40
                 [Exeunt, drums sounding.

Scene VII.

Enter Soldiers *to the battle, and after the battle enter*
Cosroe *wounded,* Tamburlaine, Theridamas, Techelles,
Usumcasane, *with others.*

Cos. Barbarous and bloody Tamburlaine,
Thus to deprive me of my crown and life!
Treacherous and false Theridamas,
Even at the morning of my happy state,
Scarce being seated in my royal throne,
To work my downfall and untimely end!
An uncouth pain torments my grieved soul
And death arrests the organ of my voice,
Who, entering at the breach thy sword hath made,
Sacks every vein and artier of my heart.—   10
Bloody and insatiate Tamburlaine!
   Tamb. The thirst of reign and sweetness of a crown,
That caus'd the eldest son of heavenly Ops
To thrust his doting father from his chair,
And place himself in the imperial heaven,
Mov'd me to manage arms against thy state.
What better precedent than mighty Jove?
Nature, that fram'd us of four elements
Warring within our breasts for regiment,
Doth teach us all to have aspiring minds: 20
Our souls, whose faculties can comprehend
The wondrous architecture of the world,
And measure every wandering planet's course,
Still climbing after knowledge infinite,
And always moving as the restless spheres,
Will us to wear ourselves, and never rest,
Until we reach the ripest fruit of all,
That perfect bliss and sole felicity,
The sweet fruition of an earthly crown.
   Ther. And that made me to join with Tambur-
     laine;   30
For he is gross and like the massy earth

That moves not upwards, nor by princely deeds
Doth mean to soar above the highest sort.

    Tech. And that made us, the friends of Tambur-
    laine,
To lift our swords against the Persian king.

    Usum. For as, when Jove did thrust old Saturn
    down,
Neptune and Dis gain'd each of them a crown,
So do we hope to reign in Asia,
If Tamburlaine be plac'd in Persia.

    Cos. The strangest men that ever nature made! 40
I know not how to take their tyrannies.
My bloodless body waxeth chill and cold,
And with my blood my life slides through my wound;
My soul begins to take her flight to hell,
And summons all my senses to depart:
The heat and moisture, which did feed each other,
For want of nourishment to feed them both,
Is dry and cold; and now doth ghastly Death
With greedy talents gripe my bleeding heart,
And like a harpy tires on my life.   50
Theridamas and Tamburlaine, I die:
And fearful vengeance light upon you both!

      [*Dies.*—Tamburlaine *takes Cosroe's crown, and
      puts it on his own head.*

    Tamb. Not all the curses which the Furies breathe
Shall make me leave so rich a prize as this.
Theridamas, Techelles, and the rest,
Who think you now is king of Persia?

    All. Tamburlaine! Tamburlaine!

    Tamb. Though Mars himself, the angry god of
    arms,
And all the earthly potentates conspire
To dispossess me of this diadem,   60
Yet will I wear it in despite of them,
As great commander of this eastern world,
If you but say that Tamburlaine shall reign.

          50 tires] preys

All. Long live Tamburlaine, and reign in Asia!
   Tamb. So, now it is more surer on my head
Than if the gods had held a parliament,
And all pronounc'd me king of Persia.   [*Exeunt.*

Act III.   Scene I.

Enter Bajazeth, *the* Kings of Fez, Morocco, *and* Argier,
with others, in great pomp.

   Baj. Great kings of Barbary, and my portly bassoes,
We hear the Tartars and the eastern thieves,
Under the conduct of one Tamburlaine,
Presume a bickering with your emperor,
And thinks to rouse us from our dreadful siege
Of the famous Grecian Constantinople.
You know our army is invincible;
As many circumcised Turks we have,
And warlike bands of Christians renied,
As hath the ocean or the Terrene sea   10
Small drops of water when the moon begins
To join in one her semicircled horns:
Yet would we not be brav'd with foreign power,
Nor raise our siege before the Grecians yield,
Or breathless lie before the city-walls.
   K. of Fez. Renowned emperor and mighty general,
What if you sent the bassoes of your guard
To charge him to remain in Asia,
Or else to threaten death and deadly arms
As from the mouth of mighty Bajazeth?   20
   Baj. Hie thee, my basso, fast to Persia;
Tell him thy lord, the Turkish emperor,
Dread lord of Afric, Europe, and Asia,
Great king and conqueror of Grecia,
The ocean, Terrene, and the Coal-black sea,
The high and highest monarch of the world,

---

  1 bassoes] bashaws or pashas   9 renied] who have denied
their faith.   10 Terrene] Mediterranean

Wills and commands, (for say not I entreat,)
Not once to set his foot in Africa,
Or spread his colours in Grecia,
Lest he incur the fury of my wrath.   30
Tell him I am content to take a truce,
Because I hear he bears a valiant mind:
But if, presuming on his silly power,
He be so mad to manage arms with me,
Then stay thou with him,—say, I bid thee so;
And if, before the sun have measur'd heaven
With triple circuit, thou regreet us not,
We mean to take his morning's next arise
For messenger he will not be reclaim'd,
And mean to fetch thee in despite of him.   40

   Bass. Most great and puissant monarch of the earth,
Your basso will accomplish your behest,
And shew your pleasure to the Persian,
As fits the legate of the stately Turk.   [*Exit.*

   K. of Arg. They say he is the king of Persia;
But, if he dare attempt to stir your siege,
'Twere requisite he should be ten times more,
For all flesh quakes at your magnificence.

   Baj. True, Argier, and tremble at my looks.

   K. of Mor. The spring is hinder'd by your smother-
    ing host;   50
For neither rain can fall upon the earth,
Nor sun reflex his virtuous beams thereon,
The ground is mantled with such multitudes.

   Baj. All this is true as holy Mahomet;
And all the trees are blasted with our breaths.

   K. of Fez. What thinks your greatness best to be
    achiev'd
In pursuit of the city's overthrow?

   Baj. I will the captive pioners of Argier
Cut off the water that by leaden pipes
Runs to the city from the mountain Carnon;   60
Two thousand horse shall forage up and down,

33 silly] empty

C

That no relief or succour come by land,
And all the sea my galleys countermand:
Then shall our footmen lie within the trench,
And with their cannons mouth'd like Orcus' gulf,
Batter the walls, and we will enter in;
And thus the Grecians shall be conquered.   [*Exeunt.*

Scene II.

Enter Zenocrate, Agydas, Anippe, *with others.*

Agyd. Madam Zenocrate, may I presume
To know the cause of these unquiet fits
That work such trouble to your wonted rest?
'Tis more than pity such a heavenly face
Should by heart's sorrow wax so wan and pale,
When your offensive rape by Tamburlaine
(Which of your whole displeasures should be most)
Hath seem'd to be digested long ago.

Zeno. Although it be digested long ago,
As his exceeding favours have deserv'd,   10
And might content the Queen of Heaven as well
As it hath chang'd my first-conceiv'd disdain;
Yet since a farther passion feeds my thoughts
With ceaseless and disconsolate conceits,
Which dyes my looks so lifeless as they are,
And might, if my extremes had full events,
Make me the ghastly counterfeit of death.

Agyd. Eternal heaven sooner be dissolv'd,
And all that pierceth Phœbe's silver eye,
Before such hap fall to Zenocrate!   20

Zeno. Ah, life and soul, still hover in his breast,
And leave my body senseless as the earth,
Or else unite you to his life and soul,
That I may live and die with Tamburlaine!

Enter, behind, Tamburlaine, *with* Techelles, *and others.*

Agyd. With Tamburlaine? Ah, fair Zenocrate,
Let not a man so vile and barbarous,

That holds you from your father in despite,
And keeps you from the honours of a queen,
Being suppos'd his worthless concubine,
Be honour'd with your love, but for necessity.   30
So, now the mighty Soldan hears of you,
Your highness needs not doubt but in short time
He will, with Tamburlaine's destruction,
Redeem you from this deadly servitude.

Zeno. Agydas, leave to wound me with these words,
And speak of Tamburlaine as he deserves:
The entertainment we have had of him
Is far from villany or servitude,
And might in noble minds be counted princely.

Agyd. How can you fancy one that looks so fierce,   40
Only disposed to martial stratagems?
Who, when he shall embrace you in his arms,
Will tell how many thousand men he slew;
And, when you look for amorous discourse,
Will rattle forth his facts of war and blood,
Too harsh a subject for your dainty ears.

Zeno. As looks the sun through Nilus' flowing stream,
Or when the morning holds him in her arms,
So looks my lordly love, fair Tamburlaine;
His talk much sweeter than the Muses' song   50
They sung for honour 'gainst Pierides,
Or when Minerva did with Neptune strive:
And higher would I rear my estimate
Than Juno, sister to the highest god,
If I were match'd with mighty Tamburlaine.

Agyd. Yet be not so inconstant in your love,
But let the young Arabian live in hope,
After your rescue to enjoy his choice.
You see, though first the king of Persia,
Being a shepherd, seem'd to love you much,   60
Now, in his majesty, he leaves those looks,
Those words of favour, and those comfortings,
And gives no more than common courtesies.

38 villany] subjection   45 facts] deeds

Zeno. Thence rise the tears that so distain my
  cheeks,
Fearing his love through my unworthiness.

  [*Tamburlaine goes to her, and takes her away lovingly
    by the hand, looking wrathfully on* Agydas, *and says
    nothing. Exeunt all except* Agydas.

  Agyd. Betray'd by fortune and suspicious love,
Threaten'd with frowning wrath and jealousy,
Surpris'd with fear of hideous revenge,
I stand aghast; but most astonied
To see his choler shut in secret thoughts,   70
And wrapt in silence of his angry soul:
Upon his brows was portray'd ugly death,
And in his eyes the fury of his heart,
That shine as comets, menacing revenge,
And casts a pale complexion on his cheeks.
As when the seaman sees the Hyades
Gather an army of Cimmerian clouds,
(Auster and Aquilon with winged steeds,
All sweating, tilt about the watery heavens,
With shivering spears enforcing thunder-claps,   80
And from their shields strike flames of lightening,)
All-fearful folds his sails, and sounds the main,
Lifting his prayers to the heavens for aid
Against the terror of the winds and waves;
So fares Agydas for the late-felt frowns,
That sent a tempest to my daunted thoughts,
And makes my soul divine her overthrow.

Re-enter Techelles *with a naked dagger, and* Usumcasane.

  Tech. See you, Agydas, how the king salutes you!
He bids you prophesy what it imports.

  Agyd. I prophesied before, and now I prove   90
The killing frowns of jealousy and love.
He needed not with words confirm my fear,
For words are vain where working tools present
The naked action of my threaten'd end.

  64 distain] stain   69 astonied] astonished

It says, Agydas, thou shalt surely die,
And of extremities elect the least;
More honour and less pain it may procure,
To die by this resolved hand of thine
Than stay the torments he and heaven have sworn.
Then haste, Agydas, and prevent the plagues   100
Which thy prolonged fates may draw on thee:
Go wander free from fear of tyrant's rage,
Removed from the torments and the hell
Wherewith he may excruciate thy soul;
And let Agydas by Agydas die,
And with this stab slumber eternally.   [*Stabs himself.*

   Tech. Usumcasane, see how right the man
Hath hit the meaning of my lord the king!

   Usum. Faith, and, Techelles, it was manly done;
And, since he was so wise and honourable,   110
Let us afford him now the bearing hence,
And crave his triple-worthy burial.

   Tech. Agreed, Casane; we will honour him.
              [*Exeunt, bearing out the body.*

Scene III.

Enter Tamburlaine, Techelles, Usumcasane, Theridamas, *a* Basso, Zenocrate, Anippe, *with others.*

   Tamb. Basso, by this thy lord and master knows
I mean to meet him in Bithynia:
See, how he comes! tush, Turks are full of brags,
And menace more than they can well perform.
He meet me in the field, and fetch thee hence!
Alas, poor Turk! his fortune is too weak
T' encounter with the strength of Tamburlaine:
View well my camp, and speak indifferently;
Do not my captains and my soldiers look
As if they meant to conquer Africa?   10

   Bas. Your men are valiant, but their number few,
And cannot terrify his mighty host:
My lord, the great commander of the world,

Besides fifteen contributory kings,
Hath now in arms ten thousand janizaries,
Mounted on lusty Mauritanian steeds,
Brought to the war by men of Tripoly;
Two hundred thousand footmen that have serv'd
In two set battles fought in Grecia;
And for the expedition of this war,   20
If he think good, can from his garrisons
Withdraw as many more to follow him.

   Tech. The more he brings, the greater is the spoil;
For, when they perish by our warlike hands,
We mean to set our footmen on their steeds,
And rifle all those stately janizars.

   Tamb. But will those kings accompany your lord?

   Bas. Such as his highness please: but some must stay
To rule the provinces he late subdu'd.

   Tamb. [*To his Officers*]. Then fight courageously:
their crowns are yours;   30
This hand shall set them on your conquering heads,
That made me emperor of Asia.

   Usum. Let him bring millions infinite of men,
Unpeopling Western Africa and Greece,
Yet we assure us of the victory.

   Ther. Even he, that in a trice vanquish'd two kings
More mighty than the Turkish emperor,
Shall rouse him out of Europe, and pursue
His scatter'd army till they yield or die.

   Tamb. Well said, Theridamas! speak in that mood;
For *will* and *shall* best fitteth Tamburlaine,   41
Whose smiling stars gives him assured hope
Of martial triumph, ere he meet his foes.
I that am term'd the scourge and wrath of God,
The only fear and terror of the world,
Will first subdue the Turk, and then enlarge
Those Christian captives which you keep as slaves,
Burdening their bodies with your heavy chains,
And feeding them with thin and slender fare,

That naked row about the Terrene sea,   50
And, when they chance to breathe and rest a space,
Are punish'd with bastones so grievously
That they lie panting on the galley's side,
And strive for life at every stroke they give.
These are the cruel pirates of Argier,
That damned train, the scum of Africa,
Inhabited with straggling runagates,
That make quick havoc of the Christian blood:
But as I live that town shall curse the time
That Tamburlaine set foot in Africa.   60

Enter Bajazeth, Bassoes, *the* Kings of Fez, Morocco,
   and Argier; Zabina *and* Ebea.

 Baj. Bassoes and janizaries of my guard,
Attend upon the person of your lord,
The greatest potentate of Africa.
 Tamb. Techelles and the rest, prepare your swords;
I mean t' encounter with that Bajazeth.
 Baj. Kings of Fez, Morocco, and Argier,
He calls me Bajazeth, whom you call lord!
Note the presumption of this Scythian slave!
I tell thee, villain, those that lead my horse
Have to their names titles of dignity,   70
And dar'st thou bluntly call me Bajazeth?
 Tamb. And know thou, Turk, that those which lead
  my horse
Shall lead thee captive thorough Africa;
And dar'st thou bluntly call me Tamburlaine?
 Baj. By Mahomet my kinsman's sepulchre,
And by the holy Alcoran I swear,
He shall be made a chaste and lustless eunuch,
And in my sarell tend my concubines;
And all his captains, that thus stoutly stand,
Shall draw the chariot of my emperess,   80
Whom I have brought to see their overthrow!
 Tamb. By this my sword that conquer'd Persia,

  52 bastones] sticks 78 sarell] seraglio

Thy fall shall make me famous through the world!
I will not tell thee how I'll handle thee,
But every common soldier of my camp
Shall smile to see thy miserable state.

 K. of Fez. What means the mighty Turkish emperor,
To talk with one so base as Tamburlaine?

 K. of Morocco. Ye Moors and valiant men of Barbary,
How can ye suffer these indignities?   90

 K. of Arg. Leave words, and let them feel your
  lances' points,
Which glided through the bowels of the Greeks.

 Baj. Well said, my stout contributory kings;
Your threefold army and my hugy host
Shall swallow up these base-born Persians.

 Tech. Puissant, renowned, and mighty Tamburlaine,
Why stay we thus prolonging all their lives?

 Ther. I long to see those crowns won by our swords,
That we may reign as kings of Africa.

 Usum. What coward would not fight for such a
  prize?   100

 Tamb. Fight all courageously, and be you kings:
I speak it, and my words are oracles.

 Baj. Zabina, mother of three braver boys
Than Hercules, that in his infancy
Did pash the jaws of serpents venomous;
Whose hands are made to gripe a warlike lance,
Their shoulders broad for complete armour fit,
Their limbs more large and of a bigger size
Than all the brats y-sprung from Typhon's loins;
Who, when they come unto their father's age,   110
Will batter turrets with their manly fists;—
Sit here upon this royal chair of state,
And on thy head wear my imperial crown,
Until I bring this sturdy Tamburlaine
And all his captains bound in captive chains.

     105 pash] dash to pieces

Zab. Such good success happen to Bajazeth!

Tamb. Zenocrate, the loveliest maid alive,
Fairer than rocks of pearl and precious stone,
The only paragon of Tamburlaine;
Whose eyes are brighter than the lamps of heaven, 120
And speech more pleasant than sweet harmony;
That with thy looks canst clear the darkened sky,
And calm the rage of thundering Jupiter;
Sit down by her, adorned with my crown,
As if thou wert the empress of the world.
Stir not, Zenocrate, until thou see
Me march victoriously with all my men,
Triumphing over him and these his kings,
Which I will bring as vassals to thy feet;
Till then, take thou my crown, vaunt of my worth, 130
And manage words with her, as we will arms.

Zeno. And may my love, the king of Persia,
Return with victory and free from wound!

Baj. Now shalt thou feel the force of Turkish arms,
Which lately made all Europe quake for fear.
I have of Turks, Arabians, Moors, and Jews,
Enough to cover all Bithynia:
Let thousands die: their slaughtered carcasses
Shall serve for walls and bulwarks to the rest;
And as the heads of Hydra, so my power,   140
Subdu'd, shall stand as mighty as before:
If they should yield their necks unto the sword,
Thy soldiers' arms could not endure to strike
So many blows as I have heads for thee.
Thou know'st not, foolish hardy Tamburlaine,
What 'tis to meet me in the open field,
That leave no ground for thee to march upon.

Tamb. Our conquering swords shall marshal us the
    way
We use to march upon the slaughtered foe,
Trampling their bowels with our horses' hoofs,   150
Brave horses bred on the white Tartarian hills.
My camp is like to Julius Cæsar's host,

That never fought but had the victory;
Nor in Pharsalia was there such hot war
As these, my followers, willingly would have.
Legions of spirits, fleeting in the air,
Direct our bullets and our weapons' points,
And make your strokes to wound the senseless air;
And when she sees our bloody colours spread,
Then Victory begins to take her flight,   160
Resting herself upon my milk-white tent.—
But come, my lords, to weapons let us fall;
The field is ours, the Turk, his wife, and all.
                              [*Exit with his followers.*
  Baj. Come, kings and bassoes, let us glut our swords,
That thirst to drink the feeble Persians' blood.
                              [*Exit with his followers.*
  Zab. Base concubine, must thou be plac'd by me
That am the empress of the mighty Turk?
  Zeno. Disdainful Turkess, and unreverend boss,
Call'st thou me concubine, that am betroth'd
Unto the great and mighty Tamburlaine?   170
  Zab. To Tamburlaine, the great Tartarian thief!
  Zeno. Thou wilt repent these lavish words of thine
When thy great basso-master and thyself
Must plead for mercy at his kingly feet,
And sue to me to be your advocates.
  Zab. And sue to thee? I tell thee, shameless girl,
Thou shalt be laundress to my waiting-maid.—
How lik'st thou her, Ebea? will she serve?
  Ebea. Madam, she thinks perhaps she is too fine;
But I shall turn her into other weeds,   180
And make her dainty fingers fall to work.
  Zeno. Hear'st thou, Anippe, how thy drudge doth
    talk?
And how my slave, her mistress, menaceth?
Both for their sauciness shall be employ'd
To dress the common soldiers' meat and drink;
For we will scorn they should come near ourselves.

          168 boss] sow, fat woman

Anip. Yet sometimes let your highness send for
them
To do the work my chambermaid disdains.
                              [*They sound to the battle within.*
Zeno. Ye gods and powers that govern Persia,
And make my lordly love her worthy king,   190
Now strengthen him against the Turkish Bajazeth,
And let his foes, like flocks of fearful roes
Pursu'd by hunters, fly his angry looks,
That I may see him issue conqueror!
Zab. Now, Mahomet, solicit God himself,
And make him rain down murthering shot from
heaven
To dash the Scythians' brains, and strike them dead,
That dare to manage arms with him
That offer'd jewels to thy sacred shrine
When first he warr'd against the Christians!   200
                              [*They sound again to the battle within.*
Zeno. By this the Turks lie weltering in their blood,
And Tamburlaine is lord of Africa.
Zab. Thou art deceiv'd. I heard the trumpets
sound
As when my emperor overthrew the Greeks,
And led them captive into Africa.
Straight will I use thee as thy pride deserves;
Prepare thyself to live and die my slave.
Zeno. If Mahomet should come from heaven and
swear
My royal lord is slain or conquered,
Yet should he not persuade me otherwise   210
But that he lives and will be conqueror.

Re-enter Bajazeth, *pursued by* Tamburlaine.

Tamb. Now, king of bassoes, who is conqueror?
Baj. Thou, by the fortune of this damned foil.
Tamb. Where are your stout contributory kings?

213 foil] defeat

Re-enter Techelles, Theridamas, *and* Usumcasane.

Tech. We have their crowns; their bodies strow the field.

Tamb. Each man a crown? why, kingly fought, i'faith.
Deliver them into my treasury.

Zeno. Now let me offer to my gracious lord
His royal crown again, so highly won.

Tamb. Nay, take the Turkish crown from her, Zenocrate,   220
And crown me emperor of Africa.

Zab. No, Tamburlaine; though now thou gat the best,
Thou shalt not yet be lord of Africa.

Ther. Give her the crown, Turkess, you were best.
                              [*Takes it from her.*

Zab. Injurious villains, thieves, runagates,
How dare you thus abuse my majesty?

Ther. Here, madam, you are empress; she is none.
                              [*Gives it to Zenocrate.*

Tamb. Not now, Theridamas; her time is past:
The pillars, that have bolstered up those terms,
Are faln in clusters at my conquering feet.   230

Zab. Though he be prisoner, he may be ransomed.

Tamb. Not all the world shall ransom Bajazeth.

Baj. Ah, fair Zabina, we have lost the field;
And never had the Turkish emperor
So great a foil by any foreign foe.
Now will the Christian miscreants be glad,
Ringing with joy their superstitious bells,
And making bonfires for my overthrow:
But, ere I die, those foul idolaters
Shall make me bonfires with their filthy bones;   240
For, though the glory of this day be lost,
Afric and Greece have garrisons enough
To make me sovereign of the earth again.

Tamb. Those walled garrisons will I subdue,

And write myself great lord of Africa:
So from the East unto the furthest West
Shall Tamburlaine extend his puissant arm.
The galleys and those pilling brigandines,
That yearly sail to the Venetian gulf,
And hover in the Straits for Christians' wreck, 250
Shall lie at anchor in the Isle Asant,
Until the Persian fleet and men-of-war,
Sailing along the oriental sea,
Have fetch'd about the Indian continent,
Even from Persepolis to Mexico,
And thence unto the Straits of Jubalter;
Where they shall meet and join their force in one,
Keeping in awe the Bay of Portingale,
And all the ocean by the British shore;
And by this means I'll win the world at last.   260
    Baj. Yet set a ransom on me, Tamburlaine.
    Tamb. What, think'st thou Tamburlaine esteems
        thy gold?
I'll make the kings of India, ere I die,
Offer their mines, to sue for peace, to me,
And dig for treasure to appease my wrath.
Come, bind them both, and one lead in the Turk;
The Turkess let my love's maid lead away.
                              [*They bind them.*
    Baj. Ah, villains, dare you touch my sacred arms?
O Mahomet! O sleepy Mahomet!
    Zab. O cursed Mahomet, that mak'st us thus 270
The slaves to Scythians rude and barbarous!
    Tamb. Come, bring them in; and for this happy
        conquest
Triumph, and solemnise a martial feast.   [*Exeunt.*

---

248 pilling] plundering   256 Jubalter] Gibraltar
                258 Portingale] Biscay

Act IV. Scene I.

Enter the Soldan of Egypt, Capolin, Lords,
and a Messenger.

Sold. Awake, ye men of Memphis! hear the clang
Of Scythian trumpets; hear the basilisks,
That, roaring, shake Damascus' turrets down!
The rogue of Volga holds Zenocrate,
The Soldan's daughter, for his concubine,
And with a troop of thieves and vagabonds,
Hath spread his colours to our high disgrace,
While you, faint-hearted base Egyptians,
Lie slumbering on the flowery banks of Nile,
As crocodiles that unaffrighted rest   10
While thundering cannons rattle on their skins.
    Mess. Nay, mighty Soldan, did your greatness see
The frowning looks of fiery Tamburlaine,
That with his terror and imperious eyes
Commands the hearts of his associates,
It might amaze your royal majesty.
    Sold. Villain, I tell thee, were that Tamburlaine
As monstrous as Gorgon, prince of hell,
The Soldan would not start a foot from him.
But speak, what power hath he?   20
    Mess. Mighty lord,
Three hundred thousand men in armour clad,
Upon their prancing steeds, disdainfully
With wanton paces trampling on the ground;
Five hundred thousand footmen threatening shot,
Shaking their swords, their spears, and iron bills,
Environing their standard round, that stood
As bristle-pointed as a thorny wood;
Their warlike engines and munition
Exceed the forces of their martial men.   30
    Sold. Nay, could their numbers countervail the
        stars,

2 basilisks] guns

Or ever-drizzling drops of April showers,
Or withered leaves that autumn shaketh down,
Yet would the Soldan by his conquering power
So scatter and consume them in his rage,
That not a man should live to rue their fall.

  Capo. So might your highness, had you time to sort
Your fighting men, and raise your royal host;
But Tamburlaine by expedition
Advantage takes of your unreadiness.   40

  Sold. Let him take all th' advantages he can:
Were all the world conspir'd to fight for him,
Nay, were he devil, as he is no man,
Yet in revenge of fair Zenocrate,
Whom he detaineth in despite of us,
This arm should send him down to Erebus,
To shroud his shame in darkness of the night.

  Mess. Pleaseth your mightiness to understand,
His resolution far exceedeth all.
The first day when he pitcheth down his tents,   50
White is their hue, and on his silver crest,
A snowy feather spangled-white he bears,
To signify the mildness of his mind,
That, satiate with spoil, refuseth blood:
But, when Aurora mounts the second time,
As red as scarlet is his furniture;
Then must his kindled wrath be quench'd with blood,
Not sparing any that can manage arms:
But if these threats move not submission,
Black are his colours, black pavilion;   60
His spear, his shield, his horse, his armour, plumes,
And jetty feathers, menace death and hell;
Without respect of sex, degree, or age,
He razeth all his foes with fire and sword.

  Sold. Merciless villain, peasant ignorant
Of lawful arms or martial discipline!
Pillage and murder are his usual trades:
The slave usurps the glorious name of war.
See, Capolin, the fair Arabian king,

That hath been disappointed by this slave   70
Of my fair daughter and his princely love,
May have fresh warning to go war with us,
And be reveng'd for her disparagement.   [*Exeunt.*

Scene II.

Enter Tamburlaine, Techelles, Theridamas, Usumcasane, Zenocrate, Anippe, *two* Moors *drawing* Bajazeth *in a cage, and* Zabina *following him.*

  Tamb. Bring out my footstool.
              [*They take* Bajazeth *out of the cage.*
  Baj. Ye holy priests of heavenly Mahomet,
That, sacrificing, slice and cut your flesh,
Staining his altars with your purple blood,
Make heaven to frown, and every fixed star
To suck up poison from the moorish fens,
And pour it in this glorious tyrant's throat!
  Tamb. The chiefest god, first mover of that sphere
Enchas'd with thousands ever-shining lamps,
Will sooner burn the glorious frame of heaven   10
Than it should so conspire my overthrow.
But, villain, thou that wishest this to me,
Fall prostrate on the low disdainful earth,
And be the footstool of great Tamburlaine,
That I may rise into my royal throne.
  Baj. First shalt thou rip my bowels with thy sword,
And sacrifice my heart to death and hell,
Before I yield to such a slavery.
  Tamb. Base villain, vassal, slave to Tamburlaine,
Unworthy to embrace or touch the ground   20
That bears the honour of my royal weight;
Stoop, villain, stoop! stoop; for so he bids
That may command thee piecemeal to be torn,
Or scatter'd like the lofty cedar-trees
Struck with the voice of thundering Jupiter.
  Baj. Then, as I look down to the damned fiends,
       7 glorious] boastful

Fiends, look on me; and thou, dread god of hell,
With ebon sceptre strike this hateful earth,
And make it swallow both of us at once!

> [*Tamburlaine gets up on him into his chair.*

  Tamb. Now clear the triple region of the air,   30
And let the Majesty of Heaven behold
Their scourge and terror tread on emperors.
Smile, stars that reign'd at my nativity,
And dim the brightness of their neighbour lamps;
Disdain to borrow light of Cynthia,
For I, the chiefest lamp of all the earth,
First rising in the east with mild aspect,
But fixed now in the meridian line,
Will send up fire to your turning spheres,
And cause the sun to borrow light of you.   40
My sword struck fire from his coat of steel,
Even in Bithynia, when I took this Turk;
As when a fiery exhalation,
Wrapt in the bowels of a freezing cloud,
Fighting for passage, makes the welkin crack,
And casts a flash of lightning to the earth:
But, ere I march to wealthy Persia,
Or leave Damascus and th' Egyptian fields,
As was the fame of Clymene's brain-sick son
That almost brent the axle-tree of heaven,   50
So shall our swords, our lances, and our shot
Fill all the air with fiery meteors;
Then, when the sky shall wax as red as blood,
It shall be said I made it red myself,
To make me think of naught but blood and war.

  Zab. Unworthy king, that by thy cruelty
Unlawfully usurp'st the Persian seat,
Dar'st thou, that never saw an emperor
Before thou met my husband in the field,
Being thy captive, thus abuse his state,   60
Keeping his kingly body in a cage,
That roofs of gold and sun-bright palaces

          50 brent] burnt

Should have prepar'd to entertain his grace?
And treading him beneath thy loathsome feet,
Whose feet the kings of Africa have kiss'd?   [lord,

Tech. You must devise some torment worse, my
To make these captives rein their lavish tongues.

Tamb. Zenocrate, look better to your slave.

Zeno. She is my handmaid's slave, and she shall
look
That these abuses flow not from her tongue: 70
Chide her, Anippe.

Anip. Let these be warnings for you then, my slave,
How you abuse the person of the king;
Or else I swear to have you whipt stark nak'd.

Baj. Great Tamburlaine, great in my overthrow,
Ambitious pride shall make thee fall as low,
For treading on the back of Bajazeth,
That should be horsed on four mighty kings.

Tamb. Thy names, and titles, and thy dignities
Are fled from Bajazeth, and remain with me,   80
That will maintain it against a world of kings.
Put him in again.   [*They put him into the cage.*

Baj. Is this a place for mighty Bajazeth?
Confusion light on him that helps thee thus.

Tamb. There, whiles he lives, shall Bajazeth be kept;
And, where I go, be thus in triumph drawn;
And thou, his wife, shall feed him with the scraps
My servitors shalt bring me from my board;
For he that gives him other food than this,
Shall sit by him, and starve to death himself: 90
This is my mind, and I will have it so.
Not all the kings and emperors of the earth,
If they would lay their crowns before my feet,
Shall ransom him, or take him from his cage:
The ages that shall talk of Tamburlaine,
Even from this day to Plato's wondrous year,
Shall talk how I have handled Bajazeth:
These Moors, that drew him from Bithynia
To fair Damascus, where we now remain,

Shall lead him with us wheresoe'er we go. 100
Techelles, and my loving followers,
Now may we see Damascus' lofty towers,
Like to the shadows of Pyramides
That with their beauties grac'd the Memphian fields.
The golden stature of their feathered bird,
That spreads her wings upon the city walls,
Shall not defend it from our battering shot:
The townsmen mask in silk and cloth of gold,
And every house is as a treasury;
The men, the treasure, and the town is ours. 110

 Ther. Your tents of white now pitch'd before the
  gates,
And gentle flags of amity display'd,
I doubt not but the governor will yield,
Offering Damascus to your majesty.

 Tamb. So shall he have his life, and all the rest:
But if he stay until the bloody flag
Be once advanc'd on my vermilion tent,
He dies, and those that kept us out so long;
And when they see me march in black array,
With mournful streamers hanging down their heads,
Were in that city all the world contain'd, 121
Not one should scape, but perish by our swords.

 Zeno. Yet would you have some pity for my sake,
Because it is my country's and my father's.

 Tamb. Not for the world, Zenocrate, if I have
  sworn.
Come; bring in the Turk. [*Exeunt.*

Scene III.

Enter Soldan, King of Arabia, Capolin, *and* Soldiers,
with streaming colours.

 Sold. Methinks we march as Meleager did,
Environed with brave Argolian knights,
To chase the savage Calydonian boar,
Or Cephalus, with lusty Theban youths,

Against the wolf that angry Themis sent
To waste and spoil the sweet Aonian fields.
A monster of five hundred thousand heads,
Compact of rapine, piracy, and spoil,
The scum of men, the hate and scourge of God,
Raves in Egyptia, and annoyeth us: 10
My lord, it is the bloody Tamburlaine,
A sturdy felon, and a base-bred thief,
By murder raised to the Persian crown,
That dares control us in our territories.
To tame the pride of this presumptuous beast,
Join your Arabians with the Soldan's power;
Let us unite our royal bands in one,
And hasten to remove Damascus' siege.
It is a blemish to the majesty
And high estate of mighty emperors,   20
That such a base usurping vagabond
Should brave a king, or wear a princely crown.

    K. of Ar. Renowned Soldan, have ye lately heard
The overthrow of mighty Bajazeth
About the confines of Bithynia?
The slavery wherewith he persecutes
The noble Turk and his great emperess?

    Sold. I have, and sorrow for his bad success;
But, noble lord of great Arabia,
Be so persuaded that the Soldan is   30
No more dismay'd with tidings of his fall,
Than in the haven when the pilot stands,
And views a stranger's ship rent in the winds,
And shivered against a craggy rock:
Yet in compassion of his wretched state,
A sacred vow to heaven and him I make,
Confirming it with Ibis' holy name,
That Tamburlaine shall rue the day, the hour,
Wherein he wrought such ignominious wrong
Unto the hallowed person of a prince,   40
Or kept the fair Zenocrate so long,
As concubine, I fear, to feed his lust.

K. of Ar. Let grief and fury hasten on revenge;
Let Tamburlaine for his offences feel
Such plagues as heaven and we can pour on him:
I long to break my spear upon his crest,
And prove the weight of his victorious arm;
For fame, I fear, hath been too prodigal
In sounding through the world his partial praise.

   Sold. Capolin, hast thou survey'd our powers?   50

   Capol. Great emperors of Egypt and Arabia,
The number of your hosts united is,
A hundred and fifty thousand horse,
Two hundred thousand foot, brave men-at-arms,
Courageous and full of hardiness,
As frolic as the hunters in the chase
Of savage beasts amid the desert woods.

   K. of Ar. My mind presageth fortunate success;
And, Tamburlaine, my spirit doth foresee
The utter ruin of thy men and thee.   60

   Sold. Then rear your standards; let your sounding
     drums
Direct our soldiers to Damascus' walls.
Now, Tamburlaine, the mighty Soldan comes,
And leads with him the great Arabian king,
To dim thy baseness and obscurity,
Famous for nothing but for theft and spoil;
To raze and scatter thy inglorious crew
Of Scythians and slavish Persians.   [*Exeunt.*

Scene IV.

A banquet set out; and to it come Tamburlaine *all in scarlet,* Zenocrate, Theridamas, Techelles, Usumcasane,
    Bajazeth *drawn in his cage,* Zabina, *and others.*

   Tamb. Now hang our bloody colours by Damascus,
Reflexing hues of blood upon their heads,
While they walk quivering on their city walls,
Half-dead for fear before they feel my wrath.
Then let us freely banquet and carouse

Full bowls of wine unto the god of war,
That means to fill your helmets full of gold,
And make Damascus' spoils as rich to you
As was to Jason Colchos' golden fleece.
And now, Bajazeth, hast thou any stomach?   10

    Baj. Ay, such a stomach, cruel Tamburlaine, as I
could willingly feed upon thy blood-raw heart.

    Tamb. Nay, thine own is easier to come by: pluck
out that, and 'twill serve thee and thy wife: well,
Zenocrate, Techelles, and the rest, fall to your
victuals.

    Baj. Fall to, and never may your meat digest!
Ye Furies, that can mask invisible,
Dive to the bottom of Avernus' pool,
And in your hands bring hellish poison up,   20
And squeeze it in the cup of Tamburlaine!
Or, winged snakes of Lerna, cast your stings,
And leave your venoms in this tyrant's dish!

    Zab. And may this banquet prove as ominous
As Progne's to th' adulterous Thracian king
That fed upon the substance of his child.

    Zeno. My lord, how can you suffer these
Outrageous curses by these slaves of yours?

    Tamb. To let them see, divine Zenocrate,
I glory in the curses of my foes,   30
Having the power from the imperial heaven
To turn them all upon their proper heads.

    Tech. I pray you, give them leave, madam; this
speech is a goodly refreshing to them.

    Ther. But, if his highness would let them be fed,
it would do them more good.

    Tamb. Sirrah, why fall you not to? are you so
daintily brought up, you cannot eat your own
flesh?   39

    Baj. First, legions of devils shall tear thee in pieces.

    Usum. Villain, knowest thou to whom thou speak-
est?

25 Progne] Procne

Tamb. Oh, let him alone. Here; eat, sir; take it from my sword's point, or I'll thrust it to thy heart.

[Bajazeth *takes the food, and stamps upon it.*

Ther. He stamps it under his feet, my lord.

Tamb. Take it up, villain, and eat it; or I will make thee slice the brawns of thy arms into carbonadoes and eat them.   49

Usum. Nay, 'twere better he killed his wife, and then she shall be sure not to be starved, and he be provided for a month's victual beforehand.

Tamb. Here is my dagger: despatch her while she is fat; for, if she live but a while longer, she will fall into a consumption with fretting, and then she will not be worth the eating.

Ther. Dost thou think that Mahomet will suffer this?

Tech. 'Tis like he will, when he cannot let it.   59

Tamb. Go to; fall to your meat. What, not a bit? belike he hath not been watered to-day: give him some drink.

[*They give* Bajazeth *water to drink, and he flings it on the ground.*

Fast, and welcome, sir, while hunger make you eat. How now, Zenocrate, doth not the Turk and his wife make a goodly show at a banquet?

Zeno. Yes, my lord.

Ther. Methinks 'tis a great deal better than a consort of music.

Tamb. Yet music would do well to cheer up Zenocrate. Pray thee tell, why art thou so sad? if thou wilt have a song, the Turk shall strain his voice: but why is it?   71

Zeno. My lord, to see my father's town besieg'd,
The country wasted, where myself was born,
How can it but afflict my very soul?
If any love remain in you, my lord,

49 carbonadoes] rashers   58 let] hinder   62 while] until

Or if my love unto your majesty
May merit favour at your highness' hands,
Then raise your siege from fair Damascus' walls,
And with my father take a friendly truce.

   Tamb. Zenocrate, were Egypt Jove's own land,   80
Yet would I with my sword make Jove to stoop.
I will confute those blind geographers
That make a triple region in the world,
Excluding regions which I mean to trace,
And with this pen reduce them to a map,
Calling the provinces, cities, and towns,
After my name and thine, Zenocrate:
Here at Damascus will I make the point
That shall begin the perpendicular:
And wouldst thou have me buy thy father's love   90
With such a loss? tell me, Zenocrate.

   Zeno. Honour still wait on happy Tamburlaine;
Yet give me leave to plead for him, my lord.

   Tamb. Content thyself: his person shall be safe,
And all the friends of fair Zenocrate,
If with their lives they will be pleas'd to yield,
Or may be forc'd to make me emperor;
For Egypt and Arabia must be mine.

   Feed, you slave; thou mayst think thyself happy to
be fed from my trencher.   100

   Baj. My empty stomach, full of idle heat,
Draws bloody humours from my feeble parts,
Preserving life by hasting cruel death.
My veins are pale; my sinews hard and dry;
My joints benumb'd; unless I eat, I die.

   Zab. Eat, Bajazeth; let us live in spite of them,
looking some happy power will pity and enlarge
us.

   Tamb. Here, Turk; wilt thou have a clean trencher?

   Baj. Ay, tyrant, and more meat.   110

   Tamb. Soft, sir, you must be dieted; too much
eating will make you surfeit.

85 pen] meaning his sword

Ther. So it would, my lord, 'specially having so small a walk and so little exercise.

> [*A second course is brought in of crowns.*

Tamb. Theridamas, Techelles, and Casane, here are the cates you desire to finger, are they not?

Ther. Ay, my lord: but none save kings must feed with these.

Tech. 'Tis enough for us to see them, and for Tamburlaine only to enjoy them.   120

Tamb. Well; here is now to the Soldan of Egypt, the King of Arabia, and the Governor of Damascus. Now, take these three crowns, and pledge me, my contributory kings. I crown you here, Theridamas, king of Argier; Techelles, king of Fez; and Usumcasane, king of Morocco. How say you to this, Turk? these are not your contributory kings.

Baj. Nor shall they long be thine, I warrant them.

Tamb. Kings of Argier, Morocco, and of Fez,   130
You that have march'd with happy Tamburlaine
As far as from the frozen place of heaven
Unto the watery morning's ruddy bower,
And thence by land unto the torrid zone,
Deserve these titles I endow you with
By valour and by magnanimity.
Your births shall be no blemish to your fame,
For virtue is the fount whence honour springs,
And they are worthy she investeth kings.

Ther. And since your highness hath so well vouch-
    saf'd,   140
If we deserve them not with higher meeds
Than erst our states and actions have retain'd,
Take them away again, and make us slaves.

Tamb. Well said, Theridamas: when holy Fates
Shall stablish me in strong Egyptia,
We mean to travel to th' antarctic pole,
Conquering the people underneath our feet,
And be renown'd as never emperors were.

Zenocrate, I will not crown thee yet,   149
Until with greater honours I be grac'd.   [*Exeunt.*

Act V. Scene I.

Enter the Governor *of* Damascus *with three or four* Citizens,
and four Virgins *with branches of laurel in their hands.*

Gov. Still doth this man, or rather god of war,
Batter our walls and beat our turrets down;
And to resist with longer stubbornness,
Or hope of rescue from the Soldan's power,
Were but to bring our wilful overthrow,
And make us desperate of our threatened lives.
We see his tents have now been altered
With terrors to the last and cruel'st hue;
His coal-black colours, everywhere advanc'd,
Threaten our city with a general spoil;   10
And if we should with common rites of arms
Offer our safeties to his clemency,
I fear the custom proper to his sword,
Which he observes as parcel of his fame,
Intending so to terrify the world,
By any innovation or remorse
Will never be dispens'd with till our deaths.
Therefore, for these our harmless virgins' sakes,
Whose honours and whose lives rely on him,
Let us have hope that their unspotted prayers,   20
Their blubbered cheeks, and hearty humble moans
Will melt his fury into some remorse,
And use us like a loving conqueror.
    First Virg. If humble suits or imprecations
(Utter'd with tears of wretchedness and blood
Shed from the heads and hearts of all our sex,
Some made your wives, and some your children,)
Might have entreated your obdurate breasts
To entertain some care of our securities
Whiles only danger beat upon our walls,   30
These more than dangerous warrants of our death

Had never been erected as they be,
Nor you depend on such weak helps as we.

  Gov. Well, lovely virgins, think our country's care,
Our love of honour, loath to be enthrall'd
To foreign powers and rough imperious yokes,
Would not with too much cowardice or fear,
Before all hope of rescue were denied,
Submit yourselves and us to servitude.
Therefore, in that your safeties and our own,   40
Your honours, liberties, and lives were weigh'd
In equal care and balance with our own,
Endure as we the malice of our stars,
The wrath of Tamburlaine and power of wars,
Or be the means the overweighing heavens
Have kept to qualify these hot extremes,
And bring us pardon in your cheerful looks.

  Sec. Virg. Then here, before the majesty of Heaven
And holy patrons of Egyptia,
With knees and hearts submissive we entreat   50
Grace to our words and pity to our looks,
That this device may prove propitious,
And through the eyes and ears of Tamburlaine
Convey events of mercy to his heart;
Grant that these signs of victory we yield
May bind the temples of his conquering head,
To hide the folded furrows of his brows,
And shadow his displeased countenance
With happy looks of ruth and lenity.
Leave us, my lord, and loving countrymen: 60
What simple virgins may persuade, we will.

  Gov. Farewell, sweet virgins, on whose safe return
Depends our city, liberty, and lives.
                       [Exeunt all except the Virgins.

Enter Tamburlaine, *all in black and very melancholy,*
    Techelles, Theridamas, Usumcasane, *with others.*

  Tamb. What, are the turtles fray'd out of their nests?
Alas, poor fools, must you be first shall feel

The sworn destruction of Damascus?
They know my custom; could they not as well
Have sent ye out when first my milk-white flags,
Through which sweet Mercy threw her gentle beams,
Reflexing them on your disdainful eyes,   70
As now when fury and incensed hate
Flings slaughtering terror from my coal-black tents,
And tells for truth submissions comes too late?
   First Vir. Most happy king and emperor of the
     earth,
Image of honour and nobility,
For whom the powers divine have made the world,
And on whose throne the holy Graces sit;
In whose sweet person is compris'd the sum
Of Nature's skill and heavenly majesty;
Pity our plights! Oh, pity poor Damascus!   80
Pity old age, within whose silver hairs
Honour and reverence evermore have reign'd!
Pity the marriage-bed, where many a lord,
In prime and glory of his loving joy,
Embraceth now with tears of ruth and blood
The jealous body of his fearful wife,
Whose cheeks and hearts, so punish'd with conceit,
To think thy puissant never-stayed arm
Will part their bodies, and prevent their souls
From heavens of comfort yet their age might bear, 90
Now wax all pale and withered to the death,
As well for grief our ruthless governor
Have thus refus'd the mercy of thy hand,
(Whose sceptre angels kiss and Furies dread,)
As for their liberties, their loves, or lives!
Oh, then, for these, and such as we ourselves,
For us, for infants, and for all our bloods,
That never nourish'd thought against thy rule,
Pity, O pity, sacred emperor,
The prostrate service of this wretched town;   100
And take in sign thereof this gilded wreath,
Whereto each man of rule hath given his hand,

And wish'd, as worthy subjects, happy means
To be investers of thy royal brows
Even with the true Egyptian diadem!

   Tamb. Virgins, in vain you labour to prevent
That which mine honour swears shall be perform'd.
Behold my sword; what see you at the point?

   First Virg. Nothing but fear and fatal steel, my lord.

   Tamb. Your fearful minds are thick and misty,
then,   110
For there sits death; there sits imperious Death,
Keeping his circuit by the slicing edge.
But I am pleas'd you shall not see him there;
He now is seated on my horsemen's spears,
And on their points his fleshless body feeds.
Techelles, straight go charge a few of them
To charge these dames, and shew my servant Death,
Sitting in scarlet on their armed spears.

   Virgins. Oh, pity us!

   Tamb. Away with them, I say, and shew them
Death.   120
    [*The* Virgins *are taken out by* Techelles *and others.*
I will not spare these proud Egyptians,
Nor change my martial observations
For all the wealth of Gihon's golden waves,
Or for the love of Venus, would she leave
The angry god of arms and lie with me.
They have refus'd the offer of their lives.
And know my customs are as peremptory
As wrathful planets, death, or destiny.

                 Re-enter Techelles.

What, have your horsemen shown the virgins Death?

   Tech. They have, my lord, and on Damascus' walls
Have hoisted up their slaughtered carcasses.   131

   Tamb. A sight as baneful to their souls, I think,
As are Thessalian drugs or mithridate:

   133 mithridate] a preservative against poisons; here, used
for these poisons.

But go, my lords, put the rest to the sword.
                     [*Exeunt all except* Tamburlaine.
Ah, fair Zenocrate!—divine Zenocrate!
Fair is too foul an epithet for thee,
That in thy passion for thy country's love,
And fear to see thy kingly father's harm,
With hair dishevell'd wip'st thy watery cheeks;
And, like to Flora in her morning's pride,   140
Shaking her silver tresses in the air,
Rain'st on the earth resolved pearl in showers,
And sprinklest sapphires on thy shining face,
Where Beauty, mother to the Muses, sits,
And comments volumes with her ivory pen,
Taking instructions from thy flowing eyes;
Eyes, when that Ebena steps to heaven,
In silence of thy solemn evening's walk,
Making the mantle of the richest night,
The moon, the planets, and the meteors, light;   150
There angels in their crystal armours fight
A doubtful battle with my tempted thoughts
For Egypt's freedom and the Soldan's life,
His life that so consumes Zenocrate,
Whose sorrows lay more siege unto my soul
Than all my army to Damascus' walls;
And neither Persia's sovereign nor the Turk
Troubled my senses with conceit of foil
So much by much as doth Zenocrate.
What is beauty, saith my sufferings, then?   160
If all the pens that ever poets held
Had fed the feeling of their masters' thoughts,
And every sweetness that inspir'd their hearts,
Their minds, and muses on admired themes;
If all the heavenly quintessence they still
From their immortal flowers of poesy,
Wherein, as in a mirror, we perceive
The highest reaches of a human wit;
If these had made one poem's period,

137 passion] sorrow

And all combin'd in beauty's worthiness,   170
Yet should there hover in their restless heads
One thought, one grace, one wonder, at the least,
Which into words no virtue can digest.
But how unseemly is it for my sex,
My discipline of arms and chivalry,
My nature, and the terror of my name,
To harbour thoughts effeminate and faint!
Save only that in beauty's just applause,
With whose instinct the soul of man is touch'd;
And every warrior that is rapt with love   180
Of fame, of valour, and of victory,
Must needs have beauty beat on his conceits:
I thus conceiving and subduing both,
That which hath stoop'd the tempest of the gods,
Even from the fiery-spangled veil of heaven,
To feel the lovely warmth of shepherds' flames,
And march in cottages of strowed weeds,
Shall give the world to note, for all my birth,
That virtue solely is the sum of glory,
And fashions men with true nobility.   190
Who's within there?

Enter Attendants.

Hath Bajazeth been fed to-day?
    Attend. Ay, my lord.
    Tamb. Bring him forth; and let us know if the
town be ransacked.   [*Exeunt* Attendants.

Enter Techelles, Theridamas, Usumcasane, *and others.*

    Tech. The town is ours, my lord, and fresh supply
Of conquest and of spoil is offer'd us.
    Tamb. That's well, Techelles. What's the news?
    Tech. The Soldan and the Arabian king together
March on us with such eager violence   200
As if there were no way but one with us.
    Tamb. No more there is not, I warrant thee,
      Techelles.

Attendants *bring in* Bajazeth *in his cage, followed by*
Zabina. *Exeunt* Attendants.

Ther. We know the victory is ours, my lord,
But let us save the reverend Soldan's life
For fair Zenocrate that so laments his state.
   Tamb. That will we chiefly see unto, Theridamas,
For sweet Zenocrate, whose worthiness
Deserves a conquest over every heart.
And now, my footstool, if I lose the field,
You hope of liberty and restitution?   210
Here let him stay, my masters, from the tents,
Till we have made us ready for the field.
Pray for us, Bajazeth; we are going.
            [*Exeunt all except* Bajazeth *and* Zabina.
   Baj. Go, never to return with victory.
Millions of men encompass thee about,
And gore thy body with as many wounds!
Sharp forked arrows light upon thy horse!
Furies from the black Cocytus lake,
Break up the earth, and with their fire-brands
Enforce the run upon the baneful pikes!   220
Volleys of shot pierce through thy charmed skin,
And every bullet dipt in poison'd drugs!
Or roaring cannons sever all thy joints,
Making thee mount as high as eagles soar!
   Zab. Let all the swords and lances in the field
Stick in his breast as in their proper rooms!
At every pore let blood come dropping forth,
That lingering pains may massacre his heart,
And madness send his damned soul to hell!
   Baj. Ah, fair Zabina, we may curse his power, 230
The heavens may frown, the earth for anger quake;
But such a star hath influence in his sword
As rules the skies and countermands the gods
More than Cimmerian Styx or Destiny:
And then shall we in this detested guise,
With shame, with hunger, and with horror ay,

Griping our bowels with retorqued thoughts,
And have no hope to end our ecstasies.

   Zab. Then is there left no Mahomet, no God,
No fiend, no fortune, nor no hope of end   240
To our infamous, monstrous slaveries?
Gape, earth, and let the fiends infernal view
A hell as hopeless and as full of fear
As are the blasted banks of Erebus,
Where shaking ghosts with ever-howling groans
Hover about the ugly ferryman,
To get a passage to Elysium!
Why should we live? Oh, wretches, beggars, slaves!
Why live we, Bajazeth, and build up nests
So high within the region of the air,   250
By living long in this oppression,
That all the world will see and laugh to scorn
The former triumphs of our mightiness
In this obscure infernal servitude?

   Baj. O life more loathsome to my vexed thoughts
Than noisome parbreak of the Stygian snakes,
Which fills the nooks of hell with standing air,
Infecting all the ghosts with cureless griefs!
O dreary engines of my loathed sight,
That sees my crown, my honour, and my name   260
Thrust under yoke and thraldom of a thief,
Why feed ye still on day's accursed beams,
And sink not quite into my tortur'd soul?
You see my wife, my queen, and emperess,
Brought up and propped by the hand of Fame,
Queen of fifteen contributory queens,
Now thrown to rooms of black abjection,
Smeared with blots of basest drudgery,
And villainess to shame, disdain, and misery.
Accursed Bajazeth, whose words of ruth,   270
That would with pity cheer Zabina's heart,
And make our souls resolve in ceaseless tears,

---

237 retorqued] bent back   256 parbreak] vomit
269 villainess] slave

Sharp hunger bites upon and gripes the root
From whence the issues of my thoughts do break:
O poor Zabina! O my queen, my queen!
Fetch me some water for my burning breast,
To cool and comfort me with longer date,
That in the shorten'd sequel of my life,
I may pour forth my soul into thine arms
With words of love; whose moaning intercourse   280
Hath hitherto been stay'd with wrath and hate
Of our expressless bann'd inflictions.

   Zab. Sweet Bajazeth, I will prolong thy life
As long as any blood or spark of breath
Can quench or cool the torments of my grief.   [*Exit.*

   Baj. Now, Bajazeth, abridge thy baneful days,
And beat thy brains out of thy conquer'd head,
Since other means are all forbidden me,
That may be ministers of my decay.
O highest lamp of ever-living Jove,   290
Accursed day, infected with my griefs,
Hide now thy stained face in endless night,
And shut the windows of the lightsome heavens.
Let ugly Darkness with her rusty coach
Engirt with tempests, wrapt in pitchy clouds,
Smother the earth with never-fading mists,
And let her horses from their nostrils breathe
Rebellious winds and dreadful thunder-claps,
That in this terror Tamburlaine may live,
And my pin'd soul, resolv'd in liquid air,   300
May still excruciate his tormented thoughts!
Then let the stony dart of senseless cold
Pierce through the centre of my withered heart,
And make a passage for my loathed life!

                [*He brains himself against the cage.*

        Re-enter Zabina.

   Zab. What do mine eyes behold? my husband
     dead!
His skull all riven in twain, his brains dash'd out!

The brains of Bajazeth, my lord and sovereign!
O Bajazeth, my husband and my lord;
O Bajazeth! O Turk! O emperor!   309
   Give him his liquor? not I. Bring milk and fire, and
my blood I bring him again.—Tear me in pieces—
give me the sword with a ball of wild-fire upon it.—
Down with him! down with him!—Go to my child;
away, away, away! ah, save that infant! save him,
save him!—I, even I, speak to her.—The sun was
down—streamers white, red, black.—Here, here,
here!—Fling the meat in his face—Tamburlaine,
Tamburlaine!—Let the soldiers be buried.—Hell,
death, Tamburlaine, hell!—Make ready my coach,
my chair, my jewels.—I come, I come, I come! 320
      [*She runs against the cage, and brains herself.*

Enter Zenocrate *with* Anippe.

Zeno. Wretched Zenocrate, that livest to see
Damascus' walls dy'd with Egyptian blood,
Thy father's subjects and thy countrymen;
Thy streets strowed with disseevered joints of men,
And wounded bodies gasping yet for life;
But most accurs'd, to see the sun-bright troop
Of heavenly virgins and unspotted maids
Whose looks might make the angry god of arms
To break his sword and mildly treat of love
On horsemen's lances to be hoisted up,   330
And guiltlessly endure a cruel death;
For every fell and stout Tartarian steed,
That stamp'd on others with their thundering hoofs,
When all their riders charg'd their quivering spears,
Began to check the ground and rein themselves,
Gazing upon the beauty of their looks.
Ah, Tamburlaine, wert thou the cause of this,
That term'st Zenocrate thy dearest love?
Whose lives were dearer to Zenocrate
Than her own life, or aught save thine own love. 340
But see, another bloody spectacle!

Ah, wretched eyes, the enemies of my heart,
How are ye glutted with these grievous objects,
And tell my soul more tales of bleeding ruth!
See, see, Anippe, if they breathe or no.

Anip. No breath, nor sense, nor motion in them
both:
Ah, madam, this their slavery hath enforc'd,
And ruthless cruelty of Tamburlaine.

Zeno. Earth, cast up fountains from thy entrails,
And wet thy cheeks for their untimely deaths;   350
Shake with their weight in sign of fear and grief!
Blush, heaven, that gave them honour at their birth,
And let them die a death so barbarous!
Those that are proud of fickle empery
And place their chiefest good in earthly pomp,
Behold the Turk and his great emperess!
Ah, Tamburlaine my love, sweet Tamburlaine,
That fights for sceptres and for slippery crowns,
Behold the Turk and his great emperess!
Thou, that in conduct of thy happy stars,   360
Sleep'st every night with conquest on thy brows,
And yet wouldst shun the wavering turns of war,
In fear and feeling of the like distress,
Behold the Turk and his great emperess!
Ah, mighty Jove and holy Mahomet,
Pardon my love! Oh, pardon his contempt
Of earthly fortune and respect of pity;
And let not conquest, ruthlessly pursu'd,
Be equally against his life incens'd
In this great Turk and hapless emperess!   370
And pardon me that was not mov'd with ruth
To see them live so long in misery!
Ah, what may chance to thee, Zenocrate?

Anip. Madam, content yourself, and be resolv'd,
Your love hath Fortune so at his command,
That she shall stay and turn her wheel no more,
As long as life maintains his mighty arm
That fights for honour to adorn your head.

Enter Philemus.

Zeno. What other heavy news now brings Philemus?

Phil. Madam, your father, and th' Arabian king,
The first affecter of your excellence,   381
Comes now, as Turnus 'gainst Æneas did,
Armed with lance into the Egyptian fields,
Ready for battle 'gainst my lord the king.

Zeno. Now shame and duty, love and fear presents
A thousand sorrows to my martyred soul!
Whom should I wish the fatal victory,
When my poor pleasures are divided thus,
And rack'd by duty from my cursed heart?
My father and my first-betrothed love   390
Must fight against my life and present love;
Wherein the change I use condemns my faith,
And makes my deeds infamous through the world:
But, as the gods, to end the Trojans' toil,
Prevented Turnus of Lavinia,
And fatally enrich'd Æneas' love,
So, for a final issue to my griefs,
To pacify my country and my love,
Must Tamburlaine by their resistless powers,
With virtue of a gentle victory,   400
Conclude a league of honour to my hope;
Then, as the powers divine have pre-ordain'd,
With happy safety of my father's life
Send like defence of fair Arabia.

> [*They sound to the battle within; and* Tamburlaine
> *enjoys the victory: after which, the* King of Arabia
> *enters wounded.*

K. of Ar. What cursed power guides the murthering
hands
Of this infamous tyrant's soldiers,
That no escape may save their enemies,
Nor fortune keep themselves from victory?
Lie down, Arabia, wounded to the death,
And let Zenocrate's fair eyes behold,   410

That, as for her thou bear'st these wretched arms,
Even so for her thou diest in these arms,
Leaving thy blood for witness of thy love.

   Zeno. Too dear a witness for such love, my lord;
Behold Zenocrate, the cursed object
Whose fortunes never mastered her griefs;
Behold her wounded in conceit for thee,
As much as thy fair body is for me!

   K. of Ar. Then shall I die with full contented heart,
Having beheld divine Zenocrate,   420
Whose sight with joy would take away my life
As now it bringeth sweetness to my wound,
If I had not been wounded as I am.
Ah, that the deadly pangs I suffer now
Would lend an hour's licence to my tongue,
To make discourse of some sweet accidents
Have chanc'd thy merits in this worthless bondage,
And that I might be privy to the state
Of thy deserv'd contentment and thy love;
But, making now a virtue of thy sight,   430
To drive all sorrow from my fainting soul,
Since death denies me further cause of joy,
Depriv'd of care, my heart with comfort dies,
Since thy desired hand shall close mine eyes.   [*Dies.*

Re-enter Tamburlaine, *leading the* Soldan; Techelles,
    Theridamas, Usumcasane, *with others.*

   Tamb. Come, happy father of Zenocrate,
A title higher than thy Soldan's name.
Though my right hand have thus enthralled thee,
Thy princely daughter here shall set thee free;
She that hath calm'd the fury of my sword,
Which had ere this been bath'd in streams of blood
As vast and deep as Euphrates or Nile.   441

   Zeno. O sight thrice-welcome to my joyful soul,
To see the king my father issue safe
From dangerous battle of my conquering love!

Sold. Well met, my only dear Zenocrate,
Though with the loss of Egypt and my crown.
   Tamb. 'Twas I, my lord, that gat the victory,
And therefore grieve not at your overthrow,
Since I shall render all into your hands,
And add more strength to your dominions   450
Than ever yet confirm'd th' Egyptian crown.
The god of war resigns his room to me,
Meaning to make me general of the world:
Jove, viewing me in arms, looks pale and wan,
Fearing my power should pull him from his throne:
Where'er I come the Fatal Sisters sweat,
And grisly Death, by running to and fro,
To do their ceaseless homage to my sword:
And here in Afric, where it seldom rains,
Since I arriv'd with my triumphant host,   460
Have swelling clouds, drawn from wide-gasping
    wounds,
Been oft resolv'd in bloody purple showers,
A meteor that might terrify the earth,
And make it quake at every drop it drinks:
Millions of souls sit on the banks of Styx,
Waiting the back-return of Charon's boat:
Hell and Elysium swarm with ghosts of men
That I have sent from sundry foughten fields
To spread my fame through hell and up to heaven:
And see, my lord, a sight of strange import,   470
Emperors and kings lie breathless at my feet;
The Turk and his great emperess, as it seems,
Left to themselves while we were at the fight,
Have desperately dispatch'd their slavish lives:
With them Arabia, too, hath left his life:
All sights of power to grace my victory;
And such are objects fit for Tamburlaine,
Wherein, as in a mirror, may be seen
His honour, that consists in shedding blood
When men presume to manage arms with him.   480
   Sold. Mighty hath God and Mahomet made thy hand,

Renowned Tamburlaine, to whom all kings
Of force must yield their crowns and emperies;
And I am pleas'd with this my overthrow,
If, as beseems a person of thy state,
Thou hast with honour us'd Zenocrate.

   Tamb. Her state and person want no pomp, you
     see,
And for all blot of foul inchastity,
I record heaven, her heavenly self is clear:
Then let me find no further time to grace   490
Her princely temples with the Persian crown;
But here these kings that on my fortunes wait,
And have been crown'd for proved worthiness
Even by this hand that shall establish them,
Shall now, adjoining all their hands with mine,
Invest her here my Queen of Persia.
What saith the noble Soldan, and Zenocrate?

   Sold. I yield with thanks and protestations
Of endless honour to thee for her love.

   Tamb. Then doubt I not but fair Zenocrate   500
Will soon consent to satisfy us both.

   Zeno. Else should I much forget myself, my lord.

   Ther. Then let us set the crown upon her head,
That long hath linger'd for so high a seat.

   Tech. My hand is ready to perform the deed;
For now her marriage-time shall work us rest.

   Usum. And here's the crown, my lord; help set it
on.

   Tamb. Then sit thou down, divine Zenocrate;
And here we crown thee Queen of Persia,
And all the kingdoms and dominions   510
That late the power of Tamburlaine subdu'd.
As Juno, when the giants were suppress'd,
That darted mountains at her brother Jove,
So looks my love, shadowing in her brows
Triumphs and trophies for my victories;
Or as Latona's daughter, bent to arms,
Adding more courage to my conquering mind.

To gratify the sweet Zenocrate,
Egyptians, Moors, and men of Asia,
From Barbary unto the Western Indie,   520
Shall pay a yearly tribute to thy sire;
And from the bounds of Afric to the banks
Of Ganges shall his mighty arm extend.
And now, my lords and loving followers,
That purchas'd kingdoms by your martial deeds,
Cast off your armour, put on scarlet robes,
Mount up your royal places of estate,
Environed with troops of noblemen,
And there make laws to rule your provinces:
Hang up your weapons on Alcides' post;   530
For Tamburlaine takes truce with all the world.
Thy first-betrothed love, Arabia,
Shall we with honour, as beseems, entomb
With this great Turk and his fair emperess.
Then, after all these solemn exequies,
We will our rites of marriage solemnise.   [*Exeunt.*

Tamburlaine the Greate.

VVith his impaſsionate furie , for the
death of his Lady and Loue faire Zenocrate : his forme of exhortation and diſcipline
to his three Sonnes, and the manner of
his owne death.

The ſecond part.

LONDON
Printed by E. A, for Ed. White, *and are to be ſolde*
at his Shop neere the little North doore of Saint Paules
Church at the Signe of the Gun.
1 6 0 6.

The Prologue

THE general welcomes Tamburlaine receiv'd,
When he arrived last upon our stage,
Hath made our poet pen his Second Part,
Where death cuts off the progress of his pomp,
And murderous Fates throws all his triumphs down.
But what became of fair Zenocrate,
And with how many cities' sacrifice
He celebrated her sad funeral,
Himself in presence shall unfold at large.

Dramatis Personæ

Tamburlaine, *King of Persia.*
Calyphas,
Amyras, } *his sons.*
Celebinus,
Theridamas, *King of Argier.*
Techelles, *King of Fez.*
Usumcasane, *King of Morocco.*
Orcanes, *King of Natolia.*
King of Trebizon.
King of Soria.
King of Jerusalem.
King of Amasia.
Gazellus, *Viceroy of Byron.*
Uribassa.
Sigismund, *King of Hungary.*
Frederick, } *lords of Buda and*
Baldwin, } *Bohemia.*

Callapine, *son to* Bajazeth, *and prisoner to* Tamburlaine.
Almeda, *his keeper.*
Governor of Babylon.
Captain of Balsera.
His Son.
Another Captain.
Maximus, Perdicas, Physicians, Lords, Citizens, Messengers, Soldiers, *and* Attendants.
Zenocrate, *wife to* Tamburlaine.
Olympia, *wife to the* Captain of Balsera.
Turkish Concubines.

The Second Part of
TAMBURLAINE THE GREAT

Act I. Scene I

Enter Orcanes *king of Natolia,* Gazellus *viceroy of Byron,*
    Uribassa, *and their train, with drums and trumpets.*

Orc. Egregious viceroys of these eastern parts,
Plac'd by the issue of great Bajazeth,
And sacred lord, the mighty Callapine,
Who lives in Egypt prisoner to that slave
Which kept his father in an iron cage,
Now have we march'd from fair Natolia
Two hundred leagues, and on Danubius' banks
Our warlike host in complete armour rest,
Where Sigismund, the king of Hungary,
Should meet our person to conclude a truce: 10
What! shall we parley with the Christian?
Or cross the stream, and meet him in the field?
Gaz. King of Natolia, let us treat of peace:
We all are glutted with the Christians' blood,
And have a greater foe to fight against,—
Proud Tamburlaine, that now in Asia,
Near Guyron's head, doth set his conquering feet,
And means to fire Turkey as he goes:
'Gainst him, my lord, must you address your power.
Uri. Besides, King Sigismund hath brought from
            Christendom   20
More than his camp of stout Hungarians,—
Slavonians, Almans, Rutters, Muffs, and Danes,
That with the halberd, lance, and murthering axe,
Will hazard that we might with surety hold.
Orc. Though from the shortest northern parallel,
Vast Gruntland, compass'd with the Frozen Sea,

22 Almans] Germans   Rutters] German troopers.
Muffs] Swiss   26 Gruntland] Greenland

Inhabited with tall and sturdy men,
Giants as big as hugy Polypheme,
Millions of soldiers cut the arctic line,
Bringing the strength of Europe to these arms,   30
Our Turkey blades shall glide through all their
        throats,
And make this champion mead a bloody fen:
Danubius' stream, that runs to Trebizon,
Shall carry, wrapt within his scarlet waves,
As martial presents to our friends at home,
The slaughtered bodies of these Christians:
The Terrene main, wherein Danubius falls,
Shall by this battle be the Bloody Sea:
The wandering sailors of proud Italy   39
Shall meet those Christians, fleeting with the tide,
Beating in heaps against their argosies,
And make fair Europe, mounted on her bull,
Trapp'd with the wealth and riches of the world,
Alight, and wear a woful mourning weed.
    Gaz. Yet, stout Orcanes, pro-rex of the world,
Since Tamburlaine hath muster'd all his men,
Marching from Cairo northward with his camp,
To Alexandria and the frontier towns,
Meaning to make a conquest of our land,
'Tis requisite to parley for a peace   50
With Sigismund, the king of Hungary,
And save our forces for the hot assaults
Proud Tamburlaine intends Natolia.
    Orc. Viceroy of Byron, wisely hast thou said.
My realm, the centre of our empery,
Once lost, all Turkey would be overthrown;
And for that cause the Christians shall have peace.
Slavonians, Almans, Rutters, Muffs, and Danes,
Fear not Orcanes, but great Tamburlaine,
Nor he, but Fortune that hath made him great.   60
We have revolted Grecians, Albanese,
Sicilians, Jews, Arabians, Turks, and Moors,

    32 champion] champaign   59 Fear] frighten

Natolians, Sorians, black Egyptians,
Illyrians, Thracians, and Bithynians,
Enough to swallow forceless Sigismund,
Yet scarce enough t' encounter Tamburlaine.
He brings a world of people to the field,
From Scythia to the oriental plage
Of India, where raging Lantchidol
Beats on the regions with his boisterous blows,   70
That never seaman yet discovered.
All Asia is in arms with Tamburlaine,
Even from the midst of fiery Cancer's tropic
To Amazonia under Capricorn;
And thence, as far as Archipelago,
All Afric is in arms with Tamburlaine:
Therefore, viceroys, the Christians must have peace.

Scene II.

Enter Sigismund, Frederick, Baldwin, *and their train,*
with drums and trumpets.

  Sig. Orcanes, (as our legates promis'd thee,)
We, with our peers, have cross'd Danubius' stream,
To treat of friendly peace or deadly war.
Take which thou wilt; for, as the Romans us'd,
I here present thee with a naked sword:
Wilt thou have war, then shake this blade at me;
If peace, restore it to my hands again,
And I will sheathe it, to confirm the same.
  Orc. Stay, Sigismund: forgett'st thou I am he
That with the cannon shook Vienna-walls,   10
And made it dance upon the continent,
As when the massy substance of the earth
Quiver about the axle-tree of heaven?
Forgett'st thou that I sent a shower of darts,
Mingled with powdered shot and feathered steel
So thick upon the blink-ey'd burghers' heads,

That thou thyself, then County Palatine,
The King of Boheme, and the Austric Duke,
Sent heralds out, which basely on their knees,
In all your names, desir'd a truce of me?   20
Forgett'st thou, that to have me raise my siege,
Waggons of gold were set before my tent,
Stamp'd with the princely fowl that in her wings
Carries the fearful thunderbolts of Jove?
How canst thou think of this, and offer war?

   Sig. Vienna was besieg'd, and I was there,
Then County Palatine, but now a king,
And what we did was in extremity.
But now, Orcanes, view my royal host,
That hides these plains, and seems as vast and wide   30
As doth the desert of Arabia
To those that stand on Badgeth's lofty tower,
Or as the ocean to the traveller
That rests upon the snowy Appenines;
And tell me whether I should stoop so low,
Or treat of peace with the Natolian king.

   Gaz. Kings of Natolia and of Hungary,
We came from Turkey to confirm a league,
And not to dare each other to the field.
A friendly parley might become ye both.   40

   Fred. And we from Europe to the same intent;
Which if your general refuse or scorn,
Our tents are pitch'd, our men stand in array,
Ready to charge you ere you stir your feet.

   Orc. So prest are we: but yet, if Sigismund
Speak as a friend, and stand not upon terms,
Here is his sword; let peace be ratified
On these conditions specified before,
Drawn with advice of our ambassadors.

   Sig. Then here I sheathe it, and give thee my hand,
Never to draw it out, or manage arms   51
Against thyself or thy confederates,
But whilst I live will be at truce with thee.

  32 Badgeth] Bagdad   45 prest] ready

Orc. But, Sigismund, confirm it with an oath,
And swear in sight of heaven and by thy Christ.

   Sig. By Him that made the world and sav'd my
     soul,
The Son of God and issue of a maid,
Sweet Jesus Christ, I solemnly protest
And vow to keep this peace inviolable.

   Orc. By sacred Mahomet, the friend of God,   60
Whose holy Alcoran remains with us,
Whose glorious body, when he left the world,
Clos'd in a coffin mounted up the air,
And hung on stately Mecca's temple-roof,
I swear to keep this truce inviolable.
Of whose conditions and our solemn oaths,
Sign'd with our hands, each shall retain a scroll,
As memorable witness of our league.
Now, Sigismund, if any Christian king
Encroach upon the confines of thy realm,   70
Send word, Orcanes of Natolia
Confirm'd this league beyond Danubius' stream,
And they will, trembling, sound a quick retreat;
So am I fear'd among all nations.

   Sig. If any heathen potentate or king
Invade Natolia, Sigismund will send
A hundred thousand horse train'd to the war,
And back'd by stout lanciers of Germany,
The strength and sinews of the imperial seat.

   Orc. I thank thee, Sigismund; but, when I war, 80
All Asia Minor, Africa, and Greece,
Follow my standard and my thundering drums.
Come, let us go and banquet in our tents:
I will despatch chief of my army hence
To fair Natolia and to Trebizon,
To stay my coming 'gainst proud Tamburlaine:
Friend Sigismund, and peers of Hungary,
Come, banquet and carouse with us a while,
And then depart we to our territories.   *[Exeunt.*

Scene III.

Enter Callapine, *and* Almeda *his keeper.*

Call. Sweet Almeda, pity the ruthful plight
Of Callapine, the son of Bajazeth,
Born to be monarch of the western world,
Yet here detain'd by cruel Tamburlaine.

Alm. My lord, I pity it, and with my heart
Wish your release; but he whose wrath is death,
My sovereign lord, renowned Tamburlaine,
Forbids you further liberty than this.

Call. Ah, were I now but half so eloquent
To paint in words what I'll perform in deeds,　　10
I know thou wouldst depart from hence with me!

Alm. Not for all Afric: therefore move me not.

Call. Yet hear me speak, my gentle Almeda.

Alm. No speech to that end, by your favour, sir.

Call. By Cairo runs—

Alm. No talk of running, I tell you, sir.

Call. A little further, gentle Almeda.

Alm. Well, sir, what of this?

Call. By Cairo runs to Alexandria-bay
Darotes' streams, wherein at anchor lies　　20
A Turkish galley of my royal fleet,
Waiting my coming to the river-side,
Hoping by some means I shall be releas'd;
Which, when I come aboard, will hoist up sail,
And soon put forth into the Terrene sea,
Where, 'twixt the isles of Cyprus and of Crete,
We quickly may in Turkish seas arrive.
Then shalt thou see a hundred kings and more,
Upon their knees, all bid me welcome home.
Amongst so many crowns of burnish'd gold,　　30
Choose which thou wilt, all are at thy command:
A thousand galleys, mann'd with Christian slaves,
I freely give thee, which shall cut the Straits,
And bring armadoes from the coasts of Spain,

Fraughted with gold of rich America:
The Grecian virgins shall attend on thee,
Skilful in music and in amorous lays,
As fair as was Pygmalion's ivory girl
Or lovely Iö metamorphosed:
With naked negroes shall thy coach be drawn,   40
And, as thou rid'st in triumph through the streets,
The pavement underneath thy chariot-wheels
With Turkey-carpets shall be covered,
And cloth of arras hung about the walls,
Fit objects for thy princely eye to pierce:
A hundred bassoes, cloth'd in crimson silk,
Shall ride before thee on Barbarian steeds;
And, when thou goest, a golden canopy
Enchas'd with precious stones, which shine as bright
As that fair veil that covers all the world,   50
When Phœbus, leaping from his hemisphere,
Descendeth downward to th' Antipodes:—
And more than this, for all I cannot tell.

   Alm. How far hence lies the galley, say you?

   Call. Sweet Almeda, scarce half a league from
     hence.

   Alm. But need we not be spied going aboard?

   Call. Betwixt the hollow hanging of a hill,
And crooked bending of a craggy rock,
The sails wrapt up, the mast and tacklings down,
She lies so close that none can find her out.   60

   Alm. I like that well: but tell me, my lord, if I
should let you go, would you be as good as your word?
shall I be made a king for my labour?

   Call. As I am Callapine the emperor,
And by the hand of Mahomet I swear,
Thou shalt be crown'd a king, and be my mate.

   Alm. Then here I swear, as I am Almeda,
Your keeper under Tamburlaine the Great,
(For that's the style and title I have yet,)
Although he sent a thousand armed men   70

56 need] must

To intercept this haughty enterprise,
Yet would I venture to conduct your grace,
And die before I brought you back again!
   Call. Thanks, gentle Almeda: then let us haste,
Lest time be past, and lingering let us both.
   Alm. When you will, my lord: I am ready.
   Call. Even straight: and farewell, cursed Tamburlaine.
Now go I to revenge my father's death.   [*Exeunt.*

Scene IV.

Enter Tamburlaine, Zenocrate, *and their three sons,*
Calyphas, Amyras, *and* Celebinus, *with drums and
trumpets.*

   Tamb. Now, bright Zenocrate, the world's fair eye,
Whose beams illuminate the lamps of heaven,
Whose cheerful looks do clear the cloudy air,
And clothe it in a crystal livery,
Now rest thee here on fair Larissa-plains,
Where Egypt and the Turkish empire parts,
Between thy sons, that shall be emperors,
And every one commander of a world.
   Zeno. Sweet Tamburlaine, when wilt thou leave
     these arms,
And save thy sacred person free from scathe,   10
And dangerous chances of the wrathful war?
   Tamb. When heaven shall cease to move on both
     the poles,
And when the ground, whereon my soldiers march,
Shall rise aloft and touch the horned moon,
And not before, my sweet Zenocrate.
Sit up, and rest thee like a lovely queen.
So, now she sits in pomp and majesty:
When these, my sons, more precious in mine eyes
Than all the wealthy kingdoms I subdued,
Plac'd by her side, look on their mother's face.   20

But yet methinks their looks are amorous,
Not martial as the sons of Tamburlaine:
Water and air, being symbolis'd in one,
Argue their want of courage and of wit;
Their hair, as white as milk, and soft as down,
(Which should be like the quills of porcupines,
As black as jet, and hard as iron or steel)
Bewrays they are too dainty for the wars;
Their fingers made to quaver on a lute,
Their arms to hang about a lady's neck,   30
Their legs to dance and caper in the air,
Would make me think them bastards, not my sons,
But that I know they issued from thy womb,
That never look'd on man but Tamburlaine.
     Zeno. My gracious lord, they have their mother's
          looks,
But when they list, their conquering father's heart.
This lovely boy, the youngest of the three,
Not long ago bestrid a Scythian steed,
Trotting the ring, and tilting at a glove,
Which when he tainted with his slender rod,   40
He rein'd him straight, and made him so curvet
As I cried out for fear he should have fall'n.
     Tamb. Well done, my boy, thou shalt have shield
          and lance,
Armour of proof, horse, helm, and curtle-axe,
And I will teach thee how to charge thy foe,
And harmless run among the deadly pikes.
If thou wilt love the wars and follow me,
Thou shalt be made a king and reign with me,
Keeping in iron cages emperors.
If thou exceed thy elder brothers' worth,   50
And shine in complete virtue more than they,
Thou shalt be king before them, and thy seed
Shall issue crowned from their mother's womb.
     Cel. Yes, father; you shall see me, if I live,
Have under me as many kings as you,

          40 tainted] touched

And march with such a multitude of men
As all the world shall tremble at their view.

   Tamb. These words assure me, boy, thou art my son.
When I am old and cannot manage arms,
Be thou the scourge and terror of the world.   60

   Amy. Why may not I, my lord, as well as he,
Be term'd the scourge and terror of the world?

   Tamb. Be all a scourge and terror to the world,
Or else you are not sons of Tamburlaine.

   Caly. But while my brothers follow arms, my lord,
Let me accompany my gracious mother:
They are enough to conquer all the world,
And you have won enough for me to keep.

   Tamb. Bastardly boy, sprung from some coward's
      loins,
And not the issue of great Tamburlaine!   70
Of all the provinces I have subdued
Thou shalt not have a foot, unless thou bear
A mind courageous and invincible;
For he shall wear the crown of Persia
Whose head hath deepest scars, whose breast most
      wounds,
Which being wroth sends lightning from his eyes,
And in the furrows of his frowning brows
Harbours revenge, war, death, and cruelty;
For in a field, whose superficies
Is covered with a liquid purple veil,   80
And sprinkled with the brains of slaughtered men,
My royal chair of state shall be advanc'd;
And he that means to place himself therein,
Must armed wade up to the chin in blood.

   Zeno. My lord, such speeches to our princely sons
Dismays their minds before they come to prove
The wounding troubles angry war affords.

   Cel. No, madam, these are speeches fit for us;
For, if his chair were in a sea of blood,
I would prepare a ship and sail to it,   90
Ere I would lose the title of a king.

Amy. And I would strive to swim through pools of
    blood
Or make a bridge of murthered carcasses,
Whose arches should be fram'd with bones of Turks,
Ere I would lose the title of a king.

Tamb. Well, lovely boys, you shall be emperors both,
Stretching your conquering arms from east to west:
And, sirrah, if you mean to wear a crown,
When we shall meet the Turkish deputy
And all his viceroys, snatch it from his head,   100
And cleave his pericranion with thy sword.

Caly. If any man will hold him, I will strike,
And cleave him to the channel with my sword.

Tamb. Hold him, and cleave him too, or I'll cleave
    thee;
For we will march against them presently.
Theridamas, Techelles, and Casane
Promis'd to meet me on Larissa-plains,
With hosts apiece against this Turkish crew;
For I have sworn by sacred Mahomet
To make it parcel of my empery.   110
The trumpets sound; Zenocrate, they come.

Enter Theridamas, *and his train, with drums and
    trumpets.*

Welcome Theridamas, king of Argier.

Ther. My lord, the great and mighty Tamburlaine,
Arch-monarch of the world, I offer here
My crown, myself, and all the power I have,
In all affection at thy kingly feet.

Tamb. Thanks, good Theridamas.

Ther. Under my colours march ten thousand
    Greeks,
And of Argier and Afric's frontier towns
Twice twenty thousand valiant men-at-arms   120

103 channel] collar-bone

All which have sworn to sack Natolia.
Five hundred brigandines are under sail,
Meet for your service on the sea, my lord,
That, launching from Argier to Tripoly,
Will quickly ride before Natolia,
And batter down the castles on the shore.
    Tamb. Well said, Argier: receive thy crown again.

        Enter Usumcasane *and* Techelles.

Kings of Morocco and of Fez, welcome.
    Usum. Magnificent and peerless Tamburlaine,
I and my neighbour king of Fez have brought,   130
To aid thee in this Turkish expedition,
A hundred thousand expert soldiers;
From Azamor to Tunis near the sea
Is Barbary unpeopled for thy sake,
And all the men in armour under me,
Which with my crown I gladly offer thee.
    Tamb. Thanks, king of Morocco: take your crown
    again.
    Tech. And, mighty Tamburlaine, our earthly god,
Whose looks make this inferior world to quake,
I here present thee with the crown of Fez,   140
And with an host of Moors train'd to the war,
Whose coal-black faces make their foes retire,
And quake for fear, as if infernal Jove,
Meaning to aid thee in these Turkish arms,
Should pierce the black circumference of hell,
With ugly Furies bearing fiery flags,
And millions of his strong tormenting spirits:
From strong Tesella unto Biledull
All Barbary is unpeopled for thy sake.
    Tamb. Thanks, king of Fez: take here thy crown
    again.   150
Your presence, loving friends and fellow-kings,
Makes me to surfeit in conceiving joy:
If all the crystal gates of Jove's high court

Were opened wide, and I might enter in
To see the state and majesty of heaven,
It could not more delight me than your sight.
Now will we banquet on these plains a while,
And after march to Turkey with our camp,
In number more than are the drops that fall
When Boreas rents a thousand swelling clouds;   160
And proud Orcanes of Natolia
With all his viceroys shall be so afraid,
That, though the stones, as at Deucalion's flood,
Were turn'd to men, he should be overcome.
Such lavish will I make of Turkish blood,
That Jove shall send his winged messenger
To bid me sheathe my sword and leave the field;
The sun, unable to sustain the sight,
Shall hide his head in Thetis' watery lap,
And leave his steeds to fair Böotes' charge;   170
For half the world shall perish in this fight.
But now, my friends, let me examine ye;
How have ye spent your absent time from me?

   Usum. My lord, our men of Barbary have march'd
Four hundred miles with armour on their backs,
And lain in leaguer fifteen months and more;
For, since we left you at the Soldan's court,
We have subdu'd the southern Guallatia,
And all the land unto the coast of Spain;
We kept the narrow Strait of Gibraltar,   180
And made Canaria call us kings and lords:
Yet never did they recreate themselves,
Or cease one day from war and hot alarms;
And therefore let them rest a while, my lord.

   Tamb. They shall, Casane, and 'tis time, i'faith.

   Tech. And I have march'd along the river Nile
To Machda, where the mighty Christian priest,
Call'd John the Great, sits in a milk-white robe,
Whose triple mitre I did take by force,
And made him swear obedience to my crown.   190
From thence unto Cazates did I march,

Where Amazonians met me in the field,
With whom, being women, I vouchsaf'd a league,
And with my power did march to Zanzibar,
The western part of Afric, where I view'd
The Ethiopian sea, rivers and lakes,
But neither man nor child in all the land:
Therefore I took my course to Manico,
Where, unresisted, I remov'd my camp;
And, by the coast of Byather, at last   200
I came to Cubar, where the negroes dwell,
And, conquering that, made haste to Nubia.
There, having sack'd Borno, the kingly seat,
I took the king and led him bound in chains
Unto Damascus, where I stay'd before.

   Tamb. Well done, Techelles. What saith Theridamas?

   Ther. I left the confines and the bounds of Afric,
And made a voyage into Europe,
Where by the river Tyros I subdu'd
Stoka, Padalia, and Codemia;   210
Then cross'd the sea and came to Oblia,
And Nigra Silva, where the devils dance,
Which, in despite of them, I set on fire.
From thence I cross'd the gulf call'd by the name
Mare Majore of the inhabitants.
Yet shall my soldiers make no period
Until Natolia kneel before your feet.

   Tamb. Then will we triumph, banquet, and carouse;
Cooks shall have pensions to provide us cates,
And glut us with the dainties of the world;   220
Lachryma Christi and Calabrian wines
Shall common soldiers drink in quaffing bowls,
Ay, liquid gold, when we have conquer'd him,
Mingled with coral and with orient pearl.
Come, let us banquet and carouse the whiles.

                                        [Exeunt.

Act II.   Scene I.

Enter Sigismund, Frederick, *and* Baldwin, *with their train.*

Sig. Now say, my lords of Buda and Bohemia,
What motion is it that inflames your thoughts,
And stirs your valours to such sudden arms?
Fred. Your majesty remembers, I am sure,
What cruel slaughter of our Christian bloods
These heathenish Turks and pagans lately made
Betwixt the city Zula and Danubius;
How through the midst of Varna and Bulgaria,
And almost to the very walls of Rome,
They have, not long since, massacred our camp.   10
It resteth now, then, that your majesty
Take all advantages of time and power,
And work revenge upon these infidels.
Your highness knows, for Tamburlaine's repair,
That strikes a terror to all Turkish hearts,
Natolia hath dismiss'd the greatest part
Of all his army, pitch'd against our power
Betwixt Cutheia and Orminius' mount,
And sent them marching up to Belgasar,
Acantha, Antioch, and Cæsarea,   20
To aid the kings of Soria and Jerusalem.
Now, then, my lord, advantage take hereof,
And issue suddenly upon the rest;
That in the fortune of their overthrow,
We may discourage all the pagan troop
That dare attempt to war with Christians.
Sig. But calls not then your grace to memory
The league we lately made with King Orcanes,
Confirm'd by oath and articles of peace,
And calling Christ for record of our truths?   30
This should be treachery and violence
Against the grace of our profession.
Bald. No whit, my lord; for with such infidels,

In whom no faith nor true religion rests,
We are not bound to those accomplishments
The holy laws of Christendom enjoin;
But as the faith which they profanely plight
Is not by necessary policy
To be esteem'd assurance for ourselves,
So what we vow to them should not infringe   40
Our liberty of arms and victory.

  Sig. Though I confess the oaths they undertake
Breed little strength to our security,
Yet those infirmities that thus defame
Their faiths, their honours, and their religion,
Should not give us presumption to the like.
Our faiths are sound, and must be consummate,
Religious, righteous, and inviolate.

  Fred. Assure your grace, 'tis superstition
To stand so strictly on dispensive faith;   50
And should we lose the opportunity
That God hath given to venge our Christians' death,
And scourge their foul blasphemous paganism,
As fell to Saul, to Balaam, and the rest,
That would not kill and curse at God's command,
So surely will the vengeance of the Highest,
And jealous anger of his fearful arm,
Be pour'd with rigour on our sinful heads,
If we neglect this offered victory.

  Sig. Then arm, my lords, and issue suddenly,   60
Giving commandment to our general host,
With expedition to assail the pagan,
And take the victory our God hath given. [*Exeunt.*

Scene II.

Enter Orcanes, Gazellus, *and* Uribassa, *with their train.*

  Orc. Gazellus, Uribassa, and the rest,
Now will we march from proud Orminius' mount
To fair Natolia, where our neighbour kings
Expect our power and our royal presence,

T' encounter with the cruel Tamburlaine,
That nigh Larissa sways a mighty host,
And with the thunder of his martial tools
Makes earthquakes in the hearts of men and heaven.

Gaz. And now come we to make his sinews shake
With greater power than erst his pride hath felt.   10
An hundred kings, by scores, will bid him arms,
And hundred thousands subjects to each score:
Which, if a shower of wounding thunderbolts
Should break out of the bowels of the clouds,
And fall as thick as hail upon our heads,
In partial aid of that proud Scythian,
Yet should our courages and steeled crests,
And numbers more than infinite of men,
Be able to withstand and conquer him.

Uri. Methinks I see how glad the Christian king   20
Is made for joy of your admitted truce,
That could not but before be terrified
With unacquainted power of our host.

Enter a Messenger.

Mess. Arm, dread sovereign, and my noble lords!
The treacherous army of the Christians,
Taking advantage of your slender power,
Comes marching on us, and determines straight
To bid us battle for our dearest lives.

Orc. Traitors, villains, damned Christians!
Have I not here the articles of peace   30
And solemn covenants we have both confirm'd,
He by his Christ, and I by Mahomet?

Gaz. Hell and confusion light upon their heads,
That with such treason seek our overthrow,
And cares so little for their prophet Christ!

Orc. Can there be such deceit in Christians,
Or treason in the fleshly heart of man,
Whose shape is figure of the highest God?
Then if there be a Christ, as Christians say,
But in their deeds deny him for their Christ,   40

If he be son to everliving Jove,
And hath the power of his outstretched arm,
If he be jealous of his name and honour
As is our holy prophet Mahomet,
Take here these papers as our sacrifice
And witness of thy servant's perjury.

[*He tears to pieces the articles of peace.*

Open, thou shining veil of Cynthia,
And make a passage from the imperial heaven,
That he that sits on high and never sleeps,
Nor in one place is circumscriptible,   50
But everywhere fills every continent
With strange infusion of his sacred vigour,
May, in his endless power and purity,
Behold and venge this traitor's perjury!
Thou Christ that art esteem'd omnipotent,
If thou wilt prove thyself a perfect God,
Worthy the worship of all faithful hearts,
Be now reveng'd upon this traitor's soul,
And make the power I have left behind
(Too little to defend our guiltless lives)   60
Sufficient to discomfort and confound
The trustless force of those false Christians.
To arms, my lords! on Christ still let us cry:
If there be Christ, we shall have victory.   [*Exeunt.*

Scene III.

Alarms of battle within. Enter Sigismund *wounded.*

Sig. Discomfited is all the Christian host,
And God hath thundered vengeance from on high,
For my accurs'd and hateful perjury.
O just and dreadful punisher of sin,
Let the dishonour of the pains I feel
In this my mortal well-deserved wound
End all my penance in my sudden death!
And let this death, wherein to sin I die,
Conceive a second life in endless mercy!   [*Dies.*

Enter Orcanes, Gazellus, Uribassa, *with others.*

Orc. Now lie the Christians bathing in their bloods,
And Christ or Mahomet hath been my friend.   11

Gaz. See, here the perjur'd traitor Hungary,
Bloody and breathless for his villany.

Orc. Now shall his barbarous body be a prey
To beasts and fowls, and all the winds shall breathe
Through shady leaves of every senseless tree,
Murmurs and hisses for his heinous sin.
Now scalds his soul in the Tartarian streams,
And feeds upon the baneful tree of hell,
That Zoacum, that fruit of bitterness,   20
That in the midst of fire is ingraft,
Yet flourisheth as Flora in her pride,
With apples like the heads of damned fiends.
The devils there, in chains of quenchless flame,
Shall lead his soul, through Orcus' burning gulf,
From pain to pain, whose change shall never end.
What say'st thou yet, Gazellus, to his foil,
Which we referr'd to justice of his Christ
And to his power, which here appears as full
As rays of Cynthia to the clearest sight?   30

Gaz. 'Tis but the fortune of the wars, my lord,
Whose power is often prov'd a miracle.

Orc. Yet in my thoughts shall Christ be honoured,
Not doing Mahomet an injury,
Whose power had share in this our victory;
And since this miscreant hath disgrac'd his faith,
And died a traitor both to heaven and earth,
We will both watch and ward shall keep his trunk
Amidst these plains for fowls to prey upon.
Go, Uribassa, give it straight in charge.   40

Uri. I will, my lord.   [*Exit.*

Orc. And now, Gazellus, let us haste and meet
Our army, and our brother of Jerusalem,
Of Soria, Trebizon, and Amasia,
And happily, with full Natolian bowls

Of Greekish wine, now let us celebrate
Our happy conquest and his angry fate.   [*Exeunt.*

Scene IV.

*The arras is drawn, and Zenocrate is discovered lying in
her bed of state;* Tamburlaine *sitting by her; three Pysi-
cians about her bed, tempering potions; her three sons*
Calyphas, Amyras, *and* Celebinus; *Theridamas,*
Techelles *and* Usumcasane.

Tamb. Black is the beauty of the brightest day;
The golden ball of heaven's eternal fire,
That danc'd with glory on the silver waves,
Now wants the fuel that inflam'd his beams,
And all with faintness, and for foul disgrace,
He binds his temples with a frowning cloud,
Ready to darken earth with endless night.
Zenocrate, that gave him light and life,
Whose eyes shot fire from their ivory bowers,
And tempered every soul with lively heat,   10
Now by the malice of the angry skies,
Whose jealousy admits no second mate,
Draws in the comfort of her latest breath,
All dazzled with the hellish mists of death.
Now walk the angels on the walls of heaven,
As sentinels to warn th' immortal souls
To entertain divine Zenocrate:
Apollo, Cynthia, and the ceaseless lamps
That gently look'd upon this loathsome earth,
Shine downwards now no more, but deck the heavens
To entertain divine Zenocrate: 21
The crystal springs, whose taste illuminates
Refined eyes with an eternal sight,
Like tried silver runs through Paradise
To entertain divine Zenocrate:
The cherubins and holy seraphins,
That sing and play before the King of Kings,
Use all their voices and their instruments

To entertain divine Zenocrate;
And in this sweet and curious harmony, 30
The god that tunes this music to our souls
Holds out his hand in highest majesty
To entertain divine Zenocrate.
Then let some holy trance convey my thoughts
Up to the palace of th' imperial heaven,
That this my life may be as short to me
As are the days of sweet Zenocrate.—
Physicians, will no physic do her good?
   First Phys. My lord, your majesty shall soon per-
     ceive:
And if she pass this fit, the worst is past. 40
   Tamb. Tell me, how fares my fair Zenocrate?
   Zeno. I fare, my lord, as other emperesses,
That, when this frail and transitory flesh
Hath suck'd the measure of that vital air
That feeds the body with his dated health,
Wane with enforc'd and necessary change.
   Tamb. May never such a change transform my love,
In whose sweet being I repose my life;
Whose heavenly presence, beautified with health,
Gives light to Phœbus and the fixed stars; 50
Whose absence makes the sun and moon as dark
As when, oppos'd in one diameter,
Their spheres are mounted on the serpent's head,
Or else descended to his winding train.
Live still, my love, and so conserve my life,
Or, dying, be the author of my death.
   Zeno. Live still, my lord; Oh, let my sovereign live!
And sooner let the fiery element
Dissolve, and make your kingdom in the sky,
Than this base earth should shroud your majesty; 60
For, should I but suspect your death by mine,
The comfort of my future happiness,
And hope to meet your highness in the heavens,
Turn'd to despair, would break my wretched breast,
And fury would confound my present rest.

But let me die, my love; yet let me die;
With love and patience let your true love die:
Your grief and fury hurts my second life.
Yet let me kiss my lord before I die,
And let me die with kissing of my lord.   70
But since my life is lengthened yet a while,
Let me take leave of these my loving sons,
And of my lords, whose true nobility
Have merited my latest memory.
Sweet sons, farewell! in death resemble me,
And in your lives your father's excellency.
Some music, and my fit will cease, my lord.
                              [They call for music.

   Tamb. Proud fury, and intolerable fit,
That dares torment the body of my love,
And scourge the scourge of the immortal God!   80
Now are those spheres, where Cupid us'd to sit,
Wounding the world with wonder and with love,
Sadly supplied with pale and ghastly death,
Whose darts do pierce the centre of my soul.
Her sacred beauty hath enchanted heaven,
And had she liv'd before the siege of Troy,
Helen, whose beauty summon'd Greece to arms,
And drew a thousand ships to Tenedos,
Had not been nam'd in Homer's Iliads;
Her name had been in every line he wrote;   90
Or, had those wanton poets, for whose birth
Old Rome was proud, but gaz'd a while on her,
Nor Lesbia nor Corinna had been nam'd—
Zenocrate had been the argument
Of every epigram or elegy.
                    [The music sounds—Zenocrate dies.
What, is she dead? Techelles, draw thy sword,
And wound the earth, that it may cleave in twain,
And we descend into th' infernal vaults,
To hale the Fatal Sisters by the hair,
And throw them in the triple moat of hell,   100
For taking hence my fair Zenocrate.

Casane and Theridamas, to arms!
Raise cavalieros higher than the clouds,
And with the cannon break the frame of heaven;
Batter the shining palace of the sun,
And shiver all the starry firmament,
For amorous Jove hath snatch'd my love from hence,
Meaning to make her stately queen of heaven.
What god soever holds thee in his arms,
Giving thee nectar and ambrosia,   110
Behold me here, divine Zenocrate,
Raving, impatient, desperate, and mad,
Breaking my steeled lance, with which I burst
The rusty beams of Janus' temple-doors,
Letting out Death and tyrannising War,
To march with me under this bloody flag!
And, if thou pitiest Tamburlaine the Great,
Come down from heaven, and live with me again!
   Ther. Ah, good my lord, be patient; she is dead,
And all this raging cannot make her live.   120
If words might serve, our voice hath rent the air;
If tears, our eyes have watered all the earth;
If grief, our murthered hearts have strain'd forth blood:
Nothing prevails, for she is dead, my lord.
   Tamb. For she is dead! thy words do pierce my soul:
Ah, sweet Theridamas, say so no more;
Though she be dead, yet let me think she lives,
And feed my mind that dies for want of her.   [me,
Where'er her soul be, thou [*To the body*] shalt stay with
Embalm'd with cassia, ambergris, and myrrh,   130
Not lapp'd in lead, but in a sheet of gold,
And till I die thou shalt not be interr'd.
Then in as rich a tomb as Mausolus'
We both will rest and have one epitaph
Writ in as many several languages
As I have conquered kingdoms with my sword.
This cursed town will I consume with fire,
Because this place bereft me of my love;

     103 cavalieros] mounds for cannon

The houses, burnt, will look as if they mourn'd;
And here will I set up her stature   140
And march about it with my mourning camp,
Drooping and pining for Zenocrate.

                              [*The arras is drawn.*

Act III.   Scene I.

Enter the Kings of Trebizon *and* Soria, *one bringing a*
sword and the other a sceptre; next, Orcanes *king of*
Natolia, *and the* King of Jerusalem *with the imperial*
crown; after, Callapine; *and, after him, other* Lords *and*
Almeda. Orcanes *and the* King of Jerusalem *crown*
          Callapine, *and the others give him the sceptre.*

Orc. Callapinus Cyricelibes, otherwise Cybelius, son
and successive heir to the late mighty emperor Bajazeth, by the aid of God and his friend Mahomet, Emperor of Natolia, Jerusalem, Trebizon, Soria, Amasia,
Thracia, Illyria, Carmania, and all the hundred and
thirty kingdoms late contributory to his mighty father.
Long live Callapinus, Emperor of Turkey!

Call. Thrice-worthy kings, of Natolia and the rest,
I will requite your royal gratitudes
With all the benefits my empire yields;   10
And were the sinews of th' imperial seat
So knit and strengthen'd as when Bajazeth,
My royal lord and father, fill'd the throne,
Whose cursed fate hath so dismember'd it,
Then should you see this thief of Scythia,
This proud usurping king of Persia,
Do us such honour and supremacy,
Bearing the vengeance of our father's wrongs,
As all the world should blot our dignities
Out of the book of base-born infamies.   20
And now I doubt not but your royal cares
Hath so provided for this cursed foe,
That, since the heir of mighty Bajazeth

        140 stature] statue. *Perhaps read* statua

(An emperor so honoured for his virtues)
Revives the spirits of true Turkish hearts,
In grievous memory of his father's shame,
We shall not need to nourish any doubt,
But that proud Fortune, who hath followed long
The martial sword of mighty Tamburlaine
Will now retain her old inconstancy,   30
And raise our honours to as high a pitch,
In this our strong and fortunate encounter;
For so hath heaven provided my escape
From all the cruelty my soul sustain'd,
By this my friendly keeper's happy means,
That Jove, surcharg'd with pity of our wrongs,
Will pour it down in showers on our heads,
Scourging the pride of cursed Tamburlaine.
   Orc. I have a hundred thousand men in arms;
Some, that in conquest of the perjur'd Christian,   40
Being a handful to a mighty host,
Think them in number yet sufficient
To drink the river Nile or Euphrates,
And for their power enow to win the world.
   K. of Jer. And I as many from Jerusalem,
Judæa, Gaza, and Scalonia's bounds,
That on mount Sinai, with their ensigns spread,
Look like the parti-coloured clouds of heaven
That show fair weather to the neighbour morn.
   K. of Treb. And I as many bring from Trebizon, 50
Chio, Famastro, and Amasia,
All bordering on the Mare-Major Sea,
Riso, Sancina, and the bordering towns
That touch the end of famous Euphrates,
Whose courages are kindled with the flames
The cursed Scythian sets on all their towns,
And vow to burn the villain's cruel heart.
   K. of Sor. From Soria with seventy thousand strong,
Ta'en from Aleppo, Soldino, Tripoly,
And so unto my city of Damascus,   60

46 Scalonia] Ascalon

I march to meet and aid my neighbour kings;
All which will join against this Tamburlaine,
And bring him captive to your highness' feet.

    Orc. Our battle, then, in martial manner pitch'd,
According to our ancient use, shall bear
The figure of the semicircled moon,
Whose horns shall sprinkle through the tainted air
The poisoned brains of this proud Scythian.

    Call. Well, then, my noble lords, for this my friend
That freed me from the bondage of my foe,   70
I think it requisite and honourable
To keep my promise and to make him king,
That is a gentleman, I know, at least.

    Alm. That's no matter, sir, for being a king; for
Tamburlaine came up of nothing.

    K. of Jer. Your majesty may choose some 'pointed time,
Performing all your promise to the full;
'Tis naught for your majesty to give a kingdom.

    Call. Then will I shortly keep my promise, Almeda.

    Alm. Why, I thank your majesty.   [*Exeunt.*

Scene II.

Enter Tamburlaine *and his three sons,* Calyphas,
Amyras, *and* Celebinus; Usumcasane; *four* Attendants
bearing the hearse of Zenocrate, *and the drums sounding a
doleful march; the town burning.*

    Tam. So, burn the turrets of this cursed town,
Flame to the highest region of the air,
And kindle heaps of exhalations,
That being fiery meteors, may presage
Death and destruction to th' inhabitants!
Over my zenith hang a blazing star,
That may endure till heaven be dissolv'd,
Fed with the fresh supply of earthly dregs,
Threatening a dearth and famine to this land!
Flying dragons, lightning, fearful thunder-claps,   10

Singe these fair plains, and make them seem as black
As is the island where the Furies mask,
Compass'd with Lethe, Styx, and Phlegethon,
Because my dear Zenocrate is dead.

   Caly. This pillar, plac'd in memory of her,
Where in Arabian, Hebrew, Greek, is writ,
This town, being burnt by Tamburlaine the Great,
Forbids the world to build it up again.

   Amy. And here this mournful streamer shall be plac'd,
Wrought with the Persian and Egyptian arms,   20
To signify she was a princess born,
And wife unto the monarch of the East.

   Cel. And here this table as a register
Of all her virtues and perfections.

   Tamb. And here the picture of Zenocrate,
To show her beauty which the world admir'd;
Sweet picture of divine Zenocrate,
That, hanging here, will draw the gods from heaven,
And cause the stars fix'd in the southern arc,
Whose lovely faces never any viewed   30
That have not pass'd the centre's latitude,
As pilgrims travel to our hemisphere,
Only to gaze upon Zenocrate.
Thou shalt not beautify Larissa-plains,
But keep within the circle of mine arms:
At every town and castle I besiege,
Thou shalt be set upon my royal tent;
And when I meet an army in the field,
Those looks will shed such influence in my camp,
As if Bellona, goddess of the war,   40
Threw naked swords and sulphur-balls of fire
Upon the heads of all our enemies.—
And now, my lords, advance your spears again;
Sorrow no more, my sweet Casane, now:
Boys, leave to mourn; this town shall ever mourn,
Being burnt to cinders for your mother's death.

   Caly. If I had wept a sea of tears for her,
It would not ease the sorrows I sustain.

Amy. As is that town, so is my heart consum'd
With grief and sorrow for my mother's death.   50

Cel. My mother's death hath mortified my mind,
And sorrow stops the passage of my speech.

Tamb. But now, my boys, leave off and list to
    me,
That mean to teach you rudiments of war.
I'll have you learn to sleep upon the ground,
March in your armour thorough watery fens,
Sustain the scorching heat and freezing cold,
Hunger and thirst, right adjuncts of the war,
And after this, to scale a castle-wall,
Besiege a fort, to undermine a town,   60
And make whole cities caper in the air:
Then next, the way to fortify your men;
In champion grounds what figure serves you best,
For which the quinque-angle form is meet,
Because the corners there may fall more flat
Whereas the fort may fittest be assail'd,
And sharpest where th' assault is desperate:
The ditches must be deep; the counterscarps
Narrow and steep; the walls made high and broad,
The bulwarks and the rampires large and strong,   70
With cavalieros and thick counterforts,
And room within to lodge six thousand men;
It must have privy ditches, countermines,
And secret issuings to defend the ditch;
It must have high argins and cover'd ways
To keep the bulwark-fronts from battery,
And parapets to hide the musketeers,
Casemates to place the great artillery,
And store of ordnance, that from every flank
May scour the outward curtains of the fort,   80
Dismount the cannon of the adverse part,
Murther the foe, and save the walls from breach.
When this is learn'd for service on the land,
By plain and easy demonstration

66 Whereas] where   75 argins] glacis, or earthwork

I'll teach you how to make the water mount,
That you may dry-foot march through lakes and
  pools,
Deep rivers, havens, creeks, and little seas,
And make a fortress in the raging waves,
Fenc'd with the concave of a monstrous rock,
Invincible by nature of the place.   90
When this is done, then are ye soldiers,
And worthy sons of Tamburlaine the Great.
  Caly. My lord, but this is dangerous to be done;
We may be slain or wounded ere we learn.
  Tamb. Villain, art thou the son of Tamburlaine,
And fear'st to die, or with a curtle-axe
To hew thy flesh and make a gaping wound?
Hast thou beheld a peal of ordnance strike
A ring of pikes, mingled with shot and horse,
Whose shattered limbs, being toss'd as high as heaven,
Hang in the air as thick as sunny motes,   101
And canst thou, coward, stand in fear of death?
Hast thou not seen my horsemen charge the foe,
Shot through the arms, cut overthwart the hands,
Dyeing their lances with their streaming blood,
And yet at night carouse within my tent,
Filling their empty veins with airy wine,
That, being concocted, turns to crimson blood,
And wilt thou shun the field for fear of wounds?
View me, thy father, that hath conquered kings,   110
And, with his host, march'd round about the earth,
Quite void of scars and clear from any wound,
That by the wars lost not a dram of blood,
And see him lance his flesh to teach you all.
                                   [*He cuts his arm.*
A wound is nothing, be it ne'er so deep;
Blood is the God of War's rich livery.
Now look I like a soldier, and this wound
As great a grace and majesty to me,
As if a chair of gold enamelled,
Enchas'd with diamonds, sapphires, rubies,   120

And fairest pearl of wealthy India,
Were mounted here under a canopy,
And I sat down, cloth'd with the massy robe
That late adorn'd the Afric potentate,
Whom I brought bound unto Damascus' walls.
Come, boys, and with your fingers search my wound,
And in my blood wash all your hands at once,
While I sit smiling to behold the sight.
Now, my boys, what think you of a wound?

   Caly. I know not what I should think of it; methinks
'tis a pitiful sight.   131

   Cel. 'Tis nothing: Give me a wound, father.

   Amy. And me another, my lord.

   Tamb. Come, sirrah, give me your arm.

   Cel. Here, father, cut it bravely, as you did your own.

   Tamb. It shall suffice thou dar'st abide a wound;
My boy, thou shalt not lose a drop of blood
Before we meet the army of the Turk;
But then run desperate through the thickest throngs,
Dreadless of blows, of bloody wounds, and death;
And let the burning of Larissa-walls,   141
My speech of war, and this my wound you see,
Teach you, my boys, to bear courageous minds,
Fit for the followers of great Tamburlaine.
Usumcasane, now come, let us march
Towards Techelles and Theridamas,
That we have sent before to fire the towns,
The towers and cities of these hateful Turks,
And hunt that coward faint-heart runaway,
With that accursed traitor Almeda,   150
Till fire and sword have found them at a bay.

   Usum. I long to pierce his bowels with my sword,
That hath betrayed my gracious sovereign,—
That curs'd and damned traitor Almeda.

   Tamb. Then let us see if coward Callapine
Dare levy arms against our puissance,
That we may tread upon his captive neck,
And treble all his father's slaveries.   [*Exeunt.*

Scene III.

Enter Techelles, Theridamas, *and their train.*

Ther. Thus have we march'd northward from
    Tamburlaine,
Unto the frontier point of Soria;
And this is Balsera, their chiefest hold,
Wherein is all the treasure of the land.

Tech. Then let us bring our light artillery,
Minions, falc'nets, and sakers, to the trench,
Filling the ditches with the walls' wide breach,
And enter in to seize upon the gold.—
How say ye, soldiers, shall we not?

Soldiers. Yes, my lord, yes; come, let's about it. 10

Ther. But stay a while; summon a parley, drum.
It may be they will yield it quietly,
Knowing two kings, the friends to Tamburlaine,
Stand at the walls with such a mighty power.

    [*A parley sounded.*—Captain *appears on the walls,*
      with Olympia *his wife, and his son.*

Capt. What require you, my masters?

Ther. Captain, that thou yield up thy hold to us.

Capt. To you! why, do you think me weary of it?

Tech. Nay, captain, thou art weary of thy life,
If thou withstand the friends of Tamburlaine.

Ther. These pioners of Argier in Africa, 20
Even in the cannon's face, shall raise a hill
Of earth and faggots higher than thy fort,
And, over thy argins and covered ways,
Shall play upon the bulwarks of thy hold
Volleys of ordinance, till the breach be made
That with his ruin fills up all the trench;
And, when we enter in, not heaven itself
Shall ransom thee, thy wife, and family. [pipes

Tech. Captain, these Moors shall cut the leaden
That bring fresh water to thy men and thee, 30

    20 pioners] pioneers

And lie in trench before thy castle-walls,
That no supply of victual shall come in,
Nor any issue forth but they shall die;
And, therefore, captain, yield it quietly.
    Capt. Were you, that are the friends of Tambur-
laine,
Brothers to holy Mahomet himself,
I would not yield it; therefore do your worst:
Raise mounts, batter, intrench, and undermine,
Cut off the water, all convoys that can,
Yet I am resolute: and so, farewell.   40
    [*Captain, Olympia, and son, retire from the walls.*
    Ther. Pioners, away! and where I stuck the stake,
Intrench with those dimensions I prescribed;
Cast up the earth towards the castle-wall,
Which, till it may defend you, labour low,
And few or none shall perish by their shot.
    Pioners. We will, my lord.   [*Exeunt* Pioners.
    Tech. A hundred horse shall scout about the plains,
To spy what force comes to relieve the hold.
Both we, Theridamas, will intrench our men,
And with the Jacob's staff measure the height   50
And distance of the castle from the trench,
That we may know if our artillery
Will carry full point-blank unto their walls.
    Ther. Then see the bringing of our ordinance
Along the trench into the battery,
Where we will have gabions of six foot broad,
To save our cannoneers from musket-shot;
Betwixt which shall our ordinance thunder forth,
And with the breach's fall, smoke, fire, and dust,
The crack, the echo, and the soldier's cry,   60
Make deaf the air and dim the crystal sky.
    Tech. Trumpets and drums, alarum presently!
And, soldiers, play the men; the hold is yours!
        [*Exeunt.*

Scene IV.

Alarms within. Enter the Captain, *with* Olympia, *and his son.*

  Olym. Come, good my lord, and let us haste from hence,
Along the cave that leads beyond the foe:
No hope is left to save this conquered hold.
  Capt. A deadly bullet gliding through my side,
Lies heavy on my heart; I cannot live:
I feel my liver pierc'd, and all my veins,
That there begin and nourish every part,
Mangled and torn, and all my entrails bath'd
In blood that straineth from their orifex.
Farewell, sweet wife! sweet son, farewell! I die.   10
                                    [Dies.
  Olym. Death, whither art thou gone, that both we live?
Come back again, sweet Death, and strike us both!
One minute end our days, and one sepulchre
Contain our bodies! Death, why com'st thou not?
Well, this must be the messenger for thee:
                        [Drawing a dagger.
Now, ugly Death, stretch out thy sable wings,
And carry both our souls where his remains.
Tell me, sweet boy, art thou content to die?
These barbarous Scythians, full of cruelty,
And Moors, in whom was never pity found,   20
Will hew us piecemeal, put us to the wheel,
Or else invent some torture worse than that;
Therefore die by thy loving mother's hand,
Who gently now will lance thy ivory throat,
And quickly rid thee both of pain and life.
  Son. Mother, despatch me, or I'll kill myself;
For think you I can live and see him dead?
Give me your knife, good mother, or strike home:
The Scythians shall not tyrannise on me:

Sweet mother, strike, that I may meet my father.   30
                              [*She stabs him, and he dies.*

  Olym. Ah, sacred Mahomet, if this be sin,
Entreat a pardon of the God of heaven,
And purge my soul before it come to thee.
          [*She burns the bodies of her husband and son, and
          then attempts to kill herself.*

  Enter Theridamas, Techelles, *and all their train.*

  Ther. How now, madam, what are you doing?
  Olym. Killing myself, as I have done my son,
Whose body, with his father's, I have burnt,
Lest cruel Scythians should dismember him.
  Tech. 'Twas bravely done, and like a soldier's wife.
Thou shalt with us to Tamburlaine the Great,
Who, when he hears how resolute thou wert,   40
Will match thee with a viceroy or a king.
  Olym. My lord deceas'd was dearer unto me
Than any viceroy, king, or emperor;
And for his sake here will I end my days.
  Ther. But, lady, go with us to Tamburlaine,
And thou shalt see a man greater than Mahomet,
In whose high looks is much more majesty,
Than from the concave superficies
Of Jove's vast palace, the imperial orb,
Unto the shining bower where Cynthia sits,   50
Like lovely Thetis, in a crystal robe;
That treadeth fortune underneath his feet,
And makes the mighty god of arms his slave;
On whom Death and the Fatal Sisters wait
With naked swords and scarlet liveries;
Before whom, mounted on a lion's back,
Rhamnusia bears a helmet full of blood,
And strows the way with brains of slaughtered men;
By whose proud side the ugly Furies run,
Hearkening when he shall bid them plague the world;
Over whose zenith, cloth'd in windy air,   61
And eagle's wings join'd to her feathered breast,

Fame hovereth, sounding of her golden trump,
That to the adverse poles of that straight line
Which measureth the glorious frame of heaven
The name of mighty Tamburlaine is spread;
And him, fair lady, shall thy eyes behold.
Come.

Olym. Take pity of a lady's ruthful tears,
That humbly craves upon her knees to stay,   70
And cast her body in the burning flame
That feeds upon her son's and husband's flesh.

Tech. Madam, sooner shall fire consume us both
Than scorch a face so beautiful as this,
In frame of which Nature hath show'd more skill
Than when she gave eternal chaos form,
Drawing from it the shining lamps of heaven.

Ther. Madam, I am so far in love with you,
That you must go with us: no remedy.

Olym. Then carry me, I care not, where you will, 80
And let the end of this my fatal journey
Be likewise end to my accursed life.

Tech. No, madam, but the beginning of your joy:
Come willingly, therefore.

Ther. Soldiers, now let us meet the general,
Who by this time is at Natolia,
Ready to charge the army of the Turk.
The gold, the silver, and the pearl ye got,
Rifling this fort, divide in equal shares:
This lady shall have twice so much again   90
Out of the coffers of our treasury.   [*Exeunt.*

Scene V.

Enter Callapine, Orcanes, *the* Kings of Jerusalem,
Trebizon, *and* Soria, *with their train,* Almeda, *and a*
Messenger.

Mess. Renowned emperor, mighty Callapine,
God's great lieutenant over all the world,
Here at Aleppo, with an host of men,

Lies Tamburlaine, this king of Persia,
In number more than are the quivering leaves
Of Ida's forest, where your highness' hounds
With open cry pursues the wounded stag,
Who means to girt Natolia's walls with siege,
Fire the town, and over-run the land.

    Call. My royal army is as great as his,   10
That, from the bounds of Phrygia to the sea
Which washeth Cyprus with his brinish waves,
Covers the hills, the valleys and the plains.
Viceroys and peers of Turkey, play the men;
Whet all your swords to mangle Tamburlaine,
His sons, his captains, and his followers:
By Mahomet, not one of them shall live.
The field wherein this battle shall be fought
For ever term the Persians' sepulchre,
In memory of this our victory.   20

    Orc. Now he that calls himself the scourge of Jove,
The emperor of the world, and earthly god,
Shall end the warlike progress he intends,
And travel headlong to the lake of hell,
Where legions of devils (knowing he must die
Here in Natolia by your highness' hands),
All brandishing their brands of quenchless fire,
Stretching their monstrous paws, grin with their
    teeth,
And guard the gates to entertain his soul.

    Call. Tell me, viceroys, the number of your men, 30
And what our army royal is esteem'd.

    K. of Jer. From Palestina and Jerusalem,
Of Hebrews three score thousand fighting men
Are come, since last we showed your majesty.

    Orc. So from Arabia Desert, and the bounds
Of that sweet land whose brave metropolis
Re-edified the fair Semiramis,
Came forty thousand warlike foot and horse,
Since last we number'd to your majesty.

    K. of Treb. From Trebizon in Asia the Less,   40

Naturalised Turks and stout Bithynians
Came to my bands full fifty thousand more,
That, fighting, knows not what retreat doth mean,
Nor e'er return but with the victory,
Since last we number'd to your majesty.

    K. of Sor. Of Sorians from Halla is repair'd,
And neighbour cities of your highness' land,
Ten thousand horse, and thirty thousand foot,
Since last we number'd to your majesty;
So that the army royal is esteem'd   50
Six hundred thousand valiant fighting men.

    Call. Then welcome, Tamburlaine, unto thy death.
Come, puissant viceroys, let us to the field
(The Persians' sepulchre), and sacrifice
Mountains of breathless men to Mahomet,
Who now, with Jove, opens the firmament
To see the slaughter of our enemies.

Enter Tamburlaine *with his three* sons, Calyphus,
    Amyras, *and* Celebinus; Usumcasane, *and others.*

    Tamb. How now, Casane? see, a knot of kings,
Sitting as if they were a-telling riddles.

    Usum. My lord, your presence makes them pale
      and wan: 60
Poor souls, they look as if their deaths were near.

    Tamb. Why, so he is, Casane; I am here:
But yet I'll save their lives, and make them slaves.
Ye petty kings of Turkey, I am come,
As Hector did into the Grecian camp,
To overdare the pride of Græcia,
And set his warlike person to the view
Of fierce Achilles, rival of his fame:
I do you honour in the simile;
For, if I should, as Hector did Achilles,   70
(The worthiest knight that ever brandish'd sword,)
Challenge in combat any of you all,
I see how fearfully ye would refuse,
And fly my glove as from a scorpion.

Orc. Now thou art fearful of thy army's strength,
Thou wouldst with overmatch of person fight:
But, shepherd's issue, base-born Tamburlaine,
Think of thy end; this sword shall lance thy throat.

Tamb. Villain, the shepherd's issue, at whose birth
Heaven did afford a gracious aspect,   80
And join'd those stars that shall be opposite
Even till the dissolution of the world,
And never meant to make a conqueror
So famous as is mighty Tamburlaine,
Shall so torment thee, and that Callapine,
That, like a roguish runaway, suborn'd
That villain there, that slave, that Turkish dog,
To false his service to his sovereign,
As ye shall curse the birth of Tamburlaine.

Call. Rail not, proud Scythian: I shall now revenge
My father's vile abuses and mine own.   91

K. of Jer. By Mahomet, he shall be tied in chains,
Rowing with Christians in a brigandine
About the Grecian isles to rob and spoil,
And turn him to his ancient trade again:
Methinks the slave should make a lusty thief.

Call. Nay, when the battle ends, all we will meet,
And sit in council to invent some pain
That most may vex his body and his soul.   99

Tamb. Sirrah Callapine, I'll hang a clog about
your neck for running away again: you shall not
trouble me thus to come and fetch you.
But as for you, viceroy, you shall have bits,
And, harness'd like my horses, draw my coach;
And, when ye stay, be lash'd with whips of wire:
I'll have you learn to feed on provender,
And in a stable lie upon the planks.

Orc. But, Tamburlaine, first thou shalt kneel to us,
And humbly crave a pardon for thy life.   [host

K. of Treb. The common soldiers of our mighty
Shall bring thee bound unto the general's tent.   111

                101 for] to prevent

K. of Sor. And all have jointly sworn thy cruel
   death,
Or bind thee in eternal torments' wrath.

Tamb. Well, sirs, diet yourselves; you know I shall
have occasion shortly to journey you.

Cel. See, father, how Almeda the jailor looks upon us.

Tamb. Villain, traitor, damned fugitive,
I'll make thee wish the earth had swallowed thee;
See'st thou not death within my wrathful looks?
Go, villain, cast thee headlong from a rock,   120
Or rip thy bowels, and rend out thy heart,
T' appease my wrath; or else I'll torture thee,
Searing thy hateful flesh with burning irons
And drops of scalding lead, while all thy joints
Be rack'd and beat asunder with the wheel;
For, if thou livest, not any element
Shall shroud thee from the wrath of Tamburlaine.

Call. Well in despite of thee, he shall be king.
Come, Almeda, receive this crown of me:
I here invest thee king of Ariadan,   130
Bordering on Mare Roso, near to Mecca.

Orc. What! take it, man.

Alm. [*to Tamb.*] Good my lord, let me take it.

Call. Dost thou ask him leave? here; take it.

Tamb. Go to, sirrah, take your crown, and make
up the half dozen. So, sirrah, now you are a king
you must give arms.

Orc. So he shall, and wear thy head in his scutcheon.

Tamb. No; let him hang a bunch of keys on his
standard, to put him in remembrance he was a jailor,
that, when I take him, I may knock out his brains
with them, and lock you in the stable, when you shall
come sweating from my chariot.

K. of Treb. Away; let us to the field, that the villain
may be slain.   145

Tamb. Sirrah, prepare whips, and bring my chariot
to my tent; for, as soon as the battle is done, I'll ride
in triumph through the camp.

Enter Theridamas, Techelles, *and their train.*

How now, ye petty kings? lo, here are bugs
Will make the hair stand upright on your heads,   150
And cast your crowns in slavery at their feet.
Welcome, Theridamas and Techelles, both:
See ye this rout, and know ye this same king?

Ther. Ay, my lord; he was Callapine's keeper.

Tamb. Well now you see he is a king. Look to him,
Theridamas, when we are fighting, lest he hide his
crown as the foolish king of Persia did.

K. of Sor. No, Tamburlaine; he shall not be put to
that exigent, I warrant thee.

Tamb. You know not, sir.—   160
But now, my followers and my loving friends,
Fight as you ever did, like conquerors,
The glory of this happy day is yours.
My stern aspect shall make fair Victory,
Hovering betwixt our armies, light on me,
Loaden with laurel-wreaths to crown us all.

Tech. I smile to think how when this field is fought
And rich Natolia ours, our men shall sweat
With carrying pearl and treasure on their backs.

Tamb. You shall be princes all, immediately;   170
Come, fight, ye Turks, or yield us victory.

Orc. No; we will meet thee, slavish Tamburlaine.
                                  [*Exeunt severally.*

Act IV.   Scene I.

Alarms within. Amyras *and* Celebinus *issue from the tent
where* Calyphas *sits asleep.*

Amy. Now in their glories shine the golden crowns
Of these proud Turks, much like so many suns
That half dismay the majesty of heaven.
Now, brother, follow we our father's sword,

                149 bugs] bugbears

That flies with fury swifter than our thoughts,
And cuts down armies with his conquering swings.

Cel. Call forth our lazy brother from the tent,
For, if my father miss him in the field,
Wrath, kindled in the furnace of his breast,
Will send a deadly lightning to his heart.   10

Amy. Brother, ho! what, given so much to sleep,
You cannot leave it, when our enemies' drums
And rattling cannons thunder in our ears
Our proper ruin and our father's foil?

Caly. Away, ye fools! my father needs not me,
Nor you, in faith, but that you will be thought
More childish-valourous than manly-wise.
If half our camp should sit and sleep with me,
My father were enough to scare the foe:
You do dishonour to his majesty,   20
To think our helps will do him any good.

Amy. What, dar'st thou then be absent from the
        fight,
Knowing my father hates thy cowardice,
And oft hath warn'd thee to be still in field,
When he himself amidst the thickest troops
Beats down our foes to flesh our taintless swords?

Caly. I know, sir, what it is to kill a man;
It works remorse of conscience in me;
I take no pleasure to be murtherous,
Nor care for blood when wine will quench my
        thirst.   30

Cel. O cowardly boy! fie, for shame, come forth!
Thou dost dishonour manhood and thy house.

Caly. Go, go, tall stripling, fight you for us both,
And take my other toward brother here,
For person like to prove a second Mars.
'Twill please my mind as well to hear both you
Have won a heap of honour in the field,
And left your slender carcasses behind,
As if I lay with you for company.

                        33 tall] brave

Amy. You will not go, then?　　40

Caly. You say true.

Amy. Were all the lofty mounts of Zona Mundi
That fill the midst of farthest Tartary
Turn'd into pearl and proffered for my stay,
I would not bide the fury of my father,
When, made a victor in these haughty arms,
He comes and finds his sons have had no shares
In all the honours he propos'd for us.

Caly. Take you the honour, I will take my ease;
My wisdom shall excuse my cowardice:　　50
I go into the field before I need?

　　　　[*Alarms within.* Amyras *and* Celebinus *run out.*
The bullets fly at random where they list;
And, should I go, and kill a thousand men,
I were as soon rewarded with a shot,
And sooner far than he that never fights;
And, should I go, and do nor harm nor good,
I might have harm, which all the good I have,
Join'd with my father's crown, would never cure.
I'll to cards.—Perdicas!

Enter Perdicas.

Perd. Here, my lord.　　60

Caly. Come, thou and I will go to cards to drive
away the time.

Perd. Content, my lord: but what shall we play for?

Caly. Who shall kiss the fairest of the Turks' concubines first, when my father hath conquered them.

Perd. Agreed, i'faith.　　　　[*They play.*

Caly. They say I am a coward, Perdicas, and I fear
as little their taratantaras, their swords, or their cannons as I do a naked lady in a net of gold, and, for
fear I should be afraid, would put it off and come to
bed with me.　　71

Perd. Such a fear, my lord, would never make ye
retire.

Caly. I would my father would let me be put in

the front of such a battle once, to try my valour.
[*Alarms within.*] What a coil they keep! I believe there
will be some hurt done anon amongst them.

Enter Tamburlaine, Theridamas, Techelles, Usumcasane; Amyras *and* Celebinus *leading in* Orcanes,
and the Kings of Jerusalem, Trebizon, *and* Soria; *and*
Soldiers.

Tamb. See now, ye slaves, my children stoops your
    pride,
And leads your glories sheep-like to the sword.
Bring them, my boys, and tell me if the wars   80
Be not a life that may illustrate gods,
And tickle not your spirits with desire
Still to be train'd in arms and chivalry?

Amy. Shall we let go these kings again, my lord,
To gather greater numbers 'gainst our power,
That they may say, it is not chance doth this,
But matchless strength and magnanimity?

Tamb. No, no, Amyras; tempt not Fortune so:
Cherish thy valour still with fresh supplies,
And glut it not with stale and daunted foes.   90
But where's this coward villain, not my son,
But traitor to my name and majesty?
                [*He goes in and brings* Calyphas *out.*
Image of sloth, and picture of a slave,
The obloquy and scorn of my renown!
How may my heart, thus fired with mine eyes,
Wounded with shame and kill'd with discontent,
Shroud any thought may hold my striving hands
From martial justice on thy wretched soul?

Ther. Yet pardon him, I pray your majesty.
Tech. and Usum. Let all of us entreat your highness'
    pardon.   100

Tamb. Stand up, ye base, unworthy soldiers!
Know ye not yet the argument of arms?

Amy. Good my lord, let him be forgiven for once
And we will force him to the field hereafter.

Tamb. Stand up, my boys, and I will teach ye
    arms,
And what the jealousy of wars must do.
O Samarcanda, where I breathed first,
And joy'd the fire of this martial flesh,
Blush, blush, fair city, at thine honour's foil,
And shame of nature, which Jaertis' stream,   110
Embracing thee with deepest of his love,
Can never wash from thy distained brows!
Here, Jove, receive his fainting soul again;
A form not meet to give that subject essence
Whose matter is the flesh of Tamburlaine,
Wherein an incorporeal spirit moves,
Made of the mould whereof thyself consists,
Which makes me valiant, proud, ambitious,
Ready to levy power against thy throne,
That I might move the turning spheres of heaven;
For earth and all this airy region   121
Cannot contain the state of Tamburlaine.

                      [Stabs Calyphas.
By Mahomet, thy mighty friend, I swear,
In sending to my issue such a soul,
Created of the massy dregs of earth,
The scum and tartar of the elements,
Wherein was neither courage, strength, or wit,
But folly, sloth, and damned idleness,
Thou hast procur'd a greater enemy
Than he that darted mountains at thy head,   130
Shaking the burthen mighty Atlas bears,
Whereat thou trembling hidd'st thee in the air,
Cloth'd with a pitchy cloud for being seen.
And now, ye canker'd curs of Asia,
That will not see the strength of Tamburlaine,
Although it shine as brightly as the sun,
Now you shall feel the strength of Tamburlaine,
And, by the state of his supremacy,
Approve the difference 'twixt himself and you.

           109 foil] disgrace

Orc. Thou show'st the difference 'twixt ourselves
In this thy barbarous damned tyranny.   [and thee,
    K. of Jer. Thy victories are grown so violent,
That shortly heaven, fill'd with the meteors
Of blood and fire thy tyrannies have made,
Will pour down blood and fire on thy head,
Whose scalding drops will pierce thy seething brains,
And, with our bloods, revenge our bloods on thee.
    Tamb. Villains, these terrors and these tyrannies
(If tyrannies war's justice ye repute),
I execute, enjoin'd me from above,   150
To scourge the pride of such as heaven abhors;
Nor am I made arch-monarch of the world,
Crown'd and invested by the hand of Jove,
For deeds of bounty or nobility;
But since I exercise a greater name,
The scourge of God and terror of the world,
I must apply myself to fit those terms,
In war, in blood, in death, in cruelty,
And plague such peasants as resist in me
The power of heaven's eternal majesty.   160
Theridamas, Techelles, and Casane,
Ransack the tents and the pavilions
Of these proud Turks, and take their concubines,
Making them bury this effeminate brat;
For not a common soldier shall defile
His manly fingers with so faint a boy:
Then bring those Turkish harlots to my tent,
And I'll dispose them as it likes me best.
Meanwhile, take him in.
    Soldiers. We will, my lord.   170
                [*Exeunt with the body of* Calyphas.
    K. of Jer. O damned monster! nay, a fiend of hell,
Whose cruelties are not so harsh as thine,
Nor yet impos'd with such a bitter hate!
    Orc. Revenge it, Rhadamanth and Æacus,
And let your hates, extended in his pains,
Excel the hate wherewith he pains our souls!

K. of Treb. May never day give virtue to his eyes,
Whose sight, compos'd of fury and of fire,
Doth send such stern affections to his heart!

K. of Sor. May never spirit, vein, or artier, feed 180
The cursed substance of that cruel heart;
But, wanting moisture and remorseful blood,
Dry up with anger, and consume with heat!

Tamb. Well, bark, ye dogs: I'll bridle all your
    tongues,
And bind them close with bits of burnish'd steel,
Down to the channels of your hateful throats;
And, with the pains my rigour shall inflict,
I'll make ye roar, that earth may echo forth
The far-resounding torments ye sustain;
As when an herd of lusty Cimbrian bulls   190
Run mourning round about the females' miss,
And, stung with fury of their following,
Fill all the air with troublous bellowing.
I will, with engines never exercis'd,
Conquer, sack, and utterly consume
Your cities and your golden palaces,
And with the flames that beat against the clouds,
Incense the heavens, and make the stars to melt,
As if they were the tears of Mahomet
For hot consumption of his country's pride;   200
And, till by vision or by speech I hear
Immortal Jove say 'Cease, my Tamburlaine,'
I will persist a terror to the world,
Making the meteors, that like armed men
Are seen to march upon the towers of heaven,
Run tilting round about the firmament,
And break their burning lances in the air,
For honour of my wondrous victories.
Come, bring them in to our pavilion.   [*Exeunt.*

182 remorseful] compassionate   191 miss] loss

Scene II.

Enter Olympia.

Olym. Distress'd Olympia, whose weeping eyes
Since thy arrival here beheld no sun,
But, clos'd within the compass of a tent,
Have stain'd thy cheeks, and made thee look like
    death,
Devise some means to rid thee of thy life,
Rather than yield to his detested suit,
Whose drift is only to dishonour thee;
And, since this earth, dew'd with thy brinish tears,
Affords no herbs whose taste may poison thee,
Nor yet this air, beat often with thy sighs,   10
Contagious smells and vapours to infect thee,
Nor thy close cave a sword to murther thee,
Let this invention be the instrument.

Enter Theridamas.

Ther. Well met, Olympia: I sought thee in my tent,
But, when I saw the place obscure and dark,
Which with thy beauty thou wast wont to light,
Enrag'd, I ran about the fields for thee,
Supposing amorous Jove had sent his son,
The winged Hermes, to convey thee hence;
But now I find thee, and that fear is past.   20
Tell me, Olympia, wilt thou grant my suit?
    Olym. My lord and husband's death, with my sweet
        son's,
With whom I buried all affections
Save grief and sorrow, which torment my heart,
Forbids my mind to entertain a thought
That tends to love, but meditate on death,
A fitter subject for a pensive soul.
    Ther. Olympia, pity him in whom thy looks
Have greater operation and more force
Than Cynthia's in the watery wilderness;   30

For with thy view my joys are at the full,
And ebb again as thou depart'st from me.

   Olym. Ah, pity me, my lord, and draw your sword,
Making a passage for my troubled soul,
Which beats against this prison to get out,
And meet my husband and my loving son.

   Ther. Nothing but still thy husband and thy son?
Leave this, my love, and listen more to me:
Thou shalt be stately queen of fair Argier,
And cloth'd in costly cloth of massy gold,   40
Upon the marble turrets of my court
Sit like to Venus in her chair of state,
Commanding all thy princely eye desires;
And I will cast off arms and sit with thee,
Spending my life in sweet discourse of love.

   Olym. No such discourse is pleasant in mine ears,
But that where every period ends with death,
And every line begins with death again:
I cannot love, to be an empress.

   Ther. Nay, lady, then, if nothing will prevail,   50
I'll use some other means to make you yield:
Such is the sudden fury of my love,
I must and will be pleas'd, and you shall yield:
Come to the tent again.

   Olym. Stay, good my lord; and, will you save my honour,
I'll give your grace a present of such price
As all the world can not afford the like.

   Ther. What is it?

   Olym. An ointment which a cunning alchemist
Distilled from the purest balsamum   60
And simplest extracts of all minerals,
In which the essential form of marble stone,
Tempered by science metaphysical,
And spells of magic from the mouths of spirits,
With which if you but 'noint your tender skin,
Nor pistol, sword, nor lance, can pierce your flesh.

Ther. Why, madam, think ye to mock me thus
palpably?

Olym. To prove it, I will 'noint my naked throat,
Which when you stab, look on your weapon's point,
And you shall see't rebated with the blow. 71

Ther. Why gave you not your husband some of it,
If you loved him, and it so precious?

Olym. My purpose was, my lord, to spend it so,
But was prevented by his sudden end;
And for a present easy proof hereof,
That I dissemble not, try it on me.

Ther. I will, Olympia, and will keep it for
The richest present of this eastern world.

> [*She anoints her throat.*

Olym. Now stab, my lord, and mark your weapon's
point, 80
That will be blunted if the blow be great.

Ther. Here, then, Olympia. [*Stabs her.*
What, have I slain her? Villain, stab thyself;
Cut off this arm that murthered my love,
In whom the learned Rabbis of this age
Might find as many wondrous miracles
As in the theoria of the world.
Now hell is fairer than Elysium;
A greater lamp than that bright eye of heaven,
From whence the stars do borrow all their light, 90
Wanders about the black circumference;
And now the damned souls are free from pain,
For every Fury gazeth on her looks;
Infernal Dis is courting of my love,
Inventing masks and stately shows for her,
Opening the doors of his rich treasury
To entertain this queen of chastity;
Whose body shall be tomb'd with all the pomp
The treasure of my kingdom may afford.

> [*Exit with the body.*

Scene III.

Enter Tamburlaine, *drawn in his chariot by the* Kings *of*
Trebizon *and* Soria, *with bits in their mouths, reins in his
left hand, and in his right hand a whip with which he
scourgeth them;* Amyras, Celebinus, Techelles, Theridamas, Usumcasane; Orcanes *king of Natolia, and the*
King *of* Jerusalem; *led by five or six common* Soldiers;
and other Soldiers.

Tamb. Holla, ye pampered jades of Asia!
What, can ye draw but twenty miles a day,
And have so proud a chariot at your heels,
And such a coachman as great Tamburlaine,
But from Asphaltis, where I conquer'd you,
To Byron here, where thus I honour you?
The horse that guide the golden eye of heaven,
And blow the morning from their nosterils,
Making their fiery gait above the clouds,
Are not so honoured in their governor   10
As you, ye slaves, in mighty Tamburlaine.
The headstrong jades of Thrace Alcides tam'd,
That King Egeus fed with human flesh,
And made so wanton that they knew their strengths,
Were not subdu'd with valour more divine
Than you by this unconquered arm of mine.
To make you fierce, and fit my appetite,
You shall be fed with flesh as raw as blood,
And drink in pails the strongest muscadel:
If you can live with it, then live, and draw   20
My chariot swifter than the racking clouds;
If not, then die like beasts, and fit for naught
But perches for the black and fatal ravens.
Thus am I right the scourge of highest Jove,
And see the figure of my dignity,
By which I hold my name and majesty!
    Amy. Let me have coach, my lord, that I may ride,
                21 racking] scudding

And thus be drawn with these two idle kings.

Tamb. Thy youth forbids such ease, my kingly boy:
They shall to-morrow draw my chariot,   30
While these their fellow-kings may be refresh'd.

Orc. O thou that sway'st the region under earth,
And art a king as absolute as Jove,
Come as thou didst in fruitful Sicily,
Surveying all the glories of the land,
And as thou took'st the fair Proserpina,
Joying the fruit of Ceres' garden-plot,
For love, for honour, and to make her queen,
So, for just hate, for shame, and to subdue
This proud contemner of thy dreadful power,   40
Come once in fury and survey his pride,
Haling him headlong to the lowest hell.

Ther. Your majesty must get some bits for these,
To bridle their contemptuous cursing tongues,
That, like unruly never-broken jades,
Break through the hedges of their hateful mouths,
And pass their fixed bounds exceedingly.

Tech. Nay, we will break the hedges of their
mouths,
And pull their kicking colts out of their pastures.

Usum. Your majesty already hath devis'd   50
A mean, as fit as may be, to restrain
These coltish coach-horse tongues from blasphemy.

Cel. How like you that, sir king? why speak you not?

K. of Jer. Ah, cruel brat, sprung from a tyrant's
loins!
How like his cursed father he begins
To practice taunts and bitter tyrannies!

Tamb. Ay, Turk, I tell thee, this same boy is he
That must (advanc'd in higher pomp than this)
Rifle the kingdoms I shall leave unsack'd,
If Jove, esteeming me too good for earth,   60
Raise me to match the fair Aldeboran,
Above the threefold astracism of heaven,

62 astracism] constellation

F

Before I conquer all the triple world.
Now fetch me out the Turkish concubines:
I will prefer them for the funeral
They have bestowed on my abortive son.

                    [*The* Concubines *are brought in.*

Where are my common soldiers now, that fought
So lion-like upon Asphaltis' plains?

    Soldiers. Here, my lord.

    Tamb. Hold ye, tall soldiers, take ye queens a-
      piece,—   70
I mean such queens as were kings' concubines;
Take them; divide them, and their jewels too,
And let them equally serve all your turns.

    Soldiers. We thank your majesty.

    Tamb. Brawl not, I warn you, for your lechery;
For every man that so offends shall die.

    Orc. Injurious tyrant, wilt thou so defame
The hateful fortunes of thy victory,
To exercise upon such guiltless dames
The violence of thy common soldiers' lust?   80

    Tamb. Live continent, then, ye slaves, and meet
      not me
With troops of harlots at your slothful heels.

    Concubines. O pity us, my lord, and save our honours.

    Tamb. Are ye not gone, ye villains, with your
      spoils? [*The* Soldiers *run away with the* Concubines.

    K. of Jer. O, merciless, infernal cruelty!

    Tamb. Save your honours! 'twere but time indeed,
Lost long before you knew what honour meant.

    Ther. It seems they meant to conquer us, my
      lord,
And make us jesting pageants for their trulls.

    Tamb. And now themselves shall make our pageant,
And common soldiers jest with all their trulls.   91
Let them take pleasure soundly in their spoils,
Till we prepare our march to Babylon,
Whither we next make expedition.

70 tall] brave

Tech. Let us not be idle then, my lord,
But presently be prest to conquer it.

Tamb. We will, Techelles. Forward, then, ye jades.
Now crouch, ye kings of greatest Asia,
And tremble when ye hear this scourge will come
That whips down cities and controlleth crowns,   100
Adding their wealth and treasure to my store.
The Euxine sea, north to Natolia,
The Terrene, west, the Caspian, north north-east,
And on the south, Sinus Arabicus,
Shall all be loaden with the martial spoils
We will convey with us to Persia.
Then shall my native city Samarcanda,
And crystal waves of fresh Jaertis' stream,
The pride and beauty of her princely seat,
Be famous through the furthest continents;   110
For there my palace royal shall be plac'd,
Whose shining turrets shall dismay the heavens,
And cast the fame of Ilion's tower to hell:
Thorough the streets, with troops of conquered kings,
I'll ride in golden armour like the sun,
And in my helm a triple plume shall spring,
Spangled with diamonds, dancing in the air,
To note me emperor of the three-fold world;
Like to an almond-tree y-mounted high
Upon the lofty and celestial mount   120
Of ever-green Selinus, quaintly deck'd
With blooms more white than Erycina's brows,
Whose tender blossoms tremble every one
At every little breath that thorough heaven is blown.
Then in my coach, like Saturn's royal son
Mounted his shining chariot gilt with fire,
And drawn with princely eagles through the path
Pav'd with bright crystal and enchas'd with stars,
When all the gods stand gazing at his pomp,
So will I ride through Samarcanda streets,   130
Until my soul, dissevered from this flesh,

96 prest] ready

Shall mount the milk-white way, and meet him there.
To Babylon, my lords, to Babylon!   [*Exeunt.*

Act V. Scene I.

Enter the Governor of Babylon, Maximus, *and others,
upon the walls.*

Gov. What saith Maximus?

Max. My lord, the breach the enemy hath made
Gives such assurance of our overthrow,
That little hope is left to save our lives,
Or hold our city from the conqueror's hands.
Then hang out flags, my lord, of humble truce,
And satisfy the people's general prayers,
That Tamburlaine's intolerable wrath
May be suppress'd by our submission.

Gov. Villain, respects thou more thy slavish life   10
Than honour of thy country or thy name?
Is not my life and state as dear to me,
The city and my native country's weal,
As any thing of price with thy conceit?
Have we not hope, for all our battered walls,
To live secure and keep his forces out,
When this our famous lake of Limnasphaltis
Makes walls a-fresh with every thing that falls
Into the liquid substance of his stream,
More strong than are the gates of death or hell?   20
What faintness should dismay our courages,
When we are thus defenc'd against our foe,
And have no terror but his threatening looks?

Enter, above, a Citizen, *who kneels to the* Governor.

Cit. My lord, if ever you did deed of ruth,
And now will work a refuge to our lives,
Offer submission, hang up flags of truce,
That Tamburlaine may pity our distress,
And use us like a loving conqueror.
Though this be held his last day's dreadful siege,

Wherein he spareth neither man nor child,   30
Yet are there Christians of Georgia here,
Whose state he ever pitied and reliev'd,
Will get his pardon, if your grace would send.

Gov. How is my soul environed!
And this eternis'd city Babylon
Fill'd with a pack of faint-heart fugitives
That thus entreat their shame and servitude!

Enter, above, a Second Citizen.

Sec. Cit. My lord, if ever you will win our hearts,
Yield up the town, save our wives and children;
For I will cast myself from off these walls,   40
Or die some death of quickest violence,
Before I bide the wrath of Tamburlaine.

Gov. Villains, cowards, traitors to our state,
Fall to the earth, and pierce the pit of hell,
That legions of tormenting spirits may vex
Your slavish bosoms with continual pains!
I care not, nor the town will never yield
As long as any life is in my breast.

Enter Theridamas *and* Techelles, *with* Soldiers.

Ther. Thou desperate governor of Babylon,
To save thy life, and us a little labour,   50
Yield speedily the city to our hands,
Or else be sure thou shalt be forc'd with pains
More exquisite than ever traitor felt.

Gov. Tyrant, I turn the traitor in thy throat,
And will defend it in despite of thee.
Call up the soldiers to defend these walls.

Tech. Yield, foolish governor; we offer more
Than ever yet we did to such proud slaves
As durst resist us till our third day's siege.
Thou seest us prest to give the last assault,   60
And that shall bide no more regard of parley.

Gov. Assault and spare not; we will never yield.
                    [*Alarms: and they scale the walls.*

Enter Tamburlaine, *drawn in his chariot (as before) by the* Kings of Trebizon *and* Soria; Amyras, Celebinus, Usumcasane; Orcanes *king of Natolia, and the* King of Jerusalem, *led by* Soldiers; *and others.*

Tamb. The stately buildings of fair Babylon,
Whose lofty pillars, higher than the clouds,
Were wont to guide the seaman in the deep,
Being carried thither by the cannon's force,
Now fill the mouth of Limnasphaltis' lake,
And make a bridge unto the battered walls.
Where Belus, Ninus, and great Alexander
Have rode in triumph, triumphs Tamburlaine,   70
Whose chariot-wheels have burst th' Assyrians' bones,
Drawn with these kings on heaps of carcasses.
Now in the place, where fair Semiramis,
Courted by kings and peers of Asia,
Hath trod the measures, do my soldiers march,
And in the streets, where brave Assyrian dames
Have rid in pomp like rich Saturnia,
With furious words and frowning visages
My horsemen brandish their unruly blades.

Re-enter Theridamas *and* Techelles, *bringing in the* Governor of Babylon.

Who have ye there, my lords?   80
Ther. The sturdy governor of Babylon,
That made us all the labour for the town,
And us'd such slender reckoning of your majesty.
Tamb. Go, bind the villain; he shall hang in chains
Upon the ruins of this conquered town.
Sirrah, the view of our vermilion tents
Which threaten'd more than if the region
Next underneath the element of fire
Were full of comets and of blazing stars,
Whose flaming trains should reach down to the earth
Could not affright you; no, nor I myself,   91
The wrathful messenger of mighty Jove,

That with his sword hath quail'd all earthly kings,
Could not persuade you to submission,
But still the ports were shut: villain, I say,
Should I but touch the rusty gates of hell,
The triple headed Cerberus would howl,
And make black Jove to crouch and kneel to me;
But I have sent volleys of shot to you.
Yet could not enter till the breach was made.   100

Gov. Nor, if my body could have stopp'd the breach,
Shouldst thou have enter'd, cruel Tamburlaine.
'Tis not thy bloody tents can make me yield,
Nor yet thyself, the anger of the highest,
For, though thy cannon shook the city-walls,
My heart did never quake, or courage faint.

Tamb. Well, now I'll make it quake; go, draw him up,
Hang him up in chains upon the city walls,
And let my soldiers shoot the slave to death.

Gov. Vile monster, born of some infernal hag,   110
And sent from hell to tyrannise on earth,
Do all thy worst; nor death, nor Tamburlaine,
Torture, or pain, can daunt my dreadless mind.

Tamb. Up with him, then; his body shall be scar'd.

Gov. But, Tamburlaine, in Limnasphaltis' lake
There lies more gold than Babylon is worth,
Which, when the city was besieg'd, I hid:
Save but my life, and I will give it thee.

Tamb. Then, for all your valour, you would save
    your life?
Whereabout lies it?   120

Gov. Under a hollow bank, right opposite
Against the western gate of Babylon.

Tamb. Go thither, some of you, and take his gold:—
                        [*Exeunt some* Attendants.
The rest forward with execution.
Away with him hence, let him speak no more.
I think I make your courage something quail.

        [*Exeunt* Attendants *with the* Governor of Babylon.

        95 ports] gates

When this is done, we'll march from Babylon,
And make our greatest haste to Persia.
These jades are broken winded and half-tir'd;
Unharness them, and let me have fresh horse.   130

> [*Attendants* unharness *the* Kings of Trebizon *and*
> Soria.

So; now their best is done to honour me,
Take them and hang them both up presently.

K. of Treb. Vild tyrant! barbarous bloody Tamburlaine!

Tamb. Take them away, Theridamas; see them
despatch'd.

Ther. I will, my lord.

> [*Exit with the* Kings of Trebizon *and* Soria.

Tamb. Come, Asian viceroys; to your tasks awhile,
And take such fortune as your fellows felt.   [limbs,

Orc. First let thy Scythian horse tear both our
Rather than we should draw thy chariot,
And, like base slaves, abject our princely minds   140
To vile and ignominious servitude.

K. of Jer. Rather lend me thy weapon, Tamburlaine,

That I may sheathe it in this breast of mine.
A thousand deaths could not torment our hearts
More than the thought of this doth vex our souls.

Amy. They will talk still, my lord, if you do not
bridle them.

Tamb. Bridle them, and let me to my coach.

> [*Attendants* bridle Orcanes *king of Natolia, and*
> *the* King of Jerusalem, *and harness them to the*
> *chariot.—The* Governor of Babylon *appears*
> *hanging in chains on the walls.—Re-enter* Theri-
> damas.

Amy. See, now, my lord, how brave the captain
hangs.

Tamb. 'Tis brave indeed, my boy: well done.
Shoot first, my lord, and then the rest shall follow.   150

133 vild] vile

Ther. Then have at him, to begin withal.

                  [*Theridamas shoots at the* Governor.

Gov. Yet save my life, and let this wound appease
The mortal fury of great Tamburlaine.

Tamb. No, though Asphaltis' lake were liquid gold,
And offer'd me as ransom for thy life,
Yet shouldst thou die. Shoot at him all at once.

                              [*They shoot.*

So, now he hangs like Bagdet's governor,
Having as many bullets in his flesh
As there be breaches in her battered wall.
Go now, and bind the burghers hand and foot,   160
And cast them headlong in the city's lake.
Tartars and Persians shall inhabit there;
And, to command the city, I will build
A citadel, that all Africa,
Which hath been subject to the Persian king,
Shall pay me tribute for in Babylon.

Tech. What shall be done with their wives and
children, my lord?

Tamb. Techelles, drown them all, man, woman,
    and child;
Leave not a Babylonian in the town.   170

Tech. I will about it straight. Come, soldiers.

                         [*Exit with* Soldiers.

Tamb. Now, Casane, where 's the Turkish Alcoran,
And all the heaps of superstitious books
Found in the temples of that Mahomet
Whom I have thought a god? they shall be burnt.

Usum. Here they are, my lord.

Tamb. Well said; let there be a fire presently.

                         [*They light a fire.*

In vain, I see, men worship Mahomet:
My sword hath sent millions of Turks to hell,
Slew all his priests, his kinsmen, and his friends,   180
And yet I live untouch'd by Mahomet.
There is a God, full of revenging wrath,
From whom the thunder and the lightning breaks,

Whose scourge I am, and him will I obey.
So, Casane; fling them in the fire.   [*They burn the books.*
Now, Mahomet, if thou have any power,
Come down thyself and work a miracle:
Thou art not worthy to be worshipped
That suffers flames of fire to burn the writ
Wherein the sum of thy religion rests: 190
Why send'st thou not a furious whirlwind down,
To blow thy Alcoran up to thy throne,
Where men report thou sitt'st by God himself?
Or vengeance on the head of Tamburlaine
That shakes his sword against thy majesty,
And spurns the abstracts of thy foolish laws?
Well, soldiers, Mahomet remains in hell;
He cannot hear the voice of Tamburlaine:
Seek out another godhead to adore;
The God that sits in heaven, if any god,   200
For he is God alone, and none but he.

Re-enter Techelles.

    Tech. I have fulfill'd your highness' will, my lord:
Thousands of men, drown'd in Asphaltis' lake,
Have made the water swell above the banks,
And fishes, fed by human carcasses,
Amaz'd, swim up and down upon the waves,
As when they swallow assafœtida,
Which makes them fleet aloft and gasp for air.
    Tamb. Well, then, my friendly lords, what now
          remains,
But that we leave sufficient garrison,   210
And presently depart to Persia,
To triumph after all our victories?
    Ther. Ay, good my lord, let us in haste to Persia;
And let this captain be remov'd the walls
To some high hill about the city here.
    Tamb. Let it be so; about it, soldiers;
But stay; I feel myself distempered suddenly.

208 fleet] float

Tech. What is it dares distemper Tamburlaine?
Tamb. Something, Techelles; but I know not what.
But, forth, ye vassals! whatsoe'er it be, 220
Sickness or death can never conquer me.

[*Exeunt.*

Scene II.

Enter Callapine, King of Amasia, a Captain, *and train,*
with drums and trumpets.

Call. King of Amasia, now our mighty host
Marcheth in Asia Major, where the streams
Of Euphrates and Tigris swiftly runs;
And here may we behold great Babylon,
Circled about with Limnasphaltis' lake,
Where Tamburlaine with all his army lies,
Which being faint and weary with the siege,
We may lie ready to encounter him
Before his host be full from Babylon,
And so revenge our latest grievous loss, 10
If God or Mahomet send any aid.

K. of Ama. Doubt not, my lord, but we shall con-
quer him:
The monster that hath drunk a sea of blood,
And yet gapes still for more to quench his thirst,
Our Turkish swords shall headlong send to hell;
And that vile carcass, drawn by warlike kings,
The fowls shall eat; for never sepulchre
Shall grace that base-born tyrant Tamburlaine.

Call. When I record my parents' slavish life,
Their cruel death, mine own captivity, 20
My viceroys' bondage under Tamburlaine,
Methinks I could sustain a thousand deaths,
To be reveng'd of all his villany.
Ah, sacred Mahomet, thou that hast seen
Millions of Turks perish by Tamburlaine,
Kingdoms made waste, brave cities sack'd and burnt,
And but one host is left to honour thee,

19 record] recall

Aid thy obedient servant Callapine,
And make him, after all these overthrows,
To triumph over cursed Tamburlaine.   30

    K. of Ama. Fear not, my lord: I see great Mahomet,
Clothed in purple clouds, and on his head
A chaplet brighter than Apollo's crown,
Marching about the air with armed men,
To join with you against this Tamburlaine.

    Capt. Renowned general, mighty Callapine,
Though God himself and holy Mahomet
Should come in person to resist your power,
Yet might your mighty host encounter all,
And pull proud Tamburlaine upon his knees   40
To sue for mercy at your highness' feet.

    Call. Captain, the force of Tamburlaine is great,
His fortune greater, and the victories
Wherewith he hath so sore dismay'd the world
Are greatest to discourage all our drifts;
Yet, when the pride of Cynthia is at full,
She wanes again; and so shall his, I hope;
For we have here the chief selected men
Of twenty several kingdoms at the least;
Nor ploughman, priest, nor merchant, stays at home;
All Turkey is in arms with Callapine;   51
And never will we sunder camps and arms
Before himself or his be conquered:
This is the time that must eternise me
For conquering the tyrant of the world.
Come, soldiers, let us lie in wait for him,
And if we find him absent from his camp,
Or that it be rejoin'd again at full,
Assail it and be sure of victory.   [*Exeunt.*

Scene III.

Enter Theridamas, Techelles, *and* Usumcasane.

    Ther. Weep, heavens, and vanish into liquid tears!
Fall, stars that govern his nativity,

And summon all the shining lamps of heaven
To cast their bootless fires to the earth,
And shed their feeble influence in the air;
Muffle your beauties with eternal clouds,
For Hell and Darkness pitch their pitchy tents,
And Death, with armies of Cimmerian spirits,
Gives battle 'gainst the heart of Tamburlaine.
Now in defiance of that wonted love   10
Your sacred virtues pour'd upon his throne,
And made his state an honour to the heavens,
These cowards invisibly assail his soul,
And threaten conquest on our sovereign;
But if he die your glories are disgrac'd,
Earth droops, and says that hell in heaven is plac'd.
   Tech. Oh, then, ye powers that sway eternal seats,
And guide this massy substance of the earth,
If you retain desert of holiness.
As your supreme estates instruct our thoughts,   20
Be not inconstant, careless of your fame,
Bear not the burthen of your enemies' joys,
Triumphing in his fall whom you advanc'd,
But as his birth, life, health, and majesty
Were strangely blest and governed by heaven,
So honour, heaven, till heaven dissolved be,
His birth, his life, his health, and majesty!
   Usum. Blush, heaven, to lose the honour of thy
      name,
To see thy footstool set upon thy head;
And let no baseness in thy haughty breast   30
Sustain a shame of such inexcellence,
To see the devils mount in angels' thrones,
And angels dive into the pools of hell!
And, though they think their painful date is out,
And that their power is puissant as Jove's,
Which makes them manage arms against thy state,
Yet make them feel the strength of Tamburlaine,
Thy instrument and note of majesty,
Is greater far than they can thus subdue;

For, if he die, thy glory is disgrac'd,   40
Earth droops, and says that hell in heaven is plac'd.

Enter Tamburlaine, *drawn in his chariot (as before) by*
Orcanes *king of Natolia, and the* King of Jerusalem,
Amyras, Celebinus, *and* Physicians.

  Tamb. What daring god torments my body thus,
And seeks to conquer mighty Tamburlaine?
Shall sickness prove me now to be a man,
That have been term'd the terror of the world?
Techelles and the rest, come, take your swords,
And threaten him whose hand afflicts my soul:
Come, let us march against the powers of heaven,
And set black streamers in the firmament,
To signify the slaughter of the gods.   50
Ah, friends, what shall I do? I cannot stand.
Come, carry me to war against the gods,
That thus envy the health of Tamburlaine.
  Ther. Ah, good my lord, leave these impatient
    words,
Which add much danger to your malady.
  Tamb. Why, shall I sit and languish in this pain?
No, strike the drums, and, in revenge of this,
Come, let us charge our spears, and pierce his breast
Whose shoulders bear the axis of the world,
That, if I perish, heaven and earth may fade.   60
Theridamas, haste to the court of Jove;
Will him to send Apollo hither straight,
To cure me, or I'll fetch him down myself.
  Tech. Sit still, my gracious lord; this grief will cease,
And cannot last, it is so violent.
  Tamb. Not last, Techelles? no, for I shall die.
See where my slave, the ugly monster Death,
Shaking and quivering, pale and wan for fear,
Stands aiming at me with his murthering dart,
Who flies away at every glance I give,   70
And, when I look away, comes stealing on.
Villain, away, and hie thee to the field!

I and mine army come to load thy bank
With souls of thousand mangled carcasses.
Look, where he goes; but see, he comes again,
Because I stay: Techelles, let us march,
And weary Death with bearing souls to hell.

    First Phy. Pleaseth your majesty to drink this potion,
Which will abate the fury of your fit,
And cause some milder spirits govern you.   80

    Tamb. Tell me what think you of my sickness now?

    First Phy. I view'd your urine, and the hypostasis
Thick and obscure, doth make your danger great:
Your veins are full of accidental heat,
Whereby the moisture of your blood is dried:
The humidum and calor, which some hold
Is not a parcel of the elements,
But of a substance more divine and pure,
Is almost clean extinguished and spent,
Which, being the cause of life, imports your death:
Besides, my lord, this day is critical,   91
Dangerous to those whose crisis is as yours:
Your artiers, which alongst the veins convey
The lively spirits which the heart engenders,
Are parch'd and void of spirit, that the soul,
Wanting those organons by which it moves,
Cannot endure, by argument of art.
Yet, if your majesty may escape this day,
No doubt but you shall soon recover all.

    Tamb. Then will I comfort all my vital parts,   100
And live, in spite of death, above a day.

                             [Alarms within.

Enter a Messenger.

    Mes. My lord, young Callapine, that lately fled
from your majesty, hath now gathered a fresh army,
and hearing your absence in the field, offers to set
upon us presently.

    Tamb. See, my physicians, now, how Jove hath sent

A present medicine to recure my pain.
My looks shall make them fly; and, might I follow,
There should not one of all the villain's power
Live to give offer of another fight.   110

   Usum. I joy, my lord, your highness is so strong,
That can endure so well your royal presence,
Which only will dismay the enemy.

   Tamb. I know it will, Casane. Draw, you slaves!
In spite of death, I will go show my face.

      [*Alarms. Exit* Tamburlaine *with all the rest (except the* Physicians), *and re-enter presently.*

   Tamb. Thus are the villains, cowards fled for fear,
Like summer's vapours vanish'd by the sun;
And, could I but a while pursue the field,
That Callapine should be my slave again.
But I perceive my martial strength is spent: 120
In vain I strive and rail against those powers
That mean t' invest me in a higher throne,
As much too high for this disdainful earth.
Give me a map; then let me see how much
Is left for me to conquer all the world,
That these, my boys, may finish all my wants.

               [*One brings a map.*

Here I began to march towards Persia,
Along Armenia and the Caspian Sea,
And thence unto Bithynia, where I took
The Turk and his great empress prisoners.   130
Then march'd I into Egypt and Arabia;
And here, not far from Alexandria,
Whereas the Terrene and the Red Sea meet,
Being distant less than full a hundred leagues,
I meant to cut a channel to them both,
That men might quickly sail to India.
From thence to Nubia near Borno-lake,
And so along the Ethiopian sea,
Cutting the tropic line of Capricorn,
I conquered all as far as Zanzibar.   140
Then, by the northern part of Africa,

I came at last to Græcia, and from thence
To Asia, where I stay against my will;
Which is from Scythia, where I first began,
Backward and forwards near five thousand leagues.
Look here, my boys; see what a world of ground
Lies westward from the midst of Cancer's line
Unto the rising of this earthly globe,
Whereas the sun, declining from our sight,
Begins the day with our Antipodes!   150
And shall I die, and this unconquered?
Lo, here, my sons, are all the golden mines,
Inestimable drugs and precious stones,
More worth than Asia and the world beside;
And from th' Antarctic Pole eastward behold
As much more land, which never was descried,
Wherein are rocks of pearl that shine as bright
As all the lamps that beautify the sky!
And shall I die, and this unconquered?
Here, lovely boys; what death forbids my life,   160
That let your lives command in spite of death.
    Amy. Alas, my lord, how should our bleeding
        hearts,
Wounded and broken with your highness' grief,
Retain a thought of joy or spark of life?
Your soul gives essence to our wretched subjects,
Whose matter is incorporate in your flesh.
    Cel. Your pains do pierce our souls; no hope sur-
        vives,
For by your life we entertain our lives.
    Tamb. But, sons, this subject, not of force enough
To hold the fiery spirit it contains,   170
Must part, imparting his impressions
By equal portions into both your breasts;
My flesh, divided in your precious shapes,
Shall still retain my spirit, though I die,
And live in all your seeds immortally.
Then now remove me, that I may resign
My place and proper title to my son.

First, take my scourge and my imperial crown,
And mount my royal chariot of estate,
That I may see thee crown'd before I die.   180
Help me, my lords, to make my last remove.

      [*They assist* Tamburlaine *to descend from the chariot.*

    Ther. A woeful change, my lord, that daunts our thoughts
More than the ruin of our proper souls!

    Tamb. Sit up, my son, let me see how well
Thou wilt become thy father's majesty.

                        [*They crown* Amyras.

    Amy. With what a flinty bosom should I joy
The breath of life and burthen of my soul,
If not resolv'd into resolved pains,
My body's mortified lineaments
Should exercise the motions of my heart,   190
Pierc'd with the joy of any dignity!
O father, if the unrelenting ears
Of Death and Hell be shut against my prayers,
And that the spiteful influence of heaven
Deny my soul fruition of her joy,
How should I step, or stir my hateful feet
Against the inward powers of my heart,
Leading a life that only strives to die,
And plead in vain unpleasing sovereignty?

    Tamb. Let not thy love exceed thine honour, son,
Nor bar thy mind that magnanimity   201
That nobly must admit necessity.
Sit up, my boy, and with these silken reins
Bridle the steeled stomachs of those jades.

    Ther. My lord, you must obey his majesty,
Since fate commands and proud necessity.

    Amy. Heavens witness me with what a broken heart   [*Mounting the chariot.*
And damned spirit I ascend this seat,
And send my soul, before my father die,
His anguish and his burning agony!   210

    Tamb. Now fetch the hearse of fair Zenocrate;

Let it be plac'd by this my fatal chair,
And serve as parcel of my funeral.

Usum. Then feels your majesty no sovereign ease,
Nor may our hearts, all drown'd in tears of blood,
Joy any hope of your recovery?

Tamb. Casane, no; the monarch of the earth,
And eyeless monster that torments my soul,
Cannot behold the tears ye shed for me,
And therefore still augments his cruelty.   220

Tech. Then let some god oppose his holy power
Against the wrath and tyranny of Death,
That his tear-thirsty and unquenched hate
May be upon himself reverberate!

        [*They bring in the hearse of* Zenocrate.
Tamb. Now, eyes, enjoy your latest benefit,
And when my soul hath virtue of your sight,
Pierce through the coffin and the sheet of gold,
And glut your longings with a heaven of joy.
So, reign, my son; scourge and control those slaves,
Guiding thy chariot with thy father's hand.   230
As precious is the charge thou undertak'st
As that which Clymene's brain-sick son did guide,
When wandering Phœbe's ivory cheeks were scorch'd,
And all the earth, like Ætna, breathing fire:
Be warn'd by him; then learn with awful eye
To sway a throne as dangerous as his;
For if thy body thrive not full of thoughts
As pure and fiery as Phyteus' beams,
The nature of these proud rebelling jades
Will take occasion by the slenderest hair,   240
And draw thee piecemeal, like Hippolytus,
Through rocks more steep and sharp than Caspian
    cliffs:
The nature of thy chariot will not bear
A guide of baser temper than myself,
More than heaven's coach the pride of Phaeton.
Farewell, my boys! my dearest friends, farewell!
My body feels, my soul doth weep to see

Your sweet desires depriv'd my company,
For Tamburlaine, the scourge of God, must die.

> *[Dies.*

  Amy. Meet heaven and earth, and here let all things
      end, 250
For earth hath spent the pride of all her fruit,
And heaven consum'd his choicest living fire.
Let earth and heaven his timeless death deplore,
For both their worths will equal him no more.

> *[Exeunt.*

253 timeless] untimely

THE
TRAGICALL
Hiſtory of D. Fauſtus.

As it hath bene Acted by the Right
Honorable the Earle of Nottingham his ſeruants.

Written by Ch. Marl.

LONDON
Printed by V.S. for Thomas Bushell. 1604.

Dramatis Personæ

The Pope.
Cardinal of Lorrain.
The Emperor of Germany.
Duke of Vanholt.
Faustus.
Valdes, }
Cornelius, } *friends to* Faustus.
Wagner, *servant to* Faustus.
Clown.
Robin.
Ralph.
Vintner.
Horse-courser.
A Knight.
An Old Man.

Scholars, Friars, *and* Atten-
    dants.

Duchess of Vanholt.

Lucifer.
Belzebub.
Mephistophilis.
Good Angel.
Evil Angel.
The Seven Deadly Sins.
Devils.
Spirits *in the shapes of* Alex-
    ander the Great, *of his*
    Paramour, *and of* Helen.
Chorus.

The Tragical History of
DOCTOR FAUSTUS

From the Quarto of 1604

Enter Chorus.

Chorus. Not marching now in fields of Thrasymene,
Where Mars did mate the Carthaginians;
Nor sporting in the dalliance of love,
In courts of kings where state is overturn'd;
Nor in the pomp of proud audacious deeds,
Intends our Muse to vaunt his heavenly verse:
Only this, gentlemen,—we must perform
The form of Faustus' fortunes, good or bad:
To patient judgments we appeal our plaud,
And speak for Faustus in his infancy.   10
Now is he born, his parents base of stock,
In Germany, within a town call'd Rhodes:
Of riper years, to Wertenberg he went,
Whereas his kinsmen chiefly brought him up.
So soon he profits in divinity,
The fruitful plot of scholarism grac'd,
That shortly he was grac'd with doctor's name,
Excelling all whose sweet delight disputes
In heavenly matters of theology;
Till swoln with cunning, of a self-conceit,   20
His waxen wings did mount above his reach,
And, melting, heavens conspir'd his overthrow;
For, falling to a devilish exercise,
And glutted now with learning's golden gifts,
He surfeits upon cursed necromancy;
Nothing so sweet as magic is to him,
Which he prefers before his chiefest bliss:
And this the man that in his study sits.   [*Exit.*

2 mate] confound
20 cunning] knowledge. Its meaning throughout the play.

Faustus discovered in his study.

Faust. Settle thy studies, Faustus, and begin
To sound the depth of that thou wilt profess: 30
Having commenc'd, be a divine in show,
Yet level at the end of every art,
And live and die in Aristotle's works.
Sweet Analytics, 'tis thou hast ravish'd me,
Bene disserere est finis logices.
Is, to dispute well, logic's chiefest end?
Affords this art no greater miracle?
Then read no more, thou hast attain'd the end:
A greater subject fitteth Faustus' wit:
Bid *on cai me on* farewell, Galen come,   40
Seeing, *Ubi desinit philosophus, ibi incipit medicus:*
Be a physician, Faustus; heap up gold,
And be eternis'd for some wondrous cure:
Summum bonum medicinæ sanitas,
The end of physic is our body's health.
Why, Faustus, hast thou not attain'd that end?
Is not thy common talk sound aphorisms?
Are not thy bills hung up as monuments,
Whereby whole cities have escap'd the plague,
And thousand desperate maladies been eas'd?   50
Yet art thou still but Faustus, and a man.
Wouldst thou make man to live eternally?
Or, being dead, raise them to life again?
Then this profession were to be esteem'd.
Physic, farewell. Where is Justinian?   [*Reads.*
Si una eademque res legatur duobus,
Alter rem, alter valorem rei, etc.
A pretty case of paltry legacies!   [*Reads.*
Exhæreditare filium non potest pater nisi:
Such is the subject of the institute   60

35 To argue well is the aim of logic.   40 ὃν καὶ μὴ ὄν
(being and not being).   41 Where the philosopher stops,
the doctor begins.   44 Health is the highest good of
medicine.   56–7 If one and the same thing is left to two
people, the thing goes to one, and its value to the other.
59 A father may not disinherit his son except . . .

And universal body of the law:
His study fits a mercenary drudge,
Who aims at nothing but external trash;
Too servile and illiberal for me.
When all is done, divinity is best:
Jerome's Bible, Faustus; view it well.   [*Reads.*
Stipendium peccati mors est. Ha! *Stipendium, etc.*
The reward of sin is death: that's hard.   [*Reads.*
Si peccasse negamus, fallimur, et nulla est in nobis veritas;
If we say that we have no sin,   70
We deceive ourselves, and there's no truth in us.
Why, then, belike
We must sin, and so consequently die:
Ay, we must die an everlasting death.
What doctrine call you this, *Che sarà, sarà,*
What will be, shall be? Divinity, adieu!
These metaphysics of magicians,
And necromantic books are heavenly;
Lines, circles, scenes, letters, and characters;
Ay, these are those that Faustus most desires.   80
Oh, what a world of profit and delight,
Of power, of honour, of omnipotence
Is promis'd to the studious artisan!
All things that move between the quiet poles
Shall be at my command: emperors and kings
Are but obey'd in their several provinces,
Nor can they raise the wind, or rend the clouds;
But his dominion that exceeds in this,
Stretcheth as far as doth the mind of man;
A sound magician is a mighty god: 90
Here, Faustus, try thy brains to gain a deity.

Enter Wagner.

Wagner, commend me to my dearest friends,
The German Valdes and Cornelius;
Request them earnestly to visit me.
     Wag. I will, sir.   [*Exit.*
     Faust. Their conference will be a greater help to me

Than all my labours, plod I ne'er so fast.

Enter Good Angel *and* Evil Angel.

  G. Ang. O, Faustus, lay that damned book aside,
And gaze not on it, lest it tempt thy soul,
And heap God's heavy wrath upon thy head.   100
Read, read the Scriptures: that is blasphemy.

  E. Ang. Go forward, Faustus, in that famous art
Wherein all Nature's treasure is contain'd:
Be thou on earth as Jove is in the sky,
Lord and commander of these elements.

                        [*Exeunt* Angels.

  Faust. How am I glutted with conceit of this!
Shall I make spirits fetch me what I please,
Resolve me of all ambiguities,
Perform what desperate enterprise I will?
I'll have them fly to India for gold,   110
Ransack the ocean for orient pearl,
And search all corners of the new-found world
For pleasant fruits and princely delicates;
I'll have them read me strange philosophy,
And tell the secrets of all foreign kings;
I'll have them wall all Germany with brass,
And make swift Rhine circle fair Wertenberg;
I'll have them fill the public schools with silk,
Wherewith the students shall be bravely clad;
I'll levy soldiers with the coin they bring,   120
And chase the Prince of Parma from our land,
And reign sole king of all our provinces;
Yea, stranger engines for the brunt of war,
Than was the fiery keel at Antwerp's bridge,
I'll make my servile spirits to invent.

Enter Valdes *and* Cornelius.

Come, German Valdes and Cornelius,
And make me blest with your sage conference.
Valdes, sweet Valdes, and Cornelius,
Know that your words have won me at the last

To practise magic and concealed arts: 130
Yet not your words only, but mine own fantasy,
That will receive no object, for my head
But ruminates on necromantic skill.
Philosophy is odious and obscure,
Both law and physic are for petty wits,
Divinity is basest of the three,
Unpleasant, harsh, contemptible, and vild:
'Tis magic, magic, that hath ravish'd me.
Then, gentle friends, aid me in this attempt;
And I, that have with concise syllogisms 140
Gravell'd the pastors of the German church,
And made the flowering pride of Wertenberg
Swarm to my problems, as the infernal spirits
On sweet Musæus when he came to hell,
Will be as cunning as Agrippa was,
Whose shadows made all Europe honour him.

   Vald. Faustus,
These books, thy wit, and our experience
Shall make all nations to canonise us.
As Indian Moors obey their Spanish lords,
So shall the subjects of every element 150
Be always serviceable to us three;
Like lions shall they guard us when we please,
Like Almain rutters with their horsemen's staves,
Or Lapland giants, trotting by our sides;
Sometimes like women, or unwedded maids,
Shadowing more beauty in their airy brows
Than has the white breasts of the queen of love:
From Venice shall they drag huge argosies,
And from America the golden fleece
That yearly stuffs old Philip's treasury; 160
If learned Faustus will be resolute.

   Faust. Valdes, as resolute am I in this
As thou to live: therefore object it not.

   Corn. The miracles that magic will perform
Will make thee vow to study nothing else.

153 rutters] troopers

He that is grounded in astrology,
Enrich'd with tongues, well seen in minerals,
Hath all the principles magic doth require:
Then doubt not, Faustus, but to be renown'd,
And more frequented for this mystery   170
Than heretofore the Delphian oracle.
The spirits tell me they can dry the sea,
And fetch the treasure of all foreign wrecks,
Ay, all the wealth that our forefathers hid
Within the massy entrails of the earth:
Then tell me, Faustus, what shall we three want?

 Faust. Nothing, Cornelius. Oh, this cheers my soul!
Come, show me some demonstrations magical,
That I may conjure in some lusty grove,
And have these joys in full possession.   180

 Vald. Then haste thee to some solitary grove,
And bear wise Bacon's and Albanus' works,
The Hebrew Psalter, and New Testament;
And whatsoever else is requisite
We will inform thee ere our conference cease.

 Corn. Valdes, first let him know the words of art;
And then, all other ceremonies learn'd,
Faustus may try his cunning by himself.

 Vald. First I'll instruct thee in the rudiments,
And then wilt thou be perfecter than I.   190

 Faust. Then come and dine with me, and, after
   meat,
We'll canvass every quiddity thereof;
For, ere I sleep, I'll try what I can do:
This night I'll conjure, though I die therefore.

           [Exeunt.

Enter two Scholars.*

 First Schol. I wonder what's become of Faustus,
that was wont to make our schools ring with *sic probo.*

 Sec. Schol. That shall we know, for see, here comes
his boy.

   * The scene is before Faustus's house.

Enter Wagner.

First Schol. How now, sirrah! where's thy master?

Wag. God in heaven knows. 200

Sec. Schol. Why, dost not thou know?

Wag. Yes, I know; but that follows not.

First Schol. Go to, sirrah! leave your jesting, and tell us where he is.

Wag. That follows not necessary by force of argument, that you, being licentiate, should stand upon't: therefore acknowledge your error, and be attentive.

Sec. Schol. Why, didst thou not say thou knewest?

Wag. Have you any witness on't? 210

First Schol. Yes, sirrah, I heard you.

Wag. Ask my fellow if I be a thief.

Sec. Schol. Well, you will not tell us?

Wag. Yes, sir, I will tell you; yet, if you were not dunces, you would never ask me such a question, for is not he *corpus naturale?* and is not that *mobile?* then wherefore should you ask me such a question? But that I am by nature phlegmatic, slow to wrath, and prone to lechery—to love, I would say,— it were not for you to come within forty foot of the place of execution, although I do not doubt to see you both hang'd the next sessions. Thus having triumphed over you, I will set my countenance like a precisian, and begin to speak thus:—Truly, my dear brethren, my master is within at dinner, with Valdes and Cornelius, as this wine, if it could speak, would inform your worships: and so the Lord bless you, preserve you, and keep you, my dear brethren, my dear brethren. [*Exit.*

First Schol. Nay, then, I fear he has fallen into that damned art for which they two are infamous through the world. 232

Sec. Schol. Were he a stranger, and not allied to me, yet should I grieve for him. But, come, let us go

and inform the Rector, and see if he by his grave
counsel can reclaim him.

First Schol. Oh, but I fear me nothing can reclaim
him.

Sec. Schol. Yet let us try what we can do.   [*Exeunt.*

Enter Faustus *to conjure.**

Faust. Now that the gloomy shadow of the earth,
Longing to view Orion's drizzling look,   241
Leaps from th' antarctic world unto the sky,
And dims the welkin with her pitchy breath,
Faustus, begin thine incantations,
And try if devils will obey thy hest,
Seeing thou hast pray'd and sacrific'd to them.
Within this circle is Jehovah's name,
Forward and backward anagrammatis'd,
The breviated names of holy saints,
Figures of every adjunct to the heavens,   250
And characters of signs and erring stars,
By which the spirits are enforc'd to rise:
Then fear not, Faustus, but be resolute,
And try the uttermost magic can perform.

*Sint mihi dei Acherontis propitii! Valeat numen triplex
Jehovæ! Ignei, aërii, aquatani spiritus, salvete! Orientis
princeps Belzebub, inferni ardentis monarcha, et Demogorgon,
propitiamus vos, ut appareat et surgat Mephistophilis, quid
tu moraris? per Jehovam, Gehennam, et consecratam aquam
quam nunc spargo, signumque crucis quod nunc facio, et per
vota nostra, ipse nunc surgat nobis dicatus Mephistophilis!*

---

* The scene is a grove.   251 erring] wandering
255-61 *Sint . . . Mephistophilis!*] Now may the gods of hell be
propitious to me: let the triple godhead of Jehovah prevail!
Hail, spirits of fire, air, and water! Belzebub, prince of the
East, king of burning hell, and Demogorgon, we propitiate
you—why do you delay in allowing Mephistophilis to rise
and appear? By Jehovah, Gehenna, and the consecrated
water that now I scatter, and the sign of the cross that now I
make, and by our vows, now let the aforesaid Mephistophilis
rise up before us!

Enter Mephistophilis.

I charge thee to return, and change thy shape; 262
Thou art too ugly to attend on me:
Go, and return an old Franciscan friar;
That holy shape becomes a devil best.
[*Exit* Mephistophilis.
I see there's virtue in my heavenly words:
Who would not be proficient in this art?
How pliant is this Mephistophilis,
Full of obedience and humility!
Such is the force of magic and my spells: 270
No, Faustus, thou art conjuror laureat,
That canst command great Mephistophilis:
Quin redis Mephistophilis fratris imagine.

Re-enter Mephistophilis *like a Franciscan friar.*

Meph. Now, Faustus, what wouldst thou have me
do?
Faust. I charge thee wait upon me whilst I live,
To do whatever Faustus shall command,
Be it to make the moon drop from her sphere,
Or the ocean to overwhelm the world.
Meph. I am a servant to great Lucifer,
And may not follow thee without his leave: 280
No more than he commands must we perform.
Faust. Did not he charge thee to appear to me?
Meph. No, I came now hither of mine own accord.
Faust. Did not my conjuring speeches raise thee?
speak.
Meph. That was the cause, but yet *per accidens*;
For when we hear one rack the name of God,
Abjure the Scriptures and his Saviour Christ,
We fly, in hope to get his glorious soul;
Nor will we come, unless he use such means
Whereby he is in danger to be damn'd. 290

273 *Quin . . . imagine*] return thou, Mephistophilis, in the
shape of a friar

Therefore the shortest cut for conjuring
Is stoutly to abjure the Trinity,
And pray devoutly to the prince of hell.

   Faust. So Faustus hath
Already done; and holds this principle,
There is no chief but Belzebub;
To whom Faustus doth dedicate himself.
This word 'damnation' terrifies not him,
For he confounds hell in Elysium:
His ghost be with the old philosophers!   300
But, leaving these vain trifles of men's souls,
Tell me what is that Lucifer thy lord?

   Meph. Arch-regent and commander of all spirits.

   Faust. Was not that Lucifer an angel once?

   Meph. Yes, Faustus, and most dearly lov'd of God.

   Faust. How comes it, then, that he is prince of
devils?

   Meph. Oh, by aspiring pride and insolence;
For which God threw him from the face of heaven.

   Faust. And what are you that live with Lucifer?

   Meph. Unhappy spirits that fell with Lucifer,   310
Conspir'd against our God with Lucifer,
And are for ever damn'd with Lucifer.

   Faust. Where are you damn'd?

   Meph. In hell.

   Faust. How comes it, then, that thou art out of
hell?

   Meph. Why, this is hell, nor am I out of it.
Think'st thou that I, who saw the face of God,
And tasted the eternal joys of heaven,
Am not tormented with ten thousand hells,
In being depriv'd of everlasting bliss?   320
Oh, Faustus, leave these frivolous demands,
Which strike a terror to my fainting soul.

   Faust. What, is great Mephistophilis so passionate
For being depriv'd of the joys of heaven?
Learn thou of Faustus manly fortitude,
And scorn those joys thou never shalt possess.

Go bear those tidings to great Lucifer:
Seeing Faustus hath incurr'd eternal death
By desperate thoughts against Jove's deity,
Say, he surrenders up to him his soul, 330
So he will spare him four-and-twenty years,
Letting him live in all voluptuousness,
Having thee ever to attend on me,
To give me whatsoever I shall ask,
To tell me whatsoever I demand,
To slay mine enemies, and aid my friends,
And always be obedient to my will.
Go and return to mighty Lucifer,
And meet me in my study at midnight,
And then resolve me of thy master's mind. 340
   Meph. I will, Faustus.   [*Exit.*
   Faust. Had I as many souls as there be stars,
I'd give them all for Mephistophilis.
By him I'll be great emperor of the world,
And make a bridge thorough the moving air,
To pass the ocean with a band of men;
I'll join the hills that bind the Afric shore,
And make that country continent to Spain,
And both contributory to my crown:
The Emperor shall not live but by my leave, 350
Nor any potentate of Germany.
Now that I have obtain'd what I desire,
I'll live in speculation of this art,
Till Mephistophilis return again.

                             [*Exit.*

Enter Wagner *and* Clown.*

   Wag. Sirrah boy, come hither.
   Clown. How, boy! swowns, boy! I hope you have
seen many boys with such pickadevaunts as I have:
boy, quotha!
   Wag. Tell me, sirrah, hast thou any comings in?

---

  * The scene is a street.   357 pickadevaunts] beards cut
to a sharp point

Clown. Ay, and goings out too; you may see else.

Wag. Alas, poor slave! see how poverty jesteth in his nakedness! the villain is bare and out of service, and so hungry, that I know he would give his soul to the devil for a shoulder of mutton, though it were blood-raw.

Clown. How! my soul to the devil for a shoulder of mutton, though 'twere blood-raw! not so, good friend: by'r lady, I had need have it well roasted, and good sauce to it, if I pay so dear.

Wag. Well, wilt thou serve me, and I'll make thee go like *Qui mihi discipulus*?   371

Clown. How, in verse?

Wag. No, sirrah; in beaten silk and staves-acre.

Clown. How, how, knaves-acre! ay, I thought that was all the land his father left him. Do ye hear? I would be sorry to rob you of your living.

Wag. Sirrah, I say in staves-acre.

Clown. Oho, oho, staves-acre! why, then, belike, if I were your man, I should be full of vermin.   379

Wag. So thou shalt, whether thou beest with me or no. But, sirrah, leave your jesting, and bind yourself presently unto me for seven years, or I'll turn all the lice about thee into familiars, and they shall tear thee in pieces.

Clown. Do you hear, sir? you may save that labour; they are too familiar with me already: swowns, they are as bold with my flesh as if they had paid for my meat and drink.

Wag. Well, do you hear, sirrah? hold, take these guilders.   [*Gives money.*

Clown. Gridirons! what be they?   391

Wag. Why, French crowns.

Clown. Mass, but for the name of French crowns, a man were as good have as many English counters. And what should I do with these?

Wag. Why, now, sirrah, thou art at an hour's

373 staves-acre] a plant used for destroying lice

warning, whensoever and wheresoever the devil shall
fetch thee.

Clown. No, no; here, take your gridirons again.

Wag. Truly I'll none of them.   400

Clown. Truly but you shall.

Wag. Bear witness I gave them him.

Clown. Bear witness I give them you again.

Wag. Well, I will cause two devils presently to
fetch thee away.—Baliol and Belcher.

Clown. Let your Balio and your Belcher come here,
and I'll knock them, they were never so knocked
since they were devils: say I should kill one of them,
what would folks say? 'Do ye see yonder tall fellow
in the round slop? he has kill'd the devil.' So I
should be call'd Kill-devil all the parish over.   411

Enter two Devils; *and the* Clown *runs up and down crying.*

Wag. Baliol and Belcher,—spirits, away!

[*Exeunt* Devils.

Clown. What, are they gone? a vengeance on them!
they have vild long nails. There was a he-devil and
a she-devil: I'll tell you how you shall know them;
all he-devils has horns, and all she-devils has clifts
and cloven feet.

Wag. Well sirrah, follow me.   418

Clown. But, do you hear? if I should serve you,
would you teach me to raise up Banios and Belcheos?

Wag. I will teach thee to turn thyself to anything,
to a dog, or a cat, or a mouse, or a rat, or anything.

Clown. How! a Christian fellow to a dog, or a cat,
a mouse, or a rat? no, no, sir, if you turn me into
anything, let it be in the likeness of a little pretty
frisking flea, that I may be here and there and everywhere: Oh, I'll tickle the pretty wenches' plackets!
I'll be amongst them, i'faith.

Wag. Well, sirrah, come.

Clown. But, do you hear, Wagner?   430

Wag. How!—Baliol and Belcher!

Clown. O Lord! I pray, sir, let Banio and Belcher go sleep.

Wag. Villain, call me Master Wagner, and let thy left eye be diametarily fixed upon my right heel, with *quasi vestigiis nostris insistere.*   [*Exit.*

Clown. God forgive me, he speaks Dutch fustian. Well, I'll follow him; I'll serve him, that's flat. [*Exit.*

Faustus *discovered in his study.*

Faust. Now, Faustus, must thou needs be damn'd,
And canst thou not be sav'd: 440
What boots it, then, to think of God or heaven?
Away with such vain fancies, and despair;
Despair in God, and trust in Belzebub:
Now go not backward; no, Faustus, be resolute:
Why waverest thou? Oh, something soundeth in mine ears,
'Abjure this magic, turn to God again!'
Ay, and Faustus will turn to God again.
To God? he loves thee not;
The god thou servest is thine own appetite,
Wherein is fix'd the love of Belzebub: 450
To him I'll build an altar and a church,
And offer lukewarm blood of new-born babes.

Enter Good Angel *and* Evil Angel.

G. Ang. Sweet Faustus, leave that execrable art.

Faust. Contrition, prayer, repentance—what of them?

G. Ang. Oh, they are means to bring thee unto heaven.

E. Ang. Rather illusions, fruits of lunacy,
That makes men foolish that do trust them most.

G. Angel. Sweet Faustus, think of heaven and heavenly things.

E. Ang. No, Faustus; think of honour and of wealth.
    [*Exeunt* Angels.

436 *quasi . . . insistere*] as if to tread in our footsteps

Faust. Of wealth! 460
Why, the signiory of Emden shall be mine.
When Mephistophilis shall stand by me,
What god can hurt thee, Faustus? thou art safe:
Cast no more doubts. Come, Mephistophilis,
And bring glad tidings from great Lucifer;
Is't not midnight? come, Mephistophilis,
Veni, veni Mephistophile!

Enter Mephistophilis.

Now tell me what says Lucifer, thy lord?
Meph. That I shall wait on Faustus whilst he lives,
So he will buy my service with his soul. 470
Faust. Already Faustus hath hazarded that for
thee.
Meph. But, Faustus, thou must bequeath it
solemnly,
And write a deed of gift with thine own blood,
For that security craves great Lucifer.
If thou deny it, I will back to hell.
Faust. Stay, Mephistophilis, and tell me, what good
Will my soul do thy lord?
Meph. Enlarge his kingdom.
Faust. Is that the reason he tempts us thus?
Meph. *Solamen miseris socios habuisse doloris.* 480
Faust. Why, have you any pain that tortures others?
Meph. As great as have the human souls of men.
But, tell me, Faustus, shall I have thy soul?
And I will be thy slave, and wait on thee,
And give thee more than thou hast wit to ask.
Faust. Ay, Mephistophilis, I give it thee.
Meph. Then stab thine arm courageously,
And bind thy soul, that at some certain day
Great Lucifer may claim it as his own;
And then be thou as great as Lucifer. 490

480 *Solamen . . . doloris*] It is a solace to the wretched to
have companions in pain

Faust. [*Stabbing his arm*] Lo, Mephistophilis, for
    love of thee,
I cut mine arm, and with my proper blood
Assure my soul to be great Lucifer's,
Chief lord and regent of perpetual night!
View here the blood that trickles from mine arm,
And let it be propitious for my wish.

Meph. But, Faustus, thou must
Write it in manner of a deed of gift.

Faust. Ay, so I will [*Writes*]. But, Mephistophilis,
My blood congeals, and I can write no more.   500

Meph. I'll fetch thee fire to dissolve it straight.

                                     [*Exit.*

Faust. Why might the staying of my blood portend?
Is it unwilling I should write this bill?
Why streams it not, that I may write afresh?
Faustus gives to thee his soul: ah, there it stay'd!
Why shouldst thou not? is not thy soul thine own?
Then write again, *Faustus gives to thee his soul.*

Re-enter Mephistophilis *with a chafer of coals.*

Meph. Here's fire; come, Faustus, set it on.

Faust. So, now the blood begins to clear again;
Now will I make an end immediately.   [*Writes.*

Meph. Oh, what will not I do to obtain his soul? 511

                                   [*Aside.*

Faust. Consummatum est; this bill is ended,
And Faustus hath bequeath'd his soul to Lucifer.
But what is this inscription on mine arm?
Homo, fuge; whither should I fly?
If unto God, he'll throw me down to hell.
My senses are deceiv'd; here's nothing writ:
I see it plain; here in this place is writ,
Homo, fuge: yet shall not Faustus fly.

Meph. I'll fetch him somewhat to delight his mind.

                          [*Aside, and then exit.*

512 *Consummatum est*] It is finished   515 *Homo, fuge*]
man, fly

Re-enter Mephistophilis *with* Devils, *who give crowns and rich apparel to* Faustus, *dance, and then depart.*

Faust. Speak, Mephistophilis, what means this show? 521

Meph. Nothing, Faustus, but to delight thy mind withal,
And to show thee what magic can perform.

Faust. But may I raise up spirits when I please?

Meph. Ay, Faustus, and do greater things than these.

Faust. Then there's enough for a thousand souls.
Here, Mephistophilis, receive this scroll,
A deed of gift of body and of soul:
But yet conditionally that thou perform
All articles prescrib'd between us both. 530

Meph. Faustus, I swear by hell and Lucifer
To effect all promises between us made.

Faust. Then hear me read them. [*Reads*] on these conditions following.

First that Faustus may be a spirit in form and substance.

Secondly, that Mephistophilis shall be his servant, and at his command.

Thirdly, that Mephistophilis shall do for him, and bring him whatsoever. 539

Fourthly, that he shall be in his chamber or house invisible.

Lastly, that he shall appear to the said John Faustus, at all times, in what form or shape soever he please.

I, John Faustus, of Wertenberg, Doctor, by these presents, do give both body and soul to Lucifer prince of the east, and his minister Mephistophilis; and furthermore grant unto them, that, twenty-four years being expired, the articles above-written inviolate, full power to fetch or carry the said John Faustus, body and soul, flesh, blood, or goods, into their habitation wheresoever.

By me, John Faustus. 550

Meph. Speak, Faustus, do you deliver this as your deed?

Faust. Ay, take it, and the devil give thee good on't!

Meph. Now, Faustus, ask what thou wilt.

Faust. First will I question with thee about hell.
Tell me, where is the place that men call hell?

Meph. Under the heavens.

Faust. Ay, but whereabout?

Meph. Within the bowels of these elements,
Where we are tortur'd and remain for ever:
Hell hath no limits, nor is circumscrib'd   560
In one self place; for where we are is hell,
And where hell is, must we ever be:
And, to conclude, when all the world dissolves,
And every creature shall be purified,
All place shall be hell that is not heaven.

Faust. Come, I think hell's a fable.

Meph. Ay, think so still, till experience change thy
    mind.

Faust. Why, think'st thou, then, that Faustus shall
    be damn'd?

Meph. Ay, of necessity, for here's the scroll
Wherein thou hast given thy soul to Lucifer.   570

Faust. Ay, and body too: but what of that?
Think'st thou that Faustus is so fond to imagine
That, after this life, there is any pain?
Tush, these are trifles and mere old wives' tales.

Meph. But, Faustus, I am an instance to prove the
    contrary,
For I am damn'd, and am now in hell.

Faust. How! now in hell! Nay, an this be hell, I'll
willingly be damn'd here: What! walking, disputing,
etc. But, leaving off this, let me have a wife, the
fairest maid in Germany, for I am wanton and
lascivious, and cannot live without a wife.   581

Meph. How! a wife? I prithee, Faustus, talk not
of a wife.

Faust. Nay, sweet Mephistophilis, fetch me one, for
I will have one.

572 fond] foolish

Meph. Well, thou wilt have one. Sit there till I
come: I'll fetch thee a wife in the devil's name. [*Exit.*

Re-enter Mephistophilis *with a* Devil *dress'd like a*
Woman, *with fireworks.*

Meph. Tell me, Faustus, how dost thou like thy
wife?

Faust. A plague on her for a hot whore!

Meph. Tut, Faustus,   590
Marriage is but a ceremonial toy;
If thou lovest me, think no more of it.
I'll cull thee out the fairest courtesans,
And bring them every morning to thy bed:
She whom thine eye shall like, thy heart shall have,
Be she as chaste as was Penelope,
As wise as Saba, or as beautiful
As was bright Lucifer before his fall.
Hold, take this book, peruse it thoroughly:

[*Gives book.*

The iterating of these lines brings gold;   600
The framing of this circle on the ground
Brings whirlwinds, tempests, thunder, and lightning;
Pronounce this thrice devoutly to thyself,
And men in armour shall appear to thee,
Ready to execute what thou desir'st.

Faust. Thanks, Mephistophilis: yet fain would I
have a book wherein I might behold all spells and incantations, that I might raise up spirits when I please.

Meph. Here they are in this book. [*Turns to them.*

Faust. Now would I have a book where I might see
all characters and planets of the heavens, that I might
know their motions and dispositions.   612

Meph. Here they are too. [*Turns to them.*

Faust. Nay, let me have one book more, and then
I have done, wherein I might see all plants, herbs,
and trees, that grow upon the earth.

Meph. Here they be.

Faust. O, thou art deceived.

Meph. Tut, I warrant thee.   [*Turns to them.*

Faust. When I behold the heavens, then I repent,
And curse thee, wicked Mephistophilis,   621
Because thou hast depriv'd me of those joys.

Meph. Why, Faustus,
Think'st thou heaven is such a glorious thing?
I tell thee, 'tis not half so fair as thou,
Or any man that breathes on earth.

Faust. How provest thou that?

Meph. It was made for man, therefore is man more
        excellent.

Faust. If it were made for man, 'twas made for me:
I will renounce this magic and repent.   630

Enter Good Angel *and* Evil Angel.

G. Ang. Faustus, repent; yet God will pity thee.

E. Ang. Thou art a spirit; God cannot pity thee.

Faust. Who buzzeth in mine ears I am a spirit?
Be I a devil, yet God may pity me;
Ay, God will pity me, if I repent.

E. Ang. Ay, but Faustus never shall repent.
                                    [*Exeunt* Angels.

Faust. My heart's so harden'd, I cannot repent:
Scarce can I name salvation, faith, or heaven,
But fearful echoes thunder in mine ears,
'Faustus, thou art damn'd!' then swords, and knives,
Poison, guns, halters, and envenom'd steel   641
Are laid before me to despatch myself;
And long ere this I should have slain myself,
Had not sweet pleasure conquer'd deep despair.
Have not I made blind Homer sing to me
Of Alexander's love and Œnon's death?
And hath not he that built the walls of Thebes
With ravishing sound of his melodious harp
Made music with my Mephistophilis?
Why should I die, then, or basely despair?   650
I am resolv'd Faustus shall ne'er repent.
Come, Mephistophilis, let us dispute again,

And argue of divine astrology.
Tell me, are there many heavens above the moon?
Are all celestial bodies but one globe,
As is the substance of this centric earth?

Meph. As are the elements, such are the spheres,
Mutually folded in each other's orb,
And, Faustus,
All jointly move upon one axletree,   660
Whose terminine is term'd the world's wide pole;
Nor are the names of Saturn, Mars, or Jupiter
Feign'd, but are erring stars.

Faust. But, tell me, have they all one motion, both
situ et tempore?

Meph. All jointly move from east to west in twenty-
four hours upon the poles of the world, but differ in
their motion upon the poles of the zodiac.

Faust. Tush,
These slender trifles Wagner can decide: 670
Hath Mephistophilis no greater skill?
Who knows not the double motion of the planets?
The first is finish'd in a natural day;

The second thus; as Saturn in thirty years; Jupiter
in twelve; Mars in four; the Sun, Venus, and Mercury
in a year; the Moon in twenty-eight days. Tush,
these are freshmen's suppositions. But, tell me, hath
every sphere a dominion or *intelligentia?*

Meph. Ay.   679

Faust. How many heavens or spheres are there?

Meph. Nine; the seven planets, the firmament, and
the imperial heaven.

Faust. Well resolve me in this question; why have
we not conjunctions, oppositions, aspects, eclipses, all
at one time, but in some years we have more, in some
less?

Meph. Per inæqualem motum respectu totius.

665 *situ et tempore*] in place and time   678 *intelligentia*] intelligence   687 *Per . . . totius*] by the inequality
of their movement in reference to the whole

Faust. Well, I am answered. Tell me who made the
    world?

Meph. I will not.

Faust. Sweet Mephistophilis, tell me.   690

Meph. Move me not, for I will not tell thee.

Faust. Villain, have I not bound thee to tell me
    anything?

Meph. Ay, that is not against our kingdom; but
    this is.
Think thou on hell, Faustus, for thou art damn'd.

Faust. Think, Faustus, upon God that made the
    world.

Meph. Remember this.   *[Exit.*

Faust. Ay, go, accursed spirit, to ugly hell!
'Tis thou hast damn'd distressed Faustus' soul
Is't not too late?

      Re-enter Good Angel *and* Evil Angel.

E. Ang. Too late.   700

G. Ang. Never too late, if Faustus can repent,

E. Ang. If thou repent, devils shall tear thee in pieces.

G. Ang. Repent, and they shall never raze thy skin.
                    [Exeunt Angels.

Faust. Ah, Christ my Saviour,
Seek to save distressed Faustus' soul!

    Enter Lucifer, Belzebub, *and* Mephistophilis.

Luc. Christ cannot save thy soul, for he is just:
There's none but I have interest in the same.

Faust. O who art thou that look'st so terrible?

Luc. I am Lucifer,
And this is my companion prince in hell.   710

Faust. O Faustus, they are come to fetch away thy
    soul!

Luc. We come to tell thee thou dost injure us;
Thou talk'st of Christ, contrary to thy promise:
Thou shouldst not think of God: think of the devil,
And of his dam too.

Faust. Nor will I henceforth: pardon me in this,
And Faustus vows never to look to heaven,
Never to name God, or to pray to Him,
To burn his Scriptures, slay his ministers,
And make my spirits pull his churches down.   720

Luc. Do so, and we will highly gratify thee.
Faustus, we are come from hell to show thee some
pastime; sit down, and thou shalt see all the Seven
Deadly Sins appear in their proper shapes.

Faust. That sight will be as pleasing unto me,
As Paradise was to Adam, the first day
Of his creation.

Luc. Talk not of Paradise nor creation; but mark
this show: talk of the devil, and nothing else. Come
away!   730

Enter the Seven Deadly Sins.

Now, Faustus, examine them of their several names
and dispositions.

Faust. What art thou, the first?

Pride. I am Pride. I disdain to have any parents.
I am like to Ovid's flea; I can creep into every corner
of a wench; sometimes, like a periwig, I sit upon her
brow; or, like a fan of feathers, I kiss her lips; indeed,
I do—what do I not? But, fie, what a scent is here!
I'll not speak another word, except the ground were
perfum'd, and covered with cloth of arras.   740

Faust. What art thou, the second?

Covet. I am Covetousness, begotten of an old churl
in an old leathern bag: and, might I have my wish,
I would desire that this house and all the people in
it were turn'd to gold, that I might lock you up in
my good chest: O my sweet gold!

Faust. What art thou, the third?

Wrath. I am Wrath. I had neither father nor
mother: I leapt out of a lion's mouth when I was
scarce half an hour old; and ever since I have run up
and down the world with this case of rapiers, wounding

myself when I had nobody to fight withal. I was born in hell; and look to it, for some of you shall be my father.

Faust. What art thou, the fourth?   754

Envy. I am Envy, begotten of a chimney-sweeper and an oyster-wife. I cannot read, and therefore wish all books were burnt. I am lean with seeing others eat. Oh, that there would come a famine through all the world, that all might die, and I live alone! then thou shouldst see how fat I would be. But must thou sit, and I stand? come down, with a vengeance!

Faust. Away, envious rascal!—What art thou, the fifth?

Glut. Who I, sir? I am Gluttony. My parents are all dead, and the devil a penny they have left me, but a bare pension, and that is thirty meals a day, and ten bevers,—a small trifle to suffice nature. Oh, I come of a royal parentage! my grandfather was a Gammon of Bacon, my grandmother a Hogshead of Claret-wine; my godfathers were these, Peter Pickle-herring and Martin Martlemas-beef; Oh, but my godmother, she was a jolly gentlewoman, and well-beloved in every good town and city; her name was Mistress Margery March-beer. Now, Faustus, thou hast heard all my progeny; wilt thou bid me to supper?

Faust. No, I'll see thee hanged: thou wilt eat up all my victuals.

Glut. Then the devil choke thee!

Faust. Choke thyself, glutton!—What art thou, the sixth?   780

Sloth. I am Sloth. I was begotten on a sunny bank, where I have lain ever since; and you have done me great injury to bring me from thence: let me be carried thither again by Gluttony and Lechery. I'll not speak another word for a king's ransom.

Faust. What are you, Mistress Minx, the seventh and last?

Lechery. Who I, sir? I am one that loves an inch

767 bevers] refreshments taken between meals

of raw mutton better than en ell of fried stock-fish;
and the first letter of my name begins with Lechery 790

Faust. Away, to hell, to hell!   [*Exeunt the* Sins.

Luc. Now, Faustus, how dost thou like this?

Faust. Oh, this feeds my soul!

Luc. Tut, Faustus, in hell is all manner of delight.

Faust. Oh, might I see hell, and return again,
How happy were I then!

Luc. Thou shalt; I will send for thee at midnight.
In meantime take this book; peruse it throughly,
And thou shalt turn thyself into what shape thou wilt.

Faust. Great thanks, mighty Lucifer.   800
This will I keep as chary as my life.

Luc. Farewell, Faustus, and think on the devil.

Faust. Farewell, great Lucifer.
               [*Exeunt* Lucifer *and* Belzebub.
    Come, Mephistophilis.   [*Exeunt.*

Enter Chorus.

Chor. Learned Faustus,
To know the secrets of astronomy
Graven in the book of Jove's high firmament,
Did mount himself to scale Olympus' top,
Being seated in a chariot burning bright,
Drawn by the strength of yoky dragons' necks. 810
He is now gone to prove cosmography,
And, as I guess, will first arrive at Rome,
To see the Pope and manner of his court,
And take some part of holy Peter's feast,
That to this day is highly solemnis'd.   [*Exit.*

Enter Faustus *and* Mephistophilis.*

Faust. Having now, my good Mephistophilis,
Pass'd with delight the stately town of Trier,
Environ'd round with airy mountain-tops,
With walls of flint, and deep-entrenched lakes,
Not to be won by any conquering prince;   820

     * The scene is the Pope's Privy Chamber

From Paris next, coasting the realm of France,
We saw the river Maine fall into Rhine,
Whose banks are set with groves of fruitful vines;
Then up to Naples, rich Campania,
Whose buildings fair and gorgeous to the eye,
The streets straight forth, and pav'd with finest brick,
Quarters the town in four equivalents:
There saw we learned Maro's golden tomb,
The way he cut, an English mile in length,
Thorough a rock of stone, in one night's space; 830
From thence to Venice, Padua, and the rest,
In one of which a sumptuous temple stands,
That threats the stars with her aspiring top.
Thus hitherto hath Faustus spent his time:
But tell me now what resting-place is this?
Hast thou, as erst I did command,
Conducted me within the walls of Rome?
    Meph. Faustus, I have; and, because we will not
be unprovided, I have taken up his Holiness' privy-
chamber for our use.   840
    Faust. I hope his Holiness will bid us welcome.
    Meph. Tut, 'tis no matter, man; we'll be bold with
his good cheer.
And now, my Faustus, that thou mayst perceive
What Rome containeth to delight thee with,
Know that this city stands upon seven hills
That underprops the groundwork of the same:
Just through the midst runs flowing Tiber's stream
With winding banks that cut it in two parts;
Over the which four stately bridges lean,
That makes safe passage to each part of Rome: 850
Upon the bridge call'd Ponte Angelo
Erected is a castle passing strong,
Within whose walls such store of ordnance are,
And double cannons fram'd of carved brass,
As match the days within one complete year;

838 because we will] so that we may   839 Taken **up**]
borrowed

Besides the gates and high pyramides,
Which Julius Cæsar brought from Africa.

Faust. Now by the kingdoms of infernal rule,
Of Styx, Acheron, and the fiery lake
Of ever-burning Phlegethon, I swear 860
That I do long to see the monuments
And situation of bright-splendent Rome:
Come, therefore, let's away.

Meph. Nay, Faustus, stay: I know you'd fain see
the Pope,
And take some part of holy Peter's feast,
Where thou shalt see a troop of bald-pate friars,
Whose *summum bonum* is in belly-cheer.

Faust. Well, I am content to compass then some
sport,
And by their folly make us merriment.
Then charm me, that I may be invisible, to do what
I please, 871
Unseen of any whilst I stay in Rome.

[*Mephistophilis charms him.*

Meph. So, Faustus; now
Do what thou wilt, thou shalt not be discerned.

Sound a Sonnet. Enter the Pope *and the* Cardinal of
Lorrain *to the banquet, with* Friars *attending.*

Pope. My lord of Lorrain, wil't please you draw near?
Faust. Fall to, and the devil choke you, an you spare!
Pope. How now! who's that which spake?—Friars,
look about.
First Friar. Here's nobody, if it like your Holiness.
Pope. My lord, here is a dainty dish was sent me
from the Bishop of Milan. 881
Faust. I thank you, sir. [*Snatches the dish.*
Pope. How now! who's that which snatch'd the
meat from me? will no man look?—My lord, this dish
was sent me from the Cardinal of Florence.

856 pyramides] obelisks

Faust. You say true; I'll ha't.   [*Snatches the dish.*

Pope. What, again!—My lord, I'll drink to your grace.

Faust. I'll pledge your grace.   [*Snatches the cup.*

C. of Lor. My lord, it may be some ghost, newly crept out of Purgatory, come to beg a pardon of your Holiness.   891

Pope. It may be so. Friars, prepare a dirge to lay the fury of this ghost. Once again, my lord, fall to.
                                    [*The* Pope *crosses himself.*

Faust. What, are you crossing of yourself?
Well, use that trick no more, I would advise you.
                            [*The* Pope *crosses himself again.*
Well, there's the second time. Aware the third;
I give you fair warning.

        [*The* Pope *crosses himself again, and* Faustus *hits
            him a box of the ear; and they all run away.*
Come on, Mephistophilis; what shall we do?

Meph. Nay, I know not: we shall be curs'd with bell, book, and candle.   900

Faust. How! bell, book, and candle,—candle, book,
    and bell,—
Forward and backward, to curse Faustus to hell!
Anon you shall hear a hog grunt, a calf bleat, and an ass bray, because it is Saint Peter's holiday.

        Re-enter all the Friars *to sing the Dirge.*

First Friar. Come, brethren, let's about our business
with good devotion.

Cursed be he that stole away his Holiness' meat from
    the table! *maledicat Dominus!*

Cursed be he that struck his Holiness a blow on the
    face! *maledicat Dominus!*

Cursed be he that took Friar Sandelo a blow on the
    pate! *maledicat Dominus!*

Cursed be he that disturbeth our holy dirge! *maledicat
    Dominus!*   910

        907 *maledicat Dominus*] may the Lord curse him

Cursed be he that took away his Holiness' wine!
  maledicat Dominus!
                    Et omnes Sancti! Amen!
        [*Mephistophilis and Faustus beat the Friars, and
        fling fireworks among them; and so exeunt.*

                    Enter Chorus.

  Chor. When Faustus had with pleasure ta'en the
        view
Of rarest things, and royal courts of kings,
He stay'd his course, and so returned home;
Where such as bear his absence but with grief,
I mean his friends and nearest companions,
Did gratulate his safety with kind words,
And in their conference of what befell,
Touching his journey through the world and air,
They put forth questions of astrology,   920
Which Faustus answer'd with such learned skill
As they admir'd and wonder'd at his wit.
Now is his fame spread forth in every land:
Amongst the rest the Emperor is one,
Carolus the Fifth, at whose palace now
Faustus is feasted 'mongst his noblemen.
What there he did, in trial of his art,
I leave untold; your eyes shall see perform'd.   [*Exit.*

    Enter Robin *the Ostler, with a book in his hand.**

  Robin. Oh, this is admirable! here I ha' stolen one
of Doctor Faustus' conjuring books, and, i'faith, I
mean to search some circles for my own use. Now
will I make all the maidens in our parish dance at
my pleasure stark naked before me; and so by that
means I shall see more than e'er I felt or saw yet.   934

              Enter Ralph, *calling* Robin.

  Ralph. Robin, prithee come away; there's a gentleman tarries to have his horse, and he would have his

          * The scene is an inn-yard

things rubb'd and made clean: he keeps such a chafing with my mistress about it, and she has set me to look thee out; prithee come away.

Robin. Keep out, keep out, or else you are blown up, you are dismember'd, Ralph: keep out, for I am about a roaring piece of work.   942

Ralph. Come, what doest thou with that same book? thou canst not read?

Robin. Yes, my master and mistress shall find that I can read, he for his forehead, she for her private study; she's born to bear with me, or else my art fails.

Ralph. Why, Robin, what book is that?

Robin. What book? why, the most intolerable book for conjuring that e'er was invented by any brimstone devil.   951

Ralph. Canst thou conjure with it?

Robin. I can do all these things easily with it; first, I can make thee drunk with ippocras at any tavern in Europe for nothing; that's one of my conjuring works.

Ralph. Our Master Parson says that's nothing.

Robin. True, Ralph: and more, Ralph, if thou hast any mind to Nan Spit, our kitchen-maid, then turn her and wind her to thy own use, as often as thou wilt, and at midnight.   960

Ralph. O brave Robin! shall I have Nan Spit, and to mine own use? On that condition I'll feed thy devil with horse-bread as long as he lives, of free cost.

Robin. No more, sweet Ralph: let's go and make clean our boots, which lie foul upon our hands, and then to our conjuring in the devil's name.   [*Exeunt.*

Enter Robin *and* Ralph *with a silver goblet.*

Robin. Come, Ralph: did not I tell thee we were for ever made by this Doctor Faustus' book? *ecce, signum!* here's a simple purchase for horse-keepers: our horses shall eat no hay as long as this lasts.   971

970 purchase] boot

Ralph. But, Robin, here comes the Vintner.

Robin. Hush! I'll gull him supernaturally.

Enter Vintner.

Drawer, I hope all is paid; God be with you;
Come, Ralph.

Vint. Soft, sir; a word with you. I must yet have
a goblet paid from you, ere you go.

Robin. I a goblet, Ralph, I a goblet! I scorn you;
and you are but a, etc. I a goblet! search me.

Vint. I mean so, sir, with your favour.   980

                [*Searches* Robin.

Robin. How say you now?

Vint. I must say somewhat to your fellow. You, sir!

Robin. Me, sir! me, sir! search your fill. [*Vintner
searches him.*] Now, sir, you may be ashamed to burden honest men with a matter of truth.

Vint. Well, t'one of you hath this goblet about you.

Robin. You lie, drawer, 'tis afore me [*Aside*].—Sirrah you, I'll teach ye to impeach honest men;—
stand by;—I'll scour you for a goblet;—stand aside
you had best, I charge you in the name of Belzebub.
Look to the goblet, Ralph [*Aside to Ralph*].   991

Vint. What mean you, sirrah?

Robin. I'll tell you what I mean. [*Reads from a
book*] *Sanctobulorum Periphrasticon*—nay, I'll tickle you,
Vintner.—Look to the goblet, Ralph [*Aside to Ralph*].
—[*Reads*] *Polypragmos Belseborams framanto pacostiphos
tostu, Mephistophilis*, etc.

Enter Mephistophilis, *sets squibs at their backs, and then
exit. They run about.*

Vint. O, *nomine Domini!* what meanest thou, Robin?
thou hast no goblet.

Ralph. Peccatum peccatorum! Here's thy goblet, good
Vintner.   [*Gives the goblet to* Vintner, *who goes out.*

    998 O, *nomine Domini*] in the name of the Lord
    1000 *Peccatum peccatorum*] sin of sins

Robin. *Misericordia pro nobis!* what shall I do? Good devil, forgive me now, and I'll never rob thy library more.   1004

Re-enter Mephistophilis.

Meph. Monarch of hell, under whose black survey
Great potentates do kneel with awful fear,
Upon whose altars thousand souls do lie,
How am I vexed with these villains' charms?
From Constantinople am I hither come,
Only for pleasure of these damned slaves.   1010

Robin. How, from Constantinople? you have had a great journey: will you take sixpence in your purse to pay for your supper, and be gone?

Meph. Well, villains, for your presumption, I transform thee into an ape, and thee into a dog; and so be gone!   [*Exit.*

Robin. How, into an ape! that's brave: I'll have fine sport with the boys; I'll get nuts and apples enow.

Ralph. And I must be a dog.   1019

Robin. I'faith, thy head will never be out of the pottage-pot.   [*Exeunt.*

Enter Emperor, Faustus, *and a* Knight, *with* Attendants.*

Emp. Master Doctor Faustus, I have heard strange report of thy knowledge in the black art, how that none in my empire nor in the whole world can compare with thee for the rare effects of magic: they say thou hast a familiar spirit, by whom thou canst accomplish what thou list. This, therefore, is my request, that thou let me see some proof of thy skill, that mine eyes may be witnesses to confirm what mine ears have heard reported: and here I swear to thee, by the honour of mine imperial crown, that,

1002 *misericordia* . . .] mercy on us   * The scene is an apartment in the Emperor's palace.

whatever thou doest, thou shalt be no ways prejudiced
or endamaged. 1033

Knight. I'faith, he looks much like a conjuror.

[*Aside.*

Faust. My gracious sovereign, though I must confess myself far inferior to the report men have published, and nothing answerable to the honour of your
imperial majesty, yet, for that love and duty binds
me thereunto, I am content to do whatsoever your
majesty shall command me. 1040

Emp. Then, Doctor Faustus, mark what I shall say.
As I was sometime solitary set
Within my closet, sundry thoughts arose
About the honour of mine ancestors,
How they had won by prowess such exploits,
Got such riches, subdued so many kingdoms,
As we that do succeed, or they that shall
Hereafter possess our throne, shall,
I fear me, never attain to that degree
Of high renown and great authority: 1050
Amongst which kings is Alexander the Great,
Chief spectacle of the world's pre-eminence,
The bright shining of whose glorious acts
Lightens the world with his reflecting beams,
As when I hear but motion made of him,
It grieves my soul I never saw the man:
If therefore thou, by cunning of thine art,
Canst raise this man from hollow vaults below,
Where lies entomb'd this famous conqueror,
And bring with him his beauteous paramour, 1060
Both in their right shapes, gesture, and attire
They us'd to wear during their time of life,
Thou shalt both satisfy my just desire,
And give me cause to praise thee whilst I live.

Faust. My gracious lord, I am ready to accomplish
your request, so far forth as by art and power of my
spirit I am able to perform.

Knight. I'faith, that's just nothing at all. [*Aside.*

Faust. But, if it like your grace, it is not in my ability to present before your eyes the true substantial bodies of those two deceased princes, which long since are consumed to dust.   1072

Knight. Ay, marry, Master Doctor, now there's a sign of grace in you, when you will confess the truth.

[*Aside.*

Faust. But such spirits as can lively resemble Alexander and his paramour shall appear before your grace, in that manner that they both liv'd in, in their most flourishing estate; which I doubt not shall sufficiently content your imperial majesty.

Emp. Go to, Master Doctor; let me see them presently.   1081

Knight. Do you hear, Master Doctor? you bring Alexander and his paramour before the Emperor!

Faust. How then, sir?

Knight. I'faith, that's as true as Diana turn'd me to a stag.

Faust. No, sir; but, when Actæon died, he left the horns for you. Mephistophilis, be gone.

[*Exit* Mephistophilis.

Knight. Nay, an you go to conjuring, I'll be gone.

[*Exit.*

Faust. I'll meet with you anon for interrupting me so. Here they are, my gracious lord!   1091

Re-enter Mephistophilis *with* Spirits *in the shapes of* Alexander *and his* Paramour.

Emp. Master Doctor, I heard this lady, while she liv'd, had a wart or mole in her neck: how shall I know whether it be so or no?

Faust. Your highness may boldly go and see.

Emp. Sure, these are no spirits, but the true substantial bodies of those two deceased princes.

[*Exeunt* Spirits.

Faust. Wil't please your highness now to send for the knight that was so pleasant with me here of late?

Emp. One of you call him forth. [*Exit* Attendant.

Re-enter the Knight *with a pair of horns on his head.*

How now, sir knight! why, I had thought thou
hadst been a bachelor, but now I see thou hast a
wife, that not only gives thee horns, but makes thee
wear them. Feel on thy head.   1104

Knight. Thou damned wretch and execrable dog,
Bred in the concave of some monstrous rock,
How dar'st thou thus abuse a gentleman?
Villain, I say, undo what thou hast done!

Faust. Oh, not so fast, sir, there's no haste: but,
good, are you remember'd how you crossed me in
my conference with the Emperor? I think I have
met with you for it.   1112

Emp. Good Master Doctor, at my entreaty release
him: he hath done penance sufficient.

Faust. My gracious lord, not so much for the injury
he offer'd me here in your presence, as to delight you
with some mirth, hath Faustus worthily requited this
injurious knight; which being all I desire, I am content to release him of his horns:—and, sir knight,
hereafter speak well of scholars. Mephistophilis,
transform him straight. [*Mephistophilis removes the
horns.*]—Now, my good lord, having done my duty,
I humbly take my leave.

Emp. Farewell, Master Doctor: yet, ere you go,
Expect from me a bounteous reward.

[*Exeunt* Emperor, Knight, *and* Attendants.

Faust. Now, Mephistophilis, the restless course
That time doth run with calm and silent foot,
Short'ning my days and thread of vital life,
Calls for the payment of my latest years:
Therefore, sweet Mephistophilis, let us   1130
Make haste to Wertenberg.

1127 The scene changes to the countryside, and then to a
room in Faustus's house

Meph. What, will you go on horse-back or on foot?

Faust. Nay, till I am past this fair and pleasant green, I'll walk on foot.

Enter a Horse-courser.*

Horse-c. I have been all this day seeking one Master Fustian: mass, see where he is! God save you Master Doctor!

Faust. What, horse-courser! you are well met.

Horse-c. Do you hear, sir? I have brought you forty dollars for your horse.   1140

Faust. I cannot sell him so: if thou lik'st him for fifty, take him.

Horse-c. Alas, sir, I have no more! I pray you, speak for me.

Meph. I pray you, let him have him: he is an honest fellow, and he has a great charge, neither wife nor child.

Faust. Well, come, give me your money [Horse-courser *gives* Faustus *the money*]: my boy will deliver him to you. But I must tell you one thing before you have him; ride him not into the water, at any hand.

Horse-c. Why, sir, will he not drink of all waters?

Faust. Oh, yes, he will drink of all waters; but ride him not into the water; ride him over hedge or ditch, or where thou wilt, but not into the water.   1155

Horse-c. Well, sir.—Now am I made man for ever: I'll not leave my horse for forty: if he had but the quality of hey-ding-ding, hey-ding-ding, I'd make a brave living on him: he has a buttock as slick as an eel [*Aside*]. Well, God b'wi'ye, sir: your boy will deliver him me: but, hark ye, sir; if my horse be sick or ill at ease, if I bring his water to you, you'll tell me what it is?

Faust. Away, you villain! what, dost think I am a horse-doctor? [*Exit* Horse-courser]. What art thou, Faustus, but a man condemn'd to die?

* Horse-dealer

Thy fatal time doth draw to final end;
Despair doth drive distrust unto my thoughts:
Confound these passions with a quiet sleep:
Tush, Christ did call the thief upon the Cross; 1170
Then rest thee, Faustus, quiet in conceit.

[Sleeps in his chair.

Re-enter Horse-courser, *all wet, crying.*

Horse-c. Alas, alas! Doctor Fustian, quotha? mass,
Doctor Lopus was never such a doctor: has given me
a purgation, has purg'd me of forty dollars; I shall
never see them more. But yet, like an ass as I was,
I would not be ruled by him, for he bade me I should
ride him into no water: now I, thinking my horse
had had some rare quality that he would not have
had me know of, I, like a venturous youth, rid him
into the deep pond at the town's end. I was no sooner
in the middle of the pond, but my horse vanish'd
away, and I sat upon a bottle of hay, never so near
drowning in my life. But I'll seek out my doctor, and
have my forty dollars again, or I'll make it the dearest
horse!—O, yonder is his snipper-snapper. Do you
hear? you, hey-pass, where's your master?

Meph. Why, sir, what would you? you cannot speak

Horse-c. But I will speak with him.   [with him.

Meph. Why, he's fast asleep: come some other time.

Horse-c. I'll speak with him now, or I'll break his
glass-windows about his ears.   1191

Meph. I tell thee, he has not slept this eight nights.

Horse-c. An he have not slept this eight weeks, I'll
speak with him.

Meph. See, where he is, fast asleep.

Horse-c. Ay, this is he.—God save you, Master
Doctor, Master Doctor, Master Doctor Fustian! forty
dollars, forty dollars for a bottle of hay!

Meph. Why, thou seest he hears thee not.   1199

Horse-c. So-ho, ho! so-ho, ho! *[Hollows in his ear.]*

1182 bottle] bundle

No, will you not wake? I'll make you wake ere I go.
[*Pulls Faustus by the leg, and pulls it away.*] Alas, I am
undone! what shall I do?

Faust. O, my leg, my leg! Help, Mephistophilis!
call the officers. My leg, my leg!

Meph. Come, villain, to the constable.

Horse-c. O Lord, sir, let me go, and I'll give you
forty dollars more.

Meph. Where be they?   1209

Horse-c. I have none about me: come to my ostry,
and I'll give them you.

Meph. Be gone quickly.   [*Horse-courser runs away.*

Faust. What, is he gone? farewell he! Faustus has
his leg again, and the Horse-courser, I take it, a
bottle of hay for his labour: well, this trick shall cost
him forty dollars more.

Enter Wagner.

How now, Wagner! what's the news with thee?

Wag. Sir, the Duke of Vanholt doth earnestly entreat your company.   1219

Faust. The Duke of Vanholt! an honourable gentleman, to whom I must be no niggard of my cunning.
Come, Mephistophilis, let's away to him.   [*Exeunt.*

Enter the Duke of Vanholt, *the* Duchess, *and* Faustus.*

Duke. Believe me, Master Doctor, this merriment
hath much pleased me.

Faust. My gracious lord, I am glad it contents you
so well. But it may be, madam, you take no delight
in this. I have heard that great-bellied women do
long for some dainties or other: what is it, madam?
tell me, and you shall have it.   1229

Duchess. Thanks, good Master Doctor: and, for I
see your courteous intent to pleasure me, I will not
hide from you the thing my heart desires; and, were

1210 ostry] hostelry   * The scene is the Court of the
Duke of Vanholt

it now summer, as it is January and the dead time of
the winter, I would desire no better meat than a dish
of ripe grapes.

Faust. Alas, madam, that's nothing!—Mephistophilis, be gone. [*Exit* Mephistophilis.] Were it a
greater thing than this, so it would content you, you
should have it.   1239

Re-enter Mephistophilis *with grapes.*

Here they be, madam: will't please you taste on them?

Duke. Believe me, Master Doctor, this makes me
wonder above the rest, that being in the dead time
of winter and in the month of January, how you
should come by these grapes.

Faust. If it like your grace, the year is divided into
two circles over the whole world, that, when it is here
winter with us, in the contrary circle it is summer
with them, as in India, Saba, and farther countries
in the east; and by means of a swift spirit that I have,
I had them brought hither, as ye see. How do you
like them, madam? be they good?   1251

Duchess. Believe me, Master Doctor, they be the
best grapes that e'er I tasted in my life before.

Faust. I am glad they content you so, madam.

Duke. Come, madam, let us in, where you must
well reward this learned man for the great kindness
he hath show'd to you.

Duchess. And so I will, my lord; and, whilst I live,
rest beholding for this courtesy.

Faust. I humbly thank your grace.   1260

Duke. Come, Master Doctor, follow us, and receive
your reward.   [*Exeunt.*

Enter Wagner.

Wag. I think my master means to die shortly,
For he hath given to me all his goods:
And yet, methinks, if that death were near,
He would not banquet, and carouse, and swill
Amongst the students, as even now he doth,

Who are at supper with such belly-cheer
As Wagner ne'er beheld in all his life.   1269
See, where they come! belike the feast is ended. [*Exit.*

    Enter Faustus *with two or three* Scholars, *and*
              Mephistophilis.*

    First Schol. Master Doctor Faustus, since our con-
ference about fair ladies, which was the beautifulest
in all the world, we have determined with ourselves
that Helen of Greece was the admirablest lady that
ever lived: therefore, Master Doctor, if you will do
us that favour, as to let us see that peerless dame of
Greece, whom all the world admires for majesty, we
should think ourselves much beholding unto you.
    Faust. Gentlemen,   1280
For that I know your friendship is unfeigned,
And Faustus' custom is not to deny
The just requests of those that wish him well,
You shall behold that peerless dame of Greece,
No otherways for pomp and majesty
Than when Sir Paris cross'd the seas with her,
And brought the spoils to rich Dardania.
Be silent, then, for danger is in words.

    [*Music sounds, and* Helen *passeth over the stage.*
    Sec. Schol. Too simple is my wit to tell her praise,
Whom all the world admires for majesty.   1290
    Third Schol. No marvel though the angry Greeks
        pursu'd
With ten years' war the rape of such a queen,
Whose heavenly beauty passeth all compare.
    First Schol. Since we have seen the pride of Nature's
        works,
And only paragon of excellence,
Let us depart; and for this glorious deed
Happy and blest be Faustus evermore.
    Faust. Gentlemen, farewell: the same I wish to
    you.   [*Exeunt* Scholars.
    * This and the following scene are inside Faustus's house

Enter an Old Man.

Old Man. Ah, Doctor Faustus, that I might prevail
To guide thy steps unto the way of life,   1300
By which sweet path thou mayst attain the goal
That shall conduct thee to celestial rest!
Break heart, drop blood, and mingle it with tears,
Tears falling from repentant heaviness
Of thy most vile and loathsome filthiness,
The stench whereof corrupts the inward soul
With such flagitious crimes of heinous sins
As no commiseration may expel,
But mercy, Faustus, of thy Saviour sweet,
Whose blood alone must wash away thy guilt.   1310
  Faust. Where art thou, Faustus? wretch, what hast
      thou done?
Damn'd art thou, Faustus, damn'd; despair and die!
Hell calls for right, and with a roaring voice
Says, 'Faustus, come; thine hour is come;'
And Faustus will come to do thee right.
                          [Mephistophilis *gives him a dagger.*
  Old Man. Ah, stay, good Faustus, stay thy despe-
      rate steps!
I see an angel hovers o'er thy head,
And, with a vial full of precious grace,
Offers to pour the same into thy soul:
Then call for mercy and avoid despair.   1320
  Faust. Ah, my sweet friend, I feel
Thy words to comfort my distressed soul.
Leave me a while to ponder on my sins.
  Old Man. I go, sweet Faustus; but with heavy
      cheer,
Fearing the ruin of thy hopeless soul.   [*Exit.*
  Faust. Accursed Faustus, where is mercy now?
I do repent; and yet I do despair:
Hell strives with grace for conquest in my breast:
What shall I do to shun the snares of death?   1329
  Meph. Thou traitor, Faustus, I arrest thy soul

For disobedience to my sovereign lord:
Revolt, or I'll in piece-meal tear thy flesh.

Faust. Sweet Mephistophilis, entreat thy lord
To pardon my unjust presumption,
And with my blood again I will confirm
My former vow I made to Lucifer.

Meph. Do it then quickly, with unfeigned heart,
Lest greater danger do attend thy drift.

Faust. Torment, sweet friend, that base and
    crooked age,
That durst dissuade me from thy Lucifer,   1340
With greatest torments that our hell affords.

Meph. His faith is great; I cannot touch his soul;
But what I may afflict his body with
I will attempt, which is but little worth.

Faust. One thing, good servant, let me crave of thee,
To glut the longing of my heart's desire,
That I might have unto my paramour
That heavenly Helen which I saw of late,
Whose sweet embracings may extinguish clean 1349
Those thoughts that do dissuade me from my vow,
And keep mine oath I made to Lucifer.

Meph. Faustus, this, or what else thou shalt desire,
Shall be perform'd in twinkling of an eye.

Re-enter Helen.

Faust. Was this the face that launch'd a thousand
    ships,
And burnt the topless towers of Ilium?
Sweet Helen, make me immortal with a kiss.

                           [*Kisses her.*
Her lips suck forth my soul: see, where it flies!—
Come, Helen, come, give me my soul again.
Here will I dwell, for heaven be in these lips,
And all is dross that is not Helena.   1360
I will be Paris, and for love of thee,
Instead of Troy, shall Wertenberg be sack'd;
And I will combat with weak Menelaus,

And wear thy colours on my plumed crest;
Yes, I will wound Achilles in the heel,
And then return to Helen for a kiss.
Oh, thou art fairer than the evening air
Clad in the beauty of a thousand stars;
Brighter art thou than flaming Jupiter
When he appear'd to hapless Semele;   1370
More lovely than the monarch of the sky
In wanton Arethusa's azur'd arms;
And none but thou shalt be my paramour.   *[Exeunt.*

Enter the Old Man.

Old Man. Accursed Faustus, miserable man,
That from thy soul exclud'st the grace of heaven,
And fly'st the throne of his tribunal-seat!

Enter Devils.

Satan begins to sift me with his pride:
As in this furnace God shall try my faith,
My faith, vile hell, shall triumph over thee.
Ambitious fiends, see how the heavens smiles   1380
At your repulse, and laughs your state to scorn!
Hence, hell! for hence I fly unto my God.   *[Exeunt.*

Enter Faustus, *with* Scholars.*

Faust. Ah, gentlemen!
First Schol. What ails Faustus?
Faust. Ah, my sweet chamber-fellow, had I lived
with thee, then had I lived still, but now I die eter-
nally. Look, comes he not? comes he not?
Sec. Schol. What means Faustus?
Third Schol. Belike he is grown into some sickness
by being over-solitary.   1390
First Schol. If it be so, we'll have physicians to cure
him. 'Tis but a surfeit; never fear, man.

---

     * The scene is a room in Faustus's house.

Faust. A surfeit of deadly sin, that hath damn'd both body and soul.

Sec. Schol. Yet, Faustus, look up to heaven; remember God's mercies are infinite.

Faust. But Faustus' offence can ne'er be pardoned: the serpent that tempted Eve may be sav'd, but not Faustus. Ah, gentlemen, hear me with patience, and tremble not at my speeches. Though my heart pants and quivers to remember that I have been a student here these thirty years, oh, would I had never seen Wertenberg, never read book! and what wonders I have done, all Germany can witness, yea, all the world; for which Faustus hath lost both Germany and the world, yea, heaven itself, heaven, the seat of God, the throne of the blessed, the kingdom of joy; and must remain in hell for ever, hell, ah, hell, for ever! Sweet friends, what shall become of Faustus, being in hell for ever?   1410

Third Schol. Yet, Faustus, call on God.

Faust. On God, whom Faustus hath abjur'd! on God, whom Faustus hath blasphemed! Ah, my God, I would weep, but the devil draws in my tears. Gush forth blood, instead of tears! yea, life and soul! Oh, he stays my tongue! I would lift up my hands; but see, they hold them, they hold them!

All. Who, Faustus?

Faust. Lucifer and Mephistophilis. Ah, gentlemen, I gave them my soul for my cunning!   1420

All. God forbid!

Faust. God forbade it, indeed; but Faustus hath done it: for vain pleasure of twenty-four years hath Faustus lost eternal joy and felicity. I writ them a bill with mine own blood: the date is expired; the time will come, and he will fetch me.

First Schol. Why did not Faustus tell us of this before, that divines might have prayed for thee? 1429

Faust. Oft have I thought to have done so, but the devil threaten'd to tear me in pieces, if I nam'd God, to fetch both body and soul, if I once gave ear to divinity: and now 'tis too late. Gentlemen, away, lest you perish with me.

Sec. Schol. Oh, what shall we do to save Faustus?

Faust. Talk not of me, but save yourselves, and depart.

Third Schol. God will strengthen me; I will stay with Faustus.

First Schol. Tempt not God, sweet friend; but let us into the next room, and there pray for him. 1440

Faust. Ay, pray for me, pray for me; and what noise soever ye hear, come not unto me, for nothing can rescue me.

Sec. Schol. Pray thou, and we will pray that God may have mercy upon thee.

Faust. Gentlemen, farewell: if I live till morning, I'll visit you; if not, Faustus is gone to hell.

All. Faustus, farewell.

[*Exeunt* Scholars.—*The clock strikes eleven.*

Faust. Ah, Faustus.

Now hast thou but one bare hour to live, 1450
And then thou must be damn'd perpetually!
Stand still, you ever-moving spheres of heaven,
That time may cease, and midnight never come;
Fair Nature's eye, rise, rise again, and make
Perpetual day; or let this hour be but
A year, a month, a week, a natural day,
That Faustus may repent and save his soul!
O lente, lente currite, noctis equi! 1458
The stars move still, time runs, the clock will strike,
The devil will come, and Faustus must be damn'd.
Oh, I'll leap up to my God! Who pulls me down?
See, see, where Christ's blood streams in the firmament!
One drop would save my soul, half a drop: ah, my Christ!
Ah, rend not my heart for naming of my Christ!

1458 *O lente . . . equi*] oh run slowly, slowly, horses of night

Yet will I call on him: Oh, spare me, Lucifer!
Where is it now? 'tis gone: and see, where God
Stretcheth out his arm, and bends his ireful brows!
Mountains and hills, come, come, and fall on me,
And hide me from the heavy wrath of God!
No, no!   1470
Then will I headlong run into the earth:
Earth, gape! Oh, no, it will not harbour me!
You stars that reign'd at my nativity,
Whose influence hath allotted death and hell,
Now draw up Faustus, like a foggy mist,
Into the entrails of yon labouring cloud,
That, when you vomit forth into the air,
My limbs may issue from your smoky mouths,
So that my soul may but ascend to heaven.
                              [*The clock strikes the half-hour.*
Ah, half the hour is past!   1480
'Twill all be past anon.
O God,
If thou wilt not have mercy on my soul,
Yet for Christ's sake, whose blood hath ransom'd me,
Impose some end to my incessant pain;
Let Faustus live in hell a thousand years,
A hundred thousand, and at last be sav'd!
Oh, no end is limited to damned souls!
Why wert thou not a creature wanting soul?
Or why is this immortal that thou hast?   1490
Ah, Pythagoras' metempsychosis, were that true,
This soul should fly from me, and I be chang'd
Unto some brutish beast! all beasts are happy,
For when they die,
Their souls are soon dissolv'd in elements;
But mine must live still to be plagu'd in hell.
Curs'd be the parents that engender'd me!
No, Faustus, curse thyself, curse Lucifer
That hath depriv'd thee of the joys of heaven.   1499
                              [*The clock strikes twelve.*
Oh, it strikes, it strikes! Now, body, turn to air,

Or Lucifer will bear thee quick to hell!
[*Thunder and lightning.*

O soul, be chang'd into little water-drops,
And fall into the ocean, ne'er be found!

Enter Devils.

My God, my God, look not so fierce on me!
Adders and serpents, let me breathe a while!
Ugly hell, gape not! come not, Lucifer!
I'll burn my books!—Ah, Mephistophilis!
[*Exeunt* Devils *with* Faustus.

Enter Chorus.

Chor. Cut is the branch that might have grown full
straight,
And burned is Apollo's laurel-bough,
That sometime grew within this learned man.   1510
Faustus is gone: regard his hellish fall,
Whose fiendful fortune may exhort the wise,
Only to wonder at unlawful things,
Whose deepness doth entice such forward wits
To practise more than heavenly power permits.
[*Exit.*

Terminat hora diem; terminat auctor opus.

1517 *Terminat . . . opus*] The hour ends the day; the author
ends the work

The Famous

TRAGEDY

OF

THE RICH IEVV

OF *MALTA.*

AS IT VVAS PLAYD
BEFORE THE KING AND
QVEENE, IN HIS MAJESTIES
Theatre at *White-Hall*, by her Majesties
Servants at the *Cock-pit.*

Written by CHRISTOPHER MARLO.

LONDON;
Printed by *I. B.* for *Nicholas Vavasour*, and are to be sold
at his Shop in the Inner-Temple, neere the
Church. 1633.

To my Worthy Friend, Master Thomas Hammon, of Gray's Inn, &c.

THIS play, composed by so worthy an author as Master Marlowe, and the part of the Jew presented by so unimitable an actor as Master Alleyn, being in this later age commended to the stage; as I usher'd it unto the court, and presented it to the Cock-pit, with these Prologues and Epilogues here inserted, so now being newly brought to the press, I was loath it should be published without the ornament of an Epistle; making choice of you unto whom to devote it; than whom, of all those gentlemen and acquaintance within the compass of my long knowledge, there is none more able to tax ignorance, or attribute right to merit. Sir, you have been pleased to grace some of mine own works with your courteous patronage: I hope this will not be the worse accepted, because commended by me, over whom none can claim more power or privilege than yourself. I had no better a new year's gift to present you with; receive it therefore as a continuance of that inviolable obligement, by which he rests still engaged, who, as he ever hath, shall always remain,

Tuissimus,
THO. HEYWOOD.

The Prologue spoken at Court

GRACIOUS and great, that we so boldly dare,
'Mongst other plays that now in fashion are,
To present this, writ many years agone,
And in that age thought second unto none,
We humbly crave your pardon. We pursue
The story of a rich and famous Jew
Who liv'd in Malta: you shall find him still,
In all his projects, a sound Machiavill;
And that's his character. He that hath past
So many censures is now come at last   10
To have your princely ears: grace you him; then
You crown the action, and renown the pen.

Epilogue

IT is our fear, dread sovereign, we have bin
Too tedious; neither can't be less than sin
To wrong your princely patience: if we have,
Thus low dejected, we your pardon crave;
And, if aught here offend your ear or sight,
We only act and speak what others write.

The Prologue to the Stage

AT THE COCK-PIT

WE know not how our play may pass this stage,
But by the best of poets *in that age   *Marlowe
The Malta Jew had being and was made,
And he then by the best of actors *play'd. *Alleyn
In *Hero and Leander* one did gain
A lasting memory; in Tamburlaine,
This Jew, with others many, th' other wan
The attribute of peerless, being a man
Whom we may rank with (doing no one wrong)
Proteus for shapes, and Roscius for a tongue,   10

2 etc.] The marginal notes are in the original edition

So could he speak, so vary; nor is't hate
To merit in him* who doth personate   *Perkins
Our Jew this day; nor is it his ambition
To exceed or equal, being of condition
More modest: this is all that he intends,
(And that too at the urgence of some friends,)
To prove his best, and, if none here gainsay it,
The part he hath studied, and intends to play it.

Epilogue

IN graving with Pygmalion to contend,
Or painting with Apelles, doubtless the end
Must be disgrace: our actor did not so,
He only aim'd to go, but not out-go.
Nor think that this day any prize was play'd;
Here were no bets at all, no wagers laid:
All the ambition that his mind doth swell,
Is but to hear from you, by me, 'twas well.

Dramatis Personæ

Ferneze, *governor of Malta.*
Lodowick, *his son.*
Selim Calymath, *son to the Grand Seignior.*
Martin Del Bosco, *vice-admiral of Spain.*
Mathias, *a gentleman.*
Jacomo, } *friars.*
Barnardine, }
Barabas, *a wealthy Jew.*
Ithamore, *a slave.*
Pilia-Borza, *a bully,* attendant *to* Bellamira.

Two Merchants.
Three Jews.
Knights, Bassoes, Officers, Guard, Slaves, Messenger, *and* Carpenters.
Katharine, *mother to* Mathias.
Abigail, *daughter to* Barabas.
Bellamira, *a courtesan.*
Abbess.
Nun.
Machiavel as Prologue-speaker.

Scene, Malta.

The Jew of Malta

Enter Machiavel.

Mach. Albeit the world think Machiavel is dead,
Yet was his soul but flown beyond the Alps;
And, now the Guise is dead, is come from France,
To view this land, and frolic with his friends.
To some perhaps my name is odious;
But such as love me, guard me from their tongues,
And let them know that I am Machiavel,
And weigh not men, and therefore not men's words.
Admir'd I am of those that hate me most:
Though some speak openly against my books,   10
Yet will they read me, and thereby attain
To Peter's chair; and when they cast me off,
Are poison'd by my climbing followers.
I count religion but a childish toy,
And hold there is no sin but ignorance.
Birds of the air will tell of murders past;
I am asham'd to hear such fooleries.
Many will talk of title to a crown:
What right had Cæsar to the empire?
Might first made kings, and laws were then most
    sure   20
When, like the Draco's, they were writ in blood.
Hence comes it that a strong-built citadel
Commands much more than letters can import:
Which maxim had Phalaris observ'd,
H'ad never bellowed in a brazen bull,
Of great ones' envy: o' th' poor petty wights
Let me be envi'd and not pitied.
But whither am I bound? I come not, I,
To read a lecture here in Britain,
But to present the tragedy of a Jew,   30
Who smiles to see how full his bags are cramm'd;
Which money was not got without my means,
I crave but this,—grace him as he deserves,

And let him not be entertain'd the worse
Because he favours me.   [*Exit.*

Act I.

Barabas *discovered in his counting house, with heaps of gold*
before him.

Bara. So that of thus much that return was made;
And of the third part of the Persian ships
There was the venture summ'd and satisfied.
As for those Samintes, and the men of Uz,
That bought my Spanish oils and wines of Greece,
Here have I purs'd their paltry silverlings.
Fie, what a trouble 'tis to count this trash!
Well fare the Arabians, who so richly pay
The things they traffic for with wedge of gold,
Whereof a man may easily in a day   10
Tell that which may maintain him all his life.
The needy groom that never finger'd groat,
Would make a miracle of thus much coin;
But he whose steel-barr'd coffers are cramm'd full,
And all his life-time hath been tired,
Wearying his fingers' ends with telling it,
Would in his age he loath to labour so,
And for a pound to sweat himself to death.
Give me the merchants of the Indian mines,
That trade in metal of the purest mould;   20
The wealthy Moor, that in the eastern rocks
Without control can pick his riches up,
And in his house heap pearl like pebble stones,
Receive them free, and sell them by the weight!
Bags of fiery opals, sapphires, amethysts,
Jacinths, hard topaz, grass-green emeralds,
Beauteous rubies, sparkling diamonds,
And seld-seen costly stones of so great price,
As one of them, indifferently rated,

4 Samintes] probably Sabaeans   11 Tell] count

And of a carat of this quantity,   30
May serve, in peril of calamity,
To ransom great kings from captivity.
This is the ware wherein consists my wealth;
And thus methinks should men of judgment frame
Their means of traffic from the vulgar trade,
And, as their wealth increaseth, so inclose
Infinite riches in a little room.
But now how stands the wind?
Into what corner peers my halcyon's bill?
Ha! to the east? yes. See how stands the vanes?   40
East and by south: why then I hope my ships
I sent for Egypt and the bordering isles
Are gotten up by Nilus' winding banks;
Mine argosy from Alexandria,
Loaden with spice and silks, now under sail,
Are smoothly gliding down by Candy-shore
To Malta, through our Mediterranean sea.
But who comes here?

Enter a Merchant.
                                    How now!
    Merch. Barabas, thy ships are safe,
Riding in Malta road: and all the merchants   50
With other merchandise are safe arriv'd,
And have sent me to know whether yourself
Will come and custom them.
    Bara. The ships are safe thou say'st, and richly
        fraught?
    Merch. They are.
    Bara. Why, then, go bid them come ashore,
And bring with them their bills of entry:
I hope our credit in the custom-house
Will serve as well as I were present there.
Go send 'em threescore camels, thirty mules,   60
And twenty wagons to bring up the ware.
But art thou master in a ship of mine,
And is thy credit not enough for that?

Merch. The very custom barely comes to more
Than many merchants of the town are worth,
And therefore far exceeds my credit, sir.

Bara. Go tell 'em the Jew of Malta sent thee, man:
Tush, who amongst 'em knows not Barabas?

Merch. I go.

Bara. So then, there's somewhat come. 70
Sirrah, which of my ships art thou master of?

Merch. Of the Speranza, sir.

Bara. And saw'st thou not
Mine argosy at Alexandria?
Thou couldst not come from Egypt, or by Caire,
But at the entry there into the sea,
Where Nilus pays his tribute to the main,
Thou needs must sail by Alexandria.

Merch. I neither saw them, nor inquir'd of them:
But this we heard some of our seamen say, 80
They wonder'd how you durst with so much wealth
Trust such a crazed vessel, and so far.

Bara. Tush, they are wise! I know her and her
    strength.
But go, go thou thy ways, discharge thy ship,
And bid my factor bring his loading in.
                              [*Exit* Merchant.
And yet I wonder at this argosy.

Enter a Second Merchant.

Sec. Merch. Thine argosy from Alexandria,
Know, Barabas, doth ride in Malta road,
Laden with riches, and exceeding store
Of Persian silks, of gold, and orient pearl. 90

Bara. How chance you came not with those other
    ships
That sail'd by Egypt?

Sec. Merch. Sir, we saw 'em not.

Bara. Belike they coasted round by Candy-shore
About their oils or other businesses.
But 'twas ill done of you to come so far

Without the aid or conduct of their ships.

   Sec. Merch. Sir, we were wafted by a Spanish fleet,
That never left us till within a league,
That had the galleys of the Turk in chase.   100

   Bara. Oh, they were going up to Sicily.
Well, go
And bid the merchants and my men despatch,
And come ashore, and see the fraught discharg'd.

   Sec. Merch. I go.   [*Exit.*

   Bara. Thus trowls our fortune in by land and sea,
And thus are we on every side enrich'd:
These are the blessings promis'd to the Jews,
And herein was old Abraum's happiness:
What more may heaven do for earthly man   110
Than thus to pour out plenty in their laps,
Ripping the bowels of the earth for them,
Making the sea their servant, and the winds
To drive their substance with successful blasts?
Who hateth me but for my happiness?
Or who is honour'd now but for his wealth?
Rather had I, a Jew, be hated thus,
Than pitied in a Christian poverty;
For I can see no fruits in all their faith,
But malice, falsehood, and excessive pride,   120
Which methinks fits not their profession.
Haply some hapless man hath conscience,
And for his conscience lives in beggary.
They say we are a scatter'd nation:
I cannot tell; but we have scambled up
More wealth by far than those that brag of faith.
There's Kirriah Jairim, the great Jew of Greece,
Obed in Bairseth, Nones in Portugal,
Myself in Malta, some in Italy,
Many in France, and wealthy every one;   130
Ay, wealthier far than any Christian.
I must confess we come not to be kings:
That's not our fault: alas, our number's few,

           125 scambled] scrambled

And crowns come either by succession,
Or urg'd by force; and nothing violent,
Oft have I heard tell, can be permanent.
Give us a peaceful rule; make Christians kings,
That thirst so much for principality.
I have no charge, nor many children,
But one sole daughter, whom I hold as dear   140
As Agamemnon did his Iphigen;
And all I have is hers. But who comes here?

Enter three Jews.*

First Jew. Tush, tell not me; 'twas done of policy.
Sec. Jew. Come, therefore, let us go to Barabas;
For he can counsel best in these affairs:
And here he comes.
Bara. Why, how now, countrymen?
Why flock you thus to me in multitudes?
What accident's betided to the Jews?
First Jew. A fleet of warlike galleys, Barabas,   150
Are come from Turkey, and lie in our road:
And they this day sit in the council-house
To entertain them and their embassy.
Bara. Why, let 'em come, so they come not to war;
Or let 'em war, so we be conquerors.—
Nay, let 'em combat, conquer, and kill all.
So they spare me, my daughter, and my wealth.
                                        [Aside.
First Jew. Were it for confirmation of a league,
They would not come in warlike manner thus.
Sec. Jew. I fear their coming will afflict us all.   160
Bara. Fond men, what dream you of their multitudes?
What need they treat of peace that are in league?
The Turks and those of Malta are in league:
Tut, tut, there is some other matter in't.
First Jew. Why, Barabas, they come for peace or war.
Bara. Haply for neither, but to pass along,
Towards Venice by the Adriatic sea,

---

    * The scene changes to a street.   161 Fond] foolish

With whom they have attempted many times,
But never could effect their stratagem.

   Third Jew. And very wisely said; it may be so. 170

   Sec. Jew. But there's a meeting in the senate-house,
And all the Jews in Malta must be there.

   Bara. Hum, all the Jews in Malta must be there?
Ay, like enough: why then let every man
Provide him, and be there for fashion-sake.
If anything shall there concern our state,
Assure yourselves I'll look—unto myself.   [*Aside.*

   First Jew. I know you will. Well, brethren, let us go.

   Sec. Jew. Let's take our leaves. Farewell, good
    Barabas.

   Bara. Farewell, Zaareth; farewell, Temainte.
                                   [*Exeunt Jews.*

And, Barabas, now search this secret out;   181
Summon thy senses, call thy wits together:
These silly men mistake the matter clean.
Long to the Turk did Malta contribute;
Which tribute all in policy, I fear,
The Turks have let increase to such a sum
As all the wealth of Malta cannot pay;
And now by that advantage thinks, belike,
To seize upon the town; ay, that he seeks.
Howe'er the world go, I'll make sure for one,   190
And seek in time to intercept the worst,
Warily guarding that which I ha' got:
Ego mihimet sum semper proximus:
Why, let 'em enter, let 'em take the town.   [*Exit.*

Enter Ferneze *governor of Malta,* Knights, *and* Officers;
    met by Calymath, *and* Bassoes *of the* Turk.*

   Fern. Now, bassoes, what demand you at our hands?

   First Bas. Know, knights of Malta, that we came
    from Rhodes,

---

* The scene is inside the Council-house.   193 *Ego . . .
proximus*] 'I am always the closest to myself.'   195 bas-
soes] Bashaws or Pashas

From Cyprus, Candy, and those other isles
That lie betwixt the Mediterranean seas.

  Fern. What's Cyprus, Candy, and those other isles
To us or Malta? what at our hands demand ye? 200

  Cal. The ten years' tribute that remains unpaid.

  Fern. Alas, my lord, the sum is over-great;
I hope your highness will consider us.

  Cal. I wish, grave governor, 'twere in my power
To favour you; but 'tis my father's cause,
Wherein I may not, nay, I dare not dally.

  Fern. Then give us leave, great Selim Calymath.

  Cal. Stand all aside, and let the knights determine;
And send to keep our galleys under sail,
For happily we shall not tarry here; 210
Now, governor, how are you resolv'd?

  Fern. Thus; since your hard conditions are such
That you will needs have ten years' tribute past,
We may have time to make collection
Amongst the inhabitants of Malta for't.

  First Bas. That's more than is in our commission.

  Cal. What, Callapine! a little courtesy;
Let's know their time; perhaps it is not long;
And 'tis more kingly to obtain by peace
Than to enforce conditions by constraint. 220
What respite ask you, governor?

  Fern. But a month.

  Cal. We grant a month, but see you keep your
    promise.
Now launch our galleys back again to sea,
Where we'll attend the respite you have ta'en,
And for the money send our messenger.
Farewell, great governor and brave knights of Malta.

  Fern. And all good fortune wait on Calymath!
                [*Exeunt* Calymath *and* Bassoes.
Go one and call those Jews of Malta hither:
Were they not summon'd to appear to-day? 230

  First Off. They were, my lord, and here they come.

210 happily] haply

Enter Barabas *and three* Jews.

First Knight. Have you determin'd what to say to
them?

Fern. Yes, give me leave:—and, Hebrews, now
come near.

From the Emperor of Turkey is arriv'd
Great Selim Calymath, his highness' son,
To levy of us ten years' tribute past:
Now then, here know that it concerneth us.

Bara. Then, good my lord, to keep your quiet still,
Your lordship shall do well to let them have it.

Fern. Soft, Barabas, there's more 'longs to't than
so.   240
To what this ten years' tribute will amount,
That we have cast, but cannot compass it
By reason of the wars, that robb'd our store;
And therefore are we to request your aid.

Bara. Alas, my lord, we are no soldiers:
And what's our aid against so great a prince?

First Knight. Tut, Jew, we know thou art no
soldier;
That art a merchant and a money'd man,
And 'tis thy money, Barabas, we seek.

Bara. How, my lord! my money?   250

Fern. Thine and the rest;
For, to be short, amongst you 't must be had.

First Jew. Alas, my lord, the most of us are poor!

Fern. Then let the rich increase your portions.

Bara. Are strangers with your tribute to be tax'd?

Sec. Knight. Have strangers leave with us to get
their wealth?
Then let them with us contribute.

Bara. How, equally?

Fern. No, Jew, like infidels;
For through our sufferance of your hateful lives,   260
Who stand accursed in the sight of heaven,
These taxes and afflictions are befall'n,

And therefore thus we are determined.
Read there the articles of our decrees.

 Officer. [reads] *First, the tribute-money of the Turks shall all be levied amongst the Jews, and each of them to pay one half of his estate.*

 Bara. How, half his estate? I hope you mean not
  mine.   [*Aside.*

 Fern. Read on.

 Officer. [reads] *Secondly, he that denies to pay, shall straight become a Christian.*   271

 Bara. How, a Christian? Hum, what's here to
  do?   [*Aside.*

 Officer. [reads] *Lastly, he that denies this, shall absolutely lose all he has.*

 Three Jews. O my lord, we will give half.

 Bara. O earth-mettled villains, and no Hebrews
  born!

And will you basely thus submit yourselves
To leave your goods to their arbitrament?

 Fern. Why, Barabas, wilt thou be christen'd?

 Bara. No, governor, I will be no convertite. 280

 Fern. Then pay thy half.

 Bara. Why, know you what you did by this
  device?

Half of my substance is a city's wealth.
Governor, it was not got so easily;
Nor will I part so slightly therewithal.

 Fern. Sir, half is the penalty of our decree,
Either pay that, or we will seize on all.

 Bara. Corpo di Dio! stay, you shall have half;
Let me be us'd but as my brethren are.

 Fern. No, Jew, thou hast denied the articles, 290
And now it cannot be recall'd.

     [*Exeunt* Officers, *on a sign from* Ferneze.

 Bara. Will you then steal my goods?
Is theft the ground of your religion?

 Fern. No, Jew, we take particularly thine
To save the ruin of a multitude:

And better one want for a common good,
Than many perish for a private man:
Yet, Barabas, we will not banish thee,
But here in Malta, where thou gott'st thy wealth,
Live still; and if thou canst, get more.   300
   Bara. Christians, what or how can I multiply?
Of naught is nothing made.
   First Knight. From naught at first thou cam'st to
     little wealth,
From little unto more, from more to most:
If your first curse fall heavy on thy head,
And make thee poor and scorn'd of all the world,
'Tis not our fault, but thy inherent sin.
   Bara. What, bring you Scripture to confirm your
     wrongs?
Preach me not out of my possessions.
Some Jews are wicked, as all Christians are;   310
But say the tribe that I descended of
Were all in general cast away for sin,
Shall I be tried by their transgression?
The man that dealeth righteously shall live;
And which of you can charge me otherwise?
   Fern. Out, wretched Barabas!
Sham'st thou not thus to justify thyself,
As if we knew not thy profession?
If thou rely upon thy righteousness,
Be patient and thy riches will increase.   320
Excess of wealth is cause of covetousness;
And covetousness, oh, 'tis a monstrous sin!
   Bara. Ay, but theft is worse: tush, take not from
     me, then,
For that is theft; and if you rob me thus,
I must be forc'd to steal, and compass more.
   First Knight. Grave governor, list not to his ex-
     claims:
Convert his mansion to a nunnery;
His house will harbour many holy nuns.
   Fern. It shall be so.

Re-enter Officers.

                    Now, officers, have you done?

First Off. Ay, my lord, we have seiz'd upon the
    goods   330
And wares of Barabas, which, being valued,
Amount to more than all the wealth in Malta:
And of the other we have seized half.

Fern. Then we'll take order for the residue.

Bara. Well then, my lord, say, are you satisfied?
You have my goods, my money, and my wealth,
My ships, my store, and all that I enjoy'd;
And, having all, you can request no more,
Unless your unrelenting flinty hearts
Suppress all pity in your stony breasts,   340
And now shall move you to bereave my life.

Fern. No, Barabas, to stain our hands with blood
Is far from us and our profession.

Bara. Why, I esteem the injury far less,
To take the lives of miserable men
Than be the causers of their misery.
You have my wealth, the labour of my life,
The comfort of mine age, my children's hope;
And therefore ne'er distinguish of the wrong.

Fern. Content thee, Barabas; thou hast naught but
    right.   350

Bara. Your extreme right does me exceeding
    wrong:
But take it to you, i' the devil's name!

Fern. Come, let us in, and gather of these goods
The money for this tribute of the Turk.

First Knight. 'Tis necessary that be look'd unto;
For, if we break our day, we break the league,
And that will prove but simple policy.

            [*Exeunt all except* Barabas *and the three* Jews.

Bara. Ay, policy! that's their profession,
And not simplicity, as they suggest.
The plagues of Egypt, and the curse of heaven,   360

Earth's barrenness, and all men's hatred
Inflict upon them, thou great *Primus Motor!*
And here upon my knees, striking the earth,
I ban their souls to everlasting pains
And extreme tortures of the fiery deep,
That thus have dealt with me in my distress.

  First Jew. Oh, yet be patient, gentle Barabas!

  Bara. O silly brethren, born to see this day,
Why stand you thus unmov'd with my laments?
Why weep you not to think upon my wrongs?   370
Why pine not I, and die in this distress?

  First Jew. Why, Barabas, as hardly can we brook
The cruel handling of ourselves in this:
Thou seest they have taken half our goods.

  Bara. Why did you yield to their extortion?
You were a multitude, and I but one;
And of me only have they taken all.

  First Jew. Yet, brother Barabas, remember Job.

  Bara. What tell you me of Job? I wot his wealth
Was written thus: he had seven thousand sheep,   380
Three thousand camels, and two hundred yoke
Of labouring oxen, and five hundred
She asses: but for every one of those,
Had they been valued at indifferent rate,
I had at home, and in mine argosy,
And other ships that came from Egypt last,
As much as would have bought his beasts and him,
And yet have kept enough to live upon;
So that not he, but I, may curse the day,
Thy fatal birthday, forlorn Barabas;   390
And henceforth wish for an eternal night,
That clouds of darkness may inclose my flesh,
And hide these extreme sorrows from mine eyes.
For only I have toil'd to inherit here
The months of vanity and loss of time,
And painful nights have been appointed me.

  Sec. Jew. Good Barabas, be patient.

  Bara. Ay, I pray leave me in my patience.

You that were ne'er possess'd of wealth, are pleas'd
   with want;
But give him liberty at least to mourn,   400
That in a field amidst his enemies,
Doth see his soldiers slain, himself disarm'd,
And knows no means of his recovery:
Ay, let me sorrow for this sudden chance;
'Tis in the trouble of my spirit I speak:
Great injuries are not so soon forgot.
   First Jew. Come, let us leave him in his ireful mood,
Our words will but increase his ecstasy.
   Sec. Jew. On, then: but trust me 'tis a misery
To see a man in such affliction.   410
Farewell, Barabas.
   Bara. Ay, fare you well.   *[Exeunt three* Jews.
See the simplicity of these base slaves,
Who, for the villains have no wit themselves,
Think me to be a senseless lump of clay,
That will with every water wash to dirt:
No, Barabas is born to better chance,
And fram'd of finer mould than common men,
That measure naught but by the present time.
A reaching thought will search his deepest wits, 420
And cast with cunning for the time to come;
For evils are apt to happen every day.

Enter Abigail.*

But whither wends my beauteous Abigail?
Oh, what has made my lovely daughter sad?
What, woman! moan not for a little loss;
Thy father has enough in store for thee.
   Abig. Not for myself, but aged Barabas;
Father, for thee lamenteth Abigail:
But I will learn to leave these fruitless tears,
And, urg'd thereto with my afflictions,   430
With fierce exclaims run to the senate-house,
And in the senate reprehend them all,

   408 ecstasy] violent emotion   * The scene is a street.

And rent their hearts with tearing of my hair,
Till they reduce the wrongs done to my father.

   Bara. No, Abigail; things past recovery
Are hardly cur'd with exclamations:
Be silent, daughter; sufferance breeds ease,
And time may yield us an occasion
Which on the sudden cannot serve the turn.
Besides, my girl, think me not all so fond   440
As negligently to forego so much
Without provision for thyself and me:
Ten thousand portagues, besides great pearls,
Rich costly jewels, and stones infinite,
Fearing the worst of this before it fell,
I closely hid.

   Abig. Where, father?

   Bara. In my house, my girl.

   Abig. Then shall they ne'er be seen of Barabas;
For they have seiz'd upon thy house and wares.   450

   Bara. But they will give me leave once more, I trow,
To go into my house.

   Abig. That may they not;
For there I left the governor placing nuns,
Displacing me; and of thy house they mean
To make a nunnery, where none but their own sect
Must enter in; men generally barr'd.

   Bara. My gold, my gold, and all my wealth is gone!
You partial heavens, have I deserv'd this plague?
What, will you thus oppose me, luckless stars,   460
To make me desperate in my poverty?
And knowing me impatient in distress,
Think me so mad as I will hang myself,
That I may vanish o'er the earth in air,
And leave no memory that e'er I was?
No, I will live; nor loathe I this my life:
And since you leave me in the ocean thus
To sink or swim, and put me to my shifts,
I'll rouse my senses, and awake myself.

   443 portagues] Portuguese gold coins   456 sect] sex

Daughter, I have it: thou perceiv'st the plight　470
Wherein these Christians have oppressed me:
Be rul'd by me, for in extremity
We ought to make bar of no policy.

  Abig. Father, whate'er it be, to injure them
That have so manifestly wronged us,
What will not Abigail attempt?

  Bara. Why, so.
Then thus: thou told'st me they have turn'd my house
Into a nunnery, and some nuns are there?

  Abig. I did.　480

  Bara. Then, Abigail, there must my girl
Entreat the abbess to be entertain'd.

  Abig. How, as a nun?

  Bara. Ay, daughter, for religion
Hides many mischiefs from suspicion.

  Abig. Ay, but, father, they will suspect me there.

  Bara. Let 'em suspect; but be thou so precise
As they may think it done of holiness:
Entreat 'em fair, and give them friendly speech,
And seem to them as if thy sins were great,　490
Till thou hast gotten to be entertain'd.

  Abig. Thus, father, shall I much dissemble.

  Bara. Tush!
As good dissemble that thou never mean'st,
As first mean truth and then dissemble it:
A counterfeit profession is better
Than unseen hypocrisy.

  Abig. Well, father, say I be entertain'd,
What then shall follow?

  Bara. This shall follow then.　500
There have I hid, close underneath the plank
That runs along the upper-chamber floor,
The gold and jewels which I kept for thee.
But here they come: be cunning, Abigail.

  Abig. Then, father, go with me.

  Bara. No, Abigail, in this
It is not necessary I be seen;

For I will seem offended with thee for't:
Be close, my girl, for this must fetch my gold.

[*They retire.*

Enter Friar Jacomo, Friar Barnardine, Abbess, *and a*
Nun.

   Friar Jac. Sisters,   510
We now are almost at the new-made nunnery.
   Abb. The better; for we love not to be seen:
'Tis thirty winters long since some of us
Did stray so far amongst the multitude.
   Friar Jac. But, madam, this house
And quarters of this new-made nunnery
Will much delight you.
   Abb. It may be so; but who comes here?

[Abigail *comes forward.*

   Abig. Grave abbess, and you happy virgins' guide,
Pity the state of a distressed maid!   520
   Abb. What art thou, daughter?
   Abig. The hopeless daughter of a hapless Jew,
The Jew of Malta, wretched Barabas,
Sometimes the owner of a goodly house,
Which they have now turn'd to a nunnery.
   Abb. Well, daughter, say, what is thy suit with us?
   Abig. Fearing the afflictions which my father feels
Proceed from sin or want of faith in us,
I'd pass away my life in penitence,
And be a novice in your nunnery,   530
To make atonement for my labouring soul.
   Friar Jac. No doubt, brother, but this proceedeth
      of the spirit
   Friar Barn. Ay, and of a moving spirit too, brother;
      but come,
Let us entreat she may be entertain'd.
   Abb. Well, daughter, we admit you for a nun.
   Abig. First let me as a novice learn to frame
My solitary life to your strait laws,
And let me lodge where I was wont to lie:

I do not doubt, by your divine precepts
And mine own industry, but to profit much.   540
   Bara. As much, I hope, as all I hid is worth. [*Aside.*
   Abb. Come, daughter, follow us.
   Bara. [*coming forward*] Why, how now, Abigail,
What mak'st thou amongst these hateful Christians?
   Friar Jac. Hinder her not, thou man of little faith,
For she has mortified herself.
   Bara. How, mortified!
   Friar Jac. And is admitted to the sisterhood.
   Bara. Child of perdition, and thy father's shame,
What wilt thou do among these hateful fiends?   550
I charge thee on my blessing that thou leave
These devils and their damned heresy!
   Abig. Father, give me—
   Bara. Nay, back, Abigail,
And think upon the jewels and the gold;
The board is marked thus that covers it.—
               [*Aside to* Abigail *in a whisper.*
Away, accursed, from thy father's sight!
   Friar Jac. Barabas, although thou art in misbelief,
And wilt not see thine own afflictions,
Yet let thy daughter be no longer blind.   560
   Bara. Blind friar, I reck not thy persuasions,—
The board is marked thus that covers it—
               [*Aside to* Abigail *in a whisper.*
For I had rather die than see her thus.—
Wilt thou forsake me too in my distress,
Seduced daughter?—Go, forget not.—
               [*Aside to her in a whisper.*
Becomes it Jews to be so credulous?—
To-morrow early I'll be at the door.—
               [*Aside to her in a whisper.*
No, come not at me; if thou wilt be damn'd,
Forget me, see me not; and so, be gone!—
Farewell; remember to-morrow morning.—
               [*Aside to her in a whisper.*
               570

Out, out, thou wretch!
    [*Exeunt.*

Enter Mathias.

Math. Who's this? fair Abigail, the rich Jew's
    daughter,
Become a nun! her father's sudden fall
Has humbled her, and brought her down to this:
Tut, she were fitter for a tale of love,
Than to be tired out with orisons;
And better would she far become a bed,
Embraced in a friendly lover's arms,
Than rise at midnight to a solemn mass.

Enter Lodowick.

Lod. Why, how now, Don Mathias! in a dump? 580
Math. Believe me, noble Lodowick, I have seen
The strangest sight, in my opinion,
That ever I beheld.
    Lod. What was't, I prithee?
    Math. A fair young maid, scarce fourteen years of
    age,
The sweetest flower in Cytherea's field,
Cropt from the pleasures of the fruitful earth,
And strangely metamorphos'd nun.
    Lod. But say, what was she?
    Math. Why, the rich Jew's daughter. 590
    Lod. What, Barabas, whose goods were lately seiz'd?
Is she so fair?
    Math. And matchless beautiful.
As, had you seen her, 'twould have mov'd your
    heart,
Though countermin'd with walls of brass, to love,
Or at the least, to pity.
    Lod. An if she be so fair as you report,
'Twere time well spent to go and visit her:
How say you, shall we?

Math. I must and will, sir; there's no remedy. 600
Lod. And so will I too, or it shall go hard.
Farewell, Mathias.

Math. Farewell, Lodowick.   [*Exeunt severally.*

Act II.

Enter Barabas, *with a light.**

Bara. Thus, like the sad presaging raven, that tolls
The sick man's passport in her hollow beak,
And in the shadow of the silent night
Doth shake contagion from her sable wings,
Vex'd and tormented runs poor Barabas
With fatal curses towards these Christians.
The incertain pleasures of swift-footed time
Have ta'en their flight, and left me in despair;
And of my former riches rests no more
But bare remembrance; like a soldier's scar,   10
That has no further comfort for his maim.
O Thou, that with a fiery pillar ledd'st
The sons of Israel through the dismal shades,
Light Abraham's offspring; and direct the hand
Of Abigail this night! or let the day
Turn to eternal darkness after this!
No sleep can fasten on my watchful eyes,
Nor quiet enter my distemper'd thoughts,
Till I have answer of my Abigail.

Enter Abigail *above.*

Abig. Now have I happily espied a time   20
To search the plank my father did appoint;
And here behold, unseen, where I have found
The gold, the pearls, and jewels, which he hid.

Bara. Now I remember those old women's words,
Who in my wealth would tell me winter's tales,
And speak of spirits and ghosts that glide by night
About the place where treasure hath been hid:

* The scene is before Barabas's house, now a nunnery.

And now methinks that I am one of those;
For, whilst I live, here lives my soul's sole hope,
And, when I die, here shall my spirit walk. 30

Abig. Now that my father's fortune were so good
As but to be about this happy place;
'Tis not so happy: yet when we parted last,
He said he would attend me in the morn.
Then, gentle Sleep, where'er his body rests,
Give charge to Morpheus that he may dream
A golden dream, and of the sudden walk,
Come and receive the treasure I have found.

Bara. Bueno para todos mi ganado no era:
As good go on, as sit so sadly thus. 40
But stay: what star shines yonder in the east?
The loadstar of my life, if Abigail.
Who's there?

Abig. Who's that?

Bara. Peace, Abigail, 'tis I.

Abig. Then, father, here receive thy happiness.

Bara. Hast thou't?

Abig. Here. [*Throws down bags*] Hast thou't?
There's more, and more, and more.

Bara. O my girl, 50
My gold, my fortune, my felicity,
Strength to my soul, death to mine enemy;
Welcome the first beginner of my bliss!
O Abigail, Abigail, that I had thee here too,
Then my desires were fully satisfied:
But I will practise thy enlargement thence:
O girl! O gold! O beauty! O my bliss! [*Hugs the bags.*

Abig. Father, it draweth towards midnight now,
And 'bout this time the nuns begin to wake;
To shun suspicion, therefore, let us part. 60

Bara. Farewell, my joy, and by my fingers take
A kiss from him that sends it from his soul.

[*Exit* Abigail *above.*

39 *Bueno . . . era*] my flock (*sc.* wealth) is not good for all
(Bennett).

478 I

Now, Phœbus, ope the eye-lids of the day,
And, for the raven, wake the morning lark,
That I may hover with her in the air,
Singing o'er these, as she does o'er her young.
Hermoso placer de los dineros.   [*Exit.*

Enter Ferneze, Martin Del Bosco, Knights,
and Officers.*

Fern. Now, captain, tell us whither thou art bound?
Whence is thy ship that anchors in our road?
And why thou cam'st ashore without our leave?   70

Bosco. Governor of Malta, hither am I bound;
My ship, the Flying Dragon, is of Spain,
And so am I; Del Bosco is my name,
Vice-admiral unto the Catholic King.

First Knight. 'Tis true, my lord; therefore entreat
him well.   [Moors;

Bosco. Our fraught is Grecians, Turks, and Afric
For late upon the coast of Corsica,
Because we vail'd not to the Turkish fleet,
Their creeping galleys had us in the chase:
But suddenly the wind began to rise,   80
And then we luff'd and tack'd, and fought at ease:
Some have we fir'd, and many have we sunk;
But one amongst the rest became our prize:
The captain's slain, the rest remain our slaves,
Of whom we would make sale in Malta here.

Fern. Martin del Bosco, I have heard of thee;
Welcome to Malta, and to all of us!
But to admit a sale of these thy Turks,
We may not, nay, we dare not give consent,
By reason of a tributary league.   [us, 90

First Knight. Del Bosco, as thou lov'st and honour'st
Persuade our governor against the Turk:
This truce we have is but in hope of gold,

67 *Hermoso . . . dineros*] The lovely thrill of coins!
  * The scene is the interior of the council-house.
75 entreat] treat

And with that sum he craves, might we wage war.
  Bosco. Will knights of Malta be in league with
       Turks,
And buy it basely too for sums of gold?
My lord, remember that, to Europe's shame,
The Christian Isle of Rhodes, from whence you came,
Was lately lost, and you were stated here
To be at deadly enmity with Turks.   100
  Fern. Captain, we know it; but our force is small.
  Bosco. What is the sum that Calymath requires?
  Fern. A hundred thousand crowns.
  Bosco. My lord and king hath title to this isle,
And he means quickly to expel you hence;
Therefore be rul'd by me, and keep the gold:
I'll write unto his majesty for aid,
And not depart until I see you free.
  Fern. On this condition shall thy Turks be sold:
Go, officers, and set them straight in show.   110
                              [*Exeunt* Officers.
Bosco, thou shalt be Malta's general;
We and our warlike knights will follow thee
Against these barbarous misbelieving Turks.
  Bosco. So shall you imitate those you succeed:
For when their hideous force environ'd Rhodes,
Small though the number was that kept the town,
They fought it out, and not a man surviv'd
To bring the hapless news to Christendom.
  Fern. So will we fight it out; come, let's away.
Proud daring Calymath, instead of gold,   120
We'll send thee bullets wrapp'd in smoke and fire:
Claim tribute where thou wilt, we are resolv'd,
Honour is bought with blood and not with gold.
                                        [*Exeunt.*

  Enter Officers, *with* Ithamore *and other* Slaves.*

  First Off. This is the market-place; here let 'em
       stand:

99 stated] instated   * The scene is the market-place.

Fear not their sale, for they'll be quickly bought.

  Sec. Off. Every one's price is written on his back,
And so much must they yield, or not be sold.

  First Off. Here comes the Jew: had not his goods
    been seiz'd,
He'd give us present money for them all.

Enter Barabas.

  Bara. In spite of these swine-eating Christians,   130
(Unchosen nation, never circumcis'd,
Such as, poor villains, were ne'er thought upon
Till Titus and Vespasian conquer'd us,)
Am I become as wealthy as I was.
They hop'd my daughter would ha' been a nun;
But she's at home, and I have bought a house
As great and fair as is the governor's:
And there, in spite of Malta, will I dwell,
Having Ferneze's hand, whose heart I'll have,
Ay, and his son's too, or it shall go hard.   140
I am not of the tribe of Levi, I,
That can so soon forget an injury.
We Jews can fawn like spaniels when we please,
And when we grin we bite, yet are our looks
As innocent and harmless as a lamb's.
I learn'd in Florence how to kiss my hand,
Heave up my shoulders when they call me dog,
And duck as low as any bare-foot friar;
Hoping to see them starve upon a stall,
Or else be gather'd for in our synagogue,   150
That, when the offering-basin comes to me,
Even for charity I may spit into't.
Here comes Don Lodowick, the governor's son,
One that I love for his good father's sake.

Enter Lodowick.

  Lod. I hear the wealthy Jew walked this way:
I'll seek him out, and so insinuate,
That I may have a sight of Abigail,

For Don Mathias tells me she is fair.

Bara. Now will I show myself to have more of the
serpent than the dove; that is, more knave than fool.
                                                    [*Aside.*

Lod. Yond' walks the Jew: now for fair Abigail.   161

Bara. Ay, ay, no doubt but she's at your command.
                                                    [*Aside.*

Lod. Barabas, thou know'st I am the governor's
son.

Bara. I would you were his father too, sir! that's
all the harm I wish you.—The slave looks like a hog's
cheek new sing'd.   [*Aside.*

Lod. Whither walk'st thou, Barabas?

Bara. No further: 'tis a custom held with us,
That when we speak with Gentiles like to you,   170
We turn into the air to purge ourselves:
For unto us the promise doth belong.

Lod. Well, Barabas, canst help me to a diamond?

Bara. Oh, sir, your father had my diamonds:
Yet I have one left that will serve your turn:—
I mean my daughter; but ere he shall have her,
I'll sacrifice her on a pile of wood:
I ha' the poison of the city for him,
And the white leprosy.   [*Aside.*

Lod. What sparkle does it give without a foil?   180

Bara. The diamond that I talk of ne'er was foil'd:—
But when he touches it, it will be foil'd:—   [*Aside.*
Lord Lodowick, it sparkles bright and fair.

Lod. Is it square or pointed? pray, let me know.

Bara. Pointed it is, good sir,—but not for you.
                                                    [*Aside.*

Lod. I like it much the better.

Bara. So do I too.

Lod. How shows it by night?

Bara. Outshines Cynthia's rays:
You'll like it better far o' nights than days.   [*Aside.*

Lod. And what's the price?   191

181 foil'd] defiled

Bara. Your life, an if you have it [*Aside*].—O my
　　lord,
We will not jar about the price; come to my house,
And I will give't your honour—with a vengeance.
　　　　　　　　　　　　　　　　　　　　[*Aside.*

Lod. No, Barabas, I will deserve it first.
Bara. Good sir,
Your father has deserv'd it at my hands,
Who, of mere charity and Christian ruth,
To bring me to religious purity,
And as it were in catechising sort,　　　　　　　　200
To make me mindful of my mortal sins,
Against my will, and whether I would or no,
Seiz'd all I had, and thrust me out o' doors,
And made my house a place for nuns most chaste.
Lod. No doubt your soul shall reap the fruit of it.
Bara. Ay, but, my lord, the harvest is far off:
And yet I know the prayers of those nuns
And holy friars, having money for their pains,
Are wondrous;—and indeed do no man good;—
　　　　　　　　　　　　　　　　　　　　[*Aside.*
And seeing they are not idle, but still doing,　　210
'Tis likely they in time may reap some fruit,
I mean, in fullness of perfection.
Lod. Good Barabas, glance not at our holy nuns.
Bara. No, but I do it through a burning zeal,—
Hoping ere long to set the house a-fire;
For, though they do awhile increase and multiply,
I'll have a saying to that nunnery.—　　[*Aside.*
As for the diamond, sir, I told you of,
Come home, and there's no price shall make us part,
Even for your honourable father's sake,—　　220
It shall go hard but I will see your death.—　[*Aside.*
But now I must be gone to buy a slave.
Lod. And, Barabas, I'll bear thee company.
Bara. Come, then; here's the market place.—
What's the price of this slave? two hundred crowns!
do the Turks weigh so much?

First Off. Sir, that's his price.

Bara. What, can he steal, that you demand so much?
Belike he has some new trick for a purse;
An if he has, he is worth three hundred plates,   230
So that, being bought, the town seal might be got
To keep him for his life-time from the gallows:
The sessions-day is critical to thieves,
And few or none escape but by being purg'd.

Lod. Ratest thou this Moor but at two hundred
plates?

First Off. No more, my lord.

Bara. Why should this Turk be dearer than that
Moor?

First Off. Because he is young, and has more
qualities.   241

Bara. What, hast the philosopher's stone? an thou
hast, break my head with it, I'll forgive thee.

Slave. No, sir; I can cut and shave.

Bara. Let me see, sirrah, are you not an old shaver?

Slave. Alas, sir, I am a very youth!

Bara. A youth? I'll buy you, and marry you to
Lady Vanity, if you do well.

Slave. I will serve you, sir.   249

Bara. Some wicked trick or other: it may be, under
colour of shaving, thou'lt cut my throat for my goods.
Tell me, hast thou thy health well?

Slave. Ay, passing well.

Bara. So much the worse: I must have one that's
sickly, an't be but for sparing victuals: 'tis not a stone
of beef a day will maintain you in these chops. Let
me see one that's somewhat leaner.

First Off. Here's a leaner; how like you him?

Bara. Where was thou born?

Itha. In Thrace; brought up in Arabia.   260

Bara. So much the better, thou art for my turn.
An hundred crowns? I'll have him; there's the coin.

[*Gives money.*

230 plates] pieces of silver coin

First Off. Then mark him, sir, and take him hence.

Bara. Ay, mark him, you were best; for this is he
That by my help shall do much villainy.   [*Aside.*
My lord, farewell. Come, sirrah; you are mine.
As for the diamond, it shall be yours:
I pray, sir, be no stranger at my house,
All that I have shall be at your command.   269

Enter Mathias *and* Katharine.

Math. What makes the Jew and Lodowick so
    private?
I fear me 'tis about fair Abigail.   [*Aside.*

Bara. [*to Lod.*] Yonder comes Don Mathias; let us
    stay:
He loves my daughter, and she holds him dear;
But I have sworn to frustrate both their hopes,
And be reveng'd upon the—governor.   [*Aside.*
                                    [*Exit* Lodowick.

Kath. This Moor is comeliest, is he not? speak, son.

Math. No, this is the better, mother, view this well.

Bara. Seem not to know me here before your
    mother,
Lest she mistrust the match that is in hand: 279
When you have brought her home, come to my house;
Think of me as thy father; son, farewell.   [you?

Math. But wherefore talk'd Don Lodowick with

Bara. Tush, man! we talk'd of diamonds, not of
    Abigail.

Kath. Tell me, Mathias, is not that the Jew?

Bara. As for the comment on the Maccabees,
I have it, sir, and 'tis at your command.

Math. Yes, madam, and my talk with him was
About the borrowing of a book or two.

Kath. Converse not with him; he is cast off from
    heaven.
Thou hast thy crowns, fellow, come, let's away.   290

Math. Sirrah Jew, remember the book.

    272 stay] break off our conversation

Bara. Marry will I, sir.

[*Exeunt* Katharine *and* Mathias.

First Off. Come, I have made
A reasonable market; let's away.

[*Exeunt* Officers *with* Slaves.

Bara. Now let me know thy name, and therewithal
Thy birth, condition, and profession.

Itha. Faith, sir, my birth is but mean; my name's
Ithamore; my profession what you please.

Bara. Hast thou no trade? then listen to my words,
And I will teach that shall stick by thee:⠀⠀⠀⠀⠀300
First, be thou void of these affections,
Compassion, love, vain hope, and heartless fear;
Be mov'd at nothing, see thou pity none,
But to thyself smile when the Christians moan.

Itha. O brave! master, I worship your nose for this.

Bara. As for myself, I walk abroad o' nights,
And kill sick people groaning under walls:
Sometimes I go about and poison wells;
And now and then, to cherish Christian thieves,
I am content to lose some of my crowns,⠀⠀⠀⠀⠀310
That I may, walking in my gallery,
See 'em go pinion'd along by my door.
Being young, I studied physic, and began
To practise first upon the Italian;
There I enrich'd the priests with burials,
And always kept the sexton's arms in ure
With digging graves and ringing dead men's knells:
And after that, was I an engineer,
And in the wars 'twixt France and Germany,
Under pretence of helping Charles the Fifth,⠀⠀⠀⠀320
Slew friend and enemy with my stratagems:
Then after that was I an usurer,
And with extorting, cozening, forfeiting,
And tricks belonging unto brokery,
I fill'd the gaols with bankrupts in a year,
And with young orphans planted hospitals,

316 ure] use

And every moon made some or other mad,
And now and then one hang himself for grief,
Pinning upon his breast a long great scroll
How I with interest tormented him.   330
But mark how I am bless'd for plaguing them;
I have as much coin as will buy the town.
But tell me now, how hast thou spent thy time?
    Itha. Faith, master,
In setting Christian villages on fire,
Chaining of eunuchs, binding galley-slaves.
One time I was an hostler in an inn,
And in the night-time secretly would I steal
To travellers' chambers, and there cut their throats:
Once at Jerusalem, where the pilgrims kneel'd,   340
I strewed powder on the marble stones,
And therewithal their knees would rankle, so
That I have laugh'd a-good to see the cripples
Go limping home to Christendom on stilts.
    Bara. Why, this is something: make account of me
As of thy fellow; we are villains both;
Both circumcised; we hate Christians both:
Be true and secret, thou shalt want no gold.
But stand aside, here comes Don Lodowick.

Enter Lodowick.*

    Lod. Oh, Barabas, well met;   350
Where is the diamond you told me of?
    Bara. I have it for you, sir: please you walk in with
        me.
What ho, Abigail! open the door, I say.

Enter Abigail, *with letters.*

    Abig. In good time, father; here are letters come
From Ormus, and the post stays here within.
    Bara. Give me the letters.—Daughter, do you hear,
Entertain Lodowick the governor's son,
With all the courtesy you can afford,

* Outside Barabas's house.

Provided that you keep your maidenhead:
Use him as if he were a Philistine;   360
Dissemble, swear, protest, vow to love him,
He is not of the seed of Abraham.—   [*Aside to her.*
I am a little busy, sir; pray, pardon me.—
Abigail, bid him welcome for my sake.

   Abig. For your sake and his own he's welcome
    hither.

   Bara. Daughter, a word more: kiss him, speak him
    fair,
And, like a cunning Jew, so cast about
That ye be both made sure ere you come out.

                          [*Aside to her.*

   Abig. O father, Don Mathias is my love.

   Bara. I know it: yet, I say, make love to him;   370
Do, it is requisite it should be so.—   [*Aside to her.*
Nay, on my life, it is my factor's hand;
But go you in, I'll think upon the account.

       [*Exeunt* Abigail *and* Lodowick *into the house.*
The account is made, for Lodowick dies.
My factor sends me word a merchant's fled
That owes me for a hundred tun of wine:
I weigh it thus much [*snapping his fingers*]! I have
wealth enough;
For now by this has he kiss'd Abigail,
And she vows love to him, and he to her.
As sure as heaven rain'd manna for the Jews,   380
So sure shall he and Don Mathias die:
His father was my chiefest enemy.

Enter Mathias.

Whither goes Don Mathias? stay a while.

   Math. Whither, but to my fair love Abigail?

   Bara. Thou know'st, and heaven can witness it is
    true,
That I intend my daughter shall be thine.

   Math. Ay, Barabas, or else thou wrong'st me much.

          368 sure] affianced

Bara. Oh, heaven forbid I should have such a
  thought.
Pardon me though I weep: the governor's son
Will, whether I will or no, have Abigail: 390
He sends her letters, bracelets, jewels, rings.

Math. Does she receive them?

Bara. She? no, Mathias, no, but sends them back,
And when he comes, she locks herself up fast;
Yet through the key-hole will he talk to her,
While she runs to the window, looking out
When you should come and hale him from the door.

Math. O treacherous Lodowick!

Bara. Even now, as I came home, he slipp'd me in,
And I am sure he is with Abigail.   400

Math. I'll rouse him thence.

Bara. Not for all Malta; therefore sheathe your
  sword;
If you love me, no quarrels in my house;
But steal you in, and seem to see him not;
I'll give him such a warning ere he goes,
As he shall have small hopes of Abigail.
Away, for here they come.

Re-enter Lodowick *and* Abigail.

Math. What, hand in hand! I cannot suffer this.

Bara. Mathias, as thou lov'st me, not a word.

Math. Well, let it pass, another time shall serve.
                          [*Exit into the house.*

Lod. Barabas, is not that the widow's son?   411

Bara. Ay, and take heed, for he hath sworn your
  death.

Lod. My death? what, is the base-born peasant
  mad?

Bara. No, no; but happily he stands in fear
Of that which you, I think, ne'er dream upon,
My daughter here, a paltry silly girl.

Lod. Why, loves she Don Mathias?

Bara. Doth she not with her smiling answer you?

Abig. He has my heart; I smile against my will.
                                           [Aside.

Lod. Barabas, thou know'st I have lov'd thy
    daughter long.   420

Bara. And so has she done you, even from a child.

Lod. And now I can no longer hold my mind.

Bara. Nor I the affection that I bear to you.

Lod. This is thy diamond; tell me, shall I have it?

Bara. Win it, and wear it, it is yet unsoil'd.
Oh, but I know your lordship would disdain
To marry with the daughter of a Jew:
And yet I'll give her many a golden cross
With Christian posies round about the ring.

Lod. 'Tis not thy wealth, but her that I esteem;
Yet crave I thy consent.   431

Bara. And mine you have, yet let me talk to her.
This offspring of Cain, this Jebusite,
That never tasted of the Passover,
Nor e'er shall see the land of Canaan,
Nor our Messias that is yet to come;
This gentle maggot, Lodowick, I mean,
Must be deluded: let him have thy hand,
But keep thy heart till Don Mathias comes.
                                      [Aside to her.

Abig. What, shall I be betroth'd to Lodowick? 440

Bara. It's no sin to deceive a Christian;
For they themselves hold it a principle,
Faith is not to be held with heretics:
But all are heretics that are not Jews;
This follows well, and therefore, daughter, fear not.
                                      [Aside to her.
I have entreated her, and she will grant.

Lod. Then, gentle Abigail, plight thy faith to me.

Abig. I cannot choose, seeing my father bids:
Nothing but death shall part my love and me.

Lod. Now have I that for which my soul hath
    long'd.   450

    428 cross] a piece of money marked with a cross

Bara. So have not I, but yet I hope I shall. [*Aside.*
Abig. O wretched Abigail, what hast thee done?
                              [*Aside.*
Lod. Why on the sudden is your colour chang'd?
Abig. I know not: but farewell, I must be gone.
Bara. Stay her, but let her not speak one word
    more.
Lod. Mute o' the sudden! here's a sudden change.
Bara. Oh, muse not at it, 'tis the Hebrews' guise,
That maidens new-betroth'd should weep awhile:
Trouble her not, sweet Lodowick, depart:
She is thy wife, and thou shalt be mine heir.   460
   Lod. Oh, is't the custom? then I am resolv'd:
But rather let the brightsome heavens be dim,
And nature's beauty choke with stifling clouds,
Than my fair Abigail should frown on me.
There comes the villain, now I'll be reveng'd.

Re-enter Mathias.

Bara. Be quiet, Lodowick, it is enough
That I have made thee sure to Abigail.
   Lod. Well, let him go.   [*Exit.*
   Bara. Well, but for me, as you went in at doors
You had been stabb'd: but not a word on't now;
Here must no speeches pass, nor swords be drawn.
   Math. Suffer me, Barabas, but to follow him.   472
   Bara. No; so shall I, if any hurt be done,
Be made an accessory of your deeds:
Revenge it on him when you meet him next.
   Math. For this I'll have his heart.
   Bara. Do so. Lo, here I give thee Abigail.
   Math. What greater gift can poor Mathias have?
Shall Lodowick rob me of so fair a love?
My life is not so dear as Abigail.   480
   Bara. My heart misgives me, that, to cross your
    love,
He's with your mother; therefore after him.
   Math. What, is he gone unto my mother?

Bara. Nay, if you will, stay till she comes herself.

Math. I cannot stay; for if my mother come,
She'll die with grief.   [*Exit.*

Abig. I cannot take my leave of him for tears.
Father, why have you thus incens'd them both?

Bara. What's that to thee?

Abig. I'll make 'em friends again.   490

Bara. You'll make 'em friends? are there not Jews enow
In Malta, but thou must dote upon a Christian?

Abig. I will have Don Mathias; he is my love.

Bara. Yes, you shall have him. Go, put her in.

Itha. Ay, I'll put her in.   [*Puts in* Abigail.

Bara. Now tell me, Ithamore, how lik'st thou
this?

Itha. Faith, master, I think by this
You purchase both their lives: is it not so?

Bara. True; and it shall be cunningly perform'd.

Itha. Oh, master, that I might have a hand in
this!   500

Bara. Ay, so thou shalt; 'tis thou must do the
deed:
Take this, and bear it to Mathias straight.
                              [*Giving a letter.*
And tell him that it comes from Lodowick.

Itha. 'Tis poison'd, is it not?

Bara. No, no, and yet it might be done that way:
It is a challenge feign'd from Lodowick.

Itha. Fear not, I'll so set his heart a-fire,
That he shall verily think it comes from him.

Bara. I cannot choose but like thy readiness:
Yet be not rash, but do it cunningly.   510

Itha. As I behave myself in this, employ me hereafter.

Bara. Away, then.   [*Exit* Ithamore.
So, now will I go in to Lodowick,
And, like a cunning spirit, feign some lie,
Till I have set 'em both at enmity.   [*Exit.*

Act III.

Enter Bellamira.*

Bell. Since this town was besieg'd, my gain grows
    cold:
The time has been, that but for one bare night
A hundred ducats have been freely given;
But now against my will I must be chaste:
And yet I know my beauty doth not fail.
From Venice merchants, and from Padua
Were wont to come rare-witted gentlemen,
Scholars I mean, learned and liberal;
And now, save Pilia-Borza, comes there none,
And he is very seldom from my house;   10
And here he comes.

Enter Pilia-Borza.

Pilia. Hold thee, wench, there's something for thee
to spend.   [*Showing a bag of silver.*
Bell. 'Tis silver; I disdain it.
Pilia. Ay, but the Jew has gold,
And I will have it, or it shall go hard.
Bell. Tell me, how cam'st thou by this?
Pilia. Faith, walking the back-lanes through the
gardens, I chanc'd to cast mine eye up to the Jew's
counting-house, where I saw some bags of money,
and in the night I clamber'd up with my hooks, and,
as I was taking my choice, I heard a rumbling in the
house; so I took only this, and run my way: But
here's the Jew's man.
Bell. Hide the bag.

Enter Ithamore.

Pilia. Look not towards him, let's away. Zoons,
what a looking thou keep'st! thou'lt betray's anon.
        Exeunt Bellamira *and* Pilia-Borza.

* The scene is the outside of Bellamira's house. She probably appears on a balcony.

Itha. Oh, the sweetest face that ever I beheld! I
know she is a courtesan by her attire: now would
I give a hundred of the Jew's crowns that I had such
a concubine.   31
Well, I have deliver'd the challenge in such sort,
As meet they will, and fighting die; brave sport.
                                              [*Exit.*

Enter Mathias.*

Math. This is the place: now Abigail shall see
Whether Mathias holds her dear or no.

Enter Lodowick *reading.*

What, dares the villain write in such base terms?
     Lod. I did it, and revenge it if thou dar'st!
                                          [*They fight.*

Enter Barabas *above.*

Bara. Oh bravely fought! and yet they thrust not
     home.
Now, Lodowick! now, Mathias!—So;   [*Both fall.*
So, now they have show'd themselves to be tall fellows.
[*Cries within*] Part 'em, part 'em!   41
     Bara. Ay, part 'em now they are dead. Farewell,
     farewell.   [*Exit above.*

Enter Ferneze, Katharine, *and* Attendants.

Fern. What sight is this? my Lodowick slain!
These arms of mine shall be thy sepulchre.
     Kath. Who is this? my son Mathias slain!
     Fern. O Lodowick, hadst thou perish'd by the Turk,
Wretched Ferneze might have veng'd thy death.
     Kath. Thy son slew mine, and I'll revenge his
     death.
     Fern. Look, Katharine, look! thy son gave mine
     these wounds.   49

     * The scene is a street.   40 tall] brave

Kath. Oh, leave to grieve me, I am griev'd enough.

Fern. Oh, that my sighs could turn to lively breath,
And these my tears to blood, that he might live.

Kath. Who made them enemies?

Fern. I know not, and that grieves me most of all.

Kath. My son lov'd thine.

Fern. And so did Lodowick him.

Kath. Lend me that weapon that did kill my son,
And it shall murder me.

Fern. Nay, madam, stay; that weapon was my
son's,
And on that rather should Ferneze die.   60

Kath. Hold, let's inquire the causers of their deaths,
That we may venge their blood upon their heads.

Fern. Then take them up, and let them be interr'd
Within one sacred monument of stone;
Upon which altar I will offer up
My daily sacrifice of sighs and tears,
And with my prayers pierce impartial heavens,
Till they reveal the causers of our smarts,
Which forc'd their hands divide united hearts.
Come, Katharina, our losses equal are;   70
Then of true grief let us take equal share.

                          [Exeunt with the bodies.

Enter Ithamore.*

Itha. Why, was there ever seen such villany,
So neatly plotted, and so well perform'd?
Both held in hand, and flatly both beguil'd?

Enter Abigail.

Abig. Why, how now, Ithamore, why laugh'st thou
so?

Itha. O mistress, ha, ha, ha!

Abig. Why, what ail'st thou?

Itha. Oh, my master!

Abig. Ha!   80

      * The scene is a room in Barabas's house.

Itha. O mistress, I have the bravest. gravest, secret,
subtle, bottle-nosed knave to my master, that ever
gentleman had.

Abig. Say, knave, why rail'st upon my father thus?

Itha. Oh, my master has the bravest policy.

Abig. Wherein?

Itha. Why, know you not?

Abig. Why, no.

Itha. Know you not of Mathias' and Don Lodowick's disaster? 90

Abig. No, what was it?

Itha. Why, the devil invented a challenge, my
master writ it, and I carried it, first to Lodowick,
and *imprimis* to Mathias;
And then they met, and, as the story says,
In doleful wise they ended both their days.

Abig. And was my father furtherer of their deaths?

Itha. Am I Ithamore?

Abig. Yes.

Itha. So sure did your father write, and I carry the
challenge. 101

Abig. Well, Ithamore, let me request thee this:
Go to the new-made nunnery, and inquire
For any of the friars of Saint Jaques,
And say, I pray them come and speak with me.

Itha. I pray, mistress, will you answer me to one
question?

Abig. Well, sirrah, what is't?

Itha. A very feeling one; have not the nuns fine
sport with the friars now and then? 110

Abig. Go to, Sirrah Sauce, is this your question?
get ye gone.

Itha. I will, forsooth, mistress. [*Exit.*

Abig. Hard-hearted father, unkind Barabas!
Was this the pursuit of thy policy,
To make me show them favour severally,
That by my favour they should both be slain?
Admit thou lov'dst not Lodowick for his sire,

Yet Don Mathias ne'er offended thee:
But thou wert set upon extreme revenge,   120
Because the Sire dispossess'd thee once,
And couldst not venge it, but upon his son,
Nor on his son, but by Mathias' means;
Nor on Mathias, but by murdering me:
But I perceive there is no love on earth,
Pity in Jews, nor piety in Turks.
But here comes cursed Ithamore with the friar.

Re-enter Ithamore *with* Friar Jacomo.

Friar Jac. Virgo, salve.

Itha. When duck you?

Abig. Welcome, grave friar; Ithamore, be gone.

[*Exit* Ithamore.

Know, holy sir, I am bold to solicit thee.   131

Friar Jac. Wherein?

Abig. To get me be admitted for a nun.

Friar Jac. Why, Abigail, it is not yet long since
That I did labour thy admission,
And then thou didst not like that holy life.

Abig. Then were my thoughts so frail and uncon-
firm'd

And I was chain'd to follies of the world:
But now experience, purchased with grief,
Has made me see the difference of things.   140
My sinful soul, alas, hath pac'd too long
The fatal labyrinth of misbelief,
Far from the sun that gives eternal life.

Friar Jac. Who taught thee this?

Abig. The abbess of the house,
Whose jealous admonition I embrace:
Oh, therefore, Jacomo, let me be one,
Although unworthy, of that sisterhood!   [more,

Friar Jac. Abigail, I will, but see thou change no
For that will be most heavy to thy soul.   150

Abig. That was my father's fault.

Friar Jac. Thy father's! how?

Abig. Nay, you shall pardon me. O Barabas,
Though thou deservest hardly at my hands,
Yet never shall these lips bewray thy life!   [*Aside.*
Friar Jac. Come, shall we go?
Abig. My duty waits on you.   [*Exeunt.*

Enter Barabas, *reading a letter.**

Bara. What, Abigail become a nun again?
False and unkind; what, hast thou lost thy father?
And all unknown and unconstrain'd of me,   160
Art thou again got to the nunnery?
Now here she writes, and wills me to repent.
Repentance? *Spurca!* what pretendeth this?
I fear she knows—'tis so—of my device
In Don Mathias' and Lodovico's deaths:
If so, 'tis time that it be seen into:
For she that varies from me in belief
Gives great presumption that she loves me not,
Or, loving, doth dislike of something done.
But who comes here?

Enter Ithamore.

O Ithamore, come near;   170
Come near, my love; come near, thy master's life,
My trusty servant, nay, my second self;
For I have now no hope but even in thee,
And on that hope my happiness is built.
When saw'st thou Abigail?
Itha. To-day.
Bara. With whom?
Itha. A friar.
Bara. A friar? false villain, he hath done the deed.
Itha. How, sir?   180
Bara. Why, made mine Abigail a nun.
Itha. That's no lie, for she sent me for him.
Bara. O unhappy day!

* The scene is the same, but there has been an interval of time.   163 pretendeth] portendeth

False, credulous, inconstant Abigail!
But let 'em go: and, Ithamore, from hence
Ne'er shall she grieve me more with her disgrace;
Ne'er shall she live to inherit aught of mine,
Be bless'd of me, nor come within my gates,
But perish underneath my bitter curse,
Like Cain by Adam for his brother's death.   190

Itha. O master—

Bara. Ithamore, entreat not for her; I am mov'd,
And she is hateful to my soul and me:
And, lest thou yield to this that I entreat,
I cannot think but that thou hat'st my life.

Itha. Who, I, master? why, I'll run to some rock,
And throw myself headlong into the sea;
Why, I'll do anything for your sweet sake.

Bara. O trusty Ithamore, no servant, but my friend;
I here adopt thee for mine only heir: 200
All that I have is thine when I am dead,
And whilst I live, use half; spend as myself;
Here, take my keys,—I'll give 'em thee anon;
Go buy thee garments; but thou shalt not want:
Only know this, that thus thou art to do—
But first go fetch me in the pot of rice
That for our supper stands upon the fire.

Itha. I hold my head my master's hungry [*Aside*].—
I go, sir.   [*Exit.*

Bara. Thus every villain ambles after wealth,   210
Although he ne'er be richer than in hope.
But, husht!

Re-enter Ithamore *with the pot.*

Itha. Here 'tis, master.

Bara. Well said, Ithamore; what, hast thou brought
the ladle with thee too?

Itha. Yes, sir, the proverb says, he that eats with
the devil had need of a long spoon; I have brought
you a ladle.

194 lest] unless

Bara. Very well, Ithamore; then now be secret;
And for thy sake, whom I so dearly love,   220
Now shalt thou see the death of Abigail,
That thou mayst freely live to be my heir.

Itha. Why, master, will you poison her with a mess
of rice-porridge? that will preserve life, make her
round and plump, and batten more than you are
aware.

Bara. Ay, but, Ithamore, seest thou this?
It is a precious powder that I bought
Of an Italian, in Ancona, once,
Whose operation is to bind, infect,   230
And poison deeply, yet not appear
In forty hours after it is ta'en.

Itha. How, master?

Bara. Thus, Ithamore:
This even they use in Malta here,—'tis call'd
Saint Jaques' Even,—and then I say they use
To send their alms unto the nunneries:
Among the rest bear this, and set it there:
There's a dark entry where they take it in,
Where they must neither see the messenger,   240
Nor make inquiry who hath sent it them.

Itha. How so?

Bara. Belike there is some ceremony in't.
There, Ithamore, must thou go place this pot:
Stay, let me spice it first.

Itha. Pray do, and let me help you, master.
Pray let me taste first.

Bara. Prithee, do. [Ithamore *tastes.*] What say'st
thou now?   249

Itha. Troth, master, I'm loath such a pot of pottage
should be spoil'd.

Bara. Peace, Ithamore, 'tis better so than spar'd.
                              [*Puts the powder into the pot.*
Assure thyself thou shalt have broth by the eye:
My purse, my coffer, and myself is thine.

Itha. Well, master, I go.

Bara. Stay, first let me stir it, Ithamore.
As fatal be it to her as the draught
Of which great Alexander drunk, and died;
And with her let it work like Borgia's wine,
Whereof his sire the Pope was poisoned.　　260
In few, the blood of Hydra, Lerna's bane,
The juice of hebon, and Cocytus' breath,
And all the poisons of the Stygian pool,
Break from the fiery kingdom, and in this
Vomit your venom, and envenom her
That, like a fiend, hath left her father thus.

Itha. What a blessing has he given't! was ever pot
of rice-porridge so sauc'd? [*Aside*] What shall I do
with it?

Bara. O my sweet Ithamore, go set it down,　　270
And come again so soon as thou hast done,
For I have other business for thee.

Itha. Here's a drench to poison a whole stable of
Flanders mares: I'll carry't to the nuns with a powder.

Bara. And the horse-pestilence to boot: away!

Itha. I am gone.
Pay me my wages, for my work is done.

　　　　　　　　　　　　　[*Exit with the pot.*

Bara. I'll pay thee with a vengeance, Ithamore.

　　　　　　　　　　　　　　　　　[*Exit.*

Enter Ferneze, Martin Del Bosco, Knights, *and* Basso.*

Fern. Welcome, great Basso: how fares Calymath?
What wind drives you thus into Malta-road?　　280

Bas. The wind that bloweth all the world besides,
Desire of gold.

Fern. Desire of gold, great sir?
That's to be gotten in the Western Inde:
In Malta are no golden minerals.

Bas. To you of Malta thus saith Calymath:
The time you took for respite is at hand

For the performance of your promise pass'd;
And for the tribute money I am sent.

Fern. Basso, in brief, shalt have no tribute here, 290
Nor shall the heathens live upon our spoil:
First will we raze the city-walls ourselves,
Lay waste the island, hew the temples down,
And, shipping off our goods to Sicily,
Open an entrance for the wasteful sea,
Whose billows beating the resistless banks,
Shall overflow it with their refluence.

Bas. Well, governor, since thou hast broke the league
By flat denial of the promis'd tribute,
Talk not of razing down your city-walls;   300
You shall not need trouble yourselves so far,
For Selim Calymath shall come himself,
And with brass bullets batter down your towers,
And turn proud Malta to a wilderness,
For these intolerable wrongs of yours;
And so farewell.

Fern. Farewell.   [*Exit* Basso.
And now, you men of Malta, look about,
And let's provide to welcome Calymath:
Close your port-cullis, charge your basilisks,   310
And as you profitably take up arms,
So now courageously encounter them,
For by this answer broken is the league,
And naught is to be look'd for now but wars,
And naught to us more welcome is than wars.
                                [*Exeunt.*

Enter Friar Jacomo *and* Friar Barnardine.*

Friar Jac. O brother, brother, all the nuns are sick,
And physic will not help them: they must die.

Friar Barn. The abbess sent for me to be confess'd:
Oh, what a sad confession will there be!

Friar Jac. And so did fair Maria send for me: 320
I'll to her lodging; hereabouts she lies.   [*Exit.*

* The scene is the interior of the convent.

Enter Abigail.

Friar Barn. What, all dead, save only Abigail?

Abig. And I shall die too, for I feel death coming.
Where is the friar that convers'd with me?

Friar Barn. Oh, he is gone to see the other nuns.

Abig. I sent for him, but seeing you are come,
Be you my ghostly father: and first know,
That in this house I liv'd religiously,
Chaste, and devout, much sorrowing for my sins;
But, ere I came—   330

Friar Barn. What then?

Abig. I did offend high heaven so grievously
As I am almost desperate for my sins:
And one offence torments me more than all.
You knew Mathias and Don Lodowick?

Friar Barn. Yes, what of them?

Abig. My father did contract me to 'em both:
First to Don Lodowick; him I never lov'd;
Mathias was the man that I held dear,
And for his sake did I become a nun.   340

Friar Barn. So, say how was their end?

Abig. Both jealous of my love, envied each other;
And by my father's practice, which is there

[*Gives writing.*

Set down at large, the gallants were both slain.

Friar Barn. O monstrous villany!

Abig. To work my peace, this I confess to thee:
Reveal it not, for then my father dies.

Friar Barn. Know that confession must not be re-
veal'd;
The canon-law forbids it, and the priest
That makes it known, being degraded first,   350
Shall be condemn'd, and then sent to the fire.

Abig. So I have heard; pray, therefore, keep it close.
Death seizeth on my heart: ah, gentle friar,
Convert my father that he may be sav'd,

342 envied] hated   343 practice] artifice

And witness that I die a Christian.   [*Dies.*

  Friar Barn. Ay, and a virgin too; that grieves me
    most.
But I must to the Jew and exclaim on him,
And make him stand in fear of me.

Re-enter Friar Jacomo.

  Friar Jac. O brother, all the nuns are dead, let's
    bury them.
  Friar Barn. First help to bury this, then go with me
And help me to exclaim against the Jew.   361
  Friar Jac. Why, what has he done?
  Friar Barn. A thing that makes me tremble to unfold.
  Friar Jac. What, has he crucified a child?
  Friar Barn. No, but a worse thing: 'twas told me in
    shrift;
Thou know'st 'tis death, an if it be reveal'd.
Come, let's away.   [*Exeunt.*

Act IV.

Enter Barabas and Ithamore.   Bells within.*

  Bara. There is no music to a Christian's knell:
How sweet the bells ring now the nuns are dead,
That sound at other times like tinkers' pans!
I was afraid the poison had not wrought,
Or, though it wrought, it would have done no good,
For every year they swell, and yet they live:
Now all are dead, not one remains alive.
  Itha. That's brave, master: but think you it will
not be known?
  Bara. How can it, if we two be secret?   10
  Itha. For my part, fear you not.
  Bara. I'd cut thy throat if I did.
  Itha. And reason too.
But here's a royal monast'ry hard by;
Good master, let me poison all the monks.

* The scene is a street.   1 to] equal *to*

Bara. Thou shalt not need, for now the nuns are
    dead,
They'll die with grief.

Itha. Do you not sorrow for your daughter's death?

Bara. No, but I grieve because she liv'd so long,
An Hebrew born, and would become a Christian: 20
Cazzo, diabolo!

Itha. Look, look, master, here comes two religious
caterpillars.

Enter Friar Jacomo *and* Friar Barnardine.

Bara. I smelt 'em ere they came.

Itha. God-a-mercy, nose! Come, let's begone.

Friar Barn. Stay, wicked Jew, repent, I say, and
    stay.

Friar Jac. Thou hast offended, therefore must be
    damn'd.

Bara. I fear they know we sent the poison'd broth.

Itha. And so do I, master; therefore speak 'em fair.

Friar Barn. Barabas, thou hast——   30

Friar Jac. Ay, that thou hast——

Bara. True, I have money, what though I have?

Friar Barn. Thou art a——

Friar Jac. Ay, that thou art, a——

Bara. What needs all this? I know I am a Jew.

Friar Barn. Thy daughter——

Friar Jac. Ay, thy daughter——

Bara. Oh, speak not of her! then I die with grief.

Friar Barn. Remember that——

Friar Jac. Ay, remember that——   40

Bara. I must needs say that I have been a great
usurer.

Friar Barn. Thou hast committed——

Bara. Fornication? but that was in another country:
And besides, the wench is dead.

Friar Barn. Ay, but, Barabas, remember Mathias
and Don Lodowick.

Bara. Why, what of them?

Friar Barn. I will not say that by a forged challenge
they met.   50
Bara. She has confess'd, and we are both undone;
My bosom's inmates!—but I must dissemble,—
                                         [*Aside to* Ithamore.
O holy friars, the burthen of my sins
Lie heavy on my soul! then pray you tell me,
Is't not too late now to turn Christian?
I have been zealous in the Jewish faith,
Hard-hearted to the poor, a covetous wretch,
That would for lucre's sake have sold my soul;
A hundred for a hundred I have ta'en;
And now for store of wealth may I compare   60
With all the Jews in Malta: but what is wealth?
I am a Jew, and therefore am I lost.
Would penance serve for this my sin,
I could afford to whip myself to death.
    Itha. And so could I; but penance will not serve.
    Bara. To fast, to pray, and wear a shirt of hair,
And on my knees creep to Jerusalem.
Cellars of wine, and sollars full of wheat,
Warehouses stuff'd with spices and with drugs,
Whole chests of gold in bullion and in coin,   70
Besides I know not how much weight in pearl,
Orient and round, have I within my house;
At Alexandria merchandise unsold:
But yesterday two ships went from this town,
Their voyage will be worth ten thousand crowns.
In Florence, Venice, Antwerp, London, Seville,
Frankfort, Lubeck, Moscow, and where not,
Have I debts owing; and in most of these,
Great sums of money lying in the banco;
All this I'll give to some religious house,   80
So I may be baptiz'd, and live therein.
    Friar Jac. O good Barabas, come to our house.
    Friar Barn. O, no, good Barabas, come to our house.
And Barabas, you know——

                    68 sollars] lofts

Bara. I know that I have highly sinn'd:
You shall convert me, you shall have all my wealth.
  Friar Jac. O Barabas, their laws are strict.
  Bara. I know they are, and I will be with you.
  Friar Jac. They wear no shirts, and they go bare-
    foot too.   89
  Bara. Then 'tis not for me; and I am resolv'd
You shall confess me, and have all my goods.
  Friar Jac. Good Barabas, come to me.
  Bara. You see I answer him, and yet he stays;
Rid him away, and go you home with me.
  Friar Barn. I'll be with you to-night.
  Bara. Come to my house at one o'clock this night.
  Friar Jac. You hear your answer, and you may be
    gone.
  Friar Barn. Why, go, get you away.
  Friar Jac. I will not go for thee.
  Friar Barn. Not! then I'll make thee, rogue.   100
  Friar Jac. How, dost call me rogue?   [*They fight.*
  Itha. Part 'em, master, part 'em.
  Bara. This is mere frailty: brethren, be content.
Friar Barnardine, go you with Ithamore:
You know my mind; let me alone with him.
  Friar Jac. Why does he go to thy house? let him be
    gone.
  Bara. I'll give him something, and so stop his mouth.
       [*Exit* Ithamore *with* Friar Barnardine.
I never heard of any man but he
Malign'd the order of the Jacobins:
But do you think that I believe his words?   110
Why, brother, you converted Abigail;
And I am bound in charity to requite it,
And so I will. O Jacomo, fail not, but come.
  Friar Jac. But, Barabas, who shall be your god-
    fathers?
For presently you shall be shriv'd.
  Bara. Marry, the Turk shall be one of my god-
    fathers,

But not a word to any of your convent.

Friar Jac. I warrant thee, Barabas.	[*Exit.*

Bara. So, now the fear is past, and I am safe;
For he that shriv'd her is within my house:	120
What if I murder'd him ere Jacomo comes?
Now I have such a plot for both their lives,
As never Jew nor Christian knew the like:
One turn'd my daughter, therefore he shall die;
The other knows enough to have my life,
Therefore 'tis not requisite he should live.
But are not both these wise men, to suppose
That I will leave my house, my goods, and all,
To fast and be well whipp'd? I'll none of that.
Now, Friar Barnardine, I come to you:	130
I'll feast you, lodge you, give you fair words,
And, after that, I and my trusty Turk—
No more, but so: it must and shall be done.

Enter Ithamore.*

Ithamore, tell me, is the friar asleep?

Itha. Yes, and I know not what the reason is,
Do what I can, he will not strip himself,
Nor go to bed, but sleeps in his own clothes;
I fear me he mistrusts what we intend.

Bara. No, 'tis an order which the friars use:
Yet if he knew our meanings, could he scape?	140

Itha. No, none can hear him, cry he ne'er so loud.

Bara. Why, true, therefore did I place him there:
The other chambers open towards the street.

Itha. You loiter, master; wherefore stay we thus?
Oh, how I long to see him shake his heels.

Bara. Come on, sirrah:
Off with your girdle, make a handsome noose.

[Ithamore *takes off his girdle, and ties a noose in it.*
Friar, awake! [*They put the noose round the Friar's neck.*

Friar Barn. What, do you mean to strangle me?

* The scene is a room in Barabas's house.

Itha. Yes, 'cause you use to confess.   150

Bara. Blame not us, but the proverb, Confess and
be hang'd. Pull hard.

Friar Barn. What, will you have my life?

Bara. Pull hard, I say. You would have had my
goods.

Itha. Ay, and our lives too: therefore pull amain.

[*They strangle the* Friar.
'Tis neatly done, sir, here's no print at all.

Bara. Then is it as it should be. Take him up.

Itha. Nay, master, be rul'd by me a little. [*Takes
the body, sets it upright against the wall, and puts a staff in
its hand.*] So, let him lean upon his staff; excellent!
he stands as if he were begging of bacon.   161

Bara. Who would not think but that this friar liv'd?
What time o' night is't now, sweet Ithamore?

Itha. Towards one.

Bara. Then will not Jacomo be long from hence.

[*Exeunt.*

Enter Friar Jacomo.*

Friar Jac. This is the hour wherein I shall proceed;
O happy hour, wherein I shall convert
An infidel, and bring his gold into
Our treasury.
But soft, is not this Barnardine? it is;   170
And, understanding I should come this way,
Stands here a purpose, meaning me some wrong,
And intercept my going to the Jew.
Barnardine!
Wilt thou not speak? thou think'st I see thee not;
Away, I'd wish thee, and let me go by:
No, wilt thou not? nay, then, I'll force my way;
And see, a staff stands ready for the purpose.
As thou lik'st that, stop me another time.

[*Takes the staff, and strikes down the body.*

* The scene continues (necessarily, since the corpse remains).

Enter Barabas *and* Ithamore.

Bara. Why, how now, Jacomo, what hast thou
    done?   180

Friar Jac. Why, stricken him that would have
    struck at me.

Bara. Who is it? Barnardine! now, out, alas,
He is slain!

Itha. Ay, master, he's slain; look how his brains
drop out on's nose.

Friar Jac. Good sirs, I have done't, but nobody
knows it but you two; I may escape.

Bara. So might my man and I hang with you for
company.

Itha. No, let us bear him to the magistrates.   190

Friar Jac. Good Barabas, let me go.

Bara. No, pardon me, the law must have his course.
I must be forc'd to give in evidence,
That, being importun'd by this Barnardine
To be a Christian, I shut him out,
And there he sate: now I, to keep my word,
And give my goods and substance to your house,
Was up thus early, with intent to go
Unto your friary, because you stay'd.   199

Itha. Fie upon 'em, master; will you turn Christian,
when holy friars turn devils and murder one
another?

Bara. No, for this example I'll remain a Jew:
Heaven bless me! what, a friar a murderer?
When shall you see a Jew commit the like?

Itha. Why, a Turk could ha' done no more.

Bara. To-morrow is the sessions; you shall to it.
Come, Ithamore, let's help to take him hence.

Friar Jac. Villains, I am a sacred person; touch me
    not.

Bara. The law shall touch you, we'll but lead you,
    we: 210
'Las, I could weep at your calamity!

Take in the staff too, for that must be shown:
Law wills that each particular be known.   [*Exeunt.*

Enter Bellamira *and* Pilia-Borza.*

Bell. Pilia-Borza, didst thou meet with Ithamore?
Pilia. I did.
Bell. And didst thou deliver my letter?
Pilia. I did.
Bell. And what think'st thou? will he come?
Pilia. I think so, and yet I cannot tell; for at the reading of the letter he look'd like a man of another world.   221
Bell. Why so?
Pilia. That such a base slave as he should be saluted by such a tall man as I am, from such a beautiful dame as you.
Bell. And what said he?
Pilia. Not a wise word; only gave me a nod, as who should say, 'Is it even so?' and so I left him, being driven to a non-plus at the critical aspect of my terrible countenance.   230
Bell. And where didst meet him?
Pilia. Upon mine own free-hold, within forty foot of the gallows, conning his neck-verse, I take it, looking of a friar's execution, whom I saluted with an old hempen proverb, *Hodie tibi, cras mihi,* and so I left him to the mercy of the hangman: but, the exercise being done, see where he comes.   237

Enter Ithamore.

Itha. I never knew a man take his death so patiently as this friar; he was ready to leap off ere the halter was about his neck; and when the hangman had put on his hempen tippet, he made such haste to his prayers, as if he had had another cure to serve. Well,

* The scene is a veranda of Bellamira's house.   236
exercise] sermon

go whither he will, I'll be none of his followers in
haste: and now I think on't, going to the execution,
a fellow met me with a muschatoes like a raven's wing,
and a dagger with a hilt like a warming pan, and he
gave me a letter from one Madam Bellamira, saluting
me in such sort as if he had meant to make clean my
boots with his lips; the effect was, that I should come
to her house: I wonder what the reason is; it may be
she sees more in me than I can find in myself, for she
writes further, that she loves me ever since she saw
me, and who would not requite such love? Here's
her house, and here she comes, and now would I
were gone! I am not worthy to look upon her.   255

   Pilia. This is the gentleman you writ to.

   Itha. Gentleman! he flouts me: what gentry can be
in a poor Turk of tenpence? I'll be gone.   [*Aside.*

   Bell. Is't not a sweet-fac'd youth, Pilia?

   Itha. Again, 'sweet youth'! [*Aside*]—Did not you,
sir, bring the sweet youth a letter?   261

   Pilia. I did, sir, and from this gentlewoman, who,
as myself and the rest of the family, stand or fall at
your service.

   Bell. Though woman's modesty should hale me
      back,
I can withhold no longer; welcome, sweet love.

   Itha. Now am I clean, or rather foully out of the
way.   [*Aside.*

   Bell. Whither so soon?

   Itha. I'll go steal some money from my master to
make me handsome [*Aside*].—Pray, pardon me, I
must go see a ship discharg'd.   272

   Bell. Canst thou be so unkind to leave me thus?

   Pilia. An ye did but know how she loves you, sir!

   Itha. Nay, I care not how much she loves me.—
Sweet Bellamira, would I had my master's wealth for
thy sake!

   Pilia. And you can have it, sir, an if you please.

   Itha. If 'twere above ground, I could and would

have it; but he hides and buries it up, as partridges
do their eggs, under the earth.   281

Pilia. And is't not possible to find it out?

Itha. By no means possible.

Bell. What shall we do with this base villain,
then?

                                        [*Aside to* Pilia-Borza.

Pilia. Let me alone; do but you speak him fair.—
                                        [*Aside to her.*

But you know some secrets of the Jew,
Which, if they were reveal'd, would do him harm.

Itha. Ay, and such as—go to, no more! I'll make
him send me half he has, and glad he scapes so,
too. Pen and ink, I'll write unto him; we'll have
money straight.   292

Pilia. Send for a hundred crowns at least.

Itha. Ten hundred thousand crowns. [*writing*]
Master Barabas,—

Pilia. Write not so submissively, but threatening
him.

Itha. [*writing*] *Sirrah Barabas, send me a hundred crowns.*

Pilia. Put in two hundred at least.

Itha. [*writing*] *I charge thee send me three hundred by
this bearer, and this shall be your warrant: if you do not—
no more, but so.*   302

Pilia. Tell him you will confess.

Itha. [*writing*] *Otherwise I'll confess all.*—Vanish, and
return in a twinkle.

Pilia. Let me alone; I'll use him in his kind.

Itha. Hang him, Jew!

                                [*Exit* Pilia-Borza *with the letter.*

Bell. Now, gentle Ithamore, lie in my lap.
Where are my maids? provide a running banquet;
Send to the merchant, bid him bring me silks;   310
Shall Ithamore, my love, go in such rags?

Itha. And bid the jeweller come hither too.

Bell. I have no husband, sweet; I'll marry thee.

309 running] hasty

Itha. Content: but we will leave this paltry land,
And sail from hence to Greece, to lovely Greece;
I'll be thy Jason, thou my golden fleece;
Where painted carpets o'er the meads are hurl'd,
And Bacchus' vineyards o'erspread the world;
Where woods and forests go in goodly green,
I'll be Adonis, thou shalt be Love's Queen.   320
The meads, the orchards, and the primrose-lanes,
Instead of sedge and reed, bear sugar-canes:
Thou in those groves, by Dis above,
Shalt live with me, and be my love.

Bell. Whither will I not go with gentle Ithamore?

Re-enter Pilia-Borza.

Itha. How now? hast thou the gold?

Pilia. Yes.

Itha. But came it freely? did the cow give down her milk freely?   329

Pilia. At reading of the letter, he star'd and stamp'd, and turn'd aside: I took him by the beard, and look'd upon him thus; told him he were best to send it: then he hugg'd and embrac'd me.

Itha. Rather for fear than love.

Pilia. Then, like a Jew, he laugh'd and jeer'd, and told me he lov'd me for your sake, and said what a faithful servant you had been.

Itha. The more villain he to keep me thus: here's goodly 'parel, is there not?

Pilia. To conclude, he gave me ten crowns.   340

[*Delivers the money to* Ithamore.

Itha. But ten? I'll not leave him worth a grey groat. Give me a ream of paper: we'll have a kingdom of gold for't.

Pilia. Write for five hundred crowns.

Itha. [*writing*] *Sirrah Jew, as you love your life, send me five hundred crowns, and give the bearer a hundred.*—Tell him I must have't.

Pilia. I warrant your worship shall have't.

Itha. And if he ask why I demand so much, tell
him I scorn to write a line under a hundred crowns.

Pilia. You'd make a rich poet, sir. I am gone.

[*Exit with the letter.*

Itha. Take thou the money; spend it for my sake.

Bell. 'Tis not thy money, but thyself I weigh:
Thus Bellamira esteems of gold; [*Throws it aside.*
But thus of thee. [*Kisses him.*

Itha. That kiss again! She runs division of my lips.
What an eye she casts on me! it twinkles like a star.

[*Aside.*

Bell. Come, my dear love, let's in and sleep together.

Itha. Oh, that ten thousand nights were put in one,
That we might sleep seven years together   360
Afore we wake!

Bell. Come, amorous wag, first banquet, and then
sleep. [*Exeunt.*

Enter Barabas, *reading a letter.**

Bara. Barabas, send me three hundred crowns;—
Plain Barabas! Oh, that wicked courtesan!
He was not wont to call me Barabas.
Or else I will confess;—ay, there it goes:
But, if I get him, *coupe de gorge* for that.
He sent a shaggy, totter'd, staring slave,
That, when he speaks, draws out his grisly beard,
And winds it twice or thrice about his ear;   370
Whose face has been a grind-stone for men's swords;
His hands are hack'd, some fingers cut quite off,
Who, when he speaks, grunts like a hog, and looks
Like one that is employ'd in catzery
And cross-biting; such a rogue
As is the husband to a hundred whores;
And I by him must send three hundred crowns.
Well, my hope is, he will not stay there still;
And, when he comes—Oh, that he were but here!

---

* Scene, a street.   356 runs division of] plays variations
on   374 catzery] knavery   375 cross-biting] swindling

Enter Pilia-Borza.

Pilia. Jew, I must ha' more gold.   380

Bara. Why, want'st thou any of thy tale?

Pilia. No; but three hundred will not serve his turn.

Bara. Not serve his turn, sir?

Pilia. No, sir; and therefore I must have five hundred more.

Bara. I'll rather——

Pilia. Oh, good words, sir, and send it you were best. See, there's his letter.   [*Gives letter.*

Bara. Might he not as well come as send? pray, bid him come and fetch it: what he writes for you, ye shall have straight.   391

Pilia. Ay, and the rest too, or else——

Bara. I must make this villain away [*Aside*]. Please you dine with me, sir—and you shall be most heartily poison'd.   [*Aside.*

Pilia. No, God-a-mercy. Shall I have these crowns?

Bara. I cannot do it, I have lost my keys.

Pilia. Oh, if that be all, I can pick ope your locks.

Bara. Or climb up to my counting-house window: you know my meaning.   400

Pilia. I know enough, and therefore talk not to me of your counting-house. The gold! or know, Jew, it is in my power to hang thee.

Bara. I am betray'd.—   [*Aside.*
'Tis not five hundred crowns that I esteem,
I am not mov'd at that: this angers me,
That he who knows I love him as myself,
Should write in this imperious vein. Why, sir,
You know I have no child, and unto whom
Should I leave all but unto Ithamore?   410

Pilia. Here's many words, but no crowns: the crowns!

Bara. Commend me to him, sir, most humbly,
And unto your good mistress as unknown.

381 tale] reckoning

Pilia. Speak, shall I have 'em, sir?

Bara. Sir, here they are.—   [*Gives money.*
Oh, that I should part with so much gold!   [*Aside.*
Here, take 'em, fellow, with as good a will——
As I would see thee hang'd [*Aside*]. Oh, love stops
　　my breath!
Never lov'd man servant as I do Ithamore.   420
Pilia. I know it, sir.
Bara. Pray, when, sir, shall I see you at my house?
Pilia. Soon enough to your cost, sir. Fare you well.
　　　　　　　　　　　　　　　　　　　　[*Exit.*
Bara. Nay, to thine own cost, villain, if thou
　　com'st!
Was ever Jew tormented as I am?
To have a shag-rag knave to come
Three hundred crowns, and then five hundred
　　crowns!
Well, I must seek a means to rid 'em all,
And presently; for in his villany
He will tell all he knows, and I shall die for't.   430
I have it:
I will in some disguise go see the slave,
And how the villain revels with my gold.   [*Exit.*

Enter Bellamira, Ithamore, *and* Pilia-Borza.*

Bell. I'll pledge thee, love, and therefore drink it
off.
Itha. Say'st thou me so? have at it; and do you
hear?   [*Whispers to her.*
Bell. Go to, it shall be so.
Itha. Of that condition I will drink it up; here's to
thee.   440
Bell. Nay, I'll have all or none.
Itha. There, if thou lov'st me, do not leave a drop.
Bell. Love thee! fill me three glasses.
Itha. Three and fifty dozen, I'll pledge thee.
Pilia. Knavely spoke, and like a knight-at-arms.

* The scene is a veranda of Bellamira's house.

Itha. Hey, *Rivo Castiliano!* a man's a man.

Bell. Now to the Jew.   [best.

Itha. Ha! to the Jew, and send me money you were

Pilia. What wouldst thou do, if he should send thee
none?   450

Itha. Do nothing: but I know what I know; he's a
murderer.

Bell. I had not thought he had been so brave a man.

Itha. You knew Mathias and the governor's son; he
and I kill'd 'em both, and yet never touch'd 'em.

Pilia. Oh, bravely done!

Itha. I carried the broth that poison'd the nuns;
and he and I, snicle hand too fast, strangled a friar.

Bell. You two alone?

Itha. We two; and 'twas never known, nor never
shall be for me.   461

Pilia. This shall with me unto the governor.
                              [*Aside to Bellamira.*

Bell. And fit it should: but first let's ha' more
       gold.—   [*Aside to Pilia-Borza.*
Come, gentle Ithamore, lie in my lap.

Itha. Love me little, love me long: let music rumble,
Whilst I in thy incony lap do tumble.

Enter Barabas, *disguised as a French musician, with a lute,
       and a nosegay in his hat.*

Bell. A French musician! Come, let's hear your
skill.

Bara. Must tuna my lute for sound, twang, twang,
first.   470

Itha. Wilt drink, Frenchman? here's to thee with a
——Pox on this drunken hiccup!

Bara. Gramercy, monsieur.

Bell. Prithee, Pilia-Borza, bid the fiddler give me
the posy in his hat there.

Pilia. Sirrah, you must give my mistress your posy.

458 snicle . . . fast] meaning uncertain; snicle = ensnare.
466 incony] dainty, sweet

Bara. A votre commandement, madame.

[*Giving nosegay.*

Bell. How sweet, my Ithamore, the flowers smell!

Itha. Like thy breath, sweetheart; no violet like 'em.

Pilia. Foh! methinks they stink like a hollyhock.

Bara. So, now I am reveng'd upon 'em all.   481
The scent thereof was death; I poison'd it.   [*Aside.*

Itha. Play, fiddler, or I'll cut your cat's guts into
chitterlings.

Bara. Pardonnez moi, be no in tune yet: so, now, now
all be in.

Itha. Give him a crown, and fill me out more wine.

Pilia. There's two crowns for thee: play.

[*Giving money.*

Bara. How liberally the villain gives me mine own
gold!   [*Aside, and then plays.*

Pilia. Methinks he fingers very well.   491

Bara. So did you when you stole my gold.   [*Aside.*

Pilia. How swift he runs!

Bara. You run swifter when you threw my gold out
of my window.   [*Aside.*

Bell. Musician, hast been in Malta long?

Bara. Two, three, four month, madam.

Itha. Dost know a Jew, one Barabas?

Bara. Very mush, monsieur; you no be his man?

Pilia. His man?   500

Itha. I scorn the peasant: tell him so.

Bara. He knows it already.   [*Aside.*

Itha. 'Tis a strange thing of that Jew, he lives upon
pickled grasshoppers and sauc'd mushrooms.

Bara. What a slave's this! the governor feeds not as
I do.   [*Aside.*

Itha. He never put on clean shirt since he was circumcis'd.

Bara. O rascal! I change myself twice a-day.

[*Aside.*

Itha. The hat he wears, Judas left under the elder
when he hang'd himself.   511

Bara. 'Twas sent me for a present from the Great
Cham.   [*Aside.*

Pilia. A nasty slave he is. Whither now, fiddler?

Bara. Pardonnez moi, monsieur; me be no well.

Pilia. Farewell, fiddler [*Exit* Barabas]. One letter
more to the Jew.

Bell. Prithee, sweet love, one more, and write it
sharp.   519

Itha. No, I'll send by word of mouth now. Bid him
deliver thee a thousand crowns, by the same token
that the nuns lov'd rice, that Friar Barnardine slept
in his own clothes; any of 'em will do it.

Pilia. Let me alone to urge it, now I know the
meaning.

Itha. The meaning has a meaning. Come, let's in:
To undo a Jew is charity, and not sin.   [*Exeunt.*

Act V.

Enter Ferneze, Knights, Martin Del Bosco, *and* Officers.*

Fern. Now, gentlemen, betake you to your arms,
And see that Malta be well fortifi'd;
And it behoves you to be resolute;
For Calymath, having hover'd here so long,
Will win the town, or die before the walls.

First Knight. And die he shall, for we will never
    yield.

Enter Bellamira *and* Pilia-Borza.

Bell. Oh, bring us to the governor.

Fern. Away with her! she is a courtesan.

Bell. Whate'er I am, yet, governor, hear me speak:
I bring thee news by whom thy son was slain: 10
Mathias did it not; it was the Jew.

Pilia. Who, besides the slaughter of these gentlemen,
Poison'd his own daughter and the nuns,

* The scene is the interior of the council-house.

Strangled a friar, and I know not what
Mischief beside.

   Fern. Had we but proof of this——

   Bell. Strong proof, my lord: his man's now at my
     lodging

That was his agent; he'll confess it all.

   Fern. Go fetch him straight [*Exeunt* Officers]. I
     always fear'd that Jew.

     Re-enter Officers *with* Barabas *and* Ithamore.

   Bara. I'll go alone; dogs, do not hale me thus.   20

   Itha. Nor me neither; I cannot out-run you, constable.—Oh, my belly!

   Bara. One dram of powder more had made all sure:
What a damn'd slave was I!   [*Aside.*

   Fern. Make fires, heat irons, let the rack be fetch'd.

   First Knight. Nay, stay, my lord; 't may be he will
confess.

   Bara. Confess! what mean you, lords? who should
confess?

   Fern. Thou and thy Turk; 'twas you that slew my
son.   31

   Itha. Guilty, my lord, I confess. Your son and
Mathias were both contracted unto Abigail: he forged
a counterfeit challenge.

   Bara. Who carried that challenge?

   Itha. I carried it, I confess, but who writ it? marry,
even he that strangled Barnardine, poison'd the nuns
and his own daughter.

   Fern. Away with him! his sight is death to me.

   Bara. For what, you men of Malta? hear me speak.
She is a courtesan, and he a thief,   41
And he my bondman: let me have law;
For none of this can prejudice my life.

   Fern. Once more, away with him; you shall have
law.

   Bara. Devils, do your worst! I live in spite of you.
                                  [*Aside.*

As these have spoke, so be it to their souls!—
I hope the poison'd flowers will work anon.   [*Aside.*
        [*Exeunt* Officers *with* Barabas *and* Ithamore;
            Bellamira, *and* Pilia-Borza.

Enter Katharine.

Kath. Was my Mathias murder'd by the Jew?
Ferneze, 'twas thy son that murder'd him.
    Fern. Be patient, gentle madam; it was he;   50
He forged the daring challenge made them fight.
    Kath. Where is the Jew? where is that murderer?
    Fern. In prison, till the law has pass'd on him.

Re-enter First Officer.

First Off. My lord, the courtesan and her man **are**
    dead;
So is the Turk and Barabas the Jew.
    Fern. Dead?
    First Off. Dead, my lord, and here they bring his
    body.
    Bosco. This sudden death of his is very strange.

Re-enter Officers, *carrying* Barabas *as dead.*

    Fern. Wonder not at it, sir; the heavens are just;
Their deaths were like their lives, then think not of
    'em.   60
Since they are dead, let them be buried:
For the Jew's body, throw that o'er the walls,
To be a prey for vultures and wild beasts.
So, now away and fortify the town.
            [*Exeunt all, leaving* Barabas *on the floor.*
    Bara. [*rising*]* What, all alone? well fare, sleepy
    drink!
I'll be reveng'd on this accursed town;
For by my means Calymath shall enter in:
I'll help to slay their children and their wives,

* The scene is outside the city walls, over which Barabas
has been thrown.

To fire the churches, pull their houses down,
Take my goods too, and seize upon my lands.   70
I hope to see the governor a slave,
And, rowing in a galley, whipp'd to death.

Enter Calymath, Bassoes, *and* Turks.

Caly. Whom have we there? a spy?

Bara. Yes, my good lord, one that can spy a place
Where you may enter, and surprise the town:
My name is Barabas; I am a Jew.

Caly. Art thou that Jew whose goods we heard were
sold
For tribute-money?

Bara. The very same, my lord:
And since that time they have hir'd a slave, my man,
To accuse me of a thousand villanies: 81
I was imprison'd, but scap'd their hands.

Caly. Didst break prison?

Bara. No, no:
I drank of poppy and cold mandrake juice;
And being asleep, belike they thought me dead,
And threw me o'er the walls: so, or how else,
The Jew is here, and rests at your command.

Caly. 'Twas bravely done: but tell me, Barabas,
Canst thou, as thou reportest, make Malta ours?   90

Bara. Fear not, my lord, for here, against the sluice,
The rock is hollow, and of purpose digg'd,
To make a passage for the running streams
And common channels of the city.
Now, whilst you give assault unto the walls,
I'll lead five hundred soldiers through the vault,
And rise with them i' th' middle of the town,
Open the gates for you to enter in,
And by this means the city is your own.

Caly. If this be true, I'll make thee governor.   100

Bara. And if it be not true, then let me die.

Caly. Thou'st doom'd thyself. Assault it presently.
[*Exeunt.*

Alarums within. Enter Calymath, Bassoes, Turks, *and*
   Barabas; *with* Ferneze *and* Knights *prisoners.**

   Caly. Now vail your pride, you captive Christians,
And kneel for mercy to your conquering foe:
Now where's the hope you had of haughty Spain?
Ferneze, speak; had it not been much better
To have kept thy promise than be thus surpris'd?

   Fern. What should I say? we are captives, and must
     yield.

   Caly. Ay, villains, you must yield, and under
     Turkish yokes
Shall groaning bear the burthen of our ire: 110
And, Barabas, as erst we promis'd thee,
For thy desert we make thee governor.
Use them at thy discretion.

   Bara. Thanks, my lord.

   Fern. O fatal day, to fall into the hands
Of such a traitor and unhallowed Jew!
What greater misery could heaven inflict?

   Caly. 'Tis our command: and, Barabas, we give,
To guard thy person, these our Janizaries:
Entreat them well, as we have used thee.   120
And now, brave bassoes, come; we'll walk about
The ruin'd town, and see the wreck we made.
Farewell, brave Jew, farewell, great Barabas!

   Bara. May all good fortune follow Calymath!
              [*Exeunt* Calymath *and* Bassoes.
And now, as entrance to our safety,
To prison with the governor and these
Captains, his consorts and confederates.

   Fern. O villain! heaven will be reveng'd on thee.

   Bara. Away! no more; let him not trouble me.
         [*Exeunt* Turks *with* Ferneze *and* Knights.
Thus hast thou gotten, by thy policy,†   130

  * The scene is an open space in the city.   120 Entreat]
Treat   † The scene is the governor's residence in the
citadel.

No simple place, no small authority:
I now am governor of Malta; true,—
But Malta hates me, and in hating thee,
My life's in danger; and what boots it thee,
Poor Barabas, to be the governor,
Whenas thy life shall be at their command?
No, Barabas, this must be look'd into;
And, since by wrong thou gott'st authority,
Maintain it bravely by firm policy,
At least, unprofitably lose it not: 140
For he that liveth in authority,
And neither gets him friends nor fills his bags,
Lives like the ass that Æsop speaketh of,
That labours with a load of bread and wine,
And leaves it off to snap on thistle tops:
But Barabas will be more circumspect.
Begin betimes; Occasion's bald behind:
Slip not thine opportunity, for fear too late
Thou seek'st for much, but canst not compass it.
Within here!   150

Enter Ferneze, *with a* Guard.

Fern. My lord?
Bara. Ay, 'lord'; thus slaves will learn.
Now, governor,—stand by there, wait within,—
                                        [*Exeunt* Guard.
This is the reason that I sent for thee:
Thou seest thy life and Malta's happiness
Are at my arbitrament; and Barabas
At his discretion may dispose of both:
Now tell me, governor, and plainly too,
What think'st thou shall become of it and thee?
Fern. This, Barabas; since things are in thy power,
I see no reason but of Malta's wreck,   161
Nor hope of thee but extreme cruelty:
Nor fear I death, nor will I flatter thee.
Bara. Governor, good words; be not so furious.
'Tis not thy life which can avail me aught;

Yet you do live, and live for me you shall:
And as for Malta's ruin, think you not
'Twere slender policy for Barabas
To dispossess himself of such a place?
For sith, as once you said, within this isle,   170
In Malta here, that I have got my goods,
And in this city still have had success,
And now at length am grown your governor,
Yourselves shall see it shall not be forgot:
For, as a friend not known but in distress,
I'll rear up Malta, now remediless.

   Fern. Will Barabas recover Malta's loss?
Will Barabas be good to Christians?

   Bara. What wilt thou give me, governor, to procure
A dissolution of the slavish bands   180
Wherein the Turk hath yok'd your land and you?
What will you give me if I render you
The life of Calymath, surprise his men,
And in an out-house of the city shut
His soldiers, till I have consum'd 'em all with fire?
What will you give him that procureth this?

   Fern. Do but bring this to pass which thou pretend-
    est,
Deal truly with us as thou intimatest,
And I will send amongst the citizens,
And by my letters privately procure   190
Great sums of money for thy recompense:
Nay, more, do this, and live thou governor still.

   Bara. Nay, do thou this, Ferneze, and be free:
Governor, I enlarge thee; live with me,
Go walk about the city, see thy friends:
Tush, send not letters to 'em, go thyself,
And let me see what money thou canst make:
Here is my hand that I'll set Malta free;
And thus we cast it: to a solemn feast
I will invite young Selim Calymath,   200
Where be thou present, only to perform
One stratagem that I'll impart to thee,

Wherein no danger shall betide thy life,
And I will warrant Malta free for ever.

Fern. Here is my hand; believe me, Barabas,
I will be there, and do as thou desirest.
When is the time?

Bara. Governor, presently;
For Calymath, when he hath view'd the town,
Will take his leave, and sail toward Ottoman.   210

Fern. Then will I, Barabas, about this coin,
And bring it with me to thee in the evening.

Bara. Do so, but fail not; now farewell, Ferneze:—
      [*Exit* Ferneze.
And thus far roundly goes the business:
Thus, loving neither, will I live with both,
Making a profit of my policy;
And he from whom my most advantage comes,
Shall be my friend.
This is the life we Jews are us'd to lead;
And reason too, for Christians do the like.   220
Well, now about effecting this device;
First, to surprise great Selim's soldiers,
And then to make provision for the feast,
That at one instant all things may be done.
My policy detests prevention:
To what event my secret purpose drives,
I know; and they shall witness with their lives. [*Exeunt.*

Enter Calymath *and* Bassoes.*

Caly. Thus have we view'd the city, seen the sack,
And caus'd the ruins to be new-repair'd,
Which with our bombards' shot and basilisk   230
We rent in sunder at our entry:
And, now I see the situation,
And how secure this conquer'd island stands
Environ'd with the Mediterranean sea,
Strong countermin'd with other petty isles,
And, toward Calabria, back'd by Sicily,

* The scene is outside the city walls.

Where Syracusian Dionysius reign'd,
Two lofty turrets that command the town.
I wonder how it could be conquer'd thus.

Enter a Messenger.

Mess. From Barabas, Malta's governor, I bring
A message unto mighty Calymath: 241
Hearing his sovereign was bound for sea,
To sail to Turkey, to great Ottoman,
He humbly would entreat your majesty
To come and see his homely citadel,
And banquet with him ere thou leav'st the isle.

Caly. To banquet with him in his citadel?
I fear me, messenger, to feast my train
Within a town of war so lately pillag'd
Will be too costly and too troublesome: 250
Yet would I gladly visit Barabas,
For well has Barabas deserv'd of us.

Mess. Selim, for that, thus saith the governor,
That he hath in store a pearl so big,
So precious, and withal so orient,
As, be it valued but indifferently,
The price thereof will serve to entertain
Selim and all his soldiers for a month;
Therefore he humbly would entreat your highness
Not to depart till he has feasted you.   260

Caly. I cannot feast my men in Malta-walls,
Except he place his tables in the streets.

Mess. Know, Selim, that there is a monastery
Which standeth as an out-house to the town;
There will he banquet them, but thee at home,
With all thy bassoes and brave followers.

Caly. Well, tell the governor we grant his suit;
We'll in this summer evening feast with him.

Mess. I shall, my lord.   [*Exit.*

Caly. And now, bold bassoes, let us to our tents,   271
And meditate how we may grace us best
To solemnise our governor's great feast.   [*Exeunt.*

Enter Ferneze, Knights, *and* Martin Del Bosco.*

Fern. In this, my countrymen, be rul'd by me:
Have special care that no man sally forth
Till you shall hear a culverin discharg'd
By him that bears the linstock, kindled thus;
Then issue out and come to rescue me,
For happily I shall be in distress,
Or you released of this servitude.
 First Knight. Rather than thus to live as Turkish
  thralls,
               280
What will we not adventure?
 Fern. On, then; be gone.
 Knights. Farewell, grave governor.
  [*Exeunt, on one side,* Knights *and* Martin Del Bosco;
   on the other, Ferneze.

Enter, above, Barabas, *with a hammer, very busy;*
   and Carpenters.†

 Bara. How stand the cords? how hang these hinges
  fast?
Are all the cranes and pulleys sure?
 First Carp. All fast.
 Bara. Leave nothing loose, all levell'd to my mind.
Why now I see that you have art, indeed:
There, carpenters, divide that gold amongst you;
           [*Giving money.*
Go, swill in bowls of sack and muscadine; 290
Down to the cellar, taste of all my wines.
 First Carp. We shall, my lord, and thank you.
         [*Exeunt* Carpenters.
 Bara. And, if you like them, drink your fill and die:
For, so I live, perish may all the world!
Now, Selim Calymath, return me word
That thou wilt come, and I am satisfied.

 * The scene is a street.   † The scene is a hall in the
citadel.

Enter Messenger.

Now, sirrah; what, will he come?

  Mess. He will; and has commanded all his men
To come ashore, and march through Malta-streets,
That thou mayst feast them in thy citadel.   300

  Bara. Then now are all things as my wish would
    have 'em;
There wanteth nothing but the governor's pelf;
And see, he brings it.

Enter Ferneze.

                    Now governor, the sum?

  Fern. With free consent, a hundred thousand
    pounds.

  Bara. Pounds say'st thou, governor? well, since it is
    no more,
I'll satisfy myself with that; nay, keep it still,
For, if I keep not promise, trust not me:
And, governor, now partake my policy:
First, for his army, they are sent before,   310
Enter'd the monastery, and underneath
In several places are field-pieces pitch'd,
Bombards, whole barrels full of gunpowder,
That on the sudden shall dissever it,
And batter all the stones about their ears,
Whence none can possibly escape alive:
Now, as for Calymath and his consorts,
Here have I made a dainty gallery,
The floor whereof, this cable being cut,
Doth fall asunder, so that it doth sink   320
Into a deep pit past recovery.
Here, hold that knife, and, when thou seest he comes,
                      [*Throws down a knife.*
And with his bassoes shall be blithely set,
A warning-piece shall be shot off from the tower,
To give thee knowledge when to cut the cord,
And fire the house. Say, will not this be brave?

Fern. Oh, excellent! here, hold thee, Barabas;
I trust thy word; take what I promis'd thee.
Bara. No, governor, I'll satisfy thee first;
Thou shalt not live in doubt of anything.   330
Stand close, for here they come.   [*Ferneze retires.*
                              Why, is not this
A kingly kind of trade to purchase towns
By treachery, and sell 'em by deceit?
Now tell me, worldlings, underneath the sun
If greater falsehood ever has been done?

Enter Calymath *and* Bassoes.

Caly. Come, my companion-bassoes: see, I pray,
How busy Barabas is there above
To entertain us in his gallery:
Let us salute him. Save thee, Barabas!
Bara. Welcome, great Calymath!   340
Fern. How the slave jeers at him!   [*Aside.*
Bara. Will't please thee, mighty Selim Calymath,
To ascend our homely stairs?
Caly. Ay, Barabas. Come, bassoes, ascend.
Fern. [*coming forward*] Stay, Calymath;
For I will show thee greater courtesy
Than Barabas would have afforded thee.
Knight. [*within*] Sound a charge there!
         [*A charge sounded within:* Ferneze *cuts the cord; the*
         floor of the gallery gives way, and Barabas *falls*
         into a cauldron placed in a pit.

Enter Knights *and* Martin Del Boscoe.

Caly. How now! what means this?
Bara. Help, help me, Christians, help!   350
Fern. See, Calymath, this was devis'd for thee.
Caly. Treason, treason! bassoes, fly!
Fern. No, Selim, do not fly:
See his end first, and fly then if thou canst.
Bara. O, help me, Selim! help me, Christians!
Governor, why stand you all so pitiless?

Fern. Should I in pity of thy plaints or thee,
Accursed Barabas, base Jew, relent?
No, thus I'll see thy treachery repaid,
But wish thou hadst behav'd thee otherwise.   360
  Bara. You will not help me, then?
  Fern. No, villain, no.
  Bara. And, villains, know you cannot help me now.
Then, Barabas, breathe forth thy latest fate,
And in the fury of thy torments strive
To end thy life with resolution.
Know, governor, 'twas I that slew thy son,
I fram'd the challenge that did make them meet:
Know, Calymath, I aim'd thy overthrow,
And had I but escap'd this stratagem,   370
I would have brought confusion on you all,
Damn'd Christians, dogs, and Turkish infidels!
But now begins the extremity of heat
To pinch me with intolerable pangs:
Die, life! fly, soul! tongue, curse thy fill, and die!
                                          [Dies.
  Caly. Tell me, you Christians, what doth this portend?
  Fern. This train he laid to have entrapp'd thy life;
Now, Selim, note the unhallowed deeds of Jews:
Thus he determin'd to have handled thee,
But I have rather chose to save thy life.   380
  Caly. Was this the banquet he prepar'd for us?
Let's hence, lest further mischief be pretended.
  Fern. Nay, Selim, stay, for since we have thee here,
We will not let thee part so suddenly:
Besides, if we should let thee go, all's one,
For with thy galleys couldst thou not get hence,
Without fresh men to rig and furnish them.
  Caly. Tush, governor, take thou no care for that;
My men are all aboard,
And do attend my coming there by this.   390
  Fern. Why, heard'st thou not the trumpet sound a
    charge?

382 pretended] intended

Caly. Yes, what of that?

Fern. Why, then the house was fir'd,
Blown up, and all thy soldiers massacred.

Caly. Oh, monstrous treason!

Fern. A Jew's courtesy;
For he that did by treason work our fall,
By treason hath delivered thee to us:
Know, therefore, till thy father hath made good
The ruins done to Malta and to us,   400
Thou canst not part; for Malta shall be freed,
Or Selim ne'er return to Ottoman.

Caly. Nay, rather, Christians, let me go to Turkey,
In person there to meditate your peace:
To keep me here will naught advantage you.

Fern. Content thee, Calymath, here thou must stay,
And live in Malta prisoner; for come all the world
To rescue thee, so will we guard us now,
As sooner shall they drink the ocean dry,
Than conquer Malta, or endanger us.   410
So, march away; and let due praise be given
Neither to Fate nor Fortune, but to Heaven.

[*Exeunt.*

The troublesome

raigne and lamentable death of
Edward *the second, King of*
England: with the tragicall
fall of proud Mortimer:

As it was sundrie times publiquely acted
in the honourable citie of London, by the
right honourable the Earle of Pem-
brooke *his seruants.*

Written by Chri. Marlow *Gent.*

Imprinted at London for. *William* Iones,
dwelling neere Holbourne conduit at the
figne of the Gunne, 1594

Dramatis Personæ

King Edward the Second.
Prince Edward, *his son, afterwards* King Edward the Third.
Kent, *brother to* King Edward the Second.
Gaveston.
Archbishop of Canterbury.
Bishop of Coventry.
Bishop of Winchester.
Warwick.
Lancaster.
Pembroke.
Arundel.
Leicester.
Berkeley.
Mortimer *the elder.*
Mortimer *the younger, his nephew.*
Spencer *the elder.*
Spencer *the younger, his son.*
Baldock.

Beaumont.
Trussel.
Gurney.
Matrevis.
Lightborn.
Sir John of Hainault.
Levune.
Rice ap Howel.
Abbot.
Monks.
Herald.
Lords, Poor Men, James, Mower, Champion, Messengers, Soldiers, *and* Attendants.

Queen Isabella, *wife to* King Edward the Second.
Niece *to* King Edward the Second, *daughter to the* Duke of Glocester.
Ladies.

Edward the Second

Enter Gaveston, *reading a letter.**

Gav. My father is deceas'd. Come, Gaveston,
And share the kingdom with thy dearest friend.
Ah, words that make me surfeit with delight!
What greater bliss can hap to Gaveston
Than live and be the favourite of a king?
Sweet prince, I come; these, these thy amorous lines
Might have enforc'd me to have swum from France,
And, like Leander, gasp'd upon the sand,
So thou wouldst smile and take me in thy arms.
The sight of London to my exiled eyes   10
Is as Elysium to a new-come soul;
Not that I love the city or the men,
But that it harbours him I hold so dear,
The king, upon whose bosom let me die,
And with the world be still at enmity.
What need the arctic people love star-light,
To whom the sun shines both by day and night?
Farewell base stooping to the lordly peers,
My knee shall bow to none but to the king.
As for the multitude that are but sparks,   20
Rak'd up in embers of their poverty—
Tanti, I'll fawn first on the wind,
That glanceth at my lips, and flieth away.

Enter three Poor Men.

But how now, what are these?
    Poor Men. Such as desire your worship's service.
    Gav. What canst thou do?
    First P. Man. I can ride.
    Gav. But I have no horses. What art thou?
    Sec. P. Man. A traveller.
    *Gav. Let me see, thou wouldst do well   30

* The scene is a street in London.

To wait at my trencher, and tell me lies at dinner-
time,
And as I like your discoursing, I'll have you
And what art thou?

    Third P. Man. A soldier, that hath serv'd against
        the Scot.

    Gav. Why, there are hospitals for such as you;
I have no war, and therefore, sir, be gone.

    Third P. Man. Farewell, and perish by a soldier's
        hand,
That wouldst reward them with an hospital.

    Gav. Ay, ay, these words of his move me as much
As if a goose should play the porcupine,   40
And dart her plumes, thinking to pierce my breast.
But yet it is no pain to speak men fair;
I'll flatter these, and make them live in hope. [*Aside.*
You know that I came lately out of France,
And yet I have not view'd my lord the king;
If I speed well, I'll entertain you all.

    All. We thank your worship.

    Gav. I have some business, leave me to myself.

    All. We will wait here about the court.

    Gav. Do.
                        [*Exeunt* Poor Men.
              These are not men for me;   50
I must have wanton poets, pleasant wits,
Musicians, that with touching of a string
May draw the pliant king which way I please:
Music and poetry is his delight,
Therefore I'll have Italian masks by night,
Sweet speeches, comedies, and pleasing shows,
And in the day, when he shall walk abroad,
Like sylvan nymphs my pages shall be clad;
My men, like satyrs grazing on the lawns,
Shall with their goat-feet dance an antic hay;   60
Sometime a lovely boy, in Dian's shape,
With hair that gilds the water as it glides,
Crownets of pearl about his naked arms,

        60 hay] A rural dance

And in his sportful hands an olive-tree,
To hide those parts which men delight to see,
Shall bathe him in a spring, and there hard by,
One like Actæon peeping through the grove,
Shall by the angry goddess be transform'd,
And running in the likeness of an hart,
By yelping hounds pull'd down, and seem to die: 70
Such things as these best please his majesty,
My lord. Here comes the king and the nobles
From the parliament. I'll stand aside. [*Retires.*

Enter King Edward, Kent, Lancaster, *the elder* Mortimer, *the younger* Mortimer, Warwick, Pembroke, *and*
Attendants.

 K. Edw. Lancaster!
 Lan. My lord?
 Gav. That Earl of Lancaster do I abhor. [*Aside.*
 K. Edw. Will you not grant me this? In spite of
them
I'll have my will, and these two Mortimers,
That cross me thus, shall know I am displeas'd.
           [*Aside.*
 E. Mor. If you love us, my lord, hate Gaveston. 80
 Gav. That villain Mortimer! I'll be his death.
           [*Aside.*
 Y. Mor. Mine uncle here, this earl, and I myself
Were sworn to your father at his death,
That he should ne'er return into the realm:
And know, my lord, ere I will break my oath,
This sword of mine, that should offend your foes,
Shall sleep within the scabbard at thy need,
And underneath thy banners march who will,
For Mortimer will hang his armour up.
 Gav. Mort dieu! [*Aside.*
 K. Edw. Well, Mortimer, I'll make thee rue these
words: 91
Beseems it thee to contradict thy king?
Frown'st thou thereat, aspiring Lancaster?

The sword shall plane the furrows of thy brows,
And hew these knees that now are grown so stiff.
I will have Gaveston, and you shall know
What danger 'tis to stand against your king.

   Gav. Well done, Ned!   [*Aside.*

   Lan. My lord, why do you thus incense your peers,
That naturally would love and honour you   100
But for that base and obscure Gaveston?
Four earldoms have I besides Lancaster,
Derby, Salisbury, Lincoln, Leicester,
These will I sell to give my soldiers pay,
Ere Gaveston shall stay within the realm;
Therefore, if he be come, expel him straight.

   Kent. Barons and earls, your pride hath made me mute,
But now I'll speak, and to the proof, I hope.
I do remember in my father's days,
Lord Percy of the North, being highly mov'd,   110
Brav'd Mowberay in presence of the king;
For which, had not his highness lov'd him well,
He should have lost his head; but with his look
The undaunted spirit of Percy was appeas'd,
And Mowberay and he were reconcil'd:
Yet dare you brave the king unto his face.
Brother, revenge it, and let these their heads
Preach upon poles, for trespass of their tongues.

   War. Oh, our heads!

   K. Edw. Ay, yours; and therefore I would wish you grant.   120

   War. Bridle thy anger, gentle Mortimer.

   Y. Mor. I cannot, nor I will not; I must speak.
Cousin, our hands I hope shall fence our heads,
And strike off his that makes you threaten us.
Come, uncle, let us leave the brain-sick king,
And henceforth parley with our naked swords.

   E. Mor. Wiltshire hath men enough to save our heads.

   War. All Warwickshire will love him for my sake.

Lan. And northward Gaveston hath many friends.
Adieu, my lord; and either change your mind,   130
Or look to see the throne where you should sit
To float in blood, and at thy wanton head
The glozing head of thy base minion thrown.

    [*Exeunt all except* King Edward, Kent, Gaveston,
      and attendants.

   K. Edw. I cannot brook these haughty menaces:
Am I a king, and must be over-rul'd?
Brother, display my ensigns in the field;
I'll bandy with the barons and the earls,
And either die or live with Gaveston.

   Gav. I can no longer keep me from my lord.

                       [*Comes forward.*

   K. Edw. What, Gaveston! welcome! Kiss not my
     hand: 140
Embrace me, Gaveston, as I do thee:
Why shouldst thou kneel, knowest thou not who I am?
Thy friend, thyself, another Gaveston.
Not Hylas was more mourned of Hercules
Than thou hast been of me since thy exile.

   Gav. And since I went from hence, no soul in hell
Hath felt more torment than poor Gaveston.

   K. Edw. I know it. Brother, welcome home my
     friend.
Now let the treacherous Mortimers conspire,
And that high-minded Earl of Lancaster: 150
I have my wish, in that I joy thy sight,
And sooner shall the sea o'erwhelm my land
Than bear the ship that shall transport thee hence.
I here create thee Lord High Chamberlain,
Chief Secretary to the state and me,
Earl of Cornwall, King and Lord of Man.

   Gav. My lord, these titles far exceed my worth.

   Kent. Brother, the least of these may well suffice
For one of greater birth than Gaveston.

137 bandy] contend   150 high-minded] haughty
151 joy] enjoy

K. Edw. Cease, brother, for I cannot brook these
  words.   160
Thy worth, sweet friend, is far above my gifts,
Therefore, to equal it, receive my heart.
If for these dignities thou be envied,
I'll give thee more, for but to honour thee,
Is Edward pleas'd with kingly regiment.
Fear'st thou thy person? thou shalt have a guard:
Wantest thou gold? go to my treasury:
Would'st thou be lov'd and fear'd? receive my seal,
Save or condemn, and in our name command
What-so thy mind affects, or fancy likes. 170
  Gav. It shall suffice me to enjoy your love,
Which whiles I have, I think myself as great
As Cæsar riding in the Roman street,
With captive kings at his triumphant car.

    Enter the Bishop of Coventry.

  K. Edw. Whither goes my Lord of Coventry so fast?
  Bish. of Cov. To celebrate your father's exequies.
But is that wicked Gaveston return'd?
  K. Edw. Ay, priest, and lives to be reveng'd on thee,
That wert the only cause of his exile. 179
  Gav. 'Tis true; and but for reverence of these robes,
Thou shouldst not plod one foot beyond this place.
  Bish. of Cov. I did no more than I was bound to do:
And, Gaveston, unless thou be reclaim'd,
As then I did incense the parliament,
So will I now, and thou shalt back to France.
  Gav. Saving your reverence, you must pardon me.
  K. Edw. Throw off his golden mitre, rend his stole,
And in the channel christen him anew.
  Kent. Ah, brother, lay not violent hands on him,
For he'll complain unto the see of Rome. 190
  Gav. Let him complain unto the see of hell,
I'll be reveng'd on him for my exile.
  K. Edw. No, spare his life, but seize upon his goods:
  165 regiment] rule 188 channel] gutter

Be thou lord bishop, and receive his rents,
And make him serve thee as thy chaplain:
I give him thee; here, use him as thou wilt.

 Gav. He shall to prison, and there die in bolts.

 K. Edw. Ay, to the Tower, the Fleet, or where thou
  wilt.

 Bish. of Cov. For this offence be thou accurs'd of
  God!

 K. Edw. Who's there? Convey this priest to the
  Tower.   200

 Bish. of Cov. True, true.

 K. Edw. But in the meantime, Gaveston, away,
And take possession of his house and goods.
Come, follow me, and thou shalt have my guard
To see it done, and bring thee safe again.

 Gav. What should a priest do with so fair a house?
A prison may beseem his holiness.   [*Exeunt.*

Enter, on one side, the elder Mortimer, *and the younger*
 Mortimer; *on the other,* Warwick, *and* Lancaster.*

 War. 'Tis true, the bishop is in the Tower,
And goods and body given to Gaveston.

 Lan. What, will they tyrannise upon the church?
Ah, wicked king! accursed Gaveston!   211
This ground, which is corrupted with their steps,
Shall be their timeless sepulchre or mine.

 Y. Mor. Well, let that peevish Frenchman guard
  him sure;
Unless his breast be sword-proof he shall die.

 E. Mor. How now! why droops the Earl of Lancaster?

 Y. Mor. Wherefore is Guy of Warwick discontent?

 Lan. That villain Gaveston is made an earl.

 E. Mor. An earl!

 War. Ay, and besides, Lord Chamberlain of the
  realm,   220
And Secretary too, and Lord of Man.

 * The scene is at Westminster. 213 timeless] untimely
 478   L

E. Mor. We may not, nor we will not suffer this.

Y. Mor. Why post we not from hence to levy men?

Lan. 'My Lord of Cornwall' now at every word;
And happy is the man whom he vouchsafes,
For vailing of his bonnet, one good look.
Thus, arm in arm, the king and he doth march:
Nay more, the guard upon his lordship waits,
And all the court begins to flatter him.   229

War. Thus leaning on the shoulder of the king,
He nods and scorns and smiles at those that pass.

E. Mor. Doth no man take exceptions at the slave?

Lan. All stomach him, but none dare speak a word.

Y. Mor. Ah, that bewrays their baseness, Lancaster!
Were all the earls and barons of my mind,
We'd hale him from the bosom of the king,
And at the court-gate hang the peasant up,
Who, swoln with venom of ambitious pride,
Will be the ruin of the realm and us.   239

War. Here comes my Lord of Canterbury's grace.

Lan. His countenance bewrays he is displeas'd.

Enter the Archbishop of Canterbury, *and an* Attendant.

Archb. of Cant. First were his sacred garments rent
    and torn,
Then laid they violent hands upon him next;
Himself imprisoned, and his goods asseiz'd:
This certify the Pope: away, take horse.

                      [*Exit* Attendant.

Lan. My lord, will you take arms against the king?

Archb. of Cant. What need I? God himself is up in
    arms,
When violence is offered to the church.

Y. Mor. Then will you join with us that be his peers,
To banish or behead that Gaveston?   250

Archb. of Cant. What else, my lords? for it concerns
    me near;
The bishopric of Coventry is his.

233 stomach] feel resentment   245 certify] inform

Enter Queen Isabella.

Y. Mor. Madam, whither walks your majesty so fast?

Q. Isab. Unto the forest, gentle Mortimer,
To live in grief and baleful discontent;
For now my lord the king regards me not,
But dotes upon the love of Gaveston.
He claps his cheeks, and hangs about his neck,
Smiles in his face, and whispers in his ears,
And when I come, he frowns, as who should say, 260
'Go whither thou wilt, seeing I have Gaveston.'

E. Mor. Is it not strange that he is thus bewitch'd?

Y. Mor. Madam, return unto the court again:
That sly inveigling Frenchman we'll exile,
Or lose our lives: and yet, ere that day come,
The king shall lose his crown; for we have power,
And courage too, to be reveng'd at full.

Archb. of Cant. But yet lift not your swords against the king.

Lan. No; but we will lift Gaveston from hence.

War. And war must be the means, or he'll stay still.

Q. Isab. Then let him stay; for rather than my lord
Shall be oppress'd with civil mutinies, 272
I will endure a melancholy life,
And let him frolic with his minion.

Archb. of Cant. My lords, to ease all this, but hear me speak:
We and the rest that are his counsellors,
Will meet, and with a general consent
Confirm his banishment with our hands and seals.

Lan. What we confirm the king will frustrate. 279

Y. Mor. Then may we lawfully revolt from him.

War. But say, my lord, where shall this meeting be?

Archb. of Cant. At the New Temple.

Y. Mor. Content.
And in the meantime, I'll entreat you all
To cross to Lambeth, and there stay with me.

Lan. Come then, let's away.

Y. Mor. Madam, farewell.

Q. Isab. Farewell, sweet Mortimer, and, for my
    sake,
Forbear to levy arms against the king.

Y. Mor. Ay, if words will serve; if not, I must.
                                   [*Exeunt.*

Enter Gaveston *and* Kent.*

Gav. Edmund, the mighty prince of Lancaster, 291
That hath more earldoms than an ass can bear,
And both the Mortimers, two goodly men,
With Guy of Warwick, that redoubted knight,
Are gone towards Lambeth: there let them remain.
                                   [*Exeunt.*

Enter Lancaster, Warwick, Pembroke, *the elder*
Mortimer, *the younger* Mortimer, *the* Archbishop of
    Canterbury, *and* Attendants.†

Lan. Here is the form of Gaveston's exile:
May it please your lordship to subscribe your name.

Archb. of Cant. Give me the paper.
       [*He subscribes, as the others do after him.*

Lan. Quick, quick, my lord; I long to write my
    name.   299

War. But I long more to see him banish'd hence.

Y. Mor. The name of Mortimer shall fright the king,
Unless he be declin'd from that base peasant.

Enter King Edward, Gaveston, *and* Kent.‡

K. Edw. What, are you mov'd that Gaveston sits
    here?
It is our pleasure; we will have it so.

Lan. Your grace doth well to place him by your
    side,

* The scene is a part of the King's palace at Westminster.
† The scene is the younger Mortimer's house at Lambeth.
‡ The scene is in the King's palace.

For nowhere else the new earl is so safe.

    E. Mor. What man of noble birth can brook this sight?

Quam male conveniunt!

See what a scornful look the peasant casts!

    Pem. Can kingly lions fawn on creeping ants? 310

    War. Ignoble vassal that, like Phaeton,

Aspir'st unto the guidance of the sun!

    Y. Mor. Their downfall is at hand, their forces down:

We will not thus be fac'd and over-peer'd.

    K. Edw. Lay hands on that traitor Mortimer!

    E. Mor. Lay hands on that traitor Gaveston!

    Kent. Is this the duty that you owe your king?

    War. We know our duties; let him know his peers.

    K. Edw. Whither will you bear him? stay, or ye shall die.

    E. Mor. We are no traitors; therefore threaten not.

    Gav. No, threaten not, my lord, but pay them home.   321

Were I a king—

    Y. Mor. Thou, villain! wherefore talks thou of a king,

That hardly art a gentleman by birth?

    K. Edw. Were he a peasant, being my minion,

I'll make the proudest of you stoop to him.

    Lan. My lord, you may not thus disparage us.

Away, I say, with hateful Gaveston!

    E. Mor. And with the Earl of Kent that favours him.   [*Attendants remove* Gaveston *and* Kent.

    K. Edw. Nay, then lay violent hands upon your king: 330

Here, Mortimer, sit thou in Edward's throne;

Warwick and Lancaster, wear you my crown.

Was ever king thus over-rul'd as I?

    Lan. Learn then to rule us better, and the realm.

308 *Quam . . . conveniunt*] How badly they suit each other!

Y. Mor. What we have done, our heart-blood shall
    maintain.

War. Think you that we can brook this upstart
    pride?

K. Edw. Anger and wrathful fury stops my speech.

Archb. of Cant. Why are you mov'd? be patient, my
    lord,
And see what we your counsellors have done.

Y. Mor. My lords, now let us all be resolute,   340
And either have our wills, or lose our lives.

K. Edw. Meet you for this, proud over-daring
    peers?
Ere my sweet Gaveston shall part from me,
This isle shall fleet upon the ocean,
And wander to the unfrequented Ind.

Archb. of Cant. You know that I am legate to the
    Pope;
On your allegiance to the see of Rome,
Subscribe, as we have done, to his exile.

Y. Mor. Curse him, if he refuse; and then may we
Depose him and elect another king.   350

K. Edw. Ay, there it goes! but yet I will not yield:
Curse me, depose me, do the worst you can.

Lan. Then linger not, my lord, but do it straight.

Archb. of Cant. Remember how the bishop was
    abus'd:
Either banish him that was the cause thereof,
Or I will presently discharge these lords
Of duty and allegiance due to thee.

K. Edw. It boots me not to threat; I must speak
    fair:
The legate of the Pope will be obey'd.   [*Aside.*
My lord, you shall be Chancellor of the realm;   360
Thou, Lancaster, High-Admiral of our fleet;
Young Mortimer and his uncle shall be earls;
And you, Lord Warwick, President of the North;
And thou of Wales. If this content you not,

344 fleet] float

Make several kingdoms of this monarchy,
And share it equally amongst you all,
So I may have some nook or corner left,
To frolic with my dearest Gaveston.

Archb. of Cant. Nothing shall alter us; we are
resolv'd.

Lan. Come, come, subscribe. 370

Y. Mor. Why should you love him, whom the
world hates so?

K. Edw. Because he loves me more than all the
world.
Ah, none but rude and savage-minded men
Would seek the ruin of my Gaveston;
You that be noble-born should pity him. [off:

War. You that are princely-born should shake him
For shame, subscribe, and let the lown depart.

E. Mor. Urge him, my lord.

Archb. of Cant. Are you content to banish him the
realm?

K. Edw. I see I must, and therefore am content. 380
Instead of ink I'll write it with my tears. [*Subscribes.*

Y. Mor. The king is love-sick for his minion.

K. Edw. 'Tis done; and now, accursed hand,
fall off!

Lan. Give it me: I'll have it published in the streets.

Y. Mor. I'll see him presently dispatched away.

Archb. of Cant. Now is my heart at ease.

War. And so is mine.

Pem. This will be good news to the common sort.

E. Mor. Be it or no, he shall not linger here.

[*Exeunt all except* King Edward.

K. Edw. How fast they run to banish him I love!
They would not stir, were it to do me good. 391
Why should a king be subject to a priest?
Proud Rome, that hatchest such imperial grooms,
For these thy superstitious taper-lights,
Wherewith thy antichristian churches blaze.

377 lown] peasant

I'll fire thy crazed buildings, and enforce
The papal towers to kiss the lowly ground,
With slaughtered priests make Tiber's channel swell,
And banks rais'd higher with their sepulchres!
As for the peers that back the clergy thus,   400
If I be king, not one of them shall live.

Re-enter Gaveston.

Gav. My lord, I hear it whispered everywhere,
That I am banish'd, and must fly the land.

K. Edw. 'Tis true, sweet Gaveston: Oh, were it
    false!
The legate of the Pope will have it so,
And thou must hence, or I shall be depos'd.
But I will reign to be reveng'd of them,
And therefore, sweet friend, take it patiently.
Live where thou wilt, I'll send thee gold enough;
And long thou shalt not stay, or if thou dost,   410
I'll come to thee; my love shall ne'er decline.

Gav. Is all my hope turn'd to this hell of grief?

K. Edw. Rend not my heart with thy too-piercing
    words:
Thou from this land, I from myself am banish'd.

Gav. To go from hence grieves not poor Gaveston,
But to forsake you, in whose gracious looks
The blessedness of Gaveston remains;
For nowhere else seeks he felicity.

K. Edw. And only this torments my wretched soul,
That, whether I will or no, thou must depart.   420
Be governor of Ireland in my stead,
And there abide till fortune call thee home.
Here take my picture, and let me wear thine:
                              [*They exchange pictures.*
Oh, might I keep thee here as I do this,
Happy were I but now most miserable.

Gav. 'Tis something to be pitied of a king.

K. Edw. Thou shalt not hence; I'll hide thee,
    Gaveston.

Gav. I shall be found, and then 'twill grieve me
  more.

K. Edw. Kind words and mutual talk makes our
  grief greater:

Therefore, with dumb embracement, let us part. 430

Stay, Gaveston, I cannot leave thee thus.

Gav. For every look, my lord drops down a tear:

Seeing I must go, do not renew my sorrow.

K. Edw. The time is little that thou hast to stay,

And, therefore, give me leave to look my fill:

But come, sweet friend, I'll bear thee on thy way.

Gav. The peers will frown.

K. Edw. I pass not for their anger. Come, let's go;

Oh, that we might as well return as go.

Enter Queen Isabella.

Q. Isab. Whither goes my lord? 440

K. Edw. Fawn not on me, French strumpet; get
  thee gone!

Q. Isab. On whom but on my husband should I
  fawn?

Gav. On Mortimer, with whom, ungentle queen,—

I say no more—judge you the rest, my lord.

Q. Isab. In saying this, thou wrong'st me, Gaveston;

Is't not enough that thou corrupts my lord,

And art a bawd to his affections,

But thou must call mine honour thus in question?

Gav. I mean not so; your grace must pardon me.

K. Edw. Thou art too familiar with that Mortimer,

And by thy means is Gaveston exil'd; 451

But I would wish thee reconcile the lords,

Or thou shalt ne'er be reconcil'd to me.

Q. Isab. Your highness knows, it lies not in my
  power.

K. Edw. Away, then! touch me not: come,
  Gaveston. [lord.

Q. Isab. Villain, 'tis thou that robb'st me of my

438 pass] care

Gav. Madam, 'tis you that rob me of my lord.

K. Edw. Speak not unto her; let her droop and
    pine.

Q. Isab. Wherein, my lord, have I deserv'd these
    words?

Witness the tears that Isabella sheds,   460
Witness this heart, that sighing for thee breaks,
How dear my lord is to poor Isabel.

K. Edw. And witness heaven how dear thou art to
    me:

There weep; for till my Gaveston be repeal'd,
Assure thyself thou com'st not in my sight.

             [Exeunt King Edward *and* Gaveston.

Q. Isab. O miserable and distressed queen!
Would, when I left sweet France and was embark'd,
That charming Circe, walking on the waves,
Had chang'd my shape, or at the marriage-day
The cup of Hymen had been full of poison,   470
Or with those arms that twin'd about my neck
I had been stifled, and not lived to see
The king my lord thus to abandon me!
Like frantic Juno will I fill the earth
With ghastly murmur of my sighs and cries;
For never doted Jove on Ganymede
So much as he on cursed Gaveston:
But that will more exasperate his wrath;
I must entreat him, I must speak him fair,
And be a means to call home Gaveston: 480
And yet he'll ever dote on Gaveston,
And so am I for ever miserable.

Re-enter Lancaster, Warwick, Pembroke, *the elder*
    Mortimer, *and the younger* Mortimer.

Lan. Look, where the sister of the king of France
Sits wringing of her hands, and beats her breast!

War. The king, I fear, hath ill-entreated her.

Pem. Hard is the heart that injures such a saint.

Y. Mor. I know 'tis 'long of Gaveston she weeps.

E. Mor. Why, he is gone.

Y. Mor. Madam, how fares your grace?

Q. Isab. Ah, Mortimer! now breaks the king's hate forth,   490
And he confesseth that he loves me not.   [him.

Y. Mor. Cry quittance, madam, then, and love not

Q. Isab. No, rather will I die a thousand deaths,
And yet I love in vain; he'll ne'er love me.

Lan. Fear ye not, madam; now his minion's gone,
His wanton humour will be quickly left.

Q. Isab. Oh never, Lancaster! I am enjoin'd
To sue unto you all for his repeal:
This wills my lord, and this must I perform,
Or else be banish'd from his highness' presence.   500

Lan. For his repeal? Madam, he comes not back,
Unless the sea cast up his shipwrack body.

War. And to behold so sweet a sight as that,
There's none here but would run his horse to death.

Y. Mor. But, madam, would you have us call him home?

Q. Isab. Ay, Mortimer, for, till he be restor'd,
The angry king hath banished me the court;
And, therefore, as thou lovest and tender'st me,
Be thou my advocate unto these peers.

Y. Mor. What, would ye have me plead for Gaveston?   510

E. Mor. Plead for him he that will, I am resolv'd.

Lan. And so am I, my lord: dissuade the queen.

Q. Isab. O Lancaster, let him dissuade the king,
For 'tis against my will he should return.

War. Then speak not for him, let the peasant go.

Q. Isab. 'Tis for myself I speak, and not for him.

Pem. No speaking will prevail, and therefore cease.

Y. Mor. Fair queen, forbear to angle for the fish
Which, being caught, strikes him that takes it dead;
I mean that vile torpedo, Gaveston,   520

---

520 torpedo] 'A fish that (as soon as ever he is struck) so
benumbs the angler that he dies.' (H. Vaughan.)

That now, I hope, floats on the Irish seas.

  Q. Isab. Sweet Mortimer, sit down by me a while,
And I will tell thee reasons of such weight
As thou wilt soon subscribe to his repeal.

  Y. Mor. It is impossible; but speak your mind.

  Q. Isab. Then thus, but none shall hear it but
    ourselves.

                     [*Talks to* Y. Mor. *apart.*

  Lan. My lords, albeit the queen win Mortimer,
Will you be resolute and hold with me?

  E. Mor. Not I, against my nephew.   529

  Pem. Fear not, the queen's words cannot alter him.

  War. No? do but mark how earnestly she pleads!

  Lan. And see how coldly his looks make denial!

  War. She smiles; now for my life his mind is
    chang'd!

  Lan. I'll rather lose his friendship, I, than grant.

  Y. Mor. Well, of necessity it must be so.
My lords, that I abhor base Gaveston,
I hope your honours make no question,
And therefore, though I plead for his repeal,
'Tis not for his sake, but for our avail:
Nay, for the realm's behoof, and for the king's.   540

  Lan. Fie, Mortimer, dishonour not thyself!
Can this be true, 'twas good to banish him?
And is this true, to call him home again?
Such reasons make white black, and dark night day.

  Y. Mor. My lord of Lancaster, mark the respect.

  Lan. In no respect can contraries be true.

  Q. Isab. Yet, good my lord, hear what he can
    allege.

  War. All that he speaks is nothing; we are resolv'd.

  Y. Mor. Do you not wish that Gaveston were dead?

  Pem. I would he were!   550

  Y. Mor. Why then, my lord, give me but leave to
    speak.

  E. Mor. But, nephew, do not play the sophister.

545 respect] consideration

Y. Mor. This which I urge is of a burning zeal
To mend the king, and do our country good.
Know you not Gaveston hath store of gold,
Which may in Ireland purchase him such friends
As he will front the mightiest of us all?
And whereas he shall live and be belov'd,
'Tis hard for us to work his overthrow.

   War. Mark you but that, my lord of Lancaster. 560

   Y. Mor. But were he here, detested as he is,
How easily might some base slave be suborn'd
To greet his lordship with a poniard,
And none so much as blame the murtherer,
But rather praise him for that brave attempt,
And in the chronicle enrol his name
For purging of the realm of such a plague!

   Pem. He saith true.

   Lan. Ay, but how chance this was not done before?

   Y. Mor. Because, my lords, it was not thought
      upon: 570
Nay, more, when he shall know it lies in us
To banish him, and then to call him home,
'Twill make him vail the top flag of his pride,
And fear to offend the meanest nobleman.

   E. Mor. But how if he do not, nephew?

   Y. Mor. Then may we with some colour rise in
      arms;
For howsoever we have borne it out,
'Tis treason to be up against the king;
So shall we have the people of our side,
Which for his father's sake lean to the king, 580
But cannot brook a night-grown mushroom,
Such a one as my Lord of Cornwall is,
Should bear us down of the nobility,
And when the commons and the nobles join,
'Tis not the king can buckler Gaveston.
We'll pull him from the strongest hold he hath.
My lords, if to perform this I be slack,

     573 vail] lower

Think me as base a groom as Gaveston.

   Lan. On that condition Lancaster will grant.

   War. And so will Pembroke and I.   590

   E. Mor. And I.

   Y. Mor. In this I count me highly gratified,
And Mortimer will rest at your command.

   Q. Isab. And when this favour Isabel forgets,
Then let her live abandon'd and forlorn.—
But see, in happy time, my lord the king,
Having brought the Earl of Cornwall on his way,
Is new return'd: this news will glad him much,
Yet not so much as me. I love him more
Than he can Gaveston; would he lov'd me   600
But half so much, then were I treble-blest.

     Re-enter King Edward, *mourning.*

   K. Edw. He's gone, and for his absence thus I
     mourn.
Did never sorrow go so near my heart
As doth the want of my sweet Gaveston;
And could my crown's revenue bring him back,
I would freely give it to his enemies,
And think I gain'd, having bought so dear a friend.

   Q. Isab. Hark, how he harps upon his minion.

   K. Edw. My heart is as an anvil unto sorrow,
Which beats upon it like the Cyclops' hammers,   610
And with the noise turns up my giddy brain,
And makes me frantic for my Gaveston:
Ah, had some bloodless Fury rose from hell,
And with my kingly sceptre struck me dead,
When I was forc'd to leave my Gaveston!

   Lan. *Diablo*, what passions call you these?

   Q. Isab. My gracious lord, I come to bring you
     news.

   K. Edw. That you have parled with your Mortimer.

   Q. Isab. That Gaveston, my lord, shall be repeal'd.

   K. Edw. Repeal'd! the news is too sweet to be true.

   Q. Isab. But will you love me, if you find it so?

K. Edw. If it be so, what will not Edward do?

Q. Isab. For Gaveston, but not for Isabel.   623

K. Edw. For thee, fair queen, if thou lovest Gaveston:
I'll hang a golden tongue about thy neck,
Seeing thou hast pleaded with so good success.

Q. Isab. No other jewels hang about my neck
Than these, my lord; nor let me have more wealth
Than I may fetch from this rich treasury:
Oh, how a kiss revives poor Isabel!   630

K. Edw. Once more receive my hand, and let this be
A second marriage 'twixt thyself and me.

Q. Isab. And may it prove more happy than the first!
My gentle lord, bespeak these nobles fair,
That wait attendance for a gracious look,
And on their knees salute your majesty.

K. Edw. Courageous Lancaster, embrace thy king,
And, as gross vapours perish by the sun,
Even so let hatred with thy sovereign's smile:
Live thou with me as my companion.   640

Lan. This salutation overjoys my heart.

K. Edw. Warwick shall be my chiefest counsellor:
These silver hairs will more adorn my court
Than gaudy silks or rich embroidery.
Chide me, sweet Warwick, if I go astray.

War. Slay me, my lord, when I offend your grace.

K. Edw. In solemn triumphs and in public shows
Pembroke shall bear the sword before the king.

Pem. And with this sword Pembroke will fight for you.

K. Edw. But wherefore walks young Mortimer aside?   650
Be thou commander of our royal fleet;
Or, if that lofty office like thee not,
I make thee here Lord Marshal of the realm.

Y. Mor. My lord, I'll marshal so your enemies,

As England shall be quiet, and you safe.

   K. Edw. And as for you, Lord Mortimer of Chirk,
Whose great achievements in our foreign war
Deserve no common place nor mean reward,
Be you the general of the levied troops
That now are ready to assail the Scots.   660

   E. Mor. In this your grace hath highly honoured me,
For with my nature war doth best agree.

   Q. Isab. Now is the king of England rich and
     strong,
Having the love of his renowned peers.

   K. Edw. Ay, Isabel, ne'er was my heart so light.
Clerk of the crown, direct our warrant forth:
For Gaveston to Ireland:

Enter Beaumont *with warrant.*

                Beaumont, fly
As fast as Iris or Jove's Mercury.

   Beau. It shall be done, my gracious lord.   [*Exit.*

   K. Edw. Lord Mortimer, we leave you to your
     charge.   670
Now let us in, and feast it royally.
Against our friend the Earl of Cornwall comes
We'll have a general tilt and tournament,
And then his marriage shall be solemnized;
For wot you not that I have made him sure
Unto our cousin, the Earl of Gloucester's heir?

   Lan. Such news we hear, my lord.

   K. Edw. That day, if not for him, yet for my sake,
Who in the triumph will be challenger,
Spare for no cost; we will requite your love.   680

   War. In this or aught your highness shall command
     us.

   K. Edw. Thanks, gentle Warwick. Come let's in
     and revel.   [*Exeunt all except the elder* Mortimer
                and the younger Mortimer.

   E. Mor. Nephew, I must to Scotland; thou stayest
     here.

Leave now to oppose thyself against the king:
Thou seest by nature he is mild and calm,
And, seeing his mind so dotes on Gaveston,
Let him without controlment have his will.
The mightiest kings have had their minions;
Great Alexander lov'd Hephæstion,
The conquering Hercules for Hylas wept,   690
And for Patroclus stern Achilles droop'd:
And not kings only, but the wisest men;
The Roman Tully loved Octavius,
Grave Socrates wild Alcibiades:
Then let his grace, whose youth is flexible,
And promiseth as much as we can wish,
Freely enjoy that vain light-headed earl,
For riper years will wean him from such toys.

  Y. Mor. Uncle, his wanton humour grieves not me;
But this I scorn, that one so basely born   700
Should by his sovereign's favour grow so pert,
And riot it with the treasure of the realm.
While soldiers mutiny for want of pay.
He wears a lord's revenue on his back,
And Midas-like, he jets it in the court,
With base outlandish cullions at his heels,
Whose proud fantastic liveries make such show
As if that Proteus, god of shapes, appear'd.
I have not seen a dapper Jack so brisk;
He wears a short Italian hooded cloak,   710
Larded with pearl, and in his Tuscan cap
A jewel of more value than the crown.
While others walk below, the king and he
From out a window laugh at such as we,
And flout our train, and jest at our attire.
Uncle, 'tis this that makes me impatient.

  E. Mor. But, nephew, now you see the king is chang'd.

  Y. Mor. Then so am I, and live to do him service:
But whiles I have a sword, a hand, a heart,

    705 jets it] struts   **706** cullions] scoundrels

I will not yield to any such upstart. 720
You know my mind; come, uncle, let's away.

[*Exeunt.*

Enter the younger Spencer *and* Baldock.*

Bald. Spencer,
Seeing that our lord th' Earl of Gloucester's dead,
Which of the nobles dost thou mean to serve?

Y. Spen. Not Mortimer, nor any of his side,
Because the king and he are enemies.
Baldock, learn this of me: a factious lord
Shall hardly do himself good, much less us;
But he that hath the favour of a king
May with one word advance us while we live. 730
The liberal Earl of Cornwall is the man
On whose good fortune Spencer's hope depends.

Bald. What, mean you then to be his follower?

Y. Spen. No, his companion; for he loves me well,
And would have once preferr'd me to the king.

Bald. But he is banish'd; there's small hope of him.

Y. Spen. Ay, for a while; but, Baldock, mark the end.
A friend of mine told me in secrecy
That he's repeal'd and sent for back again;
And even now a post came from the court 740
With letters to our lady from the king,
And as she read, she smil'd; which makes me think
It is about her lover Gaveston.

Bald. 'Tis like enough; for since he was exil'd,
She neither walks abroad nor comes in sight.
But I had thought the match had been broke off,
And that his banishment had chang'd her mind.

Y. Spen. Our lady's first love is not wavering;
My life for thine she will have Gaveston.

Bald. Then hope I by her means to be preferr'd,
Having read unto her since she was a child. 751

Y. Spen. Then, Baldock, you must cast the scholar off,
And learn to court it like a gentleman.

* The scene is a hall in the Earl of Gloucester's house.

'Tis not a black coat and a little band,
A velvet-cap'd cloak, fac'd before with serge,
And smelling to a nosegay all the day,
Or holding of a napkin in your hand,
Or saying a long grace at a table's end,
Or making low legs to a nobleman,
Or looking downward, with your eye-lids close,   760
And saying, 'Truly, an't may please your honour,'
Can get you any favour with great men:
You must be proud, bold, pleasant, resolute,
And now and then stab, as occasion serves.

    Bald. Spencer, thou know'st I hate such formal toys,
And use them but of mere hypocrisy.
Mine old lord, whiles he liv'd, was so precise
That he would take exceptions at my buttons,
And, being like pins' heads, blame me for the bigness;
Which made me curate-like in mine attire,   770
Though inwardly licentious enough,
And apt for any kind of villany.
I am none of these common pedants, I,
That cannot speak without *propterea quod.*

    Y. Spen. But one of those that saith *quandoquidem,*
And hath a special gift to form a verb.

    Bald. Leave off this jesting; here my lady comes.

                Enter King Edward's Niece.

    Niece. The grief for his exile was not so much,
As is the joy of his returning home.
This letter came from my sweet Gaveston: 780
What need'st thou, love, thus to excuse thyself?
I know thou couldst not come and visit me.   [*Reads.*
I will not long be from thee, though I die:
This argues the entire love of my lord;   [*Reads.*
When I forsake thee, death seize on my heart!
But stay thee here where Gaveston shall sleep.
                [*Puts the letter into her bosom.*

   774, 775 *propterea ... quandoquidem*] technical terms of
rhetoric

Now to the letter of my lord the king:
He wills me to repair unto the court,
And meet my Gaveston: why do I stay,
Seeing that he talks thus of my marriage day? 790
Who's there? Baldock!
See that my coach be ready; I must hence.

Bald. It shall be done, madam.

Niece. And meet me at the park-pale presently.

[*Exit* Baldock.

Spencer, stay you, and bear me company,
For I have joyful news to tell thee of;
My lord of Cornwall is a-coming over,
And will be at the court as soon as we.

Y. Spen. I knew the king would have him home
again.

Niece. If all things sort out, as I hope they will, 800
Thy service, Spencer, shall be thought upon.

Y. Spen. I humbly thank your ladyship.

Niece. Come, lead the way; I long till I am there.

[*Exeunt.*

Enter King Edward, Queen Isabella, Kent, Lancaster, *the younger* Mortimer, Warwick, Pembroke, *and* Attendants.*

K. Edw. The wind is good; I wonder why he stays;
I fear me he is wreck'd upon the sea.

Q. Isab. Look, Lancaster, how passionate he is,
And still his mind runs on his minion.

Lan. My lord,—

K. Edw. How now! what news? is Gaveston
arriv'd?

Y. Mor. Nothing but Gaveston! what means your
grace? 810
You have matters of more weight to think upon;
The King of France sets foot in Normandy.

K. Edw. A trifle! we'll expel him when we please.

800 sort] turn   * The scene is at Tynemouth.

But tell me, Mortimer, what's thy device
Against the stately triumph we decreed?

Y. Mor. A homely one, my lord, not worth the
telling.

K. Edw. Prithee, let me know it.

Y. Mor. But, seeing you are so desirous, thus it is:
A lofty cedar tree, fair flourishing,
On whose top branches kingly eagles perch,   820
And by the bark a canker creeps me up,
And gets unto the highest bough of all:
The motto, *Æque tandem.*

K. Edw. And what is yours, my Lord of Lancaster?

Lan. My lord, mine's more obscure than Mortimer's:
Pliny reports, there is a flying-fish
Which all the other fishes deadly hate,
And therefore, being pursued, it takes the air:
No sooner is it up, but there's a fowl
That seizeth it: this fish, my lord, I bear;   830
The motto this: *Undique mors est.*

Kent. Proud Mortimer! ungentle Lancaster!
Is this the love you bear your sovereign?
Is this the fruit your reconcilement bears?
Can you in words make show of amity,
And in your shields display your rancorous minds?
What call you this but private libelling
Against the Earl of Cornwall and my brother?

Q. Isab. Sweet husband, be content; they all love
you.

K. Edw. They love me not that hate my Gaveston.
I am that cedar; shake me not too much;   841
And you the eagles; soar ye ne'er so high,
I have the jesses that will pull you down;
And *Æque tandem* shall that canker cry
Unto the proudest peer of Britainy.

823 *Æque tandem*] Equally at last
831 *Undique mors est*] Death is everywhere
843 jesses] The straps round a hawk's legs, with rings
attached, to which the falconer's leash was fastened.

Thou that compar'st him to a flying-fish,
And threatenest death whether he rise or fall,
'Tis not the hugest monster of the sea,
Nor foulest harpy, that shall swallow him.

   Y. Mor. If in his absence thus he favours him, 850
What will he do whenas he shall be present?

   Lan. That shall we see: look where his lordship
   comes.

Enter Gaveston.

   K. Edw. My Gaveston!
Welcome to Tynemouth! welcome to thy friend!
Thy absence made me droop and pine away;
For, as the lovers of fair Danaë,
When she was lock'd up in a brazen tower,
Desir'd her more, and wax'd outrageous,
So did it, sure, with me: and now thy sight
Is sweeter far than was thy parting hence   860
Bitter and irksome to my sobbing heart.

   Gav. Sweet lord and king, your speech preventeth
   mine;
Yet have I words left to express my joy:
The shepherd nipp'd with biting winter's rage
Frolics not more to see the painted spring
Than I do to behold your majesty.

   K. Edw. Will none of you salute my Gaveston?

   Lan. Salute him? yes. Welcome, Lord Chamberlain!

   Y. Mor. Welcome is the good Earl of Cornwall!

   War. Welcome, Lord Governor of the Isle of
   Man!   870

   Pem. Welcome, Master Secretary!

   Kent. Brother, do you hear them?

   K. Edw. Still will these earls and barons use me
   thus?

   Gav. My lord, I cannot brook these injuries.

   Q. Isab. Ay me, poor soul, when these begin to jar!
                           [*Aside.*

K. Edw. Return it to their throats; I'll be thy
warrant.

Gav. Base, leaden earls, that glory in your birth,
Go sit at home and eat your tenants' beef;
And come not here to scoff at Gaveston,
Whose mounting thoughts did never creep so low
As to bestow a look on such as you.   881

Lan. Yet I disdain not to do this for you.

       [Draws his sword, and offers to stab Gaveston.

K. Edw. Treason! treason! where's the traitor?

Pem. Here, here!

K. Edw. Convey hence Gaveston; they'll murder
him.

Gav. The life of thee shall salve this foul disgrace.

Y. Mor. Villain, thy life! unless I miss mine aim.

                         [Wounds Gaveston.

Q. Isab. Ah, furious Mortimer, what hast thou
done?

Y. Mor. No more than I would answer, were he
slain.   *[Exit* Gaveston *with* Attendants.

K. Edw. Yes, more than thou can'st answer, though
he live;   890
Dear shall you both aby this riotous deed:
Out of my presence! come not near the court.

Y. Mor. I'll not be barr'd the court for Gaveston.

Lan. We'll hale him by the ears unto the block.

K. Edw. Look to your own heads; his is sure
enough.

War. Look to your own crown, if you back him
thus.

Kent. Warwick, these words do ill beseem thy years.

K. Edw. Nay, all of them conspire to cross me thus:
But, if I live, I'll tread upon their heads
That think with high looks thus to tread me down.
Come, Edmund, let's away, and levy men: 901
'Tis war that must abate these barons' pride.

    [Exeunt King Edward, Queen Isabella, *and* Kent.

War. Let's to our castles, for the king is mov'd.

Y. Mor. Mov'd may he be, and perish in his wrath!

Lan. Cousin, it is no dealing with him now;
He means to make us stoop by force of arms,
And therefore let us jointly here protest
To prosecute that Gaveston to the death.

Y. Mor. By heaven, the abject villain shall not live!

War. I'll have his blood, or die in seeking it.　910

Pem. The like oath Pembroke takes.

Lan. And so doth Lancaster.
Now send our heralds to defy the king;
And make the people swear to put him down.

Enter a Messenger.

Y. Mor. Letters! from whence?

Mes. From Scotland, my lord.

　　　　　　　　　　[*Giving letters to* Mortimer.

Lan. Why, how now, cousin, how fares all our friends?

Y. Mor. My uncle's taken prisoner by the Scots.

Lan. We'll have him ransom'd, man: be of good cheer.

Y. Mor. They rate his ransom at five thousand pound.　920
Who should defray the money but the king,
Seeing he is taken prisoner in his wars?
I'll to the king.

Lan. Do, cousin, and I'll bear thee company.

War. Meantime my Lord of Pembroke and myself
Will to Newcastle here, and gather head.

Y. Mor. About it then, and we will follow you.

Lan. Be resolute and full of secrecy.

War. I warrant you.　　[*Exit with* Pembroke.

Y. Mor. Cousin, an if he will not ransom him,　930
I'll thunder such a peal into his ears
As never subject did unto his king.

Lan. Content; I'll bear my part.—Holla! who's there?

Enter Guard.

Y. Mor. Ay, marry, such a guard as this doth well.
Lan. Lead on the way.
Guard. Whither will your lordships?
Y. Mor. Whither else but to the king?
Guard. His highness is dispos'd to be alone.
Lan. Why, so he may, but we will speak to him.
Guard. You may not in, my lord.   940
Y. Mor. May we not?

Enter King Edward *and* Kent.

K. Edw. How now! What noise is this?
Who have we there? is't you?   [*Going.*
     Y. Mor. Nay, stay, my lord, I come to bring you
          news;
Mine uncle's taken prisoner by the Scots.
     K. Edw. Then ransom him.
     Lan. 'Twas in your wars, you should ransom him.
     Y. Mor. And you shall ransom him, or else—
     Kent. What, Mortimer, you will not threaten him?
     K. Edw. Quiet yourself; you shall have the broad
          seal,   950
To gather for him thoroughout the realm.
     Lan. Your minion Gaveston hath taught you this.
     Y. Mor. My lord, the family of the Mortimers
Are not so poor, but, would they sell their land,
Would levy men enough to anger you.
We never beg, but use such prayers as these.
     K. Edw. Shall I still be haunted thus?
     Y. Mor. Nay, now you are here alone, I'll speak **my**
          mind.
     Lan. And so will I, and then, my lord, farewell.
     Y. Mor. The idle triumphs, masks, lascivious shows,
And prodigal gifts bestowed on Gaveston,   961
Have drawn thy treasure dry, and made thee weak;
The murmuring commons overstretched hath.
     Lan. Look for rebellion, look to be depos'd:

Thy garrisons are beaten out of France,
And, lame and poor, lie groaning at the gates;
The wild Oneil, with swarms of Irish kerns,
Lives uncontroll'd within the English pale;
Unto the walls of York the Scots made road,
And, unresisted, drove away rich spoils.   970

     Y. Mor. The haughty Dane commands the narrow seas,
While in the harbour ride thy ships unrigg'd.

     Lan. What foreign prince sends thee ambassadors?

     Y. Mor. Who loves thee, but a sort of flatterers?

     Lan. Thy gentle queen, sole sister to Valois,
Complains that thou hast left her all forlorn.

     Y. Mor. Thy court is naked, being bereft of those
That makes a king seem glorious to the world,
I mean the peers, whom thou shouldst dearly love:
Libels are cast again thee in the street,   980
Ballads and rhymes made of thy overthrow.

     Lan. The northern borderers, seeing the houses burnt,
Their wives and children slain, run up and down,
Cursing the name of thee and Gaveston.   [spread?

     Y. Mor. When wert thou in the field with banner
But once, and then thy soldiers march'd like players,
With garish robes, not armour; and thyself,
Bedaub'd with gold, rode laughing at the rest,
Nodding and shaking of thy spangled crest,
Where women's favours hung like labels down.   990

     Lan. And thereof came it that the fleering Scots,
To England's high disgrace, have made this jig;
Maids of England, sore may you mourn,
For your lemans you have lost at Bannocksbourn,—
With a heave and a ho!
What weeneth the king of England
So soon to have won Scotland!—
With a rombelow!

     967 kerns] foot soldiers   974 sort] lot   991 fleering] jeering

Y. Mor. Wigmore shall fly, to set my uncle free.

Lan. And, when 'tis gone, our swords shall purchase
more.   1000
If you be mov'd, revenge it as you can:
Look next to see us with our ensigns spread.

                        [*Exit with the younger* Mortimer.

K. Edw. My swelling heart for very anger breaks.
How oft have I been baited by these peers,
And dare not be reveng'd, for their power is great!
Yet, shall the crowing of these cockerels
Affright a lion? Edward, unfold thy paws,
And let their lives'-blood slake thy fury's hunger.
If I be cruel and grow tyrannous,
Now let them thank themselves, and rue too late.

Kent. My lord, I see your love to Gaveston   1011
Will be the ruin of the realm and you,
For now the wrathful nobles threaten wars,
And therefore, brother, banish him for ever.

K. Edw. Art thou an enemy to my Gaveston?

Kent. Ay; and it grieves me that I favoured him.

K. Edw. Traitor, be gone! whine thou with
Mortimer.

Kent. So will I, rather than with Gaveston.

K. Edw. Out of my sight, and trouble me no more!

Kent. No marvel though thou scorn thy noble peers,
When I thy brother am rejected thus.   1021

K. Edw. Away! Poor Gaveston, thou hast no friend
but me!   [*Exit* Kent.
Do what they can, we'll live in Tynemouth here,
And, so I walk with him about the walls,
What care I though the earls begirt us round?
Here comes she that's cause of all these jars.

Enter Queen Isabella, *with* Edward's Niece, *two* Ladies,
    Gaveston, Baldock, *and the younger* Spencer.

Q. Isab. My lord, 'tis thought the earls are up in
arms.

999 Wigmore] The name of young Mortimer's estate.

K. Edw. Ay, and 'tis likewise thought you favour
'em.

Q. Isab. Thus do you still suspect me without cause.

Niece. Sweet uncle, speak more kindly to the queen.

Gav. My lord, dissemble with her, speak her fair.

K. Edw. Pardon me, sweet, I forgot myself.   1032

Q. Isab. Your pardon is quickly got of Isabel.

K. Edw. The younger Mortimer is grown so brave,
That to my face he threatens civil wars.

Gav. Why do you not commit him to the Tower?

K. Edw. I dare not, for the people love him well.

Gav. Why, then we'll have him privily made away.

K. Edw. Would Lancaster and he had both carous'd
A bowl of poison to each other's health!   1040
But let them go, and tell me what are these.

Niece. Two of my father's servants whilst he liv'd:
May't please your grace to entertain them now.

K. Edw. Tell me, where wast thou born? What is
thine arms?

Bald. My name is Baldock, and my gentry
I fetch from Oxford, not from heraldry.

K. Edw. The fitter art thou, Baldock, for my turn.
Wait on me, and I'll see thou shalt not want.

Bald. I humbly thank your majesty.   1050

K. Edw. Knowest thou him, Gaveston?

Gav. Ay, my lord,
His name is Spencer, he is well allied;
For my sake let him wait upon your grace;
Scarce shall you find a man of more desert.

K. Edw. Then, Spencer, wait upon me; for his sake
I'll grace thee with a higher style ere long.

Y. Spen. No greater titles happen unto me
Than to be favoured of your majesty.

K. Edw. Cousin, this day shall be your marriage
feast;   1060
And, Gaveston, think that I love thee well,
To wed thee to our niece, the only heir
Unto the Earl of Gloucester late deceased.

Gav. I know, my lord, many will stomach me,
But I respect neither their love nor hate.

K. Edw. The headstrong barons shall not limit me;
He that I list to favour shall be great.
Come, let's away; and when the marriage ends,
Have at the rebels and their complices! [*Exeunt.*

Enter Kent, Lancaster, *the younger* Mortimer, Warwick,
Pembroke, *and others.**

Kent. My lords, of love to this our native land, 1070
I come to join with you and leave the king;
And in your quarrel and the realm's behoof
Will be the first that shall adventure life.

Lan. I fear me you are sent of policy,
To undermine us with a show of love.

War. He is your brother therefore have we cause,
To cast the worst, and doubt of your revolt.

Kent. Mine honour shall be hostage of my truth:
If that will not suffice, farewell, my lords.

Y. Mor. Stay, Edmund; never was Plantagenet
False of his word, and therefore trust we thee. 1081

Pem. But what's the reason you should leave him
now?

Kent. I have inform'd the Earl of Lancaster.

Lan. And it sufficeth. Now, my lords, know this,
That Gaveston is secretly arriv'd,
And here in Tynemouth frolics with the king.
Let us with these our followers scale the walls,
And suddenly surprise them unawares.

Y. Mor. I'll give the onset.

War. And I'll follow thee. 1090

Y. Mor. This tottered ensign of my ancestors,
Which swept the desert shore of that Dead Sea
Whereof we got the name of Mortimer,
Will I advance upon these castle walls.
Drums, strike alarum, raise them from their sport,

* The scene is near Tynemouth Castle.
1077 cast] conjecture   1091 tottered] tattered

And ring aloud the knell of Gaveston!

Lan. None be so hardy as to touch the king;
But neither spare you Gaveston nor his friends.

[*Exeunt.*

Enter, severally, King Edward *and the younger* Spencer.*

   K. Edw. Oh, tell me, Spencer, where is Gaveston?

   Y. Spen. I fear me he is slain, my gracious lord. 1100

   K. Edw. No, here he comes; now let them spoil and kill.

Enter Queen Isabella, King Edward's Niece,
Gaveston, *and* Nobles.

Fly, fly, my lords, the earls have got the hold;
Take shipping and away to Scarborough;
Spencer and I will post away by land.

   Gav. Oh, stay, my lord, they will not injure you.

   K. Edw. I will not trust them. Gaveston, away!

   Gav. Farewell, my lord.

   K. Edw. Lady, farewell.

   Niece. Farewell, sweet uncle, till we meet again.

   K. Edw. Farewell, sweet Gaveston; and farewell, niece. 1110

   Q. Isab. No farewell to poor Isabel, thy queen?

   K. Edw. Yes, yes, for Mortimer your lover's sake.

   Q. Isab. Heavens can witness I love none but you.

[*Exeunt all except* Queen Isabella.

From my embracements thus he breaks away;
Oh, that mine arms could close this isle about,
That I might pull him to me where I would!
Or that these tears, that drizzle from mine eyes,
Had power to mollify his stony heart,
That when I had him we might never part.

Enter Lancaster, Warwick, *the younger* Mortimer, *and others. Alarums within.*

   Lan. I wonder how he scap'd.

   Y. Mor. Who's this? the queen? 1120

   * The scene is inside Tynemouth Castle.

Q. Isab. Ay, Mortimer, the miserable queen,
Whose pining heart her inward sighs have blasted,
And body with continual mourning wasted:
These hands are tir'd with haling of my lord
From Gaveston, from wicked Gaveston,
And all in vain; for, when I speak him fair,
He turns away, and smiles upon his minion.

Y. Mor. Cease to lament, and tell us where's the
    king?

Q. Isab. What would you with the king? is't him
    you seek?   1130

Lan. No, madam, but that cursed Gaveston:
Far be it from the thought of Lancaster
To offer violence to his sovereign;
We would but rid the realm of Gaveston:
Tell us where he remains, and he shall die.

Q. Isab. He's gone by water unto Scarborough;
Pursue him quickly, and he cannot scape;
The king hath left him, and his train is small.

War. Forslow no time, sweet Lancaster; let's march.

Y. Mor. How comes it that the king and he is
    parted?   1140

Q. Isab. That this your army, going several ways,
Might be of lesser force, and with the power
That he intendeth presently to raise,
Be easily suppress'd: and therefore be gone.

Y. Mor. Here in the river rides a Flemish hoy;
Let's all aboard, and follow him amain.

Lan. The wind that bears him hence will fill our
    sails;
Come, come, aboard! 'tis but an hour's sailing.

Y. Mor. Madam, stay you within this castle here.

Q. Isab. No, Mortimer, I'll to my lord the king.

Y. Mor. Nay, rather sail with us to Scarborough.

Q. Isab. You know the king is so suspicious   1152
As if he hear I have but talk'd with you,
Mine honour will be call'd in question;

1139 Forslow] Delay

And therefore, gentle Mortimer, be gone.

Y. Mor. Madam, I cannot stay to answer you,
But think of Mortimer as he deserves.

                        [*Exeunt all except* Queen Isabella.

    Q.Isab. So well hast thou deserv'd, sweet Mortimer,
As Isabel could live with thee for ever.
In vain I look for love at Edward's hand,   1160
Whose eyes are fix'd on none but Gaveston:
Yet once more I'll importune him with prayers.
If he be strange and not regard my words,
My son and I will over into France,
And to the king my brother there complain
How Gaveston hath robb'd me of his love:
But yet I hope my sorrows will have end,
And Gaveston this blessed day be slain.   [*Exit.*

        Enter Gaveston, *pursued.**

    Gav. Yet, lusty lords, I have escap'd your hands,
Your threats, your 'larums, and your hot pursuits;
And, though divorced from King Edward's eyes,
Yet liveth Pierce of Gaveston unsurpris'd,   1172
Breathing in hope (malgrado all your beards,
That muster rebels thus against your king)
To see his royal sovereign once again.

Enter Warwick, Lancaster, Pembroke, *the younger*
Mortimer, Soldiers, James *and other* Attendants *of*
Pembroke.

    War. Upon him, soldiers, take away his weapons.
    Y. Mor. Thou proud disturber of thy country's
        peace,
Corrupter of thy king, cause of these broils,
Base flatterer, yield! and, were it not for shame,
Shame and dishonour to a soldier's name,   1180
Upon my weapon's point here shouldst thou fall,
And welter in thy gore.

            * The scene is the open country.
        1173 malgrado] in spite of

Lan. Monster of men,
That, like the Greekish strumpet, train'd to arms
And bloody wars so many valiant knights,
Look for no other fortune, wretch, than death!
King Edward is not here to buckler thee.

War. Lancaster, why talk'st thou to the slave?
Go, soldiers, take him hence, for, by my sword,
His head shall off: Gaveston, short warning   1190
Shall serve thy turn: it is our country's cause
That here severely we will execute
Upon thy person. Hang him at a bough.

Gav. My lord,—

War. Soldiers, have him away:
But for thou wert the favourite of a king,
Thou shalt have so much honour at our hands.

Gav. I thank you all, my lords: then I perceive
That heading is one, and hanging is the other,
And death is all.   1200

Enter Arundel.

Lan. How now, my Lord of Arundel?

Arun. My lords, King Edward greets you all by me.

War. Arundel, say your message.

Arun. His majesty,
Hearing that you had taken Gaveston,
Entreateth you by me, yet but he may
See him before he dies; for why, he says,
And sends you word, he knows that die he shall;
And if you gratify his grace so far,
He will be mindful of the courtesy.   1210

War. How now?

Gav. Renowned Edward, how thy name
Revives poor Gaveston!

War. No, it needeth not.
Arundel, we will gratify the king
In other matters; he must pardon us in this.
Soldiers, away with him.

        1184 Greekish strumpet] Helen of Troy

      M

Gav. Why, my Lord of Warwick,
Will not these delays beget my hopes?
I know it, lords, it is this life you aim at,   1220
Yet grant King Edward this.

Y. Mor.   Shalt thou appoint
What we shall grant? Soldiers, away with him:
Thus we'll gratify the king,
We'll send his head by thee; let him bestow
His tears on that, for that is all he gets
Of Gaveston, or else his senseless trunk.

Lan. Not so, my lord, lest he bestow more cost
In burying him than he hath ever earned.

Arun. My lords, it is his majesty's request,   1230
And in the honour of a king he swears,
He will but talk with him, and send him back.

War. When, can you tell? Arundel, no; we wot,
He that the care of realm remits,
And drives his nobles to these exigents
For Gaveston, will, if he seize him once,
Violate any promise to possess him.

Arun. Then, if you will not trust his grace in keep,
My lords, I will be pledge for his return.

Y. Mor. It is honourable in thee to offer this;   1240
But for we know thou art a noble gentleman,
We will not wrong thee so,
To make away a true man for a thief.

Gav. How mean'st thou, Mortimer? that is over-
base.

Y. Mor. Away, base groom, robber of king's
renown!
Question with thy companions and thy mates.

Pem. My Lord Mortimer, and you, my lords, each
one,
To gratify the king's request therein,
Touching the sending of this Gaveston,
Because his majesty so earnestly   1250
Desires to see the man before his death,
I will upon mine honour undertake

To carry him, and bring him back again,
Provided this, that you my Lord of Arundel
Will join with me.

    War. Pembroke, what wilt thou do?
Cause yet more bloodshed? is it not enough
That we have taken him, but must we now
Leave him on 'Had I wist,' and let him go?

    Pem. My lords, I will not over-woo your honours,
But if you dare trust Pembroke with the prisoner,
Upon mine oath I will return him back.   1262

    Arun. My Lord of Lancaster, what say you in this?

    Lan. Why, I say, let him go on Pembroke's word.

    Pem. And you, Lord Mortimer?

    Y. Mor. How say you, my Lord of Warwick?

    War. Nay, do your pleasures, I know how 'twill
      prove.

    Pem. Then give him me.

    Gav. Sweet sovereign, yet I come
To see thee ere I die.   1270

    War. Yet not perhaps,
If Warwick's wit and policy prevail.   [*Aside.*

    Y. Mor. My Lord of Pembroke, we deliver him you;
Return him on your honour. Sound, away!

    [*Exeunt all except* Pembroke, Arundel, Gaveston,
        James *and other* attendants *of* Pembroke.

    Pem. My lord, you shall go with me:
My house is not far hence; out of the way
A little, but our men shall go along.
We that have pretty wenches to our wives,
Sir, must not come so near and balk their lips.

    Arun. 'Tis very kindly spoke, my Lord of Pem-
      broke;   1280
Your honour hath an adamant of power
To draw a prince.

    Pem. So, my lord. Come hither, James:
I do commit this Gaveston to thee,
Be thou this night his keeper; in the morning
We will discharge thee of thy charge: be gone.

Gav. Unhappy Gaveston, whither go'st thou now?
[*Exit with* James *and other* Attendants *of* Pembroke.
Horse-boy. My lord, we'll quickly be at Cobham.
[*Exeunt.*

Enter Gaveston *mourning,* James *and other* Attendants *of*
Pembroke.*

Gav. O treacherous Warwick, thus to wrong thy
friend!
James. I see it is your life these arms pursue. 1290
Gav. Weaponless must I fall, and die in bands?
Oh, must this day be period of my life?
Centre of all my bliss! An ye be men,
Speed to the king.

Enter Warwick *and* Soldiers.

War. My Lord of Pembroke's men,
Strive you no longer, I will have that Gaveston.
James. Your lordship doth dishonour to yourself,
And wrong our lord, your honourable friend.
War. No, James, it is my country's cause I follow.
Go, take the villain; soldiers, come away,   1300
We'll make quick work. Commend me to your
master,
My friend, and tell him that I watch'd it well.
Come, let thy shadow parley with King Edward.
Gav. Treacherous earl, shall I not see the king?
War. The king of heaven perhaps, no other king.
Away! [*Exeunt* Warwick *and* Soldiers *with* Gaveston.
James. Come, fellows, it booted not for us to strive,
We will in haste go certify our lord.   [*Exeunt.*

Enter King Edward, *the younger* Spencer, Baldock, Noblemen *of the king's side, and* Soldiers *with drums and fifes.*†

K. Edw. I long to hear an answer from the barons
Touching my friend, my dearest Gaveston.   1310

* The scene changes to another part of the country.
† The scene is near Boroughbridge in Yorkshire.
1303 shadow] ghost

Ah, Spencer, not the riches of my realm
Can ransom him! ah, he is mark'd to die!
I know the malice of the younger Mortimer,
Warwick I know is rough, and Lancaster
Inexorable, and I shall never see
My lovely Pierce, my Gaveston again:
The barons overbear me with their pride.

Y. Spen. Were I King Edward, England's sovereign,
Son to the lovely Eleanor of Spain,
Great Edward Longshanks' issue, would I bear 1320
These braves, this rage, and suffer uncontroll'd
These barons thus to beard me in my land,
In mine own realm? My lord, pardon my speech:
Did you retain your father's magnanimity,
Did you regard the honour of your name,
You would not suffer thus your majesty
Be counterbuff'd of your nobility.
Strike off their heads, and let them preach on poles:
No doubt, such lessons they will teach the rest,
As by their preachments they will profit much, 1330
And learn obedience to their lawful king.

K. Edw. Yea, gentle Spencer, we have been too
    mild,
Too kind to them; but now have drawn our sword,
And if they send me not my Gaveston,
We'll steel it on their crest, and poll their tops.

Bald. This haught resolve becomes your majesty,
Not to be tied to their affection,
As though your highness were a school-boy still,
And must be aw'd and govern'd like a child.

Enter the elder Spencer *with his truncheon, and* Soldiers.

E. Spen. Long live my sovereign the noble Edward,
In peace triumphant, fortunate in wars! 1341

K. Edw. Welcome, old man, com'st thou in Ed-
    ward's aid?
Then tell thy prince of whence and what thou art.

E. Spen. Lo, with a band of bowmen and of pikes,

Brown bills and targeteers, four hundred strong,
Sworn to defend King Edward's royal right,
I come in person to your majesty,
Spencer, the father of Hugh Spencer there,
Bound to your highness everlastingly
For favours done, in him, unto us all.   1350

   K. Edw. Thy father, Spencer?

   Y. Spen. True, an it like your grace,
That pours, in lieu of all your goodness shown,
His life, my lord, before your princely feet.

   K. Edw. Welcome ten thousand times, old man,
     again.
Spencer, this love, this kindness to thy king,
Argues thy noble mind and disposition.
Spencer, I here create thee Earl of Wiltshire,
And daily will enrich thee with our favour,
That as the sunshine shall reflect o'er thee.   1360
Beside, the more to manifest our love,
Because we hear Lord Bruce doth sell his land,
And that the Mortimers are in hand withal,
Thou shalt have crowns of us t'outbid the barons:
And, Spencer, spare them not, but lay it on.
Soldiers, a largess, and thrice-welcome all!

   Y. Spen. My lord, here comes the queen.

Enter Queen Isabella, Prince Edward, *and* Levune.

   K. Edw. Madam, what news?

   Q. Isab. News of dishonour, lord, and discontent.
Our friend Levune, faithful and full of trust,   1370
Informeth us, by letters and by words,
That Lord Valois our brother, King of France,
Because your highness hath been slack in homage,
Hath seized Normandy into his hands:
These be the letters, this the messenger.

   K. Edw. Welcome, Levune. Tush, Sib, if this be all,
Valois and I will soon be friends again.
But to my Gaveston: shall I never see,
Never behold thee now? Madam, in this matter

We will employ you and your little son;   1380
You shall go parley with the King of France.
Boy, see you bear you bravely to the king,
And do your message with a majesty.

    P. Edw. Commit not to my youth things of more
      weight
Than fits a prince so young as I to bear,
And fear not, lord and father, heaven's great beams
On Atlas' shoulder shall not lie more safe
Than shall your charge committed to my trust.

    Q. Isab. Ah, boy, this towardness makes thy mother
      fear
Thou are not mark'd to many days on earth.   1390

    K. Edw. Madam, we will that you with speed be
      shipp'd,
And this our son; Levune shall follow you
With all the haste we can despatch him hence.
Choose of our lords to bear you company,
And go in peace; leave us in wars at home.

    Q. Isab. Unnatural wars, where subjects brave their
      king;
God end them once! My lord, I take my leave,
To make my preparation for France.

                       [*Exit with* Prince Edward.

Enter Arundel.

    K. Edw. What, Lord Arundel, dost thou come
      alone?

    Arun. Yea, my good lord, for Gaveston is dead.

    K. Edw. Ah, traitors, have they put my friend to
      death?   1401
Tell me, Arundel, died he ere thou cam'st,
Or didst thou see my friend to take his death?

    Arun. Neither, my lord; for, as he was surpris'd,
Begirt with weapons and with enemies round,
I did your highness' message to them all,
Demanding him of them, entreating rather,
And said, upon the honour of my name,

That I would undertake to carry him
Unto your highness, and to bring him back.   1410
    K. Edw. And tell me, would the rebels deny me
        that?
    Y. Spen. Proud recreants!
    K. Edw. Yea, Spencer, traitors all.
    Arun. I found them at the first inexorable;
The Earl of Warwick would not bide the hearing,
Mortimer hardly; Pembroke and Lancaster
Spake least: and when they flatly had denied,
Refusing to receive me pledge for him,
The Earl of Pembroke mildly thus bespake:
'My lords, because our sovereign sends for him, 1420
And promiseth he shall be safe return'd,
I will this undertake, to have him hence,
And see him re-delivered to your hands.'
    K. Edw. Well, and how fortunes it that he came
        not?
    Y. Spen. Some treason or some villainy was cause.
    Arun. The Earl of Warwick seiz'd him on his way;
For being delivered unto Pembroke's men,
Their lord rode home, thinking his prisoner safe,
But, ere he came, Warwick in ambush lay,
And bare him to his death, and in a trench   1430
Strake off his head, and march'd unto the camp.
    Y. Spen. A bloody part, flatly against law of arms!
    K. Edw. Oh, shall I speak, or shall I sigh and die!
    Y. Spen. My lord, refer your vengeance to the sword
Upon these barons; hearten up your men;
Let them not unreveng'd murther your friends:
Advance your standard, Edward, in the field,
And march to fire them from their starting-holes.
    K. Edw. [*kneeling.*] By earth, the common mother of
        us all,
By heaven, and all the moving orbs thereof,   1440
By this right hand, and by my father's sword,
And all the honours 'longing to my crown,
I will have heads and lives for him as many

As I have manors, castles, towns, and towers! [*Rises.*
Treacherous Warwick! traitorous Mortimer!
If I be England's king, in lakes of gore
Your headless trunks, your bodies will I trail,
That you may drink your fill, and quaff in blood,
And stain my royal standard with the same,
That so my bloody colours may suggest   1450
Remembrance of revenge immortally
On your accursed traitorous progeny,
You villains that have slain my Gaveston!
And in this place of honour and of trust,
Spencer, sweet Spencer, I adopt thee here,
And merely of our love we do create thee
Earl of Gloucester and Lord Chamberlain,
Despite of times, despite of enemies.

Y. Spen. My lord, here's a messenger from the
    barons
Desires access unto your majesty.   1460

K. Edw. Admit him near.

Enter Herald *with his coat of arms.*

Her. Long live King Edward, England's lawful
    lord!

K. Edw. So wish not they, I wis, that sent thee
    hither:
Thou com'st from Mortimer and his complices;
A ranker rout of rebels never was.
Well, say thy message.

Her. The barons up in arms, by me salute
Your highness with long life and happiness;
And bid me say, as plainer to your grace,
That if without effusion of blood   1470
You will this grief have ease and remedy,
That from your princely person you remove
This Spencer, as a putrifying branch
That deads the royal vine, whose golden leaves
Empale your princely head, your diadem,
Whose brightness such pernicious upstarts dim,

Say they; and lovingly advise your grace
To cherish virtue and nobility,
And have old servitors in high esteem,
And shake off smooth dissembling flatterers: 1480
This granted, they, their honours, and their lives,
Are to your highness vow'd and consecrate.

   Y. Spen. Ah, traitors, will they still display their
    pride?

   K. Edw. Away, tarry no answer, but be gone!
Rebels, will they appoint their sovereign
His sports, his pleasures, and his company?
Yet, ere thou go, see how I do divorce
                [*Embraces young* Spencer.
Spencer from me. Now get thee to thy lords,
And tell them I will come to chastise them   1489
For murdering Gaveston; hie thee, get thee gone!
Edward with fire and sword follows at thy heels.
                    [*Exit* Herald.
My lord, perceive you how these rebels swell?
Soldiers, good hearts, defend your sovereign's right,
For, now, even now, we march to make them stoop.
Away.

      [*Exeunt. Alarums, excursions, a great fight, and a
      retreat sounded, within.*

Re-enter King Edward, *the elder* Spencer, *the younger*
Spencer, Baldock, *and* Noblemen *of the king's side.*

   K. Edw. Why do we sound retreat? upon them,
    lords!
This day I shall pour vengeance with my sword
On whose proud rebels that are up in arms,
And do confront and countermand their king.   1499

   Y. Spen. I doubt it not, my lord, right will prevail.

   E. Spen. 'Tis not amiss, my liege, for either part
To breathe a while; our men, with sweat and dust
All chok'd well near, begin to faint for heat;
And this retire refresheth horse and man.

   Y. Spen. Here come the rebels.

Enter the younger Mortimer, Lancaster, Warwick,
Pembroke, *and others.*

Y. Mor. Look, Lancaster, yonder is Edward among
his flatterers.

Lan. And there let him be,
Till he pay dearly for their company.

War. And shall, or Warwick's sword shall smite in
vain.

K. Edw. What, rebels, do you shrink and sound
retreat? 1510

Y. Mor. No, Edward, no, thy flatterers faint and
fly.

Lan. Thou'd best betimes forsake them and their
trains,
For they'll betray thee, traitors as they are.

Y. Spen. Traitor on thy face, rebellious Lancaster!

Pem. Away, base upstart, brav'st thou nobles thus?

E. Spen. A noble attempt, and honourable deed,
Is it not, trow ye, to assemble aid
And levy arms against your lawful king?

K. Edw. For which, ere long, their heads shall
satisfy
T' appease the wrath of their offended king. 1520

Y. Mor. Then, Edward, thou wilt fight it to the
last,
And rather bathe thy sword in subjects' blood
Than banish that pernicious company?

K. Edw. Ay, traitors all, rather than thus be brav'd,
Make England's civil towns huge heaps of stones,
And ploughs to go about our palace gates.

War. A desperate and unnatural resolution!
Alarum to the fight!
Saint George for England, and the barons' right!

K. Edw. Saint George for England, and King
Edward's right! 1530

[*Alarums. Exeunt the two parties severally.*

1512 trains] stratagems

Enter King Edward *and his followers, with the* Barons
and Kent *captive.*∗

  K. Edw. Now, lusty lords, now not by chance of
    war,
But justice of the quarrel and the cause,
Vail'd is your pride: methinks you hang the heads,
But we'll advance them, traitors; now 'tis time
To be aveng'd on you for all your braves,
And for the murther of my dearest friend,
To whom right well you knew our soul was knit,
Good Pierce of Gaveston, my sweet favourite.
Ah, rebels, recreants, you made him away!
  Kent. Brother, in regard of thee and of thy land,
Did they remove that flatterer from thy throne. 1541
  K. Edw. So, sir, you have spoke; away, avoid our
    presence!   [*Exit* Kent.
Accursed wretches, was't in regard of us,
When we had sent our messenger to request
He might be spared to come to speak with us,
And Pembroke undertook for his return,
That thou, proud Warwick, watch'd the prisoner,
Poor Pierce, and headed him against law of arms?
For which thy head shall overlook the rest,
As much as thou in rage outwent'st the rest.   1550
  War. Tyrant, I scorn thy threats and menaces;
'Tis but temporal that thou canst inflict.
  Lan. The worst is death, and better die to live
Than live in infamy under such a king.
  K. Edw. Away with them, my lord of Winchester!
These lusty leaders, Warwick and Lancaster,
I charge you roundly, off with both their heads!
Away!
  War. Farewell, vain world!
  Lan. Sweet Mortimer, farewell.   1560
  Y. Mor. England, unkind to thy nobility,
Groan for this grief, behold how thou art maimed!

      ∗ The scene is another part of the battle-field.

K. Edw. Go, take that haughty Mortimer to the
   Tower,
There see him safe bestowed; and for the rest,
Do speedy execution on them all.
Be gone!
   Y. Mor. What, Mortimer, can ragged stony walls
Immure thy virtue that aspires to heaven?
No, Edward, England's scourge, it may not be;
Mortimer's hope surmounts his fortune far.   1570
                    [*The captive* Barons *are led off.*
   K. Edw. Sound, drums and trumpets! March with
   me, my friends.
Edward this day hath crown'd him king anew.
             [*Exeunt all except the younger* Spencer,
              Levune, *and* Baldock.
   Y. Spen. Levune, the trust that we repose in
   thee
Begets the quiet of King Edward's land:
Therefore be gone in haste, and with advice
Bestow that treasure on the lords of France,
That, therewith all enchanted, like the guard
That suffered Jove to pass in showers of gold
To Danaë, all aid may be denied
To Isabel the queen, that now in France   1580
Makes friends, to cross the seas with her young
   son,
And step into his father's regiment.
   Levune. That's it these barons and the subtle queen
Long levell'd at.
   Bal. Yea, but, Levune, thou seest
These barons lay their heads on blocks together;
What they intend, the hangman frustrates clean.
   Levune. Have you no doubts, my lords, I'll clap so
   close
Among the lords of France with England's gold,
That Isabel shall make her plaints in vain,   1590
And France shall be obdurate with her tears.

          1582 regiment] rule

Y. Spen. Then make for France amain; Levune,
    away!
Proclaim King Edward's wars and victories. [*Exeunt.*

Enter KENT.*

Kent. Fair blows the wind for France; blow gentle
    gale,
Till Edmund be arriv'd for England's good!
Nature, yield to my country's cause in this.
A brother? no, a butcher of thy friends!
Proud Edward, dost thou banish me thy presence?
But I'll to France, and cheer the wronged queen,
And certify what Edward's looseness is.   1600
Unnatural king, to slaughter noblemen
And cherish flatterers! Mortimer, I stay
Thy sweet escape.
Stand gracious, gloomy night, to his device.

Enter the younger MORTIMER *disguised.*

Y. Mor. Holla! who walketh there? Is't you, my
Kent. Mortimer, 'tis I;   [lord?
But hath thy potion wrought so happily?
Y. Mor. It hath, my lord; the warders all asleep,
I thank them, gave me leave to pass in peace:
But hath your grace got shipping unto France? 1610
Kent. Fear it not.   [*Exeunt.*

Enter QUEEN ISABELLA *and* PRINCE EDWARD.†

Q. Isab. Ah, boy, our friends do fail us all in France:
The lords are cruel, and the king unkind;
What shall we do?
P. Edw. Madam, return to England,
And please my father well, and then a fig
For all my uncle's friendship here in France.
I warrant you, I'll win his highness quickly;
'A loves me better than a thousand Spencers.
Q. Isab. Ah, boy, thou art deceiv'd, at least in this,

      * Scene—near the Tower of London.
      † Scene—Paris.

To think that we can yet be tun'd together; 1621
No, no, we jar too far. Unkind Valois!
Unhappy Isabel, when France rejects,
Whither, oh, whither dost thou bend thy steps?

Enter Sir John of Hainault.

Sir J. Madam, what cheer?

Q. Isab. Ah, good Sir John of Hainault,
Never so cheerless nor so far distress'd.

Sir J. I hear, sweet lady, of the king's unkindness;
But droop not, madam; noble minds contemn
Despair. Will your grace with me to Hainault, 1630
And there stay time's advantage with your son?
How say you, my lord, will you go with your friends,
And share of all our fortunes equally?

P. Edw. So pleaseth the queen my mother, me it
    likes:
The king of England, nor the court of France,
Shall have me from my gracious mother's side,
Till I be strong enough to break a staff;
And then have at the proudest Spencer's head.

Sir J. Well said, my lord.

Q. Isab. O my sweet heart, how do I moan thy
    wrongs, 1640
Yet triumph in the hope of thee, my joy!
Ah, sweet Sir John, even to the utmost verge
Of Europe, or the shore of Tanais,
Will we with thee to Hainault—so we will:
The marquis is a noble gentleman;
His grace, I dare presume, will welcome me.
But who are these?

Enter Kent *and the younger* Mortimer.

Kent. Madam, long may you live
Much happier than your friends in England do!

Q. Isab. Lord Edmund and Lord Mortimer alive?
Welcome to France! the news was here, my lord,
That you were dead, or very near your death. 1652

Y. Mor. Lady, the last was truest of the twain,
But Mortimer, reserv'd for better hap,
Hath shaken off the thraldom of the Tower,
And lives t' advance your standard, good my lord.

P. Edw. How mean you, and the king my father
No, my Lord Mortimer, not I, I trow.   [lives?

   Q. Isab. Not, son! why not? I would it were no
    worse.
But, gentle lords, friendless we are in France.   1660

   Y. Mor. Monsieur Le Grand, a noble friend of yours,
Told us, at our arrival, all the news,—
How hard the nobles, how unkind the king
Hath showed himself; but, madam, right makes room
Where weapons want; and though a many friends
Are made away, as Warwick, Lancaster,
And others of our party and faction,
Yet have we friends, assure your grace, in England
Would cast up caps, and clap their hands for joy,
To see us there, appointed for our foes.   1670

   Kent. Would all were well, and Edward well re-
    claim'd,
For England's honour, peace, and quietness.

   Y. Mor. But by the sword, my lord, it must be
    deserv'd;
The king will ne'er forsake his flatterers.

   Sir J. My lords of England, sith the ungentle king
Of France refuseth to give aid of arms
To this distressed queen his sister here,
Go you with her to Hainault: doubt ye not
We will find comfort, money, men, and friends
Ere long, to bid the English king a base.   1680
How say, young prince, what think you of the match?

   P. Edw. I think King Edward will outrun us all.

   Q. Isab. Nay, son, not so; and you must not dis-
    courage
Your friends that are so forward in your aid.

1670 appointed] ready equipped   1680 bid a base]
challenge an encounter

Kent. Sir John of Hainault, pardon us, I pray;
These comforts that you give our woful queen
Bind us in kindness all at your command.

Q. Isab. Yea, gentle brother; and the God of heaven
Prosper your happy motion, good Sir John.

Y. Mor. This noble gentleman, forward in arms,
Was born, I see, to be our anchor-hold.   1691
Sir John of Hainault, be it thy renown,
That England's queen and nobles in distress
Have been by thee restored and comforted.

Sir J. Madam, along, and you, my lords, with me,
That England's peers may Hainault's welcome see.
                                        [*Exeunt.*

Enter King Edward, Arundel, *the elder* Spencer, *the
    younger* Spencer, *and others.**

K. Edw. Thus after many threats of wrathful war,
Triumpheth England's Edward with his friends;
And triumph, Edward, with his friends uncontroll'd!
My Lord of Gloucester, do you hear the news?   1700

Y. Spen. What news, my lord?

K. Edw. Why, man, they say there is great execu-
    tion
Done through the realm; My Lord of Arundel,
You have the note, have you not?

Arun. From the Lieutenant of the Tower, my lord.

K. Edw. I pray, let us see it.
                          [*Takes the note from* Arundel.
What have we there?
Read it, Spencer.
    [*Gives the note to young* Spencer, *who reads their names.*
Why, so; they bark'd apace a month ago;
Now, on my life, they'll neither bark nor bite.   1710
Now, sirs, the news from France? Gloucester, I
    trow
The lords of France love England's gold so well

---

* The scene is an apartment in the King's palace at Westminster.

As Isabel gets no aid from thence.
What now remains? have you proclaimed, my lord,
Reward for them can bring in Mortimer?

Y. Spen. My lord, we have; and if he be in England,
'A will be had ere long, I doubt it not.

K. Edw. If, dost thou say? Spencer, as true as
　death,
He is in England's ground; our port-masters
Are not so careless of their king's command.　1720

Enter a Messenger.

How now, what news with thee? from whence come
　these?

Mess. Letters, my lord, and tidings forth of France;
To you, my Lord of Gloucester, from Levune.

　　　　　　　　　　　[Gives letters to young Spencer.

K. Edw. Read.

Y. Spen. [reading.] *My duty to your honour premised,
etc., I have, according to instructions in that behalf, dealt
with the King of France, his lords, and effected that the queen,
all discontented and discomforted, is gone: whither, if you ask,
with Sir John of Hainault, brother to the marquis, into
Flanders. With them are gone Lord Edmund and the Lord
Mortimer, having in their company divers of your nation, and
others; and, as constant report goeth, they intend to give King
Edward battle in England, sooner than he can look for them.
This is all the news of import.*

　　　　　　　　Your honour's in all service, Levune.

K. Edw. Ah, villains, hath that Mortimer escap'd?
With him is Edmund gone associate?
And will Sir John of Hainault lead the round?
Welcome, o' God's name, madam, and your son;
England shall welcome you and all your rout.　1740
Gallop apace, bright Phœbus, through the sky,
And, dusky Night, in rusty iron car,
Between you both shorten the time, I pray,
That I may see that most desired day,

When we may meet these traitors in the field.
Ah, nothing grieves me, but my little boy
Is thus misled to countenance their ills.
Come, friends, to Bristow, there to make us strong;
And, winds, as equal be to bring them in,   1749
As you injurious were to bear them forth!   [*Exeunt.*

    Enter Queen Isabella, Prince Edward, Kent, *the
    younger* Mortimer, *and* Sir John of Hainault.*

    Q. Isab. Now, lords, our loving friends and country-
      men,
Welcome to England all, with prosperous winds!
Our kindest friends in Belgia have we left,
To cope with friends at home: a heavy case
When force to force is knit, and sword and glaive
In civil broils makes kin and countrymen
Slaughter themselves in others, and their sides
With their own weapons gor'd. But what's the help?
Misgoverned kings are cause of all this wreck;
And, Edward, thou art one among them all,   1760
Whose looseness hath betrayed thy land to spoil,
And made the channels overflow with blood.
Of thine own people patron shouldst thou be,
But thou—
    Y. Mor. Nay, madam, if you be a warrior,
Ye must not grow so passionate in speeches.
Lords, sith that we are by sufferance of heaven
Arrived and armed in this prince's right,
Here for our country's cause swear we to him
All homage, fealty, and forwardness;   1770
And for the open wrongs and injuries
Edward hath done to us, his queen, and land,
We come in arms to wreck it with the swords;
That England's queen in peace may repossess
Her dignities and honours; and withal
We may remove these flatterers from the king,

    1748 Bristow] Bristol   1762 channels] gutters
            * The scene is near Harwich.

That havocs England's wealth and treasury.   [*march.*

   Sir J. Sound trumpets, my lord, and forward let us
Edward will think we come to flatter him.

   Kent. I would he never had been flattered more!
[*Exeunt.*

Enter King Edward, Baldock, *and the younger* Spencer.*

   Y. Spen. Fly, fly, my lord, the queen is overstrong;
Her friends do multiply, and yours do fail.   1782
Shape we our course to Ireland, there to breathe.

   K. Edw. What, was I born to fly and run away,
And leave the Mortimers conquerors behind?
Give me my horse, and let's re'nforce our troops:
And in this bed of honours die with fame.

   Bald. Oh no, my lord, this princely resolution
Fits not the time; away, we are pursu'd.   [*Exeunt.*

Enter Kent, *with a sword and target.*

   Kent. This way he fled, but I am come too late.
Edward, alas, my heart relents for thee.   1791
Proud traitor, Mortimer, why dost thou chase
Thy lawful king, thy sovereign, with thy sword?
Vile wretch! and why hast thou, of all, unkind!
Borne arms against thy brother and thy king?
Rain showers of vengeance on my cursed head,
Thou God, to whom in justice it belongs
To punish this unnatural revolt!
Edward, this Mortimer aims at thy life:
Oh, fly him, then! But, Edmund, calm this rage,
Dissemble, or thou diest; for Mortimer   1801
And Isabel do kiss, while they conspire:
And yet she bears a face of love forsooth.
Fie on that love that hatcheth death and hate!
Edmund, away! Bristow to Longshanks' blood
Is false; be not found single for suspect:
Proud Mortimer pries near into thy walks.

     ❧   1806 for suspect] for fear of suspicion
       * The scene is near Bristol.

Enter Queen Isabella, Prince Edward, *the younger*
Mortimer, *and* Sir John of Hainault.

Q. Isab. Successful battles gives the God of kings
To them that fight in right and fear his wrath.
Since then successfully we have prevailed,   1810
Thanks be heaven's great architect, and you.
Ere farther we proceed, my noble lords,
We here create our well-beloved son,
Of love and care unto his royal person,
Lord Warden of the realm, and sith the fates
Have made his father so infortunate,
Deal you, my lords, in this, my loving lords,
As to your wisdoms fittest seems in all.

Kent. Madam, without offence if I may ask,
How will you deal with Edward in his fall?   1820

P. Edw. Tell me, good uncle, what Edward do you
mean?

Kent. Nephew, your father: I dare not call him king.

Y. Mor. My Lord of Kent, what needs these questions?
'Tis not in her controlment nor in ours,
But as the realm and parliament shall please,
So shall your brother be disposed of.
I like not this relenting mood in Edmund;
Madam, 'tis good to look to him betimes.

                         [Aside to the Queen.

Q. Isab. My lord, the Mayor of Bristow knows our
mind.

Y. Mor. Yea, madam, and they scape not easily
That fled the field.   1831

Q. Isab. Baldock is with the king.
A goodly chancellor, is he not, my lord?

Sir J. So are the Spencers, the father and the son.

Y. Mor. This Edward is the ruin of the realm.

Enter Rice ap Howel *and the* Mayor of Bristow *with the*
elder *Spencer* prisoner, *and* Attendants.

Rice. God save Queen Isabel and her princely son!
Madam, the Mayor and citizens of Bristow,

In sign of love and duty to this presence,
Present by me this traitor to the state,
Spencer, the father to that wanton Spencer,   1840
That, like the lawless Catiline of Rome,
Revell'd in England's wealth and treasury.

Q. Isab. We thank you all.

Y. Mor. Your loving care in this
Deserveth princely favours and rewards.
But where's the king and the other Spencer fled?

Rice. Spencer the son, created Earl of Gloucester,
Is with that smooth-tongu'd scholar Baldock gone,
And shipp'd but late for Ireland with the king.

Y. Mor. Some whirlwind fetch them back, or sink
them all!—   [*Aside.*
They shall be started thence, I doubt it not.   1851

P. Edw. Shall I not see the king my father yet?

Kent. Unhappy Edward, chas'd from England's
bounds!   [*Aside.*

Sir J. Madam, what resteth? why stand ye in a
muse?

Q. Isab. I rue my lord's ill-fortune; but, alas,
Care of my country call'd me to this war.

Y. Mor. Madam, have done with care and sad
complaint,
Your king hath wrong'd your country and himself,
And we must seek to right it as we may.
Meanwhile have hence this rebel to the block,   1860
Your lordship cannot privilege your head.

E. Spen. Rebel is he that fights against his prince;
So fought not they that fought in Edward's right.

Y. Mor. Take him away, he prates;

[*Exeunt* Attendants *with the elder* Spencer.
    You, Rice ap Howel,
Shall do good service to her majesty,
Being of countenance in your country here,
To follow these rebellious runagates.
We in mean while, madam, must take advice.
How Baldock, Spencer, and their complices,

May in their fall be followed to their end.   [*Exeunt.*

Enter the Abbot, Monks, King Edward, *the younger*
    Spencer, *and* Baldock (*the three latter disguised*).*

Abbot. Have you no doubt, my lord; have you no
As silent and as careful will we be   [fear:
To keep your royal person safe with us,   1873
Free from suspect, and fell invasion
Of such as have your majesty in chase,
Yourself, and those your chosen company,
As danger of this stormy time requires.

K. Edw. Father, thy face should harbour no deceit.
Oh, hadst thou ever been a king, thy heart,
Pierced deeply with sense of my distress,   1880
Could not but take compassion of my state.
Stately and proud, in riches and in train,
Whilom I was powerful and full of pomp:
But what is he whom rule and empery
Have not in life or death made miserable?
Come, Spencer, come, Baldock, come, sit down by me
Make trial now of that philosophy
That in our famous nurseries of arts
Thou suckedst from Plato and from Aristotle.
Father, this life contemplative is heaven.   1890
Oh, that I might this life in quiet lead!
But we, alas, are chas'd; and you, my friends,
Your lives and my dishonour they pursue.
Yet, gentle monks, for treasure, gold, nor fee,
Do you betray us and our company.

First Monk. Your grace may sit secure, if none but we
Do wot of your abode.

Y. Spen. Not one alive, but shrewdly I suspect
A gloomy fellow in a mead below.
'A gave a long look after us, my lord;   1900
And all the land, I know, is up in arms,
Arms that pursue our lives with deadly hate.

Bald. We were embark'd for Ireland; wretched we,

* The scene is the Abbey of Neath.

With awkward winds and sore tempests driven,
To fall on shore, and here to pine in fear
Of Mortimer and his confederates.

K. Edw. Mortimer! who talks of Mortimer?
Who wounds me with the name of Mortimer,
That bloody man? Good father, on thy lap
Lay I this head, laden with mickle care.   1910
Oh, might I never ope these eyes again,
Never again lift up this drooping head,
Oh, never more lift up this dying heart!

Y. Spen. Look up, my lord. Baldock, this drowsiness
Betides no good; here even we are betrayed.

Enter, with Welsh hooks, Rice ap Howel, *a* Mower, *and*
Leicester.

Mow. Upon my life, those be the men ye seek.

Rice. Fellow, enough.—My lord, I pray be short,
A fair commission warrants what we do.

Leices. The queen's commission, urg'd by Mortimer;
What cannot gallant Mortimer with the queen? 1920
Alas, see where he sits, and hopes unseen
T'escape their hands that seek to reave his life.
Too true it is, *Quem dies vidit veniens superbum,*
Hunc dies vidit fugiens jacentem.
But, Leicester, leave to grow so passionate.
Spencer and Baldock, by no other names,
I arrest you of high treason here.
Stand not on titles, but obey th' arrest;
'Tis in the name of Isabel the queen.
My lord, why droop you thus?   1930

K. Edw. O day, the last of all my bliss on earth,
Centre of all misfortune! O my stars,
Why do you lour unkindly on a king?
Comes Leicester then, in Isabella's name,
To take my life, my company from me?
Here, man, rip up this panting breast of mine,

1923-4 *Quem . . . jacentem*] Whom the approaching day
saw in his pride, the parting day saw cast down

And take my heart in rescue of my friends.

   Rice. Away with them!

   Y. Spen. It may become thee yet

To let us take our farewell of his grace.   1940

   Abbot. My heart with pity earns to see this sight,

A king to bear these words and proud commands!

                                    [Aside.

   K. Edw. Spencer, ah, sweet Spencer, thus then must
     we part?

   Y. Spen. We must, my lord, so will the angry
heavens.

   K. Edw. Nay, so will hell and cruel Mortimer;

The gentle heavens have not to do in this.

   Bald. My lord, it is in vain to grieve or storm.

Here humbly of your grace we take our leaves;

Our lots are cast; I fear me, so is thine.

   K. Edw. In heaven we may, in earth never shall we
     meet: 1950

And, Leicester, say, what shall become of us?

   Leices. Your majesty must go to Killingworth.

   K. Edw. Must! 'tis somewhat hard when kings
     must go.

   Leices. Here is a litter ready for your grace,

That waits your pleasure, and the day grows old.

   Rice. As good be gone, as stay and be benighted.

   K. Edw. A litter hast thou? lay me in a hearse,

And to the gates of hell convey me hence;

Let Pluto's bells ring out my fatal knell,

And hags howl for my death at Charon's shore, 1960

For friends hath Edward none but these, and these,

And these must die under a tyrant's sword.

   Rice. My lord, be going; care not for these,

For we shall see them shorter by the heads.

   K. Edw. Well, that shall be, shall be: part we must,

Sweet Spencer, gentle Baldock, part we must.

Hence feigned weeds! unfeigned are my woes;

                   [Throwing off his disguise.

   1941 earns] yearns   1952 Killingworth] Kenilworth

Father, farewell. Leicester, thou stay'st for me,
And go I must. Life, farewell, with my friends.

              [Exeunt King Edward *and* Leicester.

    Y. Spen. Oh, is he gone? is noble Edward gone?
Parted from hence, never to see us more,   1971
Rent, sphere of heaven! and, fire, forsake thy orb!
Earth, melt to air! gone is my sovereign,
Gone, gone, alas, never to make return.

    Bald. Spencer, I see our souls are fleeted hence;
We are depriv'd the sunshine of our life:
Make for a new life, man; throw up thy eyes,
And heart and hand to heaven's immortal throne;
Pay nature's debt with cheerful countenance;
Reduce we all our lessons unto this,   1980
To die, sweet Spencer, therefore live we all;
Spencer, all live to die, and rise to fall.

    Rice. Come, come, keep these preachments till you
come to the place appointed. You, and such as you
are, have made wise work in England. Will your
lordships away?

    Mow. Your worship I trust will remember me?

    Rice. Remember thee, fellow? what else? Follow
me to the town.   *[Exeunt.*

      Enter King Edward, Leicester, *the* Bishop of
            Winchester, *and* Trussel.*

    Leices. Be patient, good my lord, cease to lament,
Imagine Killingworth Castle were your court,   1991
And that you lay for pleasure here a space,
Not of compulsion or necessity.

    K. Edw. Leicester, if gentle words might com-
        fort me,
Thy speeches long ago had eas'd my sorrows,
For kind and loving hast thou always been.
The griefs of private men are soon allay'd,
But not of kings. The forest deer, being struck,
Runs to an herb that closeth up the wounds;

    * The scene is an apartment in Kenilworth Castle.

But when the imperial lion's flesh is gor'd,   2000
He rends and tears it with his wrathful paw,
And, highly scorning that the lowly earth
Should drink his blood, mounts up into the air:
And so it fares with me, whose dauntless mind
The ambitious Mortimer would seek to curb,
And that unnatural queen, false Isabel,
That thus hath pent and mew'd me in a prison;
For such outrageous passions cloy my soul,
As, with the wings of rancour and disdain,
Full often am I soaring up to heaven,   2010
To plain me to the gods against them both.
But when I call to mind I am a king,
Methinks I should revenge me of the wrongs
That Mortimer and Isabel have done.
But what are kings, when regiment is gone,
But perfect shadows in a sunshine day?
My nobles rule, I bear the name of king;
I wear the crown, but am controll'd by them,
By Mortimer, and my unconstant queen,
Who spots my nuptial bed with infamy,   2020
Whilst I am lodg'd within this cave of care,
Where sorrow at my elbow still attends,
To company my heart with sad laments,
That bleeds within me for this strange exchange.
But tell me, must I now resign my crown,
To make usurping Mortimer a king?

   Bish. of Win. Your grace mistakes; it is for Eng-
     land's good
And princely Edward's right we crave the crown.

   K. Edw. No, 'tis for Mortimer, not Edward's head;
For he's a lamb, encompassed by wolves,   2030
Which in a moment will abridge his life.
But if proud Mortimer do wear this crown,
Heavens turn it to a blaze of quenchless fire!
Or like the snaky wreath of Tisiphon,
Engirt the temples of his hateful head;
So shall not England's vine be perished.

But Edward's name survives, though Edward dies.

Leices. My lord, why waste you thus the time away?
They stay your answer; will you yield your crown?

K. Edw. Ah, Leicester, weigh how hardly I can
    brook   2040
To lose my crown and kingdom without cause;
To give ambitious Mortimer my right,
That like a mountain overwhelms my bliss,
In which extreme my mind here murthered is.
But what the heavens appoint, I must obey.
Here, take my crown; the life of Edward too,
                         [Taking off the crown.
Two kings in England cannot reign at once.
But stay awhile, let me be king till night,
That I may gaze upon this glittering crown;
So shall my eyes receive their last content,   2050
My head, the latest honour due to it,
And jointly both yield up their wished right.
Continue ever thou celestial sun;
Let never silent night possess this clime:
Stand still, you watches of the element;
All times and seasons, rest you at a stay,
That Edward may be still fair England's king!
But day's bright beams doth vanish fast away,
And needs I must resign my wished crown.
Inhuman creatures, nurs'd with tiger's milk,   2060
Why gape you for your sovereign's overthrow?
My diadem, I mean, and guiltless life.
See, monsters, see, I'll wear my crown again.
                         [Putting on the crown.
What, fear you not the fury of your king?
But, hapless Edward, thou art fondly led;
They pass not for thy frowns as late they did,
But seek to make a new-elected king,
Which fills my mind with strange despairing thoughts,
Which thoughts are martyred with endless torments,
And in this torment comfort find I none,   2070

2065 fondly] foolishly   2066 pass] care

But that I feel the crown upon my head;
And therefore let me wear it yet a while.

   Trus. My lord, the parliament must have present
     news,
And therefore say, will you resign or no?
                         [*The* King *rageth.*

   K. Edw. I'll not resign, but, whilst I live be king.
Traitors, be gone, and join you with Mortimer.
Elect, conspire, install, do what you will:
Their blood and yours shall seal these treacheries.

   Bish. of Win. This answer we'll return; and so
     farewell.   [*Going with* Trussel.

   Leices. Call them again, my lord, and speak them
     fair;   2080
For if they go, the prince shall lose his right.

   K. Edw. Call thou them back, I have no power to
     speak.

   Leices. My lord, the king is willing to resign.

   Bish. of Win. If he be not, let him choose.

   K. Edw. Oh, would I might! but heavens and earth
     conspire
To make me miserable. Here receive my crown.
Receive it? no, these innocent hands of mine
Shall not be guilty of so foul a crime.
He of you all that most desires my blood,
And will be called the murtherer of a king,   2090
Take it. What, are you mov'd? pity you me?
Then send for unrelenting Mortimer,
And Isabel, whose eyes being turn'd to steel
Will sooner sparkle fire than shed a tear.
Yet stay, for rather than I will look on them,
Here, here! [*Gives the crown.*] Now, sweet God of
     heaven,
Make me despise this transitory pomp,
And sit for aye enthronised in heaven!
Come, death, and with thy fingers close my eyes,
Or if I live, let me forget myself.   2100

   Bish. of Win. My lord,—

K. Edw. Call me not lord;
Away, out of my sight: ah, pardon me,
Grief makes me lunatic.
Let not that Mortimer protect my son;
More safety there is in a tiger's jaws
Than his embracements. Bear this to the queen,
Wet with my tears, and dried again with sighs;

                      [*Gives a handkerchief.*

If with the sight thereof she be not moved,
Return it back and dip it in my blood.   2110
Commend me to my son, and bid him rule
Better than I: yet how have I transgress'd,
Unless it be with too much clemency?

    Trus. And thus most humbly do we take our leave.

    K. Edw. Farewell;

        [*Exeunt the* Bishop of Winchester *and* Trussel
           with the crown.

          I know the next news that they bring
Will be my death; and welcome shall it be:
To wretched men death is felicity.

    Leices. Another post! what news brings he?

    Enter Berkeley, *who gives a paper to* Leicester.

    K. Edw. Such news as I expect. Come, Berkeley,
      come,   2120
And tell thy message to my naked breast.

    Berk. My lord, think not a thought so villanous
Can harbour in a man of noble birth.
To do your highness service and devoir,
And save you from your foes, Berkeley would die.

    Leices. My lord, the council of the queen commands
That I resign my charge.

    K. Edw. And who must keep me now? Must you,
      my lord?

    Berk. Ay, my most gracious lord, so 'tis decreed.

    K. Edw. [*Taking the paper.*] By Mortimer, whose
      name is written here!   2130
Well may I rent his name that rends my heart. [*Tears it.*

This poor revenge hath something eas'd my mind.
So may his limbs be torn as is this paper!
Hear me, immortal Jove, and grant it too!

Berk. Your grace must hence with me to Berkeley
    straight.

K. Edw. Whither you will: all places are alike,
And every earth is fit for burial.

Leices. Favour him, my lord, as much as lieth in
    you.

Berk. Even so betide my soul as I use him.

K. Edw. Mine enemy hath pitied my estate,   2140
And that's the cause that I am now remov'd.

Berk. And thinks your grace that Berkeley will be
    cruel?

K. Edw. I know not; but of this am I assured,
That death ends all, and I can die but once.
Leicester, farewell.

Leices. Not yet, my lord; I'll bear you on your way.
                                        [*Exeunt.*

Enter Queen Isabella *and the younger* Mortimer.*

Y. Mor. Fair Isabel, now have we our desire;
The proud corrupters of the light-brain'd king
Have done their homage to the lofty gallows,
And he himself lies in captivity.   2150
Be rul'd by me, and we will rule the realm.
In any case take heed of childish fear,
For now we hold an old wolf by the ears,
That, if he slip, will seize upon us both,
And gripe the sorer, being grip'd himself.
Think therefore, madam, that imports us much
To erect your son with all the speed we may,
And that I be protector over him;
For our behoof will bear the greater sway
Whenas a king's name shall be under-writ.   2160

Q. Isab. Sweet Mortimer, the life of Isabel,
Be thou persuaded that I love thee well,

* The scene is an apartment of the royal palace.

And therefore, so the prince my son be safe,
Whom I esteem as dear as these mine eyes,
Conclude against his father what thou wilt,
And I myself will willingly subscribe.

   Y. Mor. First would I hear news that he were
     depos'd,
And then let me alone to handle him.

Enter Messenger.

Letters! from whence?

   Mess. From Killingworth, my lord.   2170
   Q. Isab. How fares my lord the king?
   Mess. In health, madam, but full of pensiveness.
   Q. Isab. Alas, poor soul, would I could ease his
     grief!
   Enter the Bishop of Winchester *with the crown.*
Thanks, gentle Winchester.

          Sirrah, be gone.   [*Exit* Messenger.
   Bish. of Win. The king hath willingly resign'd his
     crown.
   Q. Isab. Oh, happy news! send for the prince my
     son.
   Bish. of Win. Further, or this letter was sealed,
     Lord Berkeley came,
So that he now is gone from Killingworth;
And we have heard that Edmund laid a plot
To set his brother free; no more but so.   2180
The Lord of Berkeley is so pitiful
As Leicester that had charge of him before.

   Q. Isab. Then let some other be his guardian.
   Y. Mor. Let me alone, here is the privy-seal.

                 [*Exit the* Bish. of Win.
Who's there? Call hither Gurney and Matrevis.

               [*To* Attendants *within.*
To dash the heavy-headed Edmund's drift,
Berkeley shall be discharg'd, the king remov'd,
And none but we shall know where he lieth.

   Q. Isab. But, Mortimer, as long as he survives,

What safety rests for us or for my son?   2190
 Y. Mor. Speak, shall he presently be despatch'd and
  die?
 Q. Isab. I would he were, so 'twere not by my
  means.

Enter Matrevis* and Gurney.

 Y. Mor. Enough.—Matrevis, write a letter presently
Unto the Lord of Berkeley from ourself
That he resign the king to thee and Gurney;
And when 'tis done, we will subscribe our name.
 Mat. It shall be done, my lord.   *[Writes.*
 Y. Mor. Gurney.
 Gur. My lord?   2199
 Y. Mor. As thou intendest to rise by Mortimer,
Who now makes Fortune's wheel turn as he please,
Seek all the means thou canst to make him droop,
And neither give him kind word nor good look.
 Gur. I warrant you, my lord.
 Y. Mor. And this above the rest: because we hear
That Edmund casts to work his liberty,
Remove him still from place to place by night,
Till at the last he come to Killingworth,
And then from thence to Berkeley back again:
And by the way, to make him fret the more,   2210
Speak curstly to him; and in any case
Let no man comfort him if he chance to weep,
But amplify his grief with bitter words.
 Mat. Fear not, my lord, we'll do as you command.
 Y. Mor. So now away; post thitherwards amain.
 Q. Isab. Whither goes this letter? to my lord the
  king?
Commend me humbly to his majesty,
And tell him that I labour all in vain
To ease his grief and work his liberty: 2219
And bear him this as witness of my love. *[Gives ring.*

2191 presently] immediately * Sir John Maltravers.
     2206 casts] plots

Mat. I will, madam.   [*Exit with* Gurney.

Y. Mor. Finely dissembled. Do so still, sweet queen.
Here comes the young prince with the Earl of Kent.

Q. Isab. Something he whispers in his childish ears.

Y. Mor. If he have such access unto the prince,
Our plots and stratagems will soon be dash'd.

Q. Isab. Use Edmund friendly, as if all were well.

Enter Prince Edward, *and* Kent *talking with him.*

Y. Mor. How fares my honourable Lord of Kent?

Kent. In health, sweet Mortimer: How fares your
     grace?   2229

Q. Isab. Well, if my lord your brother were enlarg'd.

Kent. I hear of late he hath depos'd himself.

Q. Isab. The more my grief.

Y. Mor. And mine.

Kent. Ah, they do dissemble!   [*Aside.*

Q. Isab. Sweet son, come hither, I must talk with
     thee.

Y. Mor. Thou being his uncle and the next of
     blood,
Do look to be protector over the prince.

Kent. Not I, my lord; who should protect the son,
But she that gave him life? I mean the queen.

P. Edw. Mother, persuade me not to wear the
     crown: 2240
Let him be king; I am too young to reign.

Q. Isab. But be content, seeing it is his highness'
     pleasure.

P. Edw. Let me but see him first, and then I will.

Kent. Ay, do, sweet nephew.

Q. Isab. Brother, you know it is impossible.

P. Edw. Why, is he dead?

Q. Isab. No, God forbid.

Kent. I would those words proceeded from your
     heart.

Y. Mor. Inconstant Edmund, dost thou favour him,
That wast a cause of his imprisonment?   2250

Kent. The more cause now have I now to make
  amends.

  Y. Mor. [*aside to* Q. Isab.] I tell thee, 'tis not meet
    that one so false
Should come about the person of a prince.
My lord, he hath betrayed the king his brother,
And therefore trust him not.

  P. Edw. But he repents, and sorrows for it now.

  Q. Isab. Come, son, and go with this gentle lord
    and me.

  P. Edw. With you I will, but not with Mortimer.

  Y. Mor. Why, youngling, 'sdain'st thou so of
    Mortimer?
Then I will carry thee by force away.   2260

  P. Edw. Help, uncle Kent! Mortimer will wrong
    me.

  Q. Isab. Brother Edmund, strive not; we are his
    friends;
Isabel is nearer than the Earl of Kent.

  Kent. Sister, Edward is my charge, redeem him.

  Q. Isab. Edward is my son, and I will keep him.

  Kent. Mortimer shall know that he hath wrong'd me.
Hence will I haste to Killingworth Castle,
And rescue aged Edward from his foes,
To be reveng'd on Mortimer and thee.   [*Aside.*
  [*Exeunt, on one side,* Queen Isabella, Prince Edward,
    and the younger Mortimer; *on the other,* Kent.

Enter Matrevis, Gurney, *and* Soldiers, *with*
    King Edward.*

  Mat. My lord, be not pensive, we are your friends:
Men are ordain'd to live in misery,   2271
Therefore come; dalliance dangereth our lives.

  K. Edw. Friends, whither must unhappy Edward go?
Will hateful Mortimer appoint no rest?
Must I be vexed like the nightly bird,
Whose sight is loathsome to all winged fowls?

  * The scene is near Kenilworth Castle.

When will the fury of his mind assuage?
When will his heart be satisfied with blood?
If mine will serve, unbowel straight this breast,
And give my heart to Isabel and him;   2280
It is the chiefest mark they level at.

   Gur. Not so, my liege, the queen hath given this
     charge
To keep your grace in safety;
Your passions make your dolours to increase.

   K. Edw. This usage makes my misery increase.
But can my air of life continue long,
When all my senses are annoy'd with stench?
Within a dungeon England's king is kept,
Where I am starv'd for want of sustenance.
My daily diet is heart-breaking sobs,   2290
That almost rents the closet of my heart.
Thus lives old Edward not reliev'd by any,
And so must die, though pitied by many.
Oh, water, gentle friends, to cool my thirst,
And clear my body from foul excrements!

   Mat. Here's channel-water, as our charge is given;
Sit down, for we'll be barbers to your grace.

   K. Edw. Traitors, away! what, will you murther me,
Or choke your sovereign with puddle-water?

   Gur. No, but wash your face, and shave away your
     beard,   2300
Lest you be known, and so be rescued.

   Mat. Why strive you thus? your labour is in vain.

   K. Edw. The wren may strive against the lion's
     strength,
But all in vain: so vainly do I strive
To seek for mercy at a tyrant's hand.

       [*They wash him with puddle-water, and shave his
        beard away.*

Immortal powers, that know the painful cares
That waits upon my poor distressed soul,
Oh, level all your looks upon these daring men

       2296 channel] gutter

That wrongs their liege and sovereign, England's king!
O Gaveston, it is for thee that I am wrong'd, 2310
For me both thou and both the Spencers died;
And for your sakes a thousand wrongs I'll take.
The Spencers' ghosts, wherever they remain,
Wish well to mine; then, tush, for them I'll die.

Mat. 'Twixt theirs and yours shall be no enmity.
Come, come, away; now put the torches out,
We'll enter in by darkness to Killingworth.

Gur. How now, who comes there?

Enter Kent.

Mat. Guard the king sure: it is the Earl of Kent.

K. Edw. O gentle brother, help to rescue me! 2320

Mat. Keep them asunder; thrust in the king.

Kent. Soldiers, let me but talk to him one word.

Gur. Lay hands upon the earl for this assault.

Kent. Lay down your weapons, traitors! yield the
king.

Mat. Edmund, yield thou thyself, or thou shalt die.

Kent. Base villains, wherefore do you gripe me thus?

Gur. Bind him and so convey him to the court.

Kent. Where is the court but here? here is the king,
And I will visit him; why stay you me? 2329

Mat. The court is where Lord Mortimer remains;
Thither shall your honour go; and so farewell.

[*Exeunt* Matrevis *and* Gurney *with* King Edward.

Kent. Oh, miserable is that common-weal where
lords
Keep courts, and kings are lock'd in prison!

First Sold. Wherefore stay we? on, sirs, to the court.

Kent. Ay, lead me whither you will, even to my death,
Seeing that my brother cannot be releas'd. [*Exeunt.*

Enter the younger Mortimer.*

Y. Mor. The king must die, or Mortimer goes down;
The commons now begin to pity him:

* The scene is an apartment of the royal palace.

Yet he that is the cause of Edward's death,
Is sure to pay for it when his son is of age;   2340
And therefore will I do it cunningly.
This letter, written by a friend of ours,
Contains his death, yet bids them save his life.

[*Reads.*

Edwardum occidere nolite timere, bonum est,
Fear not to kill the king, 'tis good he die:
But read it thus, and that's another sense:
Edwardum occidere nolite, timere bonum est,
Kill not the king, 'tis good to fear the worst.
Unpointed as it is, thus shall it go,
That, being dead, if it chance to be found,   2350
Matrevis and the rest may bear the blame,
And we be quit that caus'd it to be done.
Within this room is lock'd the messenger
That shall convey it, and perform the rest:
And by a secret token that he bears,
Shall he be murdered when the deed is done.
Lightborn,
Come forth!

Enter Lightborn.

                    Art thou as resolute as thou wast?
Light. What else, my lord? and far more resolute.
Y. Mor. And hast thou cast how to accomplish it?
Light. Ay, ay, and none shall know which way he
    died.   2361
Y. Mor. But at his looks, Lightborn, thou wilt
    relent.
Light. Relent! ha, ha! I use much to relent!
Y. Mor. Well, do it bravely, and be secret.
Light. You shall not need to give instructions;
'Tis not the first time I have killed a man:
I learn'd in Naples how to poison flowers;
To strangle with a lawn thrust through the throat;
To pierce the windpipe with a needle's point;
Or whilst one is asleep, to take a quill   2370

And blow a little powder in his ears:
Or open his mouth and pour quick-silver down.
But yet I have a braver way than these.

  Y. Mor. What's that?

  Light. Nay, you shall pardon me; none shall know
    my tricks.

  Y. Mor. I care not how it is, so it be not spi'd.
Deliver this to Gurney and Matrevis.   [*Gives letter.*
At every ten miles end thou hast a horse.
Take this [*Gives money*]: away, and never see me more.

  Light. No?   2380

  Y. Mor. No; unless thou bring me news of Edward's
    death.

  Light. That will I quickly do. Farewell, my lord.
                                     [*Exit.*

  Y. Mor. The prince I rule, the queen do I com-
    mand,
And with a lowly congé to the ground
The proudest lords salute me as I pass;
I seal, I cancel, I do what I will.
Fear'd am I more than lov'd; let me be fear'd,
And when I frown, make all the court look pale.
I view the prince with Aristarchus' eyes,
Whose looks were as a breeching to a boy.   2390
They thrust upon me the protectorship,
And sue to me for that that I desire;
While at the council-table, grave enough,
And not unlike a bashful puritan,
First I complain of imbecility,
Saying it is *onus quam gravissimum;*
Till, being interrupted by my friends,
Suscepi that *provinciam,* as they term it;
And to conclude, I am Protector now.
Now is all sure: the queen and Mortimer   2400
Shall rule the realm, the king, and none rule us.
Mine enemies will I plague, my friends advance,

2395 imbecility] weakness   2396 a very heavy burden
                  2398 undertake that province

And what I list command who dare control?
Major sum quam cui possit fortuna nocere.
And that this be the coronation-day,
It pleaseth me and Isabel the queen.

                                                    [*Trumpets within.*
The trumpets sound, I must go take my place.

Enter King Edward the Third, Queen Isabella, *the*
Archbishop of Canterbury, Champion, *and* Nobles.*

    Archb. of Cant.   Long live King Edward, by the
        grace of God
King of England and Lord of Ireland!   2409
    Cham.   If any Christian, Heathen, Turk, or Jew,
Dares but affirm that Edward's not true king,
And will avouch his saying with the sword,
I am the Champion that will combat him.
    Y. Mor.   None comes, sound trumpets.   [*Trumpets.*
    K. Edw. Third.   Champion, here's to thee.
                                                    [*Gives purse.*
    Q. Isab.   Lord Mortimer, now take him to your
    charge.

        Enter Soldiers *with* Kent *prisoner.*

    Y. Mor.   What traitor have we there with blades
    and bills?
    First Sold.   Edmund the Earl of Kent.
    K. Edw. Third.   What hath he done?
    First Sold.   'A would have taken the king away per-
    force,   2420
As we were bringing him to Killingworth.
    Y. Mor.   Did you attempt his rescue, Edmund?
    speak.
    Kent.   Mortimer, I did; he is our king,
And thou compell'st this prince to wear the crown.
    Y. Mor.   Strike off his head: he shall have martial
    law.

  2404 *Major . . . nocere*] I am too great for fortune to hurt
        * The scene is at Westminster.

Kent. Strike off my head! base traitor, I defy thee!

K. Edw. Third. My lord, he is my uncle, and shall live.

Y. Mor. My lord, he is your enemy, and shall die.

Kent. Stay, villains!

K. Edw. Third. Sweet mother, if I cannot pardon him,
Entreat my Lord Protector for his life.   2431

Q. Isab. Son, be content; I dare not speak a word.

K. Edw. Third. Nor I, and yet methinks I should command;
But, seeing I cannot, I'll entreat for him.—
My lord, if you will let my uncle live,
I will requite it when I come to age.

Y. Mor. 'Tis for your highness' good and for the realm's.—
How often shall I bid you bear him hence?

Kent. Art thou king? must I die at thy command?

Y. Mor. At our command.—Once more away with him.   2440

Kent. Let me but stay and speak; I will not go.
Either my brother or his son is king,
And none of both them thirst for Edmund's blood:
And therefore, soldiers, whither will you hale me?

[*Soldiers hale* Kent *away, and carry him to be beheaded.*

K. Edw. Third. What safety may I look for at his
If that my uncle shall be murthered thus?   [hands,

Q. Isab. Fear not, sweet boy, I'll guard thee from thy foes;
Had Edmund liv'd, he would have sought thy death.
Come, son, we'll ride a-hunting in the park.

K. Edw. Third. And shall my uncle Edmund ride with us?   2450

Q. Isab. He is a traitor; think not on him; come.

    [*Exeunt.*

Enter Matrevis *and* Gurney.*

Mat. Gurney, I wonder the king dies not,
Being in a vault up to the knees in water,

    * The scene is Berkeley Castle.

To which the channels of the castle run,
From whence a damp continually ariseth,
That were enough to poison any man,
Much more a king brought up so tenderly.

   Gur. And so do I, Matrevis: yesternight
I opened but the door to throw him meat,
And I was almost stifled with the savour.   2460

   Mat. He hath a body able to endure
More than we can inflict: and therefore now
Let us assail his mind another while.

   Gur. Send for him out thence, and I will anger him.

   Mat. But stay, who's this?

Enter Lightborn.

   Light. My Lord Protector greets you.   *[Gives letter.*

   Gur. What's here? I know not how to construe it.

   Mat. Gurney, it was left unpointed for the nonce;
Edwardum occidere nolite timere,
That's his meaning.   2470

   Light. Know you this token? I must have the king.
                          [Gives token.

   Mat. Ay, stay a while, thou shalt have answer
    straight.
This villain's sent to make away the king.   *[Aside.*

   Gur. I thought as much.   *[Aside.*

   Mat. And when the murther's done,
See how he must be handled for his labour.
Pereat iste! Let him have the king.   *[Aside.*
What else? Here is the keys, this is the lake,
Do as you are commanded by my lord.   2479

   Light. I know what I must do. Get you away:
Yet be not far off; I shall need your help.
See that in the next room I have a fire,
And get me a spit, and let it be red-hot.

   Mat. Very well.

   Gur. Need you anything besides?

   Light. What else? a table and a feather-bed.

     2477 *Pereat iste*] Let this man perish

Gur. That's all?

Light. Ay, ay: so, when I call, you bring it in.

Mat. Fear not you that.

Gur. Here's a light to go into the dungeon.　2490

[*Gives light to* Lightborn, *and then exit with* Matrevis.

Light. So now must I about this gear: ne'er was
　　there any

So finely handled as this king shall be.

Foh, here's a place indeed with all my heart!

　　K. Edw. Who's there? what light is that? where-
　　fore comes thou?

　　Light. To comfort you, and bring you joyful news.

　　K. Edw. Small comfort finds poor Edward in thy
　　looks.

Villain, I know thou com'st to murther me.

　　Light. To murther you, my most gracious lord?

Far is it from my heart to do you harm.

The queen sent me to see how you were used,　2500

For she relents at this your misery:

And what eyes can refrain from shedding tears,

To see a king in this most piteous state?

　　K. Edw. Weep'st thou already? list a-while to me,

And then thy heart, were it as Gurney's is,

Or as Matrevis', hewn from the Caucasus,

Yet will it melt ere I have done my tale.

This dungeon where they keep me is the sink

Wherein the filth of all the castle falls.

　　Light. O villains!　2510

　　K. Edw. And there in mire and puddle have I stood

This ten days' space; and, lest that I should sleep,

One plays continually upon a drum.

They give me bread and water, being a king;

So that, for want of sleep and sustenance,

My mind's distempered, and my body's numb'd,

And whether I have limbs or no I know not.

Oh, would my blood dropp'd out from every vein,

As doth this water from my tattered robes.

Tell Isabel the queen, I look'd not thus,　2520

When for her sake I ran at tilt in France,
And there unhors'd the Duke of Cleremont.
    Light. Oh, speak no more, my lord! this breaks my
      heart.
Lie on this bed, and rest yourself a while.
    K. Edw. These looks of thine can harbour naught
but death.
I see my tragedy written in thy brows.
Yet stay a while, forbear thy bloody hand,
And let me see the stroke before it comes,
That even then when I shall lose my life,
My mind may be more steadfast on my God.   2530
    Light. What means your highness to mistrust me
      thus?
    K. Edw. What means thou to dissemble with me
      thus?
    Light. These hands were never stain'd with innocent
      blood,
Nor shall they now be tainted with a king's.
    K. Edw. Forgive my thought for having such a
      thought.
One jewel have I left; receive thou this.
                      [Giving jewel.
Still fear I, and I know not what's the cause,
But every joint shakes as I give it thee.
Oh, if thou harbour'st murther in thy heart,
Let this gift change thy mind, and save thy soul! 2540
Know that I am a king: Oh, at that name
I feel a hell of grief! where is my crown?
Gone, gone, and do I remain alive?
    Light. You're overwatch'd, my lord: lie down and
      rest.
    K. Edw. But that grief keeps me waking, I should
sleep;
For not these ten days have these eyes' lids clos'd.
Now as I speak they fall, and yet with fear
Open again. Oh, wherefore sits thou here?
    Light. If you mistrust me, I'll be gone, my lord.

K. Edw. No, no, for if thou mean'st to murther me,
Thou wilt return again, and therefore stay.   [*Sleeps.*
    Light. He sleeps.   2552
    K. Edw. [*waking*] Oh, let me not die yet! Oh, stay
        a while!
    Light. How now, my lord?
    K. Edw. Something still buzzeth in mine ears,
And tells me if I sleep I never wake;
This fear is that which makes me tremble thus.
And therefore tell me, wherefore art thou come?
    Light. To rid thee of thy life. Matrevis, come!

        Enter Matrevis *and* Gurney.

    K. Edw. I am too weak and feeble to resist.   2560
Assist me, sweet God, and receive my soul.
    Light. Run for the table.
    K. Edw. Oh, spare me, or dispatch me in a trice.
        [*Matrevis* brings in a table. *King Edward is*
            murdered by holding him down on the bed with the
            table, and stamping on it.
    Light. So, lay the table down, and stamp on it,
But not too hard, lest that you bruise his body.
    Mat. I fear me that this cry will raise the town,
And therefore let us take horse and away.
    Light. Tell me, sirs, was it not bravely done?
    Gur. Excellent well: take this for thy reward.
                            [*Stabs* Lightborn, *who dies.*
Come, let us cast the body in the moat,   2570
And bear the king's to Mortimer our lord:
Away!   [*Exeunt with the bodies.*

        Enter the younger Mortimer *and* Matrevis.*

    Y. Mor. Is't done, Matrevis, and the murtherer
        dead?
    Mat. Ay, my good lord; I would it were undone.
    Y. Mor. Matrevis, if thou now growest penitent,
I'll be thy ghostly father; therefore choose,

        * The scene is an apartment in the royal palace.

Whether thou wilt be secret in this,
Or else die by the hand of Mortimer.

Mat. Gurney, my lord, is fled, and will, I fear,
Betray us both; therefore let me fly. 2580

Y. Mor. Fly to the savages!

Mat. I humbly thank your honour. [*Exit.*

Y. Mor. As for myself, I stand as Jove's huge tree,
And others are but shrubs compar'd to me.
All tremble at my name, and I fear none;
Let's see who dare impeach me for his death!

Enter Queen Isabella.

Q. Isab. Ah, Mortimer, the king my son hath news
His father's dead, and we have murthered him!

Y. Mor. What if he have? the king is yet a child.

Q. Isab. Ay, ay, but he tears his hair, and wrings
his hands, 2590
And vows to be reveng'd upon us both.
Into the council-chamber he is gone,
To crave the aid and succour of his peers.
Ay me, see where he comes, and they with him;
Now, Mortimer, begins our tragedy.

Enter King Edward the Third, Lords, *and* Attendants.

First Lord. Fear not, my lord, know that you are a
king.

K. Edw. Third. Villain!—

Y. Mor. How now, my lord!

K. Edw. Third. Think not that I am frighted with
thy words:
My father's murthered through thy treachery; 2600
And thou shalt die, and on his mournful hearse
Thy hateful and accursed head shall lie,
To witness to the world that by thy means
His kingly body was too soon interr'd.

Q. Isab. Weep not, sweet son.

K. Edw. Third. Forbid not me to weep; he was my
father,
And had you lov'd him half so well as I,

You could not bear his death thus patiently.
But you, I fear, conspir'd with Mortimer.

   First Lord. Why speak you not unto my lord the
     king?   2610

   Y. Mor. Because I think scorn to be accus'd.
Who is the man dare say I murthered him?

   K. Edw. Third. Traitor, in me my loving father
     speaks,
And plainly saith, 'twas thou that murther'dst him.

   Y. Mor. But hath your grace no other proof than
     this?

   K. Edw. Third. Yes, if this be the hand of Mortimer.
                             [Showing letter.

   Y. Mor. False Gurney hath betray'd me and him-
     self.   *[Aside to* Queen Isabella.

   Q. Isab. I fear'd as much; murther cannot be hid.

   Y. Mor. It is my hand; what gather you by this?

   K. Edw. Third. That thither thou didst send a
     murtherer.   2620

   Y. Mor. What murtherer? bring forth the man I sent.

   K. Edw. Third. Ah, Mortimer, thou knowest that
     he is slain;
And so shalt thou be too.—Why stays he here?
Bring him unto a hurdle, drag him forth;
Hang him, I say, and set his quarters up;
But bring his head back presently to me.

   Q. Isab. For my sake, sweet son, pity Mortimer.

   Y. Mor. Madam, entreat not, I will rather die,
Than sue for life unto a paltry boy.

   K. Edw. Third. Hence with the traitor, with the
     murtherer!   2630

   Y. Mor. Base Fortune, now I see, that in thy wheel
There is a point, to which when men aspire,
They tumble headlong down: that point I touch'd,
And, seeing there was no place to mount up higher,
Why should I grieve at my declining fall?
Farewell, fair queen; weep not for Mortimer,
That scorns the world, and, as a traveller,

Goes to discover countries yet unknown.

　K Edw. Third. What, suffer you the traitor to delay?

　　　[*Exit the younger* Mortimer *with* First Lord *and some of the* Attendants.

　Q. Isab. As thou receivedst thy life from me,　2640
Spill not the blood of gentle Mortimer!

　K. Edw. Third. This argues that you spilt my
　　father's blood,
Else would you not entreat for Mortimer.

　Q. Isab. I spill his blood! no.

　K. Edw. Third. Ay, madam, you; for so the rumour
　　runs.

　Q. Isab. That rumour is untrue; for loving thee
Is this report rais'd on poor Isabel.

　K. Edw. Third. I do not think her so unnatural.

　Sec. Lord. My lord, I fear me it will prove too true.

　K. Edw. Third. Mother, you are suspected for his
　　death,　2650
And therefore we commit you to the Tower
Till further trial may be made thereof.
If you be guilty, though I be your son,
Think not to find me slack or pitiful.

　Q. Isab. Nay, to my death, for too long have I lived
Whenas my son thinks to abridge my days.

　K. Edw. Third. Away with her, her words enforce
　　these tears,
And I shall pity her if she speak again.

　Q. Isab. Shall I not mourn for my beloved lord,
And with the rest accompany him to his grave?　2660

　Sec. Lord. Thus, madam, 'tis the king's will you
　　shall hence.

　Q. Isab. He hath forgotten me; stay, I am his
　　mother.

　Sec. Lord. That boots not; therefore, gentle madam,
　　go.

　Q. Isab. Then come, sweet death, and rid me of this
　　grief.

　　　[*Exit with* Second Lord *and some of the* Attendants.

Re-enter First Lord, *with the head of the younger*
Mortimer.

First Lord. My lord, here is the head of Mortimer.

K. Edw. Third. Go fetch my father's hearse, where
    it shall lie;
And bring my funeral robes.   [*Exeunt* Attendants.
                    Accursed head,
Could I have rul'd thee then, as I do now,
Thou hadst not hatch'd this monstrous treachery!
Here comes the hearse: help me to mourn, my lords.

Re-enter Attendants, *with the hearse and funeral robes.*

Sweet father, here unto thy murthered ghost   2671
I offer up the wicked traitor's head;
And let these tears, distilling from mine eyes,
Be witness of my grief and innocency.   [*Exeunt.*

THE
MASSACRE
AT PARIS:

With the Death of the Duke
of Guise.

As it was plaide by the right honourable the
Lord high *Admirall* his Seruants.

Written by *Christopher Marlow*.

AT LONDON

Printed by *E. A.* for *Edward White*, dwelling neere
the little North doore of S. Paules
Church, at the signe of
the Gun.

Dramatis Personæ

Charles the Ninth, *King of France.*

Duke of Anjou, *his brother, afterwards* King Henry the Third.

King of Navarre.

Prince of Condé, *his cousin.*

Duke of Guise,
Cardinal of Lorraine,
Duke Dumaine,
} *brothers.*

Son to the Duke of Guise, *a boy.*

The Lord High Admiral.

Duke Joyeux.

Epernoun.

Pleshé.

Bartus.

Two Lords of Poland.

Gonzago.

Retes.

Mountsorrell.

Mugeroun.

The Cutpurse.

Loreine, *a preacher.*

Seroune.

Ramus.

Talæus.

Friar.

Surgeon.

English Agent.

Apothecary.

Captain of the Guard, Protestants, Schoolmasters, Soldiers, Murderers, Attendants, *etc.*

Catherine, *the Queen-Mother of France.*

Margaret, *her daughter, wife to the* King of Navarre.

The Old Queen of Navarre.

Duchess of Guise.

Wife *to* Seroune.

Maid *to the* Duchess of Guise.

The Massacre at Paris

Enter Charles, *the French king;* Catherine, *the Queen-Mother; the* King of Navarre; Margaret, *Queen of Navarre; the* Prince of Condé; *the* Lord High Admiral; *the* Old Queen of Navarre; *with others.**

Char. Prince of Navarre, my honourable brother,
Prince Condé, and my good Lord Admiral,
I wish this union and religious league,
Knit in these hands, thus join'd in nuptial rites,
May not dissolve till death dissolve our lives;
And that the native sparks of princely love,
That kindled first this motion in our hearts,
May still be fuell'd in our progeny.
   Nav. The many favours which your grace hath
    shown,
From time to time, but specially in this,   10
Shall bind me ever to your highness' will,
In what Queen-Mother or your grace commands.
   Cath. Thanks, son Navarre. You see we love you
    well,
That link you in marriage with our daughter here;
And, as you know, our difference in religion
Might be a means to cross you in your love.
   Char. Well, madam, let that rest.
And now, my lords, the marriage-rites perform'd,
We think it good to go and consummate
The rest with hearing of a holy mass.   20
Sister, I think yourself will bear us company.
   Mar. I will, my good lord.
   Char. The rest that will not go, my lords, may stay.
Come, mother,
Let us go to honour this solemnity.
   Cath. Which I'll dissolve with blood and cruelty.
                           [Aside.

      * The scene is in the royal palace.

[*Exeunt all except the* King of Navarre, Condé,
    and the Admiral.

Nav. Prince Condé and my good Lord Admiral,
Now Guise may storm, but do us little hurt,
Having the king, Queen-mother on our sides,
To stop the malice of his envious heart,   30
That seeks to murder all the Protestants.
Have you not heard of late how he decreed,
If that the king had given consent thereto,
That all the protestants that are in Paris
Should have been murdered the other night?
    Adm. My lord, I marvel that th' aspiring Guise
Dares once adventure, without the king's consent,
To meddle or attempt such dangerous things.
    Con. My lord, you need not marvel at the Guise,
For what he doth the Pope will ratify,   40
In murder, mischief, or in tyranny.
    Nav. But he that sits and rules above the clouds
Doth hear and see the prayers of the just,
And will revenge the blood of innocents,
That Guise hath slain by treason of his heart,
And brought by murder to their timeless ends.
    Adm. My lord, but did you mark the Cardinal,
The Guise's brother, and the Duke Dumaine,
How they did storm at these your nuptial rites,
Because the house of Bourbon now comes in,   50
And joins your lineage to the crown of France?
    Nav. And that's the cause that Guise so frowns
        at us,
And beats his brains to catch us in his trap,
Which he hath pitch'd within his deadly toil.
Come, my lords, let's go to the church, and pray
That God may still defend the right of France,
And make his Gospel flourish in this land.   [*Exeunt.*

Enter Guise.*

Guise. If ever Hymen lour'd at marriage-rites,

    * The scene is probably in Guise's house.

And had his altars deck'd with dusky lights;
If ever sun stain'd heaven with bloody clouds,   60
And made it look with terror on the world;
If ever day were turn'd to ugly night,
And night made semblance of the hue of hell;
This day, this hour, this fatal night,
Shall fully show the fury of them all.
Apothecary!

Enter Apothecary.

Apoth. My lord?
Guise. Now shall I prove and guerdon to the full
The love thou bear'st unto the house of Guise.
Where are those perfumed gloves which I sent   70
To be poisoned? hast thou done them? speak;
Will every savour breed a pang of death?
Apoth. See where they be, my good lord,
And he that smells but to them, dies.
Guise. Then thou remainest resolute?
Apoth. I am, my lord, in what your grace com-
Till death.   [mands.
Guise. Thanks, my good friend, I will requite thy
      love.
Go, then, present them to the Queen Navarre;
For she is that huge blemish in our eye,   80
That makes these upstart heresies in France:
Be gone, my friend, present them to her straight.
                                    [*Exit* Apothecary.
Soldier!

Enter a Soldier.

Sold. My lord?
Guise. Now come thou forth and play thy tragic
      part.
Stand in some window opening near the street,
And when thou see'st the Admiral ride by,
Discharge thy musket and perform his death;
And then I'll guerdon thee with store of crowns.   89
Sold. I will, my lord.   [*Exit.*

Guise. Now, Guise, begin those deep-engender'd
    thoughts
To burst abroad those never-dying flames
Which cannot be extinguish'd but by blood.
Oft have I levell'd, and at last have learn'd
That peril is the chiefest way to happiness,
And resolution honour's fairest aim.
What glory is there in a common good,
That hangs for every peasant to achieve?
That like I best that flies beyond my reach.
Set me to scale the high Pyramides,   100
And thereon set the diadem of France,
I'll either rend it with my nails to naught,
Or mount the top with my aspiring wings,
Although my downfall be the deepest hell.
For this I wake, when others think I sleep;
For this I wait, that scorns attendance else;
For this, my quenchless thirst, whereon I build,
Hath often pleaded kindred to the king;
For this, this head, this heart, this hand and sword,
Contrives, imagines, and fully executes   110
Matters of import aim'd at by many,
Yet understood by none;
For this, hath heaven engender'd me of earth;
For this, this earth sustains my body's weight,
And with this weight I'll counterpoise a crown,
Or with seditions weary all the world;
For this, from Spain the stately Catholics
Sends Indian gold to coin me French ecues;
For this, have I a largess from the Pope,
A pension, and a dispensation too;   120
And by that privilege to work upon,
My policy hath fram'd religion.
Religion! *O Diabole!*
Fie, I am asham'd, however that I seem,
To think a word of such a simple sound
Of so great matter should be made the ground.
The gentle king, whose pleasure uncontroll'd

Weak'neth his body, and will waste his realm,
If I repair not what he ruinates,
Him, as a child, I daily win with words,   130
So that for proof he barely bears the name:
I execute, and he sustains the blame.
The Mother-Queen works wonders for my sake,
And in my love entombs the hope of France,
Rifling the bowels of her treasury,
To supply my wants and necessity.
Paris hath full five hundred colleges,
As monasteries, priories, abbeys, and halls,
Wherein are thirty thousand able men,
Besides a thousand sturdy student Catholics,   140
And more,—of my knowledge, in one cloister keeps
Five hundred fat Franciscan friars and priests—,
All this and more, if more may be compris'd,
To bring the will of our desires to end.
Then, Guise,
Since thou hast all the cards within thy hands,
To shuffle or cut, take this as surest thing,
That, right or wrong, thou deal thyself a king.
Ay, but, Navarre, Navarre,—'tis but a nook of
    France,
Sufficient yet for such a petty king,   150
That, with a rabblement of his heretics,
Blinds Europe's eyes, and troubleth our estate.
Him will we—[*Pointing to his sword.*]
But first let's follow those in France
That hinder our possession to the crown.
As Cæsar to his soldiers, so say I,—
Those that hate me will I learn to loathe.
Give me a look, that, when I bend the brows,
Pale death may walk in furrows of my face;
A hand, that with a grasp may gripe the world;   160
An ear to hear what my detractors say;
A royal seat, a sceptre, and a crown;
That those which do behold, they may become
As men that stand and gaze against the sun.

The plot is laid, and things shall come to pass
Where resolution strives for victory.   [*Exit.*

Enter the King of Navarre, Queen Margaret, *the* Old
Queen of Navarre, *the* Prince of Condé, *and the*
Admiral; *they are met by the* Apothecary *with the gloves,
which he gives to the* Old Queen.*

 Apoth. Madam, I beseech your grace to accept this
  simple gift.
 Old. Q. of Nav. Thanks, my good friend. Hold, take
  thou this reward.   [*Gives a purse.*
 Apoth. I humbly thank your majesty.   [*Exit.*
 Old. Q. of Nav. Methinks the gloves have a very
  strong perfume,   170
The scent whereof doth make my head to ache.
 Nav. Doth not your grace know the man that gave
  them you?   [man.
 Old Q. of Nav. Not well; but do remember such a
 Adm. Your grace was ill-advis'd to take them, then,
Considering of these dangerous times.
 Old Q. of Nav. Help, son Navarre, I am poisoned!
 Mar. The heavens forbid your highness such mis-
  hap!
 Nav. The late suspicion of the Duke of Guise
Might well have moved your highness to beware
How you did meddle with such dangerous gifts. 180
 Mar. Too late it is, my lord, if that be true,
To blame her highness; but I hope it be
Only some natural passion makes her sick.
 Old Q. of Nav. Oh no, sweet Margaret, the fatal
  poison
Works within my head; my brain-pan breaks;
My heart doth faint; I die!   [*Dies.*
 Nav. My mother poisoned here before my face!
O gracious God, what times are these!
Oh, grant, sweet God, my days may end with hers,

   * Scene—a street outside the palace.
    183 passion] ailment

That I with her may die and live again.   190

   Mar. Let not this heavy chance, my dearest lord,
(For whose effects my soul is massacred),
Infect thy gracious breast with fresh supply
To aggravate our sudden misery.

   Adm. Come, my lords, let us bear her body hence,
And see it honoured with just solemnity.

      [*As they are going out, the* Soldier *dischargeth his
       musket at the* Admiral.

   Con. What, are you hurt, my Lord High Admiral?

   Adm. Ay, my good lord, shot through the arm.

   Nav. We are betray'd! Come, my lords, and let us
Go tell the king of this.   200

   Adm. These are
The cursed Guisians that do seek our death.
Oh, fatal was this marriage to us all.

      [*Exeunt, bearing out the body of the* Old Queen
      of Navarre.

   Enter King Charles, Catherine *the Queen-Mother,*
      Guise, Anjou, *and* Dumaine.*

   Cath. My noble son, and princely Duke of Guise,
Now have we got the fatal, straggling deer
Within the compass of a deadly toil,
And, as we late decreed, we may perform.

   Char. Madam, it will be noted through the world
An action bloody and tyrannical;
Chiefly, since under safety of our word   210
They justly challenge their protection:
Besides, my heart relents that noblemen,
Only corrupted in religion,
Ladies of honour, knights, and gentlemen,
Should for their conscience taste such ruthless ends.

   Anj. Though gentle minds should pity others' pains,
Yet will the wisest note their proper griefs,
And rather seek to scourge their enemies
Than be themselves base subjects to the whip.   219

     * The scene is in the royal palace.

Guise. Methinks, my Lord, Anjou hath well advis'd
Your highness to consider of the thing,
And rather choose to seek your country's good
Than pity or relieve these upstart heretics.

Cath. I hope these reasons may serve my princely
To have some care for fear of enemies.   [son

Char. Well, madam, I refer it to your majesty,
And to my nephew here, the Duke of Guise:
What you determine, I will ratify.

Cath. Thanks to my princely son.—Then tell me,
Guise,
What order will you set down for the massacre? 230

Guise. Thus, madam.
They that shall be actors in this massacre
Shall wear white crosses on their burgonets,
And tie white linen scarfs about their arms:
He that wants these, and is suspected of heresy,
Shall die, be he king or emperor. Then I'll have
A peal of ordnance shot from the tower, at which
They all shall issue out and set the streets,
And then, the watchword being given, a bell shall
ring,
Which when they hear, they shall begin to kill, 240
And never cease until that bell shall cease,
Then breathe a while.

Enter the Admiral's Serving-Man.

Char. How now, fellow, what news?

Serv.-M. And it please your grace, the Lord High
Admiral,
Riding the streets, was traitorously shot,
And most humbly entreats your majesty
To visit him, sick in his bed,

Char. Messenger, tell him I will see him straight.
[*Exit Serv.-M.*
What shall we do now with the Admiral?

Cath. Your majesty were best go visit him, 250

233 burgonets] helmets   238 set] beset

And make a show as if all were well.

   Char. Content; I will go visit the Admiral.

   Guise. And I will go take order for his death.

                         [*Exeunt* Catherine *and* Guise.

             Enter the Admiral *in his bed.**

   Char. How fares it with my Lord High Admiral?
Hath he been hurt with villains in the street?
I vow and swear, as I am King of France,
To find and to repay the man with death,
With death delay'd and torments never us'd,
That durst presume for hope of any gain
To hurt the nobleman his sovereign loves.   260

   Adm. Ah, my good lord, these are the Guisians,
That seek to massacre our guiltless lives.

   Char. Assure yourself, my good Lord Admiral,
I deeply sorrow for your treacherous wrong;
And that I am not more secure myself
Than I am careful you should be preserved.
Cousin, take twenty of our strongest guard,
And under your direction, see they keep
All treacherous violence from our noble friend,
Repaying all attempts with present death   270
Upon the cursed breakers of our peace.
And so be patient, good Lord Admiral,
And every hower I will visit you.

   Adm. I humbly thank your royal majesty.

                [*Exeunt* Charles, *&c. Scene closes.*

   Enter Guise, Anjou, Dumaine, Gonzago, Retes,
     Mountsorrell, *and* Soldiers, *to the massacre.*†

   Guise. Anjou, Dumaine, Gonzago, Retes, swear
By the argent crosses in your burgonets,
To kill all that you suspect of heresy.

   Dum. I swear by this to be unmerciful.

   Anj. I am disguis'd, and none knows who I am,

---

  * The scene is the Admiral's house.   273 hower] hour
    † The scene is a street outside the Admiral's house.

And therefore mean to murder all I meet.   280

Gon. And so will I.

Retes. And I.

Guise. Away, then, break into the Admiral's house.

Retes. Ay, let the Admiral be first despatch'd.

Guise. The Admiral,

Chief standard-bearer to the Lutherans,

Shall in the entrance of this massacre

Be murdered in his bed. Gonzago,

Conduct them thither, and then

Beset his house, that not a man may live.   290

Anj. That charge is mine. Switzers, keep you the streets,

And at each corner shall the king's guard stand.

Gon. Come, sirs, follow me.

                    [*Exit* Gonzago *and others with him.*

Anj. Cousin, the captain of the Admiral's guard,

Plac'd by my brother, will betray his lord.

Now, Guise, shall Catholics flourish once again;

The head being off, the members cannot stand.

Retes. But look, my lord, there's some in the Admiral's house.

         [*The* Admiral *discovered in bed;* Gonzago *and others in the house.*

Anj. In lucky time: come, let us keep this lane,

And slay his servants that shall issue out.   300

Gon. Where is the Admiral?

Adm. Oh, let me pray before I die!

Gon. Then pray unto our Lady; kiss this cross.

                                   [*Stabs him.*

Adm. O God, forgive my sins!   [*Dies.*

Guise. Gonzago, what, is he dead?

Gon. Ay, my lord.

Guise. Then throw him down.

             [*The body of the* Admiral *is thrown down.*

Anj. Now, cousin, view him well:

It may be it is some other, and he escap'd.

Guise. Cousin, 'tis he; I know him by his look: 310

See where my soldier shot him through the arm;
He miss'd him near, but we have struck him now.
Ah, base Chatillon and degenerate,
Chief standard-bearer to the Lutherans,
Thus, in despite of thy religion,
The Duke of Guise stamps on thy lifeless bulk!

Anj. Away with him! cut off his head and hands,
And send them for a present to the Pope;
And, when this just revenge is finished,
Unto Mount Faucon will we drag his corse, 320
And he, that living hated so the Cross,
Shall, being dead, be hang'd thereon in chains.

Guise. Anjou, Gonzago, Retes, if that you three
Will be as resolute as I and Dumaine,
There shall not a Huguenot breathe in France.

Anj. I swear by this cross, we'll not be partial,
But slay as many as we can come near.

Guise. Mountsorrell, go shoot the ordnance off,
That they, which have already set the street,
May know their watchword; then toll the bell, 330
And so let's forward to the massacre.

Mount. I will, my lord.   [*Exit.*

Guise. And now, my lords, let's closely to our
 business.

Anj. Anjou will follow thee.

Dum. And so will Dumaine.
    [*The ordnance being shot off, the bell tolls.*

Guise. Come then, let's away.   [*Exeunt.*

Enter Guise, *and the rest, with their swords drawn, chasing
the Protestants.*

Guise. Tuez, tuez, tuez!
Let none escape! murder the Huguenots!

Anj. Kill them! kill them!   [*Exeunt.*

Enter Loreine, *running;* Guise *and the rest pursuing him.*

Guise. Loreine, Loreine! follow Loreine!—Sirrah,
Are you a preacher of these heresies? 341

Lor. I am a preacher of the word of God;
And thou a traitor to thy soul and him.

    Guise. 'Dearly beloved brother,'—thus 'tis written.
　　　　　　　　　　　　　[Stabs Loreine, *who dies.*

    Anj. Stay, my lord, let me begin the psalm.

    Guise. Come, drag him away, and throw him in a
    ditch.　　　　　　　　　　*[Exeunt with the body.*

Enter Mountsorrell, *and knocks at* Seroune's *door.**

    Seroune's Wife [within]. Who is that which knocks
    there?

    Mount. Mountsorrell, from the Duke of Guise.

    Seroune's Wife [within]. Husband, come down;
    here's one would speak with you
From the Duke of Guise.　　　　　　　　　　350

Enter Seroune *from the house.*

    Ser. To speak with me, from such a man as he?

    Mount. Ay, ay, for this, Seroune; and thou shalt
    ha't.　　　　　　　　　　*[Showing his dagger.*

    Ser. Oh, let me pray before I take my death!

    Mount. Dispatch, then, quickly.

    Ser. O Christ my Saviour!

    Mount. Christ, villain?
Why, darest thou presume to call on Christ,
Without the intercession of some saint?
Sanctus Jacobus, he was my saint; pray to him.

    Ser. Oh, let me pray unto my God!　　　　360

    Mount. Then take this with you.
　　　　　　　[Stabs Seroune, *who dies; and then exit.*

Enter Ramus, *in his study.†*

    Ramus. What fearful cries comes from the river
    Seine,
That frights poor Ramus sitting at his book!

---

    * The scene is a street.
    † The scene is in Ramus's house.

I fear the Guisians have pass'd the bridge,
And mean once more to menace me.

Enter Talæus.

Tal. Fly, Ramus, fly, if thou wilt save thy life!
Ramus. Tell me, Talæus, wherefore should I fly?
Tal. The Guisians are
Hard at thy door, and mean to murder us:
Hark, hark, they come! I'll leap out at the window.
Ramus. Sweet Talæus, stay.   371

Enter Gonzago *and* Retes.

Gon. Who goes there?
Retes. 'Tis Talæus, Ramus' bedfellow.
Gon. What art thou?
Tal. I am, as Ramus is, a Christian.
Retes. Oh, let him go, he is a Catholic.
                                    [*Exit* Talæus.
Gon. Come, Ramus, more gold, or thou shalt have
    the stab.
Ramus. Alas,
I am a scholar, how should I have gold?
All that I have is but my stipend from the king,   380
Which is no sooner receiv'd but it is spent.

Enter Guise, Anjou, Dumaine, Mountsorrell, *and*
                    Soldiers.

Anj. Who have you there?
Retes. 'Tis Ramus, the king's Professor of Logic.
Guise. Stab him.
Ramus. O good my lord,
Wherein hath Ramus been so offensious?
Guise. Marry, sir, in having a smack in all,
And yet didst never sound anything to the depth.
Was it not thou that scoff'dst the *Organon*,
And said it was a heap of vanities?   390
He that will be a flat dichotomist,
And seen in nothing but epitomes,
Is in your judgment thought a learned man;

And he, forsooth, must go and preach in Germany,
Excepting against doctors' axioms,
And *ipse dixi* with this quiddity,
Argumentum testimonii est inartificiale.
To contradict which, I say, Ramus shall die:
How answer you that? your *nego argumentum*
Cannot serve, sirrah. Kill him.   400

   Ramus. O good my lord, let me but speak a word!
   Anj. Well, say on.
   Ramus. Not for my life do I desire this pause;
But in my latter hour to purge myself,
In that I know the things that I have wrote,
Which, as I hear, one Scheckius takes it ill,
Because my places, being but three, contains all his.
I knew the *Organon* to be confus'd,
And I reduc'd it into better form:
And this for Aristotle will I say,   410
That he that despiseth him can ne'er
Be good in logic or philosophy;
And that's because the blockish Sorbonnists
Attribute as much unto their works
As to the service of the eternal God.

   Guise. Why suffer you that peasant to declaim?
Stab him, I say, and send him to his friends in hell.
   Anj. Ne'er was there collier's son so full of pride.
                   [*Stabs* Ramus, *who dies.*

   Guise. My Lord of Anjou, there are a hundred Protestants,
Which we have chas'd into the river Seine,   420
That swim about, and so preserve their lives:
How may we do? I fear me they will live.

   Dum. Go place some men upon the bridge,
With bows and darts, to shoot at them they see,
And sink them in the river as they swim.

---

   396 *ipse dixi*] I have said it myself
   397 *Argumentum . . . inartificiale*] The argument of the evidence is not according to the rules
   399 *nego argumentum*] I deny the argument

Guise. 'Tis well advis'd, Dumaine; go see it straight
    be done.   [*Exit* Dumaine.
And in the meantime, my lord, could we devise
To get those pedants from the King Navarre,
That are tutors to him and the Prince of Condé—

Anj. For that, let me alone, cousin; stay you here,
And when you see me in, then follow hard.   431

Anjou *knocketh at the door; and enter the* King of Navarre
and the Prince of Condé, *with their two* Schoolmasters.*

How now, my lords! how fare you?

Nav. My lord, they say
That all the Protestants are massacred.

Anj. Ay, so they are; but yet, what remedy?
I have done what I could to stay this broil.

Nav. But yet, my lord, the report doth run,
That you were one that made this massacre.

Anj. Who, I? you are deceived; I rose but now.

Guise, Gonzago, Retes, Mountsorrell, *and* Soldiers,
come forward.

Guise. Murder the Huguenots! take those pedants
    hence!   440
Nav. Thou traitor, Guise, lay off thy bloody hands!
Con. Come, let us go tell the king.
               [*Exit with the* King of Navarre.
Guise. Come sirs,
I'll whip you to death with my poniard's point.
            [*Stabs the* Schoolmasters, *who die.*
Anj. Away with them both!
        [*Exeunt* Anjou *and* Soldiers *with the bodies.*
Guise. And now, sirs, for this night let our fury stay.
Yet will we not that the massacre shall end:
Gonzago, post you to Orleans,
Retes to Dieppe, Mountsorrell unto Rouen,
And spare not one that you suspect of heresy.   450
And now stay

    * The scene is outside the King of Navarre's apartment.

That bell, that to the devil's matins rings.
Now every man put off his burgonet,
And so convey him closely to his bed.   [*Exeunt.*

Enter Anjou, *with two* Lords of Poland.*

Anj. My lords of Poland, I must needs confess
The offer of your Prince Electors far
Beyond the reach of my deserts:
For Poland is, as I have been inform'd,
A martial people, worthy such a king
As hath sufficient counsel in himself   460
To lighten doubts, and frustrate subtle foes;
And such a king, whom practice long hath taught
To please himself with manage of the wars,
The greatest wars within our Christian bounds,
I mean our wars against the Muscovites,
And, on the other side, against the Turk,
Rich princes both, and mighty emperors.
Yet, by my brother Charles, our king of France,
And by his grace's council, it is thought
That, if I undertake to wear the crown   470
Of Poland, it may prejudice their hope
Of my inheritance to the crown of France;
For, if th' Almighty take my brother hence,
By due descent the regal seat is mine.
With Poland, therefore, must I covenant thus,—
That, if, by death of Charles, the diadem
Of France be cast on me, then, with your leaves,
I may retire me to my native home.
If your commission serve to warrant this,
I thankfully shall undertake the charge   480
Of you and yours, and carefully maintain
The wealth and safety of your kingdom's right.
    First Lord. All this, and more, your highness shall
        command,
For Poland's crown and kingly diadem.
    Anj. Then, come, my lords, let's go.   [*Exeunt.*

    * The scene is in Anjou's part of the palace.

Enter two Men, *with the* Admiral's *body.**

First Man. Now, sirrah, what shall we do with the
Admiral?

Sec. Man. Why, let us burn him for an heretic.

First Man. Oh no, his body will infect the fire,
and the fire the air, and so we shall be poisoned with
him.   491

Sec. Man. What shall we do, then?

First Man. Let's throw him into the river.

Sec. Man. Oh, 'twill corrupt the water, and the
water the fish, and by the fish ourselves, when we
eat them.

First Man. Then throw him into the ditch.

Sec. Man. No, no. To decide all doubts, be rul'd by
me: let's hang him here upon this tree.

First Man. Agreed.   500

    [*They hang up the body on a tree, and then exeunt.*

Enter Guise, Catherine *the Queen-Mother, and the*
Cardinal of Lorraine, *with Attendants.*

Guise. Now, madam, how like you our lusty
Admiral?

Cath. Believe me, Guise, he becomes the place so
    well
As I could long ere this have wish'd him there.
But come, let's walk aside, th' air's not very sweet.

Guise. No, by my faith, madam.—
Sirs, take him away, and throw him in some ditch.

      [*The* Attendants *bear off the* Admiral's *body.*
And now, madam, as I understand,
There are a hundred Huguenots and more,
Which in the woods do hold their synagogue,
And daily meet about this time of day,   510
And thither will I, to put them to the sword.

Cath. Do so, sweet Guise; let us delay no time;
For, if these stragglers gather head again,

    * The scene is a park near the palace.

And disperse themselves throughout the realm of
    France,
It will be hard for us to work their deaths.
Be gone, delay no time, sweet Guise.
  Guise. Madam,
I go as whirlwinds rage before a storm.   [*Exit.*
  Cath. My Lord of Lorraine, have you mark'd of
    late,
How Charles our son begins for to lament   520
For the late night's work which my Lord of Guise
Did make in Paris amongst the Huguenots?
  Card. Madam, I have heard him solemnly vow,
With the rebellious King of Navarre,
For to revenge their deaths upon us all.
  Cath. Ay, but, my lord, let me alone for that,
For Catherine must have her will in France.
As I do live, so surely shall he die,
And Henry then shall wear the diadem;
And, if he grudge or cross his mother's will,   530
I'll disinherit him and all the rest;
For I'll rule France, but they shall wear the crown,
And if they strive, I then may pull them down.
Come, my lord, let us go.   [*Exeunt.*

Enter five or six Protestants, *with books, and kneel together.*
    Then enter Guise *and others.**

  Guise. Down with the Huguenots! murder them!
  First Pro. O Monsieur de Guise, hear me but speak!
  Guise. No, villain, that tongue of thine,
That hath blasphem'd the holy Church of Rome,
Shall drive no plaints into the Guise's ears,
To make the justice of my heart relent.   540
Tuez, tuez, tuez! let none escape.
                [*They kill the* Protestants.
So, drag them away.   [*Exeunt with the bodies.*

    * The scene is another part of the park.

Enter King Charles, *supported by the* King of Navarre *and* Epernoun; Catherine *the* Queen-Mother, *the* Cardinal of Lorraine, Pleshé, *and* Attendants.*

   Char. Oh, let me stay and rest me here a while.
A griping pain hath seiz'd upon my heart;
A sudden pang, the messenger of death.
   Cath. Oh say not so! thou kill'st thy mother's heart.
   Char. I must say so; pain forceth me complain.
   Nav. Comfort yourself, my lord, and have no doubt
But God will sure restore you to your health.
   Char. Oh no, my loving brother of Navarre!   550
I have deserv'd a scourge, I must confess,
Yet is there patience of another sort
Than to misdo the welfare of their king:
God grant my nearest friends may prove no worse!
Oh, hold me up! my sight begins to fail,
My sinews shrink, my brains turn upside down,
My heart doth break: I faint and die.   [*Dies.*
   Cath. What, art thou dead, sweet son? speak to thy mother!
Oh, no, his soul is fled from out his breast,
And he nor hears nor sees us what we do!   560
My lords, what resteth there now for to be done,
But that we presently despatch ambassadors
To Poland, to call Henry back again,
To wear his brother's crown and dignity?
Epernoun, go see it presently be done,
And bid him come without delay to us.
   Eper. Madam, I will.   [*Exit.*
   Cath. And now, my lords, after these funerals be done,
We will with all the speed we can provide
For Henry's coronation from Polony.   570
Come, let us take his body hence.
      [*The body of* King Charles *is borne out; and exeunt all except the* King of Navarre *and* Pleshé.

     * The scene is in the King's palace.

Nav. And now, Pleshé, whilst that these broils do
 last,
My opportunity may serve me fit
To steal from France, and hie me to my home.
For here's no safety in the realm for me,
And now that Henry is call'd from Poland,
It is my due, by just succession;
And therefore, as speedily as I can perform,
I'll muster up an army secretly,
For fear that Guise, join'd with the king of Spain,
Might seek to cross me in mine enterprise.   581
But God, that always doth defend the right,
Will show his mercy and preserve us still.
 Pleshé. The virtues of our true religion
Cannot but march, with many graces more,
Whose army shall discomfort all your foes,
And, at the length, in Pampeluna crown,
In spite of Spain, and all the popish power,
That holds it from your highness wrongfully,
Your majesty her rightful lord and sovereign.   590
 Nav. Truth, Pleshé; and God so prosper me in all,
As I intend to labour for the truth,
And true profession of his holy word!
Come, Pleshé, let's away whilst time doth serve.
            [*Exeunt.*

Trumpets sounded within, and a cry of 'Vive le Roi', two or
three times. Enter Anjou *crowned as King Henry the Third;*
Catherine *the Queen-Mother, the* Cardinal of Lorraine,
Guise, Epernoun, Mugeroun, *the* Cutpurse, *and others.*

 All. Vive le Roi, Vive le Roi!   [*A flourish of trumpets.*
 Cath. Welcome from Poland, Henry, once again,
Welcome to France, thy father's royal seat!
Here hast thou a country void of fears,
A warlike people to maintain thy right,
A watchful senate for ordaining laws,   600
A loving mother to preserve thy state,
And all things that a king may wish besides:

All this, and more, hath Henry with his crown.
   Card. And long may Henry enjoy all this, and more!
   All. Vive le Roi, Vive le Roi! [*A flourish of trumpets.*
   Henry. Thanks to you all. The guider of all crowns
Grant that our deeds may well deserve your loves;
And so they shall, if fortune speed my will,
And yield your thoughts to height of my deserts.
What says our minions? think they Henry's heart
Will not both harbour love and majesty?   611
Put off that fear, they are already join'd:
No person, place, or time, or circumstance,
Shall slack my love's affections from his bent:
As now you are, so shall you still persist,
Removeless from the favours of your king.
   Mug. We know that noble minds change not their
     thoughts
For wearing of a crown, in that your grace
Hath worn the Poland diadem before
You were invested in the crown of France.   620
   Henry. I tell thee, Mugeroun, we will be friends,
And fellows too, whatever storms arise.
   Mug. Then may it please your majesty to give me
     leave
To punish those that do profane this holy feast.
   Henry. How mean'st thou that?
     [*Mugeroun cuts off the* Cutpurse's *ear, for cutting*
     the gold buttons off his cloak.
   Cutp. O Lord, mine ear!
   Mug. Come, sir, give me my buttons, and here's
     your ear.
   Guise. Sirrah, take him away.
   Henry. Hands off, good fellow; I will be his bail
For this offence.—Go, sirrah, work no more   630
Till this our coronation-day be past.—
And now,
Our solemn rites of coronation done,
What now remains but for a while to feast,
And spend some days in barriers, tourney, tilt,

And like disports, such as do fit the court?
Let's go, my lords; our dinner stays for us.
      [*Exeunt all except* Catherine *the Queen-Mother and
         the* Cardinal of Lorraine.

  Cath. My Lord Cardinal of Lorraine, tell me,
How likes your grace my son's pleasantness?
His mind, you see, runs on his minions,   640
And all his heaven is to delight himself;
And, whilst he sleeps securely thus in ease,
Thy brother Guise and we may now provide
To plant ourselves with such authority
As not a man may live without our leaves.
Then shall the Catholic faith of Rome
Flourish in France, and none deny the same.
  Card. Madam, as in secrecy I was told,
My brother Guise hath gathered a power of men,
Which are, he saith, to kill the Puritans;   650
But 'tis the house of Bourbon that he means.
Now, madam, must you insinuate with the king,
And tell him that 'tis for his country's good,
And common profit of religion.
  Cath. Tush, man, let me alone with him,
To work the way to bring this thing to pass;
And, if he do deny what I do say,
I'll despatch him with his brother presently,
And then shall Monsieur wear the diadem.
Tush, all shall die unless I have my will,   660
For, while she lives, Catherine will be queen.
Come, my lord, let us go seek the Guise,
And then determine of this enterprise.   [*Exeunt.*

    Enter the Duchess of Guise *and her* Maid.*

  Duch. of G. Go fetch me pen and ink,—
  Maid. I will, madam.   [*Exit* Maid.
  Duch. That I may write unto my dearest lord.
Sweet Mugeroun, 'tis he that hath my heart,
And Guise usurps it 'cause I am his wife:
    * The scene is the apartment of the Duke of Guise.

Fain would I find some means to speak with him,
But cannot, and therefore am enforc'd to write,   670
That he may come and meet me in some place,
Where we may one enjoy the other's sight.

Re-enter the Maid, *with pen, ink, and paper.*

So, set it down, and leave me to myself.

      [*Exit* Maid. *The* Duchess *writes.*

Oh, would to God this quill that here doth write,
Had late been pluck'd from out fair Cupid's wing,
That it might print these lines within his heart!

Enter Guise.

 Guise. What, all alone, my love? and writing too?
I prithee, say to whom thou writes.

 Duch. To such a one, my lord, as when she reads my lines,
Will laugh, I fear me, at their good array.   680

 Guise. I pray thee, let me see.

 Duch. Oh no, my lord; a woman only must
Partake the secrets of my heart.

 Guise. But, madam, I must see.   [*Seizes the paper.*
Are these your secrets that no man must know?

 Duch. Oh, pardon me, my lord!

 Guise. Thou trothless and unjust, what lines are
these?
Am I grown old, or is thy lust grown young?
Or hath my love been so obscur'd in thee,
That others needs to comment on my text?   690
Is all my love forgot which held thee dear,
Ay, dearer than the apple of mine eye?
Is Guise's glory but a cloudy mist,
In sight and judgment of thy lustful eye?
Mort Dieu! were not the fruit within thy womb,
Of whose increase I set some longing hope,
This wrathful hand should strike thee to the heart.
Hence, strumpet! hide thy head for shame,

And fly my presence, if thou look to live!

          [Exit Duchess.

O wicked sex, perjured and unjust,   700
Now do I see that from the very first
Her eyes and looks sow'd seeds of perjury.
But villain he to whom these lines should go,
Shall buy her love even with his dearest blood.

          [Exit.

Enter the King of Navarre, Pleshé, Bartus, *and train,
with drums and trumpets.**

  Nav. My lords, sith in a quarrel just and right
We undertake to manage these our wars
Against the proud disturbers of the faith,
I mean the Guise, the Pope, and king of Spain,
Who set themselves to tread us under foot,
And rent our true religion from this land;   710
But for you know our quarrel is no more
But to defend their strange inventions,
Which they will put us to with sword and fire,
We must with resolute minds resolve to fight,
In honour of our God and country's good.
Spain is the council-chamber of the Pope,
Spain is the place where he makes peace and
    war,
And Guise for Spain hath now incens'd the king
To send his power to meet us in the field.
  Bar. Then in this bloody brunt they may behold
The sole endeavour of your princely care,   721
To plant the true succession of the faith,
In spite of Spain and all his heresies.
  Nav. The power of vengeance now encamps itself
Upon the haughty mountains of my breast;
Plays with her gory colours of revenge,
Whom I respect as leaves of boasting green,
That change their colour when the winter comes,
When I shall vaunt as victor in revenge.

    * The scene is in the King of Navarre's palace.

Enter a Messenger.

How now, sirrah, what news? 730

Mes. My lord, as by our scouts we understand,
A mighty army comes from France with speed;
Which are already mustered in the land,
And means to meet your highness in the field.

Nav. In God's name, let them come!
This is the Guise that hath incens'd the king
To levy arms and make these civil broils.
But canst thou tell who is their general?

Mes. Not yet, my lord, for thereon do they stay:
But, as report doth go, the Duke of Joyeux 740
Hath made great suit unto the king therefore.

Nav. It will not countervail his pains, I hope.
I would the Guise in his stead might have come,
But he doth lurk within his drowsy couch,
And makes his footstool on security:
So he be safe, he cares not what becomes
Of king or country; no, not for them both.
But come, my lords, let us away with speed,
And place ourselves in order for the fight. [*Exeunt.*

Enter King Henry, Guise, Epernoun, *and* Joyeux.*

Henry. My sweet Joyeux, I make thee general 750
Of all my army now in readiness
To march against the rebellious King Navarre;
At thy request I am content thou go,
Although my love to thee can hardly suffer
Regarding still the danger of thy life. [*leave.*

Joyeux. Thanks to your majesty: and so, I take my
Farewell to my Lord of Guise, and Epernoun.

Guise. Health and hearty farewell to my Lord
Joyeux. [*Exit* Joyeux.

Henry. So kindly, cousin of Guise, you and your
wife
Do both salute our lovely minions. 760

* The scene is the camp of the French army.

Remember you the letter, gentle sir,
Which your wife writ
To my dear minion, and her chosen friend?

[*Makes horns at* Guise.

Guise. How now, my lord! faith, this is more than
Am I thus to be jested at and scorn'd?   [need.
'Tis more than kingly or emperious:
And, sure, if all the proudest kings
In Christendom should bear me such derision,
They should know how I scorn'd them and their
    mocks.
I love your minions! dote on them yourself;   770
I know none else but holds them in disgrace;
And here, by all the saints in heaven, I swear,
That villain for whom I bear this deep disgrace,
Even for your words that have incens'd me so,
Shall buy that strumpet's favour with his blood!
Whether he have dishonoured me or no,
Par la mort Dieu, il mourra!   [*Exit.*

Henry. Believe me, this jest bites sore.
Eper. My lord, 'twere good to make them friends,
For his oaths are seldom spent in vain.

Enter Mugeroun.

Henry. How now, Mugeroun! met'st thou not the
    Guise at the door?   781
Mug. Not I, my lord; what if I had?
Henry. Marry, if thou hadst, thou mightst have had
    the stab,
For he hath solemnly sworn thy death.
Mug. I may be stabb'd, and live till he be dead:
But wherefore bears he me such deadly hate?
Henry. Because his wife bears thee such kindly
    love.
Mug. If that be all, the next time that I meet her,
I'll make her shake off love with her heels.
But which way is he gone? I'll go make a walk   790
On purpose from the court to meet with him. [*Exit.*

Henry. I like not this. Come, Epernoun,
Let's go seek the duke, and make them friends.
                                        [*Exeunt.*

Alarums, within, and a cry—'The Duke Joyeux is slain.'
      Enter the King of Navarre, Bartus, *and train.**

  Nav. The duke is slain, and all his power dispers'd,
And we are grac'd with wreaths of victory.
Thus God, we see, doth ever guide the right,
To make his glory great upon the earth.

  Bar. The terror of this happy victory,
I hope, will make the king surcease his hate,
And either never manage army more,   800
Or else employ them in some better cause.

  Nav. How many noblemen have lost their lives
In prosecution of these cruel arms,
Is ruth, and almost death to call to mind.
But God we know will always put them down
That lift themselves against the perfect truth,
Which I'll maintain so long as life doth last,
And with the Queen of England join my force
To beat the papal monarch from our lands,
And keep those relics from our countries' coasts. 810
Come, my lords, now that this storm is overpast,
Let us away with triumph to our tents.   [*Exeunt.*

Enter a Soldier.†

  Sold. Sir, to you, sir, that dares make the duke a
cuckold, and use a counterfeit key to his privy-
chamber door; and although you take out nothing
but your own, yet you put in that which displeaseth
him, and so forestall his market, and set up your
standing where you should not; and whereas he is
your landlord, you will take upon you to be his, and
till the ground that he himself should occupy, which is
his own free land, if it be not too free—there's the question; and though I come not to take possession (as I

  * Scene—a battlefield.   † Scene—outside the Louvre.

would I might!) yet I mean to keep you out; which
I will, if this gear hold.   824

Enter Mugeroun.

What, are ye come so soon? have at ye, sir!
                              [*Shoots at* Mugeroun *and kills him.*

Enter Guise *and* Attendants.

Guise. [*Giving a purse*]. Hold thee, tall soldier, take
    thee this, and fly.   [*Exit* Soldier.
Lie there, the king's delight, and Guise's scorn!
Revenge it, Henry, as thou list or dare,
I did it only in despite of thee.
                              [*Attendants* bear off Mugeroun's *body.*

Enter King Henry *and* Epernoun.

Henry. My Lord of Guise, we understand   830
That you have gathered a power of men.
What your intent is yet we cannot learn,
But we presume it is not for our good.
Guise. Why, I am no traitor to the crown of France:
What I have done, 'tis for the Gospel sake.
Eper. Nay, for the Pope's sake, and thine own
    benefit.
What peer in France but thou, aspiring Guise,
Durst be in arms without the king's consent?
I challenge thee for treason in the cause.
Guise. Ah, base Epernoun, were not his highness
    here,   840
Thou shouldst perceive the Duke of Guise is mov'd.
Henry. Be patient, Guise, and threat not Epernoun,
Lest thou perceive the king of France be mov'd.
Guise. Why, I am a prince of the Valois's line,
Therefore an enemy to the Bourbonites;
I am a juror in the holy league,
And therefore hated of the Protestants:
What should I do but stand upon my guard?

826 tall] brave

And, being able, I'll keep an host in pay.

   Eper. Thou able to maintain an host in pay,   850
That liv'st by foreign exhibition!
The Pope and King of Spain are thy good friends,
Else all France knows how poor a duke thou art.

   Henry. Ay, those are they that feed him with their gold,
To countermand our will, and check our friends.

   Guise. My lord, to speak more plainly, thus it is.
Being animated by religious zeal,
I mean to muster all the power I can,
To overthrow those sexious Puritans:
And know, my lord, the Pope will sell his triple crown,
Ay, and the Catholic Philip, king of Spain,   861
Ere I shall want, will cause his Indians
To rip the golden bowels of America.
Navarre, that cloaks them underneath his wings,
Shall feel the house of Lorraine is his foe.
Your highness needs not fear mine army's force;
'Tis for your safety, and your enemies' wreck.

   Henry. Guise, wear our crown, and be thou king of France,
And, as dictator, make or war or peace,
Whilst I cry *placet*, like a senator.   870
I cannot brook thy haughty insolence:
Dismiss thy camp, or else by our edict
Be thou proclaim'd a traitor throughout France.

   Guise. The choice is hard; I must dissemble.—
                                [Aside.
My lord, in token of my true humility,
And simple meaning to your majesty,
I kiss your grace's hand, and take my leave,
Intending to dislodge my camp with speed.

   Henry. Then farewell, Guise, the king and thou are friends.   *[Exit Guise.*

   Eper. But trust him not, my lord, for had your highness   880

859 sexious] sectarian

Seen with what a pomp he enter'd Paris,
And how the citizens with gifts and shows
Did entertain him,
And promised to be at his command—
Nay, they fear'd not to speak in the streets,
That the Guise durst stand in arms against the
king,
For not effecting of his holiness' will.
  Henry. Did they of Paris entertain him so?
Then means he present treason to our state.
Well, let me alone.—Who's within there?   890

Enter an Attendant.

Make a discharge of all my council straight,
And I'll subscribe my name, and seal it straight.
                              [Attendant *writes.*
My head shall be my council; they are false;
And, Epernoun, I will be rul'd by thee.
  Eper. My lord,
I think, for safety of your royal person,
It would be good the Guise were made away,
And so to quit your grace of all suspect.
  Henry. First let us set our hand and seal to this,
And then I'll tell thee what I mean to do.— [*Writes.*
So; convey this to the council presently.   901
                              [*Exit* Attendant.
And, Epernoun, though I seem mild and calm,
Think not but I am tragical within.
I'll secretly convey me unto Blois;
For, now that Paris takes the Guise's part,
Here is no staying for the king of France,
Unless he mean to be betray'd and die:
But, as I live, so sure the Guise shall die.   [*Exeunt.*

Enter the King of Navarre, *reading a letter, and* Bartus.*

  Nav. My lord, I am advertised from France
That the Guise hath taken arms against the king,

* The scene is the King of Navarre's palace.

And that Paris is revolted from his grace.   911

  Bar. Then hath your grace fit opportunity
To show your love unto the king of France,
Offering him aid against his enemies,
Which cannot but be thankfully receiv'd.

  Nav. Bartus, it shall be so: post then to France,
And there salute his highness in our name;
Assure him all the aid we can provide
Against the Guisians and their complices.
Bartus, be gone: commend me to his grace,   920
And tell him, ere it be long, I'll visit him.

  Bar. I will, my lord.   [*Exit.*

  Nav. Pleshé!

Enter Pleshé.

  Pleshé. My lord!

  Nav. Pleshé, go muster up our men with speed,
And let them march away to France amain,
For we must aid the king against the Guise.
Be gone, I say, 'tis time that we were there.

  Pleshé. I go, my lord.   [*Exit.*

  Nav. That wicked Guise, I fear me much, will be
The ruin of that famous realm of France;   931
For his aspiring thoughts aim at the crown,
And takes his vantage on religion,
To plant the Pope and popelings in the realm,
And bind it wholly to the see of Rome.
But, if that God do prosper mine attempts,
And send us safely to arrive in France,
We'll beat him back, and drive him to his death,
That basely seeks the ruin of his realm.   [*Exit.*

Enter the Captain of the Guard, and three Murderers*

  Cap. Come on, sirs. What, are you resolutely bent,
Hating the life and honour of the Guise?   941
What, will you not fear, when you see him come?

  First Murd. Fear him, said you? tush, were he here,
we would kill him presently.

      * The scene is the King of France's palace.

Sec. Murd. Oh, that his heart were leaping in my
    hand!

Third Murd. But when will he come, that we may
    murther him?

Cap. Well, then, I see you are resolute.

First Murd. Let us alone, I warrant you.

Cap. Then, sirs, take your standings within this
    chamber,

For anon the Guise will come.   950

All three Murderers. You will give us our money?

Cap. Ay, ay, fear not: stand close: so; be resolute.

                  [Exeunt Murderers.

Now falls the star whose influence governs France,
Whose light was deadly to the Protestants:
Now must he fall and perish in his height.

Enter King Henry *and* Epernoun.

Henry. Now, captain of my guard, are these mur-
    therers ready?

Cap. They be, my good lord.

Henry. But are they resolute, and arm'd to kill,
Hating the life and honour of the Guise?

Cap. I warrant ye, my lord.   *[Exit.*

Henry. Then come, proud Guise, and here disgorge
    thy breast,   961

Surcharg'd with surfeit of ambitious thoughts:
Breathe out that life wherein my death was hid,
And end thy endless treasons with thy death.

                  [Knocking within.

Guise. [*within*]. Holà, varlet, hé!—Epernoun, where
    the king?

Eper. Mounted his royal cabinet.

Guise. [*within*]. I prithee tell him that the Guise is
    here.

Eper. An please your grace, the Duke of Guise
    doth crave

Access unto your highness.

Henry. Let him come in.   970

Come, Guise, and see thy traitorous guile outreach'd,
And perish in the pit thou mad'st for me.

Enter Guise.

Guise. Good morrow to your majesty.

Henry. Good morrow to my loving cousin of Guise:
How fares it this morning with your excellence?

Guise. I heard your majesty was scarcely pleas'd,
That in the court I bare so great a train.

Henry. They were to blame that said I was dis-
pleas'd,
And you, good cousin, to imagine it.
'Twere hard with me, if I should doubt my kin, 980
Or be suspicious of my dearest friends.
Cousin, assure you I am resolute,
Whatsoever any whisper in mine ears,
Not to suspect disloyalty in thee:
And so, sweet coz, farewell.   [*Exit with* Epernoun.

Guise. So;
Now sues the king for favour to the Guise,
And all his minions stoop when I command:
Why, this 'tis to have an army in the field.
Now by the holy sacrament I swear,   990
As ancient Romans over their captive lords,
So will I triumph over this wanton king,
And he shall follow my proud chariot's wheels.
Now do I but begin to look about,
And all my former time was spent in vain.
Hold, sword,
For in thee is the Duke of Guise's hope.

Re-enter Third Murderer.

Villain, why dost thou look so ghastly? speak.   998

Third Murd. Oh, pardon me, my Lord of Guise!

Guise. Pardon thee! why, what hast thou done?

Third Murd. O my lord, I am one of them that is
set to murder you.

Guise. To murder me, villain?

Third Murd. Ay, my lord: the rest have ta'en their
standings in the next room; therefore, good my
lord, go not forth.

Guise. Yet Cæsar shall go forth.
Let mean conceits and baser men fear death:
Tut, they are peasants; I am Duke of Guise;
And princes with their looks engender fear.   1010

First Murd. [*within*]. Stand close, he is coming; I
know him by his voice.

Guise. As pale as ashes! nay, then, 'tis time
To look about.

      Enter First *and* Second Murderers.

First and Sec. Murderers. Down with him, down with
    him!   [*They stab* Guise.

Guise. Oh, I have my death's wound! give me leave
    to speak.

Sec. Murd. Then pray to God, and ask forgiveness
    of the king.

Guise. Trouble me not, I ne'er offended him,
Nor will I ask forgiveness of the king.
Oh, that I have not power to stay my life,   1020
Nor immortality to be reveng'd!
To die by peasants, what a grief is this!
Ah, Sixtus, be reveng'd upon the king;
Philip and Parma, I am slain for you:
Pope, excommunicate, Philip, depose
The wicked branch of curs'd Valois his line.
Vive la messe! perish Huguenots!
Thus Cæsar did go forth, and thus he died.   [*Dies.*

      Enter the Captain of the Guard.

Cap. What, have you done?
Then stay a while, and I'll go call the king.   1030
But see, where he comes.

    Enter King Henry, Epernoun, *and* Attendants.
My lord, see where the Guise is slain.

Henry. Ah, this sweet sight is physic to my soul!

Go fetch his son for to behold his death.

[*Exit an* Attendant.

Surcharg'd with guilt of thousand massacres,
Monsieur of Lorraine, sink away to hell!
And in remembrance of those bloody broils,
To which thou didst allure me, being alive,
And here in presence of you all I swear,
I ne'er was king of France until this hour.   1040
This is the traitor that hath spent my gold
In making foreign wars and civil broils.
Did he not draw a sort of English priests
From Douay to the seminary at Rheims,
To hatch forth treason 'gainst their natural queen?
Did he not cause the king of Spain's huge fleet
To threaten England, and to menace me?
Did he not injure Monsieur that's deceas'd?
Hath he not made me in the Pope's defence
To spend the treasure, that should strength my land,
In civil broils between Navarre and me?   1051
Tush, to be short, he meant to make me monk,
Or else to murder me, and so be king.
Let Christian princes, that shall hear of this,
(As all the world shall know our Guise is dead),
Rest satisfied with this, that here I swear,
Ne'er was there king of France so yok'd as I.

Eper. My lord, here is his son.

Enter Guise's Son.

Henry. Boy, look where your father lies.   1059
G.'s Son. My father slain! who hath done this deed?
Henry. Sirrah, 'twas I that slew him; and will slay
Thee too, an thou prove such a traitor.
G.'s Son. Art thou king, and hast done this bloody
deed?
I'll be reveng'd.   [*Offers to throw his dagger.*
Henry. Away to prison with him! I'll clip his wings
Or e'er he pass my hands. Away with him.

[*Some of the* Attendants *bear off* Guise's Son.

But what availeth that this traitor's dead,
When Duke Dumaine, his brother, is alive,
And that young cardinal that is grown so proud?
Go to the governor of Orleans,   1070
And will him, in my name, to kill the duke.

                      [*To the* Captain of the Guard.
Get you away, and strangle the cardinal.

                           [*To the* Murderers.
      [*Exeunt* Captain of the Guard *and* Murderers.
These two will make one entire Duke of Guise,
Especially with our old mother's help.

   Eper. My lord, see where she comes, as if she
To hear these news.   [droop'd
   Henry. And let her droop; my heart is light enough.

          Enter Catherine *the* Queen-Mother.

Mother, how like you this device of mine?
I slew the Guise, because I would be king.
   Cath. King! why, so thou wert before: 1080
Pray God thou be a king now this is done!
   Henry. Nay, he was king, and countermanded me:
But now I will be king, and rule myself,
And make the Guisians stoop that are alive.
   Cath. I cannot speak for grief.—When thou wast
    born,
I would that I had murdered thee, my son!
My son? thou art a changeling, not my son:
I curse thee, and exclaim thee miscreant,
Traitor to God and to the realm of France.
   Henry. Cry out, exclaim, howl till thy throat be
    hoarse!   1090
The Guise is slain, and I rejoice therefore:
And now will I to arms. Come, Epernoun,
And let her grieve her heart out, if she will.

                      [*Exit with* Epernoun.
   Cath. Away! leave me alone to meditate.

                        [*Exeunt* Attendants.
Sweet Guise, would he had died, so thou wert here!

To whom shall I bewray my secrets now,
Or who will help to build religion?
The Protestants will glory and insult;
Wicked Navarre will get the crown of France;
The Popedom cannot stand; all goes to wreck;   1100
And all for thee, my Guise! What may I do?
But sorrow seize upon my toiling soul,
For since the Guise is dead, I will not live.   [*Exit.*

Enter two Murderers, *dragging in the* Cardinal.*

Card. Murder me not; I am a cardinal.
First Murd. Wert thou the Pope, thou mightst not
    'scape from us.
Card. What, will you file your hands with church-
    men's blood?
Sec. Murd. Shed your blood! O Lord, no, for we
    intend to strangle you.
Card. Then there is no remedy, but I must die?
First Murd. No remedy; therefore prepare yourself.
Card. Yet lives   1110
My brother Duke Dumaine, and many moe,
To revenge our deaths upon that cursed king,
Upon whose heart may all the Furies gripe,
And with their paws drench his black soul in hell!
First Murd. Yours, my Lord Cardinal, you should
    have said.   [*They strangle him.*
So, pluck amain:
He is hard-hearted, therefore pull with violence.
Come, take him away.   [*Exeunt with the body.*

Enter Dumaine, *reading a letter; with others.†*

Dum. My noble brother murdered by the king?
Oh, what may I do for to revenge thy death?   1120
The king's alone, it cannot satisfy.
Sweet Duke of Guise, our prop to lean upon,

---

* The scene is the residence of the Cardinal of Lorraine.
1106 file] defile   1111 moe] more
† The scene is Duke Dumaine's residence.

Now thou art dead, here is no stay for us.
I am thy brother, and I'll revenge thy death,
And root Valois his line from forth of France,
And beat proud Bourbon to his native home,
That basely seeks to join with such a king,
Whose murderous thoughts will be his overthrow.
He will'd the governor of Orleans, in his name,
That I with speed should have been put to death,
But that's prevented, for to end his life,   1131
And all those traitors to the Church of Rome
That durst attempt to murder noble Guise.

Enter Friar.

Fri. My lord, I come to bring you news that your
brother the Cardinal of Lorraine, by the king's consent, is lately strangled unto death.

Dum. My brother Cardinal slain, and I alive?
O words of power to kill a thousand men!—
Come, let us away, and levy men;
'Tis war that must assuage this tyrant's pride.   1140

Fri. My lord, hear me but speak.
I am a friar of the order of the Jacobins,
That for my conscience' sake will kill the king.

Dum. But what doth move thee, above the rest, to
do the deed?

Fri. O my lord, I have been a great sinner in my
days, and the deed is meritorious.

Dum. But how wilt thou get opportunity?

Fri. Tush, my lord, let me alone for that.

Dum. Friar, come with me,   1150
We will go talk more of this within.   [*Exeunt.*

Drums and Trumpets. Enter King Henry, *the* King of
Navarre, Epernoun, Bartus, Pleshé, Soldiers, *and*
Attendants.*

Henry. Brother of Navarre, I sorrow much
That ever I was prov'd your enemy,

* The scene is outside the walls of **Paris.**

And that the sweet and princely mind you bear
Was ever troubled with injurious wars.
I vow, as I am lawful King of France,
To recompense your reconciled love
With all the honours and affections
That ever I vouchsaf'd my dearest friends.

    Nav. It is enough if that Navarre may be   1160
Esteemed faithful to the King of France,
Whose service he may still command till death.

    Henry. Thanks to my kingly brother of Navarre.
Then here we'll lie before Lutetia walls,
Girting this strumpet city with our siege,
Till, surfeiting with our afflicting arms,
She cast her hateful stomach to the earth.

Enter a Messenger.

    Mess. An it please your majesty, here is a friar of
the order of the Jacobins, sent from the President of
Paris, that craves access unto your grace.   1170

    Henry. Let him come in.   [*Exit* Messenger.

Enter Friar, *with a letter.*

    Eper. I like not this friar's look:
'Twere not amiss, my lord, if he were search'd.

    Henry. Sweet Epernoun, our friars are holy men,
And will not offer violence to their king
For all the wealth and treasure of the world.
Friar, thou dost acknowledge me thy king?

    Fri. Ay, my good lord, and will die therein.

    Henry. Then come thou near, and tell what news
    thou bring'st.

    Fri. My lord,   1180
The President of Paris greets your grace
And sends his duty by these speedy lines,
Humbly craving your gracious reply.   [*Gives letter.*

    Henry. I'll read them, friar, and then I'll answer thee.

    Fri. Sancte Jacobe, now have mercy upon me!

1164 Lutetia] Paris

[*Stabs the king with a knife, as he reads the letter;
and then the king gets the knife, and kills him.*

Eper. O my lord, let him live a while!

Henry. No, let the villain die, and feel in hell
Just torments for his treachery.

Nav. What, is your highness hurt? 1189

Henry. Yes, Navarre; but not to death, I hope.

Nav. God shield your grace from such a sudden
death!
Go call a surgeon hither straight.

[*Exit an* Attendant.

Henry. What irreligious pagan's parts be these,
Of such as hold them of the holy church!
Take hence that damned villain from my sight.

[*Attendants* carry out the Friar's *body.*

Eper. Ah, had your highness let him live,
We might have punish'd him to his deserts!

Henry. Sweet Epernoun, all rebels under heaven
Shall take example by his punishment,
How they bear arms against their sovereign. 1200
Go call the English agent hither straight:

[*Exit an* Attendant.

I'll send my sister England news of this,
And give her warning of her treacherous foes.

Enter a Surgeon.

Nav. Pleaseth your grace to let the surgeon search
your wound?

Henry. The wound, I warrant ye, is deep, my lord.
Search, surgeon, and resolve me what thou see'st.

[*The* Surgeon *searches the wound.*

Enter the English Agent.

Agent for England, send thy mistress word
What this detested Jacobin hath done.
Tell her, for all this, that I hope to live;
Which if I do, the papal monarch goes 1210
To wreck, and antichristian kingdom falls:
These bloody hands shall tear his triple crown.

And fire accursed Rome about his ears;
I'll fire his crazed buildings, and enforce
The papal towers to kiss the lowly earth.
Navarre, give me thy hand: I here do swear
To ruinate that wicked Church of Rome,
That hatcheth up such bloody practices,
And here protest eternal love to thee,
And to the Queen of England specially,   1220
Whom God hath bless'd for hating papistry.

  Nav. These words revive my thoughts, and comforts me,
To see your highness in this virtuous mind.

  Henry. Tell me, surgeon, shall I live?

  Surg. Alas, my lord, the wound is dangerous,
For you are stricken with a poisoned knife.

  Henry. A poisoned knife! what, shall the French king die,
Wounded and poisoned both at once?

  Eper. Oh, that that damned villain were alive again,
That we might torture him with some new-found death!   1230

  Bar. He died a death too good: the devil of hell
Torture his wicked soul!

  Henry. Ah, curse him not, sith he is dead. Oh,
The fatal poison works within my breast.
Tell me, surgeon, and flatter not—may I live?

  Surg. Alas, my lord, your highness cannot live!

  Nav. Surgeon, why say'st thou so? the king may live.

  Henry. Oh no, Navarre! thou must be king of France!

  Nav. Long may you live, and still be king of France!

  Eper. Or else, die Epernoun!   1240

  Henry. Sweet Epernoun, thy king must die.—My lords,
Fight in the quarrel of this valiant prince,

For he is your lawful king, and my next heir;
Valois's line ends in my tragedy.
Now let the house of Bourbon wear the crown,
And may it never end in blood, as mine hath done!
Weep not, sweet Navarre, but revenge my death.
Ah, Epernoun, is this thy love to me?
Henry, thy king, wipes off these childish tears,
And bids thee whet thy sword on Sixtus' bones, 1250
That it may keenly slice the Catholics.
He loves me not that sheds most tears,
But he that makes most lavish of his blood.
Fire Paris, where these treacherous rebels lurk.
I die, Navarre; come bear me to my sepulchre.
Salute the Queen of England in my name,
And tell her, Henry dies her faithful friend.   [*Dies.*
    Nav. Come, lords, take up the body of the king,
That we may see it honourably interr'd:
And then I vow for to revenge his death,   1260
As Rome and all those popish prelates there,
Shall curse the time that e'er Navarre was king,
And rul'd in France by Henry's fatal death.

   [*They march out, with the body of* King Henry
      lying on four men's shoulders, with a dead march,
      drawing weapons on the ground.

THE
Tragedie of Dido
Queene of Carthage:
Played by the Children of her
Maiesties Chappell.

Written by Christopher Marlowe, and
Thomas Nash. Gent.

Actors

Iupiter.	*Ascanius.*
Ganimed.	*Dido.*
Venus.	*Anna.*
Cupid.	*Achates.*
Iuno.	*Ilioneus.*
Mercurie,	*Iarbas.*
Hermes.	*Cloanthes.*
Æneas.	*Sergestus.*

AT LONDON,
Printed, by the Widdowe *Orwin*, for *Thomas Woodcocke*, and
are to be solde at his shop, in Paules Church-yeard, at
the signe of the blacke Beare. 1594.

Dramatis Personæ

Jupiter.
Ganymede.
Hermes.
Cupid.

Juno.
Venus.

Æneas.
Ascanius, *his son.*
Achates.

Ilioneus.
Cloanthus.
Sergestus.
Other Trojans.
Iarbas.
Carthaginian Lords.

Dido.
Anna, *her sister.*
Nurse.

The Tragedy of
DIDO, QUEEN OF CARTHAGE

Act I. Scene I.

Here the curtains draw; there is discovered Jupiter *dandling*
  Ganymede *upon his knee, and* Hermes *lying asleep.*

Jup. Come, gentle Ganymede, and play with me;
I love thee well, say Juno what she will.
  Gan. I am much better for your worthless love,
That will not shield me from her shrewish blows!
To day, whenas I fill'd into your cups,
And held the cloth of pleasance whiles you drank,
She reach'd me such a rap for that I spill'd,
As made the blood run down about mine ears.
  Jup. What, dares she strike the darling of my
      thoughts?
By Saturn's soul, and this earth-threat'ning hair, 10
That, shaken thrice, makes nature's buildings quake,
I vow, if she but once frown on thee more,
To hang her, meteor-like, 'twixt heaven and earth,
And bind her, hand and foot, with golden cords,
As once I did for harming Hercules!
  Gan. Might I but see that pretty sport a-foot,
Oh, how would I with Helen's brother laugh,
And bring the gods to wonder at the game!
Sweet Jupiter, if e'er I pleas'd thine eye,
Or seemed fair, wall'd-in with eagle's wings, 20
Grace my immortal beauty with this boon,
And I will spend my time in thy bright arms.
  Jup. What is't, sweet wag, I should deny thy youth?
Whose face reflects such pleasure to mine eyes,
As I, exhal'd with thy fire-darting beams,
Have oft driven back the horses of the Night,
Whenas they would have hal'd thee from my sight.

17 Helen's brother] Castor or Pollux

Sit on my knee, and call for thy content,
Control proud Fate, and cut the thread of Time:
Why, are not all the gods at thy command,   30
And heaven and earth the bounds of thy delight?
Vulcan shall dance to make thee laughing sport,
And my nine daughters sing when thou art sad;
From Juno's bird I'll pluck her spotted pride,
To make thee fans wherewith to cool thy face;
And Venus' swans shall shed their silver down,
To sweeten out the slumbers of thy bed;
Hermes no more shall show the world his wings,
If that thy fancy in his feathers dwell,
But, as this one, I'll tear them all from him,   40
                [*Plucks a feather from* Hermes' *wings.*
Do thou but say, 'their colour pleaseth me.'
Hold here, my little love, these linked gems,
                      [*Gives jewels.*
My Juno ware upon her marriage-day,
Put thou about thy neck, my own sweet heart,
And trick thy arms and shoulders with my theft.
   Gan. I would have a jewel for mine ear,
And a fine brooch to put in my hat,
And then I'll hug with you an hundred times. [love.
   Jup. And shalt have, Ganymede, if thou wilt be my
               Enter Venus.
   Ven. Ay, this is it: you can sit toying there,   50
And playing with that female wanton boy,
Whiles my Æneas wanders on the seas,
And rests a prey to every billow's pride.
Juno, false Juno, in her chariot's pomp,
Drawn through the heavens by steeds of Boreas'
    brood,
Made Hebe to direct her airy wheels
Into the windy country of the clouds,
Where, finding Æolus entrench'd with storms,
And guarded with a thousand grisly ghosts,
She humbly did beseech him for our bane,   60
And charg'd him drown my son with all his train.

Then gan the winds break ope their brazen doors,
And all Æolia to be up in arms:
Poor Troy must now be sack'd upon the sea,
And Neptune's waves be envious men of war;
Epeus' horse, to Ætna's hill transform'd,
Prepared stands to wreck their wooden walls,
And Æolus, like Agamemnon, sounds
The surges, his fierce soldiers, to the spoil:
See how the night, Ulysses-like, comes forth,   70
And intercepts the day, as Dolon erst!
Ay, me! the stars surpris'd, like Rhesus' steeds,
Are drawn by darkness forth Astræus' tents.
What shall I do to save thee, my sweet boy?
Whenas the waves do threat our crystal world,
And Proteus, raising hills of floods on high,
Intends, ere long, to sport him in the sky.
False Jupiter, reward'st thou virtue so?
What, is not piety exempt from woe?
Then die, Æneas, in thine innocence,   80
Since that religion hath no recompense.
    Jup. Content thee, Cytherea, in thy care,
Since thy Æneas' wand'ring fate is firm,
Whose weary limbs shall shortly make repose
In those fair walls I promis'd him of yore.
But first in blood must his good fortune bud,
Before he be the lord of Turnus' town,
Or force her smile that hitherto hath frown'd:
Three winters shall he with the Rutiles war,
And in the end subdue them with his sword;   90
And full three summers likewise shall he waste
In managing those fierce barbarian minds;
Which once perform'd, poor Troy, so long suppress'd,
From forth her ashes shall advance her head,
And flourish once again, that erst was dead.
But bright Ascanius, beauty's better work,
Who with the sun divides one radiant shape,
Shall build his throne amidst those starry towers
That earth-born Atlas, groaning, underprops:

No bounds but heaven shall bound his empery,　　100
Whose azured gates enchased with his name
Shall make the Morning haste her grey uprise,
To feed her eyes with his engraven fame.
Thus in stout Hector's race three hundred years
The Roman sceptre royal shall remain,
Till that a princess-priest conceiv'd by Mars,
Shall yield to dignity a double birth,
Who will eternish Troy in their attempts.

Ven. How may I credit these thy flattering terms,
When yet both sea and sands beset their ships,　　110
And Phœbus, as in Stygian pools, refrains
To taint his tresses in the Tyrrhene main?

Jup. I will take order for that presently.
Hermes awake, and haste to Neptune's realm,
Whereas the wind-god, warring now with fate,
Besiege the offspring of our kingly loins:
Charge him from me to turn his stormy powers,
And fetter them in Vulcan's sturdy brass,
That durst thus proudly wrong our kinsman's peace.
　　　　　　　　　　　　　　　　[*Exit* Hermes.

Venus, farewell, thy son shall be our care.　　120
Come, Ganymede, we must about this gear.
　　　　　　　　　　　[*Exeunt* Jupiter *and* Ganymede.

Ven. Disquiet seas, lay down your swelling looks,
And court Æneas with your calmy cheer,
Whose beauteous burden well might make you
　　proud,　　　　　　　　　　　　　　[clouds,
Had not the heavens, conceived with hell-born
Veil'd his resplendent glory from your view.
For my sake pity him, Oceanus,
That erstwhile issued from thy wat'ry loins,
And had my being from thy bubbling froth.
Triton, I know, hath fill'd his trump with Troy,　　130
And therefore will take pity on his toil,
And call both Thetis and Cymothoe
To succour him in this extremity.

　　　　108 eternish] make eternal　　　112 taint] stain

Enter Æneas, Ascanius, Achates, and others.

What, do I see my son now come on shore?
Venus, how art thou compass'd with content,
The while thine eyes attract their sought-for joys!
Great Jupiter, still honour'd may'st thou be
For this so friendly aid in time of need!
Here in this bush disguised will I stand,
Whiles my Æneas spends himself in plaints,   140
And heaven and earth with his unrest acquaints.

Æn. You sons of care, companions of my course,
Priam's misfortune follows us by sea,
And Helen's rape doth haunt ye at the heels.
How many dangers have we overpass'd!
Both barking Scylla, and the sounding rocks,
The Cyclops' shelves, and grim Ceraunia's seat,
Have you o'ergone, and yet remain alive.
Pluck up your hearts, since Fate still rests our friend,
And changing heavens may those good days return,
Which Pergama did vaunt in all her pride.   151

Ach. Brave prince of Troy, thou only art our god,
That by thy virtues free'st us from annoy,
And makes our hopes survive to coming joys:
Do thou but smile, and cloudy heaven will clear,
Whose night and day descendeth from thy brows:
Though we be now in extreme misery,
And rest the map of weather-beaten woe,
Yet shall the aged sun shed forth his hair,
To make us live unto our former heat,   160
And every beast the forest doth send forth
Bequeath her young ones to our scanted food.

Asc. Father, I faint; good father, give me meat.

Æn. Alas, sweet boy, thou must be still a while,
Till we have fire to dress the meat we kill'd.
Gentle Achates, reach the tinder box,
That we may make a fire to warm us with,
And roast our new-found victuals on this shore.

Ven. See what strange arts necessity finds out! 169

How near, my sweet Æneas, art thou driven! [*Aside.*

Æn. Hold; take this candle, and go light a fire;
You shall have leaves and windfall boughs enow,
Near to these woods, to roast your meat withal.
Ascanius, go and dry thy drenched limbs,
Whiles I with my Achates rove abroad,
To know what coast the wind hath driven us on,
Or whether men or beasts inhabit it.

                       [*Exeunt* Ascanius *and others.*

Ach. The air is pleasant, and the soil most fit
For cities' and society's supports;
Yet much I marvel that I cannot find   180
No steps of men imprinted in the earth.

Ven. Now is the time for me to play my part.—

                           [*Aside.*

Ho, young men! saw you, as you came,
Any of all my sisters wand'ring here,
Having a quiver girded to her side,
And clothed in a spotted leopard's skin?

Æn. I neither saw nor heard of any such.
But what may I, fair virgin, call your name,
Whose looks set forth no mortal form to view,
Nor speech bewrays aught human in thy birth?   190
Thou art a goddess that delud'st our eyes,
And shrouds thy beauty in this borrow'd shape;
But whether thou the Sun's bright sister be,
Or one of chaste Diana's fellow nymphs,
Live happy in the height of all content,
And lighten our extremes with this one boon,
As to instruct us under what good heaven
We breathe as now, and what this world is call'd
On which by tempests' fury we are cast:
Tell us, oh, tell us, that are ignorant,   200
And this right hand shall make thy altars crack
With mountain-heaps of milk-white sacrifice.

Ven. Such honour, stranger, do I not affect:
It is the use for Tyrian maids to wear
Their bow and quiver in this modest sort

And suit themselves in purple for the nonce,
That they may trip more lightly o'er the lawnds,
And overtake the tusked boar in chase.
But for the land whereof thou dost inquire,
It is the Punic kingdom, rich and strong,   210
Adjoining on Agenor's stately town,
The kingly seat of Southern Libya,
Whereas Sidonian Dido rules as queen.
But what are you that ask of me these things?
Whence may you come, or whither will you go?

Æn. Of Troy am I, Æneas is my name,
Who, driven by war from forth my native world,
Put sails to sea to seek out Italy;
And my divine descent from sceptred Jove:
With twice twelve Phrygian ships I ploughed the
And made that way my mother Venus led;   [deep,
But of them all scarce seven do anchor safe,
And they so wreck'd and welter'd by the waves,
As every tide tilts 'twixt their oaken sides;
And all of them, unburdened of their load,
Are ballassed with billows' wat'ry weight.
But hapless I, God wot, poor and unknown,
Do trace these Libyan deserts, all despis'd,
Exil'd forth Europe and wide Asia both,
And have not any coverture but heaven.   230

Ven. Fortune hath favour'd thee, whate'er thou be,
In sending thee unto this courteous coast.
A' God's name, on! and haste thee to the court,
Where Dido will receive ye with her smiles:
And for thy ships, which thou supposest lost,
Not one of them hath perish'd in the storm,
But are arrived safe, not far from hence:
And so I leave thee to thy fortune's lot,
Wishing good luck unto thy wandering steps.   [*Exit.*

Æn. Achates, 'tis my mother that is fled;   240
I know her by the movings of her feet.
Stay, gentle Venus, fly not from thy son!

207 lawnds] glades

Too cruel, why wilt thou forsake me thus,
Or in these shades deceiv'st mine eye so oft?
Why talk we not together hand in hand,
And tell our griefs in more familiar terms?
But thou art gone and leav'st me here alone
To dull the air with my discursive moan. [*Exeunt.*

Scene II.

Enter Iarbas, *followed by* Ilioneus, Cloanthus,
Sergestus, *and others.*

Ili. Follow, ye Trojans, follow this brave lord,
And plain to him the sum of your distress.

Iar. Why, what are you, or wherefore do you sue?

Ili. Wretches of Troy, envied of the winds,
That crave such favour at your honour's feet,
As poor distressed misery may plead:
Save, save, oh save our ships from cruel fire,
That do complain the wounds of thousand waves,
And spare our lives, whom every spite pursues.
We come not, we, to wrong your Libyan gods,   10
Or steal your household Lares from their shrines;
Our hands are not prepar'd to lawless spoil,
Nor armed to offend in any kind;
Such force is far from our unweaponed thoughts,
Whose fading weal, of victory forsook,
Forbids all hope to harbour near our hearts.

Iar. But tell me, Trojans, Trojans if you be,
Unto what fruitful quarters were ye bound,
Before that Boreas buckled with your sails?

Clo. There is a place, Hesperia term'd by us,   20
An ancient empire, famoused for arms,
And fertile in fair Ceres' furrowed wealth,
Which now we call Italia, of his name
That in such peace long time did rule the same.
Thither made we,
When, suddenly, gloomy Orion rose,
And led our ships into the shallow sands,

Whereas the southern wind, with brackish breath,
Dispers'd them all amongst the wreckful rocks:
From thence a few of us escap'd to land;   30
The rest, we fear, are folded in the floods.

 Iar. Brave men-at-arms, abandon fruitless fears,
Since Carthage knows to entertain distress.

 Serg. Ay, but the barbarous sort do threat our ships,
And will not let us lodge upon the sands;
In multitudes they swarm unto the shore,
And from the first earth interdict our feet.

 Iar. Myself will see they shall not trouble ye:
Your men and you shall banquet in our court,
And every Trojan be as welcome here   40
As Jupiter to silly Baucis' house.
Come in with me; I'll bring you to my queen,
Who shall confirm my words with further deeds.

 Serg. Thanks, gentle lord, for such unlook'd-for
  grace:
Might we but once more see Æneas' face,
Then would we hope to quite such friendly turns
As shall surpass the wonder of our speech.   [*Exeunt.*

Act II. Scene I.

Enter Æneas, Achates, Ascanius, and others.

 Æn. Where am I now? these should be Carthage
  walls.

 Ach. Why stands my sweet Æneas thus amaz'd?

 Æn. O my Achates, Theban Niobe,
Who for her sons' death wept out life and breath,
And, dry with grief, was turn'd into a stone,
Had not such passions in her head as I.
Methinks that town there should be Troy, yon Ida's
  hill,
There Xanthus' stream, because here's Priamus;
And when I know it is not, then I die.

 Ach. And in this humour is Achates too;   10
I cannot choose but fall upon my knees,

And kiss his hand. Oh, where is Hecuba?
Here she was wont to sit; but, saving air,
Is nothing here; and what is this but stone?

Æn. Oh, yet this stone doth make Æneas weep,
And would my prayers, as Pygmalion's did,
Could give it life, that under his conduct
We might sail back to Troy, and be reveng'd
On these hard-hearted Grecians, which rejoice
That nothing now is left of Priamus!   20
Oh, Priamus is left, and this is he!
Come, come aboard; pursue the hateful Greeks.

Ach. What means Æneas?

Æn. Achates, though mine eyes say this is stone,
Yet thinks my mind that this is Priamus:
And when my grieved heart sighs and says no,
Then would it leap out to give Priam life.
Oh, were I not at all, so thou mightst be!
Achates, see, King Priam wags his hand!
He is alive; Troy is not overcome!   30

Ach. Thy mind, Æneas, that would have it so,
Deludes thy eyesight; Priamus is dead.

Æn. Ah, Troy is sack'd, and Priamus is dead!
And why should poor Æneas be alive?

Asc. Sweet father, leave to weep, this is not he,
For, were it Priam, he would smile on me.

Ach. Æneas, see, here come the citizens:
Leave to lament, lest they laugh at our fears.

Enter Cloanthus, Sergestus, Ilioneus, *and others.*

Æn. Lords of this town, or whatsoever style
Belongs unto your name, vouchsafe of ruth   40
To tell us who inhabits this fair town,
What kind of people, and who governs them:
For we are strangers driven on this shore,
And scarcely know within what clime we are.

Ili. I hear Æneas' voice, but see him not,
For none of these can be our general.

Ach. Like Ilioneus speaks this nobleman,

But Ilioneus goes not in such robes.

   Serg. You are Achates, or I deceiv'd.

   Ach. Æneas, see, Sergestus, or his ghost!   50

   Ili. He names Æneas; let us kiss his feet.

   Clo. It is our captain; see, Ascanius!

   Serg. Live long Æneas and Ascanius!

   Æn. Achates, speak, for I am overjoyed.

   Ach. O Ilioneus, art thou yet alive?

   Ili. Blest be the time I see Achates' face!

   Clo. Why turns Æneas from his trusty friends?

   Æn. Sergestus, Ilioneus, and the rest,
Your sight amaz'd me. Oh, what destinies
Have brought my sweet companions in such plight?
Oh tell me, for I long to be resolv'd!   61

   Ili. Lovely Æneas, these are Carthage walls,
And here Queen Dido wears th' imperial crown,
Who for Troy's sake hath entertain'd us all,
And clad us in these wealthy robes we wear.
Oft hath she ask'd us under whom we serv'd,
And when we told her, she would weep for grief,
Thinking the sea had swallowed up thy ships;
And, now she sees thee, how will she rejoice!

   Serg. See, where her servitors pass through the hall
Bearing a banquet: Dido is not far.   71

   Ili. Look where she comes; Æneas, view her well.

   Æn. Well may I view her; but she sees not me.

Enter Dido, Anna, Iarbas, *and train.*

   Dido. What stranger art thou, that dost eye me
thus?

   Æn. Sometime I was a Trojan, mighty queen:
But Troy is not:—what shall I say I am?

   Ili. Renowned Dido, 'tis our general,
Warlike Æneas.

   Dido. Warlike Æneas, and in these base robes?
Go fetch the garment which Sichæus ware.   80

     [Exit an Attendant *who brings in the garment,
      which* Æneas *puts on.*

Brave prince, welcome to Carthage and to me,
Both happy that Æneas is our guest.
Sit in this chair, and banquet with a queen:
Æneas is Æneas, were he clad
In weeds as bad as ever Irus ware.

Æn. This is no seat for one that's comfortless:
May it please your grace to let Æneas wait;
For though my birth be great, my fortune's mean,
Too mean to be companion to a queen.

Dido. Thy fortune may be greater than thy birth:
Sit down, Æneas, sit in Dido's place,   91
And, if this be thy son, as I suppose,
Here let him sit.—Be merry, lovely child.

Æn. This place beseems me not; O pardon me!

Dido. I'll have it so; Æneas, be content.

Asc. Madam, you shall be my mother.

Dido. And so I will, sweet child.—Be merry, man:
Here's to thy better fortune and good stars. [*Drinks.*

Æn. In all humility, I thank your grace.

Dido. Remember who thou art; speak like thyself:
Humility belongs to common grooms.   101

Æn. And who so miserable as Æneas is?

Dido. Lies it in Dido's hands to make thee blest?
Then be assured thou art not miserable.

Æn. O Priamus, O Troy, O Hecuba!

Dido. May I entreat thee to discourse at large,
And truly too, how Troy was overcome?
For many tales go of that city's fall,
And scarcely do agree upon one point:
Some say Antenor did betray the town,   110
Others report 'twas Sinon's perjury,
But all in this, that Troy is overcome,
And Priam dead; yet how, we hear no news.

Æn. A woful tale bids Dido to unfold,
Whose memory, like pale Death's stony mace,
Beats forth my senses from this troubled soul,
And makes Æneas sink at Dido's feet.

Dido. What, faints Æneas to remember Troy,

In whose defence he fought so valiantly?
Look up, and speak.   120
    Æn. Then speak, Æneas, with Achilles' tongue:
And, Dido, and you Carthaginian peers,
Hear me; but yet with Myrmidon's harsh ears,
Daily inur'd to broils and massacres,
Lest you be mov'd too much with my sad tale.
The Grecian soldiers, tir'd with ten years' war,
Began to cry, 'Let us unto our ships,
Troy is invincible, why stay we here?'
With whose outcries Atrides being appall'd,
Summoned the captains to his princely tent,   130
Who, looking on the scars we Trojans gave,
Seeing the number of their men decreas'd,
And the remainder weak and out of heart,
Gave up their voices to dislodge the camp,
And so in troops all march'd to Tenedos:
Where when they came, Ulysses on the sand
Assay'd with honey words to turn them back;
And as he spoke to further his intent,
The winds did drive huge billows to the shore,
And heaven was darken'd with tempestuous clouds:
Then he alleg'd the gods would have them stay,   141
And prophesied Troy should be overcome:
And therewithal he call'd false Sinon forth,
A man compact of craft and perjury,
Whose ticing tongue was made of Hermes' pipe,
To force an hundred watchful eyes to sleep;
And him, Epeus having made the horse,
With sacrificing wreaths upon his head,
Ulysses sent to our unhappy town;
Who, grovelling in the mire of Xanthus' banks,   150
His hands bound at his back, and both his eyes
Turn'd up to heaven, as one resolv'd to die,
Our Phrygian shepherds haled within the gates,
And brought unto the court of Priamus;
To whom he used action so pitiful,
Looks so remorseful, vows so forcible,

As therewithal the old man overcome,
Kiss'd him, embrac'd him, and unloos'd his bands,
And then—O Dido, pardon me!

  Dido. Nay, leave not here; resolve me of the rest.

  Æn. Oh, th' enchanting words of that base slave 161
Made him to think Epeus' pine-tree horse
A sacrifice t' appease Minerva's wrath!
The rather, for that one Laocoon,
Breaking a spear upon his hollow breast,
Was with two winged serpents stung to death.
Whereat aghast, we were commanded straight
With reverence to draw it into Troy:
In which unhappy work was I employ'd;
These hands did help to hale it to the gates, 170
Through which it could not enter, 'twas so huge,—
Oh, had it never enter'd, Troy had stood!
But Priamus, impatient of delay,
Enforc'd a wide breach in that rampir'd wall
Which thousand battering-rams could never pierce,
And so came in this fatal instrument:
At whose accursed feet, as overjoyed,
We banqueted, till, overcome with wine,
Some surfeited, and others soundly slept.
Which Sinon viewing, caus'd the Greekish spies 180
To haste to Tenedos, and tell the camp:
Then he unlock'd the horse, and suddenly
From out his entrails, Neoptolemus,
Setting his spear upon the ground, leapt forth,
And after him a thousand Grecians more,
In whose stern faces shin'd the quenchless fire
That after burnt the pride of Asia.
By this, the camp was come unto the walls,
And through the breach did march into the streets,
Where, meeting with the rest, 'Kill, kill!' they cried.
Frighted with this confused noise, I rose, 191
And looking from a turret, might behold
Young infants swimming in their parents' blood,
Headless carcases piled up in heaps,

Virgins half-dead, dragged by their golden hair,
And with main force flung on a ring of pikes,
Old men with swords thrust through their aged sides,
Kneeling for mercy to a Greekish lad,
Who with steel pole-axes dash'd out their brains.
Then buckled I mine armour, drew my sword,   200
And thinking to go down, came Hector's ghost,
With ashy visage, blueish sulphur eyes,
His arms torn from his shoulders, and his breast
Furrow'd with wounds, and, that which made me weep,
Thongs at his heels, by which Achilles' horse
Drew him in triumph through the Greekish camp,
Burst from the earth, crying 'Æneas, fly,
Troy is a-fire, the Grecians have the town!'
  Dido. O Hector, who weeps not to hear thy name?
  Æn. Yet flung I forth, and desperate of my life
Ran in the thickest throngs, and with this sword   211
Sent many of their savage ghosts to hell.
At last came Pyrrhus, fell and full of ire,
His harness dropping blood, and on his spear
The mangled head of Priam's youngest son,
And after him his band of Myrmidons,
With balls of wild-fire in their murdering paws,
Which made the funeral flame that burnt fair Troy:
All which hemm'd me about, crying, 'This is he!'
  Dido. Ah, how could poor Æneas scape their hands?
  Æn. My mother Venus, jealous of my health,   221
Convey'd me from their crooked nets and bands;
So I escap'd the furious Pyrrhus' wrath:
Who then ran to the palace of the king,
And at Jove's altar finding Priamus,
About whose withered neck hung Hecuba,
Folding his hand in hers, and jointly both
Beating their breasts and falling on the ground,
He, with his falchion's point rais'd up at once,
And with Megæra's eyes, stared in their face,   230
Threat'ning a thousand deaths at every glance:
To whom the aged king thus trembling spoke;

'Achilles' son, remember what I was,
Father of fifty sons, but they are slain;
Lord of my fortune, but my fortune's turn'd;
King of this city, but my Troy is fired;
And now am neither father, lord, nor king:
Yet who so wretched but desires to live?
Oh, let me live, great Neoptolemus!'
Not mov'd at all, but smiling at his tears,   240
This butcher, whilst his hands were yet held up,
Treading upon his breast, struck off his hands.

    Dido. Oh, end, Æneas! I can hear no more.

    Æn. At which the frantic queen leap'd on his face,
And in his eyelids hanging by the nails,
A little while prolong'd her husband's life.
At last, the soldiers pull'd her by the heels,
And swung her howling in the empty air,
Which sent an echo to the wounded king:
Whereat he lifted up his bed-rid limbs,   250
And would have grappled with Achilles' son,
Forgetting both his want of strength and hands;
Which he, disdaining, whisk'd his sword about,
And with the wind thereof the king fell down:
Then from the navel to the throat at once
He ripp'd old Priam; at whose latter gasp
Jove's marble statue gan to bend the brow,
As loathing Pyrrhus for this wicked act.
Yet he, undaunted, took his father's flag,
And dipp'd it in the old king's chill cold blood, 260
And then in triumph ran into the streets,
Through which he could not pass for slaughter'd men;
So, leaning on his sword, he stood stone still,
Viewing the fire wherewith rich Ilion burnt.
By this, I got my father on my back,
This young boy in mine arms, and by the hand
Led fair Creusa, my beloved wife;
When thou, Achates, with thy sword mad'st way,
And we were round-environ'd with the Greeks:
Oh, there I lost my wife! and had not we   270

Fought manfully, I had not told this tale.
Yet manhood would not serve; of force we fled;
And as we went unto our ships, thou knowest
We saw Cassandra sprawling in the streets,
Whom Ajax ravish'd in Diana's fane,
Her cheeks swollen with sighs, her hair all rent,
Whom I took up to bear unto our ships;
But suddenly the Grecians followed us,
And I, alas, was forc'd to let her lie.
Then got we to our ships, and, being aboard,   280
Polyxena cried out, 'Æneas, stay,
The Greeks pursue me; stay, and take me in!'
Moved with her voice, I leap'd into the sea,
Thinking to bear her on my back aboard,
For all our ships were launch'd into the deep,
And, as I swom, she, standing on the shore,
Was by the cruel Myrmidons surpris'd
And after by that Pyrrhus sacrific'd.
    Dido. I die with melting ruth; Æneas, leave.
    Anna. Oh, what became of aged Hecuba?   290
    Iar. How got Æneas to the fleet again?
    Dido. But how scap'd Helen, she that caus'd this
        war?
    Æn. Achates, speak; sorrow hath tired me quite.
    Ach. What happened to the queen we cannot show,
We hear they led her captive into Greece:
As for Æneas, he swom quickly back;
And Helena betrayed Deiphobus,
Her lover, after Alexander died,
And so was reconcil'd to Menelaus.
    Dido. Oh, had that ticing strumpet ne'er been
        born!   300
Trojan, thy ruthful tale hath made me sad:
Come, let us think upon some pleasing sport,
To rid me from these melancholy thoughts.
            [*Exeunt all except* Ascanius, *whom* Venus, *entering
                with* Cupid *at another door, takes by the sleeve as
                he is going off.*

Ven. Fair child, stay thou with Dido's waiting maid:
I'll give thee sugar almonds, sweet conserves,
A silver girdle, and a golden purse,
And this young prince shall be thy playfellow.

Asc. Are you Queen Dido's son?

Cup. Ay; and my mother gave me this fine bow.

Asc. Shall I have such a quiver and a bow?   310

Ven. Such bow, such quiver, and such golden shafts,
Will Dido give to sweet Ascanius.
For Dido's sake I take thee in my arms,
And stick these spangled feathers in thy hat:
Eat comfits in mine arms, and I will sing.   [*Sings.*
Now is he fast asleep, and in this grove,
Amongst green brakes, I'll lay Ascanius,
And strew him with sweet-smelling violets,
Blushing roses, purple hyacinth:
These milk-white doves shall be his centronels,   320
Who, if that any seek to do him hurt,
Will quickly fly to Cytherea's fist.
Now, Cupid, turn thee to Ascanius' shape,
And go to Dido, who, instead of him,
Will set thee on her lap, and play with thee:
Then touch her white breast with this arrow head,
That she may dote upon Æneas' love,
And by that means repair his broken ships,
Victual his soldiers, give him wealthy gifts,
And he at last depart to Italy,   330
Or else in Carthage make his kingly throne.

Cup. I will, fair mother; and so play my part
As every touch shall wound Queen Dido's heart.
    [*Exit.*

Ven. Sleep, my sweet nephew, in these cooling shades,
Free from the murmur of these running streams,
The cry of beasts, the rattling of the winds,
Or whisking of these leaves: all shall be still,
And nothing interrupt thy quiet sleep,
Till I return, and take thee hence again.   [*Exit.*

Act III. Scene I.

Enter Cupid *as* Ascanius.

Cup. Now, Cupid, cause the Carthaginian queen
To be enamour'd of thy brother's looks;
Convey this golden arrow in thy sleeve,
Lest she imagine thou art Venus' son;
And when she strokes thee softly on the head,
Then shall I touch her breast and conquer her.

Enter Dido, Anna, *and* Iarbas.

Iar. How long, fair Dido, shall I pine for thee?
'Tis not enough that thou dost grant me love,
But that I may enjoy what I desire:
That love is childish which consists in words.   10
Dido. Iarbas, know that thou of all my wooers,—
And yet have I had many mightier kings,—
Hast had the greatest favours I could give.
I fear me, Dido hath been counted light
In being too familiar with Iarbas;
Albeit the gods do know no wanton thought
Had ever residence in Dido's breast.
Iar. But Dido is the favour I request.
Dido. Fear not, Iarbas; Dido may be thine.
Anna. Look, sister, how Æneas' little son   20
Plays with your garments and embraceth you.
Cup. No, Dido will not take me in her arms;
I shall not be her son, she loves me not.
Dido. Weep not, sweet boy; thou shalt be Dido's
     son,
Sit in my lap, and let me hear thee sing.
                                   [Cupid *sings.*
No more, my child; now talk another while,
And tell me where learn'st thou this pretty song.
Cup. My cousin Helen taught it me in Troy.
Dido. How lovely is Ascanius when he smiles!
Cup. Will Dido let me hang about her neck?   30

Dido. Ay, wag, and give thee leave to kiss her too.

Cup. What will you give me? Now I'll have this fan.

Dido. Take it, Ascanius, for thy father's sake.

Iar. Come, Dido, leave Ascanius; let us walk.

Dido. Go thou away; Ascanius shall stay.

Iar. Ungentle queen, is this thy love to me?

Dido. O stay, Iarbas, and I'll go with thee.

Cup. An if my mother go, I'll follow her.

Dido. Why stay'st thou here? thou art no love of mine.

Iar. Iarbas, die, seeing she abandons thee!   40

Dido. No, live, Iarbas: what hast thou deserv'd,
That I should say thou art no love of mine?
Something thou hast deserv'd.—Away, I say!
Depart from Carthage; come not in my sight.

Iar. Am I not king of rich Gætulia?

Dido. Iarbas, pardon me, and stay a while.

Cup. Mother, look here.

Dido. What tell'st thou me of rich Gætulia?
Am not I queen of Libya? then depart.

Iar. I go to feed the humour of my love,   50
Yet not from Carthage for a thousand worlds.

Dido. Iarbas!

Iar. Doth Dido call me back?

Dido. No, but I charge thee never look on me.

Iar. Then pull out both mine eyes, or let me die.
                                                    [*Exit.*

Anna. Wherefore doth Dido bid Iarbas go?

Dido. Because his loathsome sight offends mine eye,
And in my thoughts is shrin'd another love.
O Anna, didst thou know how sweet love were,
Full soon wouldst thou abjure this single life.   60

Anna. Poor soul, I know too well the sour of love:
Oh, that Iarbas could but fancy me!   [*Aside.*

Dido. Is not Æneas fair and beautiful?

Anna. Yes, and Iarbas foul and favourless.

Dido. Is he not eloquent in all his speech?

Anna. Yes, and Iarbas rude and rustical.

Dido. Name not Iarbas: but, sweet Anna, say,
Is not Æneas worthy Dido's love?

Anna. O sister, were you empress of the world,
Æneas well deserves to be your love! 70
So lovely is he, that where'er he goes,
The people swarm to gaze him in the face.

Dido. But tell them none shall gaze on him but I,
Lest their gross eye-beams taint my lover's cheeks.
Anna, good sister Anna, go for him,
Lest with these sweet thoughts I melt clean away.

Anna. Then, sister, you'll abjure Iarbas' love?

Dido. Yet must I hear that loathsome name again?
Run for Æneas, or I'll fly to him.   [*Exit* Anna.

Cup. You shall not hurt my father when he comes.

Dido. No, for thy sake I'll love thy father well.
O dull-conceited Dido, that till now
Didst never think Æneas beautiful!
But now, for quittance of this oversight,
I'll make me bracelets of his golden hair;
His glistening eyes shall be my looking-glass,
His lips an altar, where I'll offer up
As many kisses as the sea hath sands;
Instead of music I will hear him speak,
His looks shall be my only library; 90
And thou, Æneas, Dido's treasury,
In whose fair bosom I will lock more wealth
Than twenty thousand Indias can afford.
Oh, here he comes! Love, love, give Dido leave
To be more modest than her thoughts admit,
Lest I be made a wonder to the world.

Enter Æneas, Achates, Sergestus, Ilioneus, *and*
Cloanthus.

Achates, how doth Carthage please your lord?

Ach. That will Æneas show your majesty.

Dido. Æneas, art thou there?

Æn. I understand your highness sent for me. 100

Dido. No; but now thou art here, tell me, in sooth,

In what might Dido highly pleasure thee.

Æn. So much have I receiv'd at Dido's hands,
As, without blushing, I can ask no more:
Yet, queen of Afric, are my ships unrigg'd,
My sails all rent in sunder with the wind,
My oars broken, and my tackling lost,
Yea, all my navy split with rocks and shelves;
Nor stern nor anchor have our maimed fleet,
Our masts the furious winds struck overboard: 110
Which piteous wants if Dido will supply,
We will account her author of our lives.

Dido. Æneas, I'll repair thy Trojan ships,
Conditionally that thou wilt stay with me,
And let Achates sail to Italy:
I'll give thee tackling made of rivell'd gold,
Wound on the barks of odoriferous trees;
Oars of massy ivory, full of holes,
Through which the water shall delight to play;
Thy anchors shall be hewed from crystal rocks,   120
Which, if thou lose, shall shine above the waves;
The masts, whereon thy swelling sails shall hang,
Hollow pyramides of silver plate;
The sails of folded lawn, where shall be wrought
The wars of Troy, but not Troy's overthrow;
For ballass, empty Dido's treasury,
Take what ye will, but leave Æneas here.
Achates, thou shalt be so meanly clad,
As sea-born nymphs shall swarm about thy ships,
And wanton mermaids court thee with sweet songs,
Flinging in favours of more sovereign worth   131
Than Thetis hangs about Apollo's neck,
So that Æneas may but stay with me.

Æn. Wherefore would Dido have Æneas stay?

Dido. To war against my bordering enemies.
Æneas, think not Dido is in love;
For if that any man could conquer me,
I had been wedded ere Æneas came:

116 rivell'd] twisted

See, where the pictures of my suitors hang;
And are not these as fair as fair may be?   140
  Ach. I saw this man at Troy, ere Troy was sack'd.
  Serg. I this in Greece, when Paris stole fair Helen.
  Ili. This man and I were at Olympus' games.
  Serg. I know this face; he is a Persian born:
I travell'd with him to Ætolia.
  Cloan. And I in Athens with this gentleman,
Unless I be deceiv'd, disputed once.
  Dido. But speak, Æneas; know you none of these?
  Æn. No, madam; but it seems that these are kings.
  Dido. All these, and others which I never saw,   150
Have been most urgent suitors for my love;
Some came in person, others sent their legates,
Yet none obtain'd me: I am free from all;
And yet, God knows, entangled unto one.
This was an orator, and thought by words
To compass me, but yet he was deceiv'd:
And this a Spartan courtier, vain and wild,
But his fantastic humours pleas'd not me:
This was Alcion, a musician,
But, play'd he ne'er so sweet, I let him go: 160
This was the wealthy king of Thessaly,
But I had gold enough, and cast him off:
This, Meleager's son, a warlike prince,
But weapons gree not with my tender years:
The rest are such as all the world well knows,
Yet now I swear, by heaven and him I love,
I was as far from love as they from hate.
  Æn. Oh, happy shall he be whom Dido loves!
  Dido. Then never say that thou art miserable,
Because it may be thou shalt be my love: 170
Yet boast not of it, for I love thee not,—
And yet I hate thee not.—Oh, if I speak,
I shall betray myself! [*Aside*]—Æneas, speak:
We two will go a-hunting in the woods;
But not so much for thee,—thou art but one,—
As for Achates and his followers.   [*Exeunt.*

Scene II.

Enter Juno *to* Ascanius, *who lies asleep.*

Juno. Here lies my hate, Æneas' cursed brat,
The boy wherein false Destiny delights,
The heir of Fury, the favourite of the Fates,
That ugly imp that shall outwear my wrath,
And wrong my deity with high disgrace.
But I will take another order now,
And raze th' eternal register of Time:
Troy shall no more call him her second hope,
Nor Venus triumph in his tender youth;
For here, in spite of heaven, I'll murder him,   10
And feed infection with his let-out life.
Say, Paris, now shall Venus have the ball?
Say, vengeance, now shall her Ascanius die?
Oh, no! God wot, I cannot watch my time,
Nor quit good turns with double fee down-told!
Tut, I am simple, without mind to hurt,
And have no gall at all to grieve my foes.
But lustful Jove and his adulterous child
Shall find it written on confusion's front,
That only Juno rules in Rhamnus' town.   20

Enter Venus.

Ven. What should this mean? my doves are back
     return'd,
Who warn me of such danger prest at hand
To harm my sweet Ascanius' lovely life.
Juno, my mortal foe, what make you here?
Avaunt, old witch, and trouble not my wits.
Juno. Fie, Venus, that such causeless words of wrath
Should e'er defile so fair a mouth as thine!
Are not we both sprung of celestial race,
And banquet as two sisters with the gods?
Why is it then, displeasure should disjoin   30
Whom kindred and acquaintance co-unites?

22 prest] near

Ven. Out, hateful hag, thou wouldst have slain my son,
Had not my doves discover'd thy intent:
But I will tear thy eyes fro forth thy head,
And feast the birds with their blood-shotten balls,
If thou but lay thy fingers on my boy.

   Juno. Is this, then, all the thanks that I shall have
For saving him from snakes' and serpents' stings,
That would have kill'd him, sleeping as he lay?
What though I was offended with thy son,   40
And wrought him mickle woe on sea and land,
When, for the hate of Trojan Ganymede,
That was advanced by my Hebe's shame,
And Paris' judgment of the heavenly ball,
I muster'd all the winds unto his wreck,
And urg'd each element to his annoy?
Yet now I do repent me of his ruth,
And wish that I had never wrong'd him so.
Bootless, I saw, it was to war with fate
That hath so many unresisted friends: 50
Wherefore I change my counsel with the time,
And planted love where envy erst had sprung.

   Ven. Sister of Jove, if that thy love be such
As these thy protestations do paint forth,
We two, as friends, one fortune will divide:
Cupid shall lay his arrows in thy lap,
And to a sceptre change his golden shafts;
Fancy and modesty shall live as mates,
And thy fair peacocks by my pigeons perch:
Love my Æneas, and desire is thine;   60
The day, the night, my swans, my sweets, are thine.

   Juno. More than melodious are these words to me,
That overcloy my soul with their content:
Venus, sweet Venus, how may I deserve
Such amorous favours at thy beauteous hand?
But that thou mayst more easily perceive
How highly I do prize this amity,
Hark to a motion of eternal league,
Which I will make in quittance of thy love.

Thy son, thou knowest, with Dido now remains   70
And feeds his eyes with favours of her court;
She, likewise, in admiring spends her time,
And cannot talk nor think of aught but him;
Why should not they, then, join in marriage,
And bring forth mighty kings to Carthage town,
Whom casualty of sea hath made such friends?
And, Venus, let there be a match confirm'd
Betwixt these two, whose loves are so alike,
And both our deities, conjoin'd in one,
Shall chain felicity unto their throne.   80

Ven. Well could I like this reconcilement's means,
But much I fear, my son will ne'er consent,
Whose armed soul, already on the sea,
Darts forth her light to Lavinia's shore.

Juno. Fair queen of love, I will divorce these doubts,
And find the way to weary such fond thoughts.
This day they both a-hunting forth will ride
Into these woods adjoining to these walls;
When, in the midst of all their gamesome sports,
I'll make the clouds dissolve their wat'ry works,   90
And drench Silvanus' dwellings with their showers;
Then in one cave the queen and he shall meet,
And interchangeably discourse their thoughts,
Whose short conclusion will seal up their hearts
Unto the purpose which we now propound.

Ven. Sister, I see you savour of my wiles;
Be it as you will have it for this once.
Meantime Ascanius shall be my charge,
Whom I will bear to Ida in mine arms,
And couch him in Adonis' purple down.   [*Exeunt.*

Scene III.

Enter Dido, Æneas, Anna, Iarbas, Achates,
Cupid *as* Ascanius, *and* Followers.

Dido. Æneas, think not but I honour thee,
That thus in person go with thee to hunt:

My princely robes, thou see'st, are laid aside,
Whose glittering pomp Diana's shrouds supplies;
All fellows now, dispos'd alike to sport;
The woods are wide, and we have store of game:
Fair Trojan, hold my golden bow a while,
Until I gird my quiver to my side:
Lords, go before; we two must talk alone.

    Iar. Ungentle, can she wrong Iarbas so?   10
I'll die before a stranger have that grace.
'We two will talk alone'—what words be these? [*Aside.*

    Dido. What makes Iarbas here of all the rest?
We could have gone without your company.

    Æn. But love and duty led him on perhaps
To press beyond acceptance to your sight.

    Iar. Why, man of Troy, do I offend thine eyes?
Or art thou griev'd thy betters press so nigh?

    Dido. How now, Gætulian, are ye grown so brave,
To challenge us with your comparisons?   20
Peasant, go seek companions like thyself,
And meddle not with any that I love.
Æneas, be not mov'd at what he says,
For otherwhile he will be out of joint.

    Iar. Women may wrong by privilege of love;
But should that man of men, Dido except,
Have taunted me in these opprobrious terms,
I would have either drunk his dying blood,
Or else I would have given my life in gage.

    Dido. Huntsmen, why pitch you not your toils
apace,   30
And rouse the light-foot deer from forth their lair?

    Anna. Sister, see, see Ascanius in his pomp,
Bearing his hunt-spear bravely in his hand!

    Dido. Yea, little son, are you so forward now?

    Cup. Ay, mother; I shall one day be a man,
And better able unto other arms;
Meantime these wanton weapons serve my war,
Which I will break betwixt a lion's jaws.

    Dido. What, dar'st thou look a lion in the face?

Cup. Ay, and outface him too, do what he can. 40
Anna. How like his father speaketh he in all!
Æn. And mought I live to see him sack rich Thebes,
And load his spear with Grecian princes' heads,
Then would I wish me with Anchises' tomb,
And dead to honour that hath brought me up.
Iar. And might I live to see thee shipp'd away,
And hoist aloft on Neptune's hideous hills,
Then would I wish me in fair Dido's arms,
And dead to scorn that hath pursued me so. [*Aside.*
Æn. Stout friend Achates, dost thou know this
wood? 50
Ach. As I remember, here you shot the deer
That sav'd your famish'd soldiers' lives from death,
When first you set your foot upon the shore;
And here we met fair Venus, virgin-like,
Bearing her bow and quiver at her back.
Æn. Oh, how these irksome labours now delight,
And overjoy my thoughts with their escape!
Who would not undergo all kind of toil,
To be well stor'd with such a winter's tale?
Dido. Æneas, leave these dumps, and let's away,
Some to the mountains, some unto the soil, 61
You to the valleys, thou [*to Iarbas*] unto the house.
[*Exeunt all except Iarbas.*
Iar. Ay, this it is which wounds me to the death,
To see a Phrygian, far-fet o' the sea,
Preferr'd before a man of majesty.
O love! O hate! O cruel women's hearts,
That imitate the moon in every change,
And like the planets, ever love to range!
What shall I do, thus wronged with disdain?
Revenge me on Æneas or on her? 70
On her? fond man, that were to war 'gainst heaven,
And with one shaft provoke ten thousand darts.
This Trojan's end will be thy envy's aim,
Whose blood will reconcile thee to content,
And make love drunken with thy sweet desire.

But Dido, that now holdeth him so dear,
Will die with very tidings of his death:
But time will discontinue her content,
And mould her mind unto new fancy's shapes.
O God of heaven, turn the hand of Fate   80
Unto that happy day of my delight!
And then—what then? Iarbas shall but love:
So doth he now, though not with equal gain;
That resteth in the rival of thy pain,
Who ne'er will cease to soar till he be slain.   [*Exit.*

Scene IV.

The storm. Enter Æneas and Dido *in the cave,*
at several times.

Dido. Æneas!
Æn. Dido!
Dido. Tell me, dear love, how found you out this
     cave?
Æn. By chance, sweet queen, as Mars and Venus
     met.
Dido. Why, that was in a net, where we are loose;
And yet I am not free,—Oh, would I were!
Æn. Why, what is it that Dido may desire
And not obtain, be it in human power?
Dido. The thing that I will die before I ask,
And yet desire to have before I die.   10
Æn. It is not aught Æneas may achieve?
Dido. Æneas! no, although his eyes do pierce.
Æn. What, hath Iarbas anger'd her in aught?
And will she be avenged on his life?
Dido. Not anger'd me, except in ang'ring thee.
Æn. Who, then, of all so cruel may he be
That should detain thy eye in his defects?
Dido. The man that I do eye where'er I am,
Whose amorous face, like Pæan, sparkles fire,
Whenas he butts his beams on Flora's bed,   20
Prometheus hath put on Cupid's shape,

And I must perish in his burning arms:
Æneas, O Æneas, quench these flames!

Æn. What ails my queen? is she fall'n sick of late?

Dido. Not sick, my love; but sick I must conceal
The torment that it boots me not reveal:
And yet I'll speak, and yet I'll hold my peace.
Do shame her worst, I will disclose my grief:
Æneas, thou art he—what did I say?
Something it was that now I have forgot.   30

Æn. What means fair Dido by this doubtful speech?

Dido. Nay, nothing; but Æneas loves me not.

Æn. Æneas' thoughts dare not ascend so high
As Dido's heart, which monarchs might not scale.

Dido. It was because I saw no king like thee,
Whose golden crown might balance my content;
But now that I have found what to affect,
I follow one that loveth fame 'fore me,
And rather had seem fair to Sirens' eyes,
Than to the Carthage queen that dies for him.   40

Æn. If that your majesty can look so low
As my despised worths that shun all praise,
With this my hand I give to you my heart,
And vow, by all the gods of hospitality,
By heaven and earth, and my fair brother's bow,
By Paphos, Capys, and the purple sea
From whence my radiant mother did descend,
And by this sword that saved me from the Greeks,
Never to leave these new-upreared walls,
Whiles Dido lives and rules in Juno's town,   50
Never to like or love any but her!

Dido. What more than Delian music do I hear,
That calls my soul from forth his living seat
To move unto the measures of delight?
Kind clouds, that sent forth such a courteous storm
As made disdain to fly to fancy's lap!
Stout love, in mine arms make thy Italy,
Whose crown and kingdom rests at thy command:
Sichæus, not Æneas, be thou call'd;

The king of Carthage, not Anchises' son: 60
Hold, take these jewels at thy lover's hand,

             [Giving jewels, &c.

These golden bracelets, and this wedding-ring,
Wherewith my husband woo'd me yet a maid,
And be thou king of Libya by my gift.

             [Exeunt to the cave.

Act IV. Scene I.

Enter Achates, Cupid *as* Ascanius, Iarbas, *and* Anna.

   Ach. Did ever men see such a sudden storm,
Or day so clear so suddenly o'ercast?

   Iar. I think some fell enchantress dwelleth here,
That can call them forth whenas she please,
And dive into black tempests' treasury,
Whenas she means to mask the world with clouds.

   Anna. In all my life I never knew the like;
It hail'd, it snow'd, it lighten'd, all at once.

   Ach. I think it was the devil's revelling night,
There was such hurly-burly in the heavens: 10
Doubtless Apollo's axle-tree is crack'd,
Or aged Atlas' shoulder out of joint,
The motion was so over-violent.

   Iar. In all this coil, where have ye left the queen?

   Asc. Nay, where is my warlike father, can you tell?

   Anna. Behold where both of them come forth the
     cave.

   Iar. Come forth the cave! can heaven endure this
     sight?

Iarbas, curse that unrevenging Jove,
Whose flinty darts slept in Typhœus' den,
Whiles these adulterers surfeited with sin.   20
Nature, why mad'st me not some poisonous beast,
That with the sharpness of my edged sting
I might have stak'd them both unto the earth,
Whilst they were sporting in this darksome cave?

Enter, from the cave, Æneas and Dido.

Æn. The air is clear, and southern winds are whist.
Come, Dido, let us hasten to the town,
Since gloomy Æolus doth cease to frown.
  Dido. Achates and Ascanius, well met.
  Æn. Fair Anna, how escap'd you from the shower?
  Anna. As others did, by running to the wood.   30
  Dido. But where were you, Iarbas, all this while?
  Iar. Not with Æneas in the ugly cave.
  Dido. I see Æneas sticketh in your mind,
But I will soon put by that stumbling-block,
And quell those hopes that thus employ your cares.
                                            [*Exeunt.*

Scene II.

Enter Iarbas *to sacrifice.*

  Iar. Come, servants, come; bring forth the sacrifice,
That I may pacify that gloomy Jove,
Whose empty altars have enlarg'd our ills.
          [*Servants* bring in the sacrifice, and then exeunt.
Eternal Jove, great master of the clouds,
Father of gladness and all frolic thoughts,
That with thy gloomy hand corrects the heaven,
When airy creatures war amongst themselves:
Hear, hear, oh hear Iarbas' plaining prayers,
Whose hideous echoes make the welkin howl,
And all the woods Eliza to resound: 10
The woman that thou will'd us entertain,
Where, straying in our borders up and down,
She crav'd a hide of ground to build a town,
With whom we did divide both laws and land,
And all the fruits that plenty else sends forth,
Scorning our loves and royal marriage-rites,
Yields up her beauty to a stranger's bed;
Who, having wrought her shame, is straightway fled:
Now, if thou be'st a pitying god of power,
On whom ruth and compassion ever waits,   20

Redress these wrongs, and warn him to his ships,
That now afflicts me with his flattering eyes.

Enter Anna.

Anna. How now, Iarbas! at your prayers so hard?
Iar. Ay, Anna: is there aught you would with me?
Anna. Nay, no such weighty business of import,
But may be slack'd until another time:
Yet if you would partake with me the cause
Of this devotion that detaineth you,
I would be thankful for such courtesy.
Iar. Anna, against this Trojan do I pray,   30
Who seeks to rob me of thy sister's love,
And dive into her heart by coloured looks.
Anna. Alas, poor king, that labours so in vain
For her that so delighteth in thy pain!
Be rul'd by me, and seek some other love,
Whose yielding heart may yield thee more relief.
Iar. Mine eye is fix'd where fancy cannot start:
O leave me, leave me to my silent thoughts,
That register the numbers of my ruth,
And I will either move the thoughtless flint,   40
Or drop out both mine eyes in drizzling tears,
Before my sorrow's tide have any stint.
Anna. I will not leave Iarbas, whom I love,
In this delight of dying pensiveness.
Away with Dido! Anna be thy song;
Anna, that doth admire thee more than heaven.
Iar. I may nor will list to such loathsome change,
That intercepts the course of my desire.
Servants, come fetch these empty vessels here,
For I will fly from these alluring eyes,   50
That do pursue my peace where'er it goes.
[*Exit.*—Servants *re-enter, and carry out the vessels, etc.*
Anna. Iarbas, stay, loving Iarbas, stay!
For I have honey to present thee with.
Hard-hearted, wilt not deign to hear me speak?

    32 coloured] feigned   37 start] change

Q

I'll follow thee with outcries ne'ertheless,
And strew thy walks with my dishevell'd hair. [*Exit.*

Scene III.

Enter Æneas.

Æn. Carthage, my friendly host, adieu,
Since destiny doth call me from the shore:
Hermes this night, descending in a dream,
Hath summon'd me to fruitful Italy:
Jove wills it so; my mother wills it so;
Let my Phœnissa grant, and then I go.
Grant she or no, Æneas must away,
Whose golden fortunes, clogg'd with courtly ease,
Cannot ascend to Fame's immortal house,
Or banquet in bright Honour's burnish'd hall,   10
Till he hath furrowed Neptune's glassy fields,
And cut a passage through his topless hills.
Achates, come forth! Sergestus, Ilioneus,
Cloanthus, haste away! Æneas calls.

Enter Achates, Cloanthus, Sergestus, *and* Ilioneus.

Ach. What wills our lord, or wherefore did he call?
Æn. The dreams, brave mates, that did beset my
        bed,
When sleep but newly had embrac'd the night,
Commands me leave these unrenowned realms,
Whereas nobility abhors to stay,
And none but base Æneas will abide.   20
Aboard, aboard! since Fates do bid aboard,
And slice the sea with sable-coloured ships,
On whom the nimble winds may all day wait,
And follow them, as footmen, through the deep.
Yet Dido casts her eyes, like anchors, out,
To stay my fleet from loosing forth the bay:
'Come back, come back,' I hear her cry a-far,
'And let me link thy body to my lips,

That, tied together by the striving tongues,
We may, as one, sail into Italy.'   30

 Ach. Banish that ticing dame from forth your
  mouth,
And follow your foreseeing stars in all:
This is no life for men-at-arms to live,
Where dalliance doth consume a soldier's strength,
And wanton motions of alluring eyes
Effiminate our minds, inur'd to war.

 Ili. Why, let us build a city of our own,
And not stand lingering here for amorous looks.
Will Dido raise old Priam forth his grave,
And build the town again the Greeks did burn?   40
No, no; she cares not how we sink or swim,
So she may have Æneas in her arms.

 Clo. To Italy, sweet friends, to Italy,
We will not stay a minute longer here.

 Æn. Trojans, aboard, and I will follow you.
      [Exeunt all except Æneas.
I fain would go, yet beauty calls me back:
To leave her so, and not once say farewell,
Were to transgress against all laws of love.
But if I use such ceremonious thanks
As parting friends accustom on the shore,   50
Her silver arms will coll me round about,
And tears of pearl cry, 'Stay, Æneas, stay!'
Each word she says will then contain a crown,
And every speech be ended with a kiss:
I may not dure this female drudgery:
To sea, Æneas! find out Italy!   *[Exit.*

Scene IV.

Enter Dido *and* Anna.

 Dido. O Anna, run unto the water side,
They say Æneas' men are going aboard;
It may be, he will steal away with them:

Stay not to answer me, run, Anna, run! [*Exit* Anna.
O foolish Trojans, that would steal from hence,
And not let Dido understand their drift!
I would have given Achates store of gold,
And Ilioneus gum and Libyan spice;
The common soldiers rich embroidered coats,
And silver whistles to control the winds,   10
Which Circe sent Sichæus when he lived;
Unworthy are they of a queen's reward.
See where they come: how might I do to chide?

Re-enter Anna, *with* Æneas, Achates, Cloanthus,
Ilioneus, Sergestus, *and* Carthaginian Lords.

Anna. 'Twas time to run; Æneas had been gone;
The sails were hoising up, and he aboard.
Dido. Is this thy love to me?
Æn. O princely Dido, give me leave to speak!
I went to take my farewell of Achates.
Dido. How haps Achates bid me not farewell?
Acha. Because I fear'd your grace would keep me
here.   20
Dido. To rid thee of that doubt, aboard again:
I charge thee put to sea, and stay not here.
Ach. Then let Æneas go aboard with us.
Dido. Get you aboard; Æneas means to stay.
Æn. The sea is rough, the winds blow to the shore.
Dido. O false Æneas, now the sea is rough,
But when you were aboard, 'twas calm enough:
Thou and Achates meant to sail away.
Æn. Hath not the Carthage queen mine only son?
Thinks Dido I will go and leave him here?   30
Dido. Æneas, pardon me, for I forgot
That young Ascanius lay with me this night;
Love made me jealous, but to make amends,
Wear the imperial crown of Libya,
                              [*Giving him her crown and sceptre.*
Sway thou the Punic sceptre in my stead,
And punish me, Æneas, for this crime.

Æn. This kiss shall be fair Dido's punishment.

Dido. Oh, how a crown becomes Æneas' head!
Stay here, Æneas, and command as king.

Æn. How vain am I to wear this diadem,   40
And bear this golden sceptre in my hand!
A burgonet of steel, and not a crown,
A sword, and not a sceptre, fits Æneas.

Dido. Oh keep them still, and let me gaze my fill!
Now looks Æneas like immortal Jove:
Oh where is Ganymede, to hold his cup,
And Mercury, to fly for what he calls?
Ten thousand Cupids hover in the air,
And fan it in Æneas' lovely face!
Oh that the clouds were here wherein thou flee'st,   50
That thou and I unseen might sport ourselves!
Heaven, envious of our joys, is waxen pale,
And when we whisper, then the stars fall down,
To be partakers of our honey talk.

Æn. O Dido, patroness of all our lives,
When I leave thee, death be my punishment!
Swell, raging seas! frown, wayward Destinies!
Blow, winds! threaten, ye rocks and sandy shelves!
This is the harbour that Æneas seeks,
Let's see what tempests can annoy me now.   60

Dido. Not all the world can take thee from mine
        arms.
Æneas may command as many Moors
As in the sea are little water drops:
And now, to make experience of my love,
Fair sister Anna, lead my lover forth,
And, seated on my jennet, let him ride
As Dido's husband through the Punic streets;
And will my guard, with Mauritanian darts,
To wait upon him as their sovereign lord.

Anna. What if the citizens repine thereat?   70

Dido. Those that dislike what Dido gives in charge,
Command my guard to slay for their offence.
Shall vulgar peasants storm at what I do?

The ground is mine that gives them sustenance,
The air wherein they breathe, the water, fire,
All that they have, their lands, their goods, their lives,
And I, the goddess of all these, command
Æneas ride as Carthaginian king.

Ach. Æneas, for his parentage, deserves
As large a kingdom as is Libya.   80

Æn. Ay, and, unless the Destinies be false,
I shall be planted in as rich a land.

Dido. Speak of no other land; this land is thine;
Dido is thine, henceforth I'll call thee lord.—
Do as I bid thee, sister; lead the way;
And from a turret I'll behold my love.

Æn. Then here in me shall flourish Priam's race,
And thou and I, Achates, for revenge
For Troy, for Priam, for his fifty sons,
Our kinsmen's loves and thousand guiltless souls, 90
Will lead an host against the hateful Greeks,
And fire proud Lacedæmon o'er their heads.

    [*Exeunt all except* Dido *and* Carthaginian Lords.

Dido. Speaks not Æneas like a conqueror?
O blessed tempests that did drive him in!
O happy sand that made him run aground!
Henceforth you shall be our Carthage gods.
Ay, but it may be, he will leave my love,
And seek a foreign land call'd Italy:
Oh that I had a charm to keep the winds
Within the closure of a golden ball;   100
Or that the Tyrrhene sea were in mine arms,
That he might suffer shipwreck on my breast,
As oft as he attempts to hoist up sail!
I must prevent him; wishing will not serve.
Go bid my nurse take young Ascanius,
And bear him in the country to her house;
Æneas will not go without his son,
Yet, lest he should, for I am full of fear,
Bring me his oars, his tackling, and his sails.

    [*Exit* First Lord.

What if I sink his ships? Oh, he will frown! 110
Better he frown than I should die for grief.
I cannot see him frown; it may not be:
Armies of foes resolv'd to win this town,
Or impious traitors vow'd to have my life,
Affright me not; only Æneas' frown
Is that which terrifies poor Dido's heart:
Not bloody spears appearing in the air,
Presage the downfall of my empery,
Nor blazing comets threatens Dido's death;
It is Æneas' frown that ends my days. 120
If he forsake me not, I never die,
For in his looks I see eternity,
And he'll make me immortal with a kiss.

Re-enter First Lord, *with* Attendants *carrying*
tackling, etc.

First Lord. Your nurse is gone with young Ascanius,
And here's Æneas' tackling, oars, and sails.
Dido. Are these the sails that, in despite of me,
Pack'd with the winds to bear Æneas hence?
I'll hang ye in the chamber where I lie;
Drive, if you can, my house to Italy:
I'll set the casement open that the winds 130
May enter in and once again conspire
Against the life of me, poor Carthage queen:
But, though he go, he stays in Carthage still,
And let rich Carthage fleet upon the seas,
So I may have Æneas in mine arms.
Is this the wood that grew in Carthage plains,
And would be toiling in the wat'ry billows
To rob their mistress of her Trojan guest?
O cursed tree, hadst thou but wit or sense,
To measure how I prize Æneas' love, 140
Thou wouldst have leapt from out the sailors' hands,
And told me that Æneas meant to go!
And yet I blame thee not, thou art but wood.

127 Pack'd] conspired 134 fleet] float

The water, which our poets term a nymph,
Why did it suffer thee to touch her breast,
And shrunk not back, knowing my love was there?
The water is an element, no nymph.
Why should I blame Æneas for his flight?
O Dido, blame not him, but break his oars,
These were the instruments that launch'd him forth.
There's not so much as this base tackling too,   151
But dares to heap up sorrow to my heart:
Was it not you that hoised up these sails?
Why burst you not, and they fell in the seas?
For this will Dido tie ye full of knots,
And shear ye all asunder with her hands:
Now serve to chastise shipboys for their faults;
Ye shall no more offend the Carthage queen.
Now let him hang my favours on his masts,
And see if those will serve instead of sails;   160
For tackling, let him take the chains of gold
Which I bestow'd upon his followers;
Instead of oars, let him use his hands,
And swim to Italy. I'll keep these sure.
Come, bear them in.   [*Exeunt.*

Scene V.

Enter Nurse, *with* Cupid *as* Ascanius.

Nurse. My Lord Ascanius, ye must go with me.
Cup. Whither must I go? I'll stay with my mother.
Nurse. No, thou shalt go with me unto my house.
I have an orchard that hath store of plums,
Brown almonds, services, ripe figs, and dates,
Dewberries, apples, yellow oranges;
A garden where are bee-hives full of honey,
Musk-roses, and a thousand sort of flowers,
And in the midst doth run a silver stream,
Where thou shalt see the red-gill'd fishes leap,   10
White swans, and many lovely water-fowls.

5 services] pears

Now speak, Ascanius, will ye go or no?

  Cup. Come, come, I'll go. How far hence is your
    house?   [straight.

  Nurse. But hereby, child; we shall get thither

  Cup. Nurse, I am weary; will you carry me?

  Nurse. Ay, so you'll dwell with me, and call me
    mother.

  Cup. So you'll love me, I care not if I do.

  Nurse. That I might live to see this boy a man!

How prettily he laughs! Go, ye wag,

You'll be a twigger when you come to age.   20

Say Dido what she will, I am not old;

I'll be no more a widow; I am young;

I'll have a husband, or else a lover.

  Cup. A husband, and no teeth!   [thoughts?

  Nurse. Oh, what mean I to have such foolish

Foolish is love, a toy.—O sacred love!

If there be any heaven in earth, 'tis love,

Especially in women of your years.

Blush, blush for shame! why shouldst thou think of
    love?   30

A grave, and not a lover, fits thy age.

A grave, why? I may live a hundred years;

Fourscore is but a girl's age: love is sweet.

My veins are withered, and my sinews dry:

Why do I think of love, now I should die?

  Cup. Come, nurse.

  Nurse. Well, if he come a-wooing, he shall speed:

Oh, how unwise was I to say him nay!   [*Exeunt.*

Act V. Scene I.

*Enter Æneas, with a paper in his hand, drawing the platform
of the city; Achates, Sergestus, Cloanthus, and Ilioneus.*

  Æn. Triumph, my mates, our travels are at end;

Here will Æneas build a statelier Troy

V. i. heading *platform*] plan

Than that which grim Atrides overthrew.
Carthage shall vaunt her petty walls no more,
For I will grace them with a fairer frame,
And clad her in a crystal livery,
Wherein the day may evermore delight;
From golden India Ganges will I fetch,
Whose wealthy streams may wait upon her towers,
And triple-wise entrench her round about;   10
The sun from Egypt shall rich odours bring,
Wherewith his burning beams, like labouring bees
That load their thighs with Hybla's honey's spoils,
Shall here unburden their exhaled sweets,
And plant our pleasant suburbs with her fumes.

    Ach. What length or breadth shall this brave town
      contain?
    Æn. Not past four thousand paces at the most.
    Ili. But what shall it be call'd? Troy, as before?
    Æn. That have I not determin'd with myself.
    Clo. Let it be term'd Ænea, by your name.   20
    Serg. Rather Ascania, by your little son.
    Æn. Nay, I will have it call'd Anchisæon,
Of my old father's name.

Enter Hermes *with* Ascanius.

    Her. Æneas, stay; Jove's herald bids thee stay.
    Æn. Whom do I see? Jove's winged messenger!
Welcome to Carthage' new-erected town.
    Her. Why, cousin, stand you building cities here,
And beautifying the empire of this queen,
While Italy is clean out of thy mind?
Too too forgetful of thine own affairs,   30
Why wilt thou so betray thy son's good hap?
The king of gods sent me from highest heaven,
To sound this angry message in thine ears:
Vain man, what monarchy expect'st thou here?
Or with what thought sleep'st thou in Libya shore?
If that all glory hath forsaken thee,
And thou despise the praise of such attempts,

Yet think upon Ascanius' prophecy,
And young Iulus' more than thousand years,
Whom I have brought from Ida, where he slept, 40
And bore young Cupid unto Cyprus' isle.

Æn. This was my mother that beguil'd the queen,
And made me take my brother for my son:
No marvel, Dido, though thou be in love,
That daily dandlest Cupid in thy arms.
Welcome, sweet child: where hast thou been this
    long?

Asc. Eating sweet comfits with Queen Dido's maid,
Who ever since hath lull'd me in her arms.

Æn. Sergestus, bear him hence unto our ships,
Lest Dido, spying him, keep him for a pledge. 50
        [*Exit* Sergestus *with* Ascanius.

Her. Spend'st thou thy time about this little boy,
And givest not ear unto the charge I bring?
I tell thee thou must straight to Italy,
Or else abide the wrath of frowning Jove. [*Exit.*

Æn. How should I put into the raging deep,
Who have no sails nor tackling for my ships?
What, would the gods have me, Deucalion-like,
Float up and down where'er the billows drive?
Though she repair'd my fleet and gave me ships,
Yet hath she ta'en away my oars and masts, 60
And left me neither sail nor stern aboard.

Enter Iarbas.

Iar. How now, Æneas! sad! what means these
    dumps?

Æn. Iarbas, I am clean besides myself;
Jove hath heap'd on me such a desperate charge,
Which neither art nor reason may achieve,
Nor I devise by what means to contrive.

Iar. As how, I pray? may I entreat you tell?

Æn. With speed he bids me sail to Italy,
Whenas I want both rigging for my fleet,
And also furniture for these my men. 70

Iar. If that be all, then cheer thy drooping looks,
For I will furnish thee with such supplies.
Let some of those thy followers go with me,
And they shall have what thing soe'er thou need'st.

Æn. Thanks, good Iarbas, for thy friendly aid:
Achates and the rest shall wait on thee,
Whilst I rest thankful for this courtesy.

          [Exeunt all except Æneas.

Now will I haste unto Lavinian shore,
And raise a new foundation to old Troy.
Witness the gods, and witness heaven and earth,   80
How loth I am to leave these Libyan bounds,
But that eternal Jupiter commands!

      Enter Dido.

Dido. I fear I saw Æneas' little son
Led by Achates to the Trojan fleet.
If it be so, his father means to fly:—
But here he is; now, Dido, try thy wit.—   [*Aside.*
Æneas, wherefore go thy men aboard?
Why are thy ships new-rigg'd? or to what end,
Launch'd from the haven, lie they in the road?
Pardon me, though I ask; love makes me ask.   90

Æn. Oh, pardon me, if I resolve thee why!
Æneas will not feign with his dear love.
I must from hence: this day swift Mercury,
When I was laying a platform for these walls,
Sent from his father Jove, appear'd to me,
And in his name rebuk'd me bitterly
For lingering here, neglecting Italy.

Dido. But yet Æneas will not leave his love.

Æn. I am commanded by immortal Jove
To leave this town and pass to Italy;   100
And therefore must of force.

Dido. These words proceed not from Æneas' heart.

Æn. Not from my heart, for I can hardly go;
And yet I may not stay. Dido, farewell.

Dido. Farewell! is this the 'mends for Dido's love?

Do Trojans use to quit their lovers thus?
Fare well may Dido, so Æneas stay;
I die, if my Æneas say farewell.

 Æn. Then let me go, and never say farewell:

 Dido. 'Let me go; farewell, I must from hence.' 110
These words are poison to poor Dido's soul:
Oh, speak like my Æneas, like my love!
Why look'st thou toward the sea? the time hath been
When Dido's beauty chain'd thine eyes to her.
Am I less fair than when thou sawest me first?
Oh, then, Æneas, 'tis for grief of thee!
Say thou wilt stay in Carthage with thy queen,
And Dido's beauty will return again.
Æneas, say, how canst thou take thy leave?
Wilt thou kiss Dido? Oh, thy lips have sworn 120
To stay with Dido! canst thou take her hand?
Thy hand and mine have plighted mutual faith;
Therefore, unkind Æneas, must thou say,
'Then let me go, and never say farewell'?

 Æn. O queen of Carthage, wert thou ugly-black,
Æneas could not choose but hold thee dear!
Yet must he not gainsay the gods' behest.

 Dido. The gods! what gods be those that seek my
  death?
Wherein have I offended Jupiter,
That he should take Æneas from mine arms? 130
Oh no! the gods weigh not what lovers do:
It is Æneas calls Æneas hence,
And woful Dido, by these blubber'd cheeks,
By this right hand, and by our spousal rites,
Desires Æneas to remain with her;
Si bene quid de te merui, fuit aut tibi quidquam
Dulce meum, miserere domus labentis, et istam,
Oro, si quis adhuc precibus locus, exue mentem.

136–8 *Si . . . mentem*] If I have deserved well of you at all,
if anything of mine has been sweet to you, have pity on this
falling house, and put away your purpose, I entreat, if entreaty
may still be used.

Æn. *Desine meque tuis incendere teque querelis;*
Italiam non sponte sequor.   140

Dido. Hast thou forgot how many neighbour kings
Were up in arms, for making thee my love?
How Carthage did rebel, Iarbas storm,
And all the world calls me a second Helen,
For being entangled by a stranger's looks?
So thou wouldst prove as true as Paris did,
Would, as fair Troy was, Carthage might be sack'd,
And I be call'd a second Helena!
Had I son by thee, the grief were less,
That I might see Æneas in his face: 150
Now if thou go'st, what canst thou leave behind,
But rather will augment than ease my woe?

Æn. In vain, my love, thou spend'st thy fainting
      breath:
If words might move me, I were overcome.

Dido. And wilt thou not be mov'd with Dido's
      words?
Thy mother was no goddess, perjur'd man,
Nor Dardanus the author of thy stock;
But thou art sprung from Scythian Caucasus,
And tigers of Hyrcania gave thee suck.
Ah, foolish Dido, to forbear this long!   160
Wast thou not wreck'd upon this Libyan shore,
And cam'st to Dido like a fisher swain?
Repair'd not I thy ships, made thee a king,
And all thy needy followers noblemen?
O serpent, that came creeping from the shore,
And I for pity harbour'd in my bosom,
Wilt thou now slay me with thy venomed sting,
And hiss at Dido for preserving thee?
Go, go, and spare not; seek out Italy:
I hope that that which love forbids me do,   170
The rocks and sea-gulfs will perform at large,

139-40 *Desine . . . sequor*] Cease to set both yourself and me
on fire by lamentations; I do not follow after Italy of my own .
will.

And thou shalt perish in the billows' ways,
To whom poor Dido doth bequeath revenge:
Ay, traitor! and the waves shall cast thee up,
Where thou and false Achates first set foot;
Which if it chance, I'll give ye burial,
And weep upon your lifeless carcasses,
Though thou nor he will pity me a whit.
Why star'st thou in my face? If thou wilt stay,
Leap in mine arms; mine arms are open wide;   180
If not, turn from me, and I'll turn from thee;
For though thou hast the heart to say farewell,
I have not the power to stay thee.   [*Exit* Æneas.
                                    Is he gone?
Ay, but he'll come again; he cannot go;
He loves me too too well to serve me so:
Yet he that in my sight would not relent,
Will, being absent, be obdurate still.
By this is he got to the water-side;
And see, the sailors take him by the hand;
But he shrinks back; and now, rememb'ring me,   190
Returns amain: welcome, welcome, my love!
But where's Æneas? ah, he's gone, he's gone!

Enter Anna.

   Anna. What means my sister, thus to rave and cry?
   Dido. O Anna, my Æneas is aboard,
And leaving me, will sail to Italy!
Once didst thou go, and he came back again:
Now bring him back, and thou shalt be a queen,
And I will live a private life with him.
   Anna. Wicked Æneas!
   Dido. Call him not wicked, sister: speak him fair,
And look upon him with a mermaid's eye;   201
Tell him, I never vow'd at Aulis' gulf
The desolation of his native Troy,
Nor sent a thousand ships unto the walls,
Nor ever violated faith to him;
Request him gently, Anna, to return:

I crave but this, he stay a tide or two,
That I may learn to bear it patiently;
If he depart thus suddenly, I die.
Run, Anna, run; stay not to answer me. 210

Anna. I go, fair sister: heavens grant good success!
[*Exit.*

Enter Nurse.

Nurse. O Dido, your little son Ascanius
Is gone! he lay with me last night,
And in the morning he was stol'n from me:
I think some fairies have beguiled me.

Dido. O cursed hag and false dissembling wretch,
That slayest me with thy harsh and hellish tale!
Thou for some petty gift hast let him go,
And I am thus deluded of my boy.
Away with her to prison presently, 220

Enter Attendants.

Traitress too keend and cursed sorceress!

Nurse. I know not what you mean by treason, I;
I am as true as any one of yours.

Dido. Away with her! suffer her not to speak.
[*Exit Nurse with* Attendants.
My sister comes: I like not her sad looks.

Re-enter Anna.

Anna. Before I came, Æneas was aboard,
And, spying me, hoist up the sails amain;
But I cried out, 'Æneas, false Æneas, stay!'
Then gan he wag his hand, which, yet held up,
Made me suppose he would have heard me speak:
Then gan they drive into the ocean: 231
Which when I view'd, I cried, 'Æneas, stay!
Dido, fair Dido wills Æneas stay!'
Yet he, whose heart of adamant or flint,
My tears nor plaints could mollify a whit.
Then carelessly I rent my hair for grief,

221 keend] cruel

Which seen to all, though he beheld me not,
They gan to move him to redress my ruth,
And stay a while to hear what I could say;
But he, clapp'd under hatches, sail'd away.   240

    Dido. O Anna, Anna, I will follow him!
    Anna. How can ye go, when he hath all your fleet?
    Dido. I'll frame me wings of wax, like Icarus,
And o'er his ships will soar unto the sun,
That they may melt, and I fall in his arms;
Or else I'll make a prayer unto the waves,
That I may swim to him, like Triton's niece.
O Anna, fetch Arion's harp,
That I may tice a dolphin to the shore,
And ride upon his back unto my love!   250
Look, sister, look! lovely Æneas' ships!
See, see, the billows heave him up to heaven,
And now down falls the keels into the deep.
O sister, sister, take away the rocks,
They'll break his ships. O Proteus, Neptune, Jove,
Save, save Æneas, Dido's liefest love!
Now he is come on shore, safe without hurt:
But, see, Achates wills him put to sea,
And all the sailors merry make for joy;
But he, rememb'ring me, shrinks back again: 260
See, where he comes! welcome, welcome, my love!

    Anna. Ah, sister, leave these idle fantasies!
Sweet sister, cease; remember who you are.
    Dido. Dido I am, unless I be deceiv'd,
And must I rave thus for a runagate?
Must I make ships for him to sail away?
Nothing can bear me to him but a ship,
And he hath all my fleet. What shall I do,
But die in fury of this oversight?
Ay, I must be the murderer of myself: 270
No, but I am not; yet I will be, straight.   [*Aside.*
Anna, be glad; now have I found a mean
To rid me from these thoughts of lunacy:
Not far from hence

There is a woman famoused for arts,
Daughter unto the nymphs Hesperides,
Who will'd me sacrifice his ticing relics:
Go, Anna, bid my servants bring me fire.

> [*Exit* Anna.

Enter Iarbas.

Iar. How long will Dido mourn a stranger's flight
That hath dishonour'd her and Carthage both? 280
How long shall I with grief consume my days,
And reap no guerdon for my truest love?

Enter Attendants *with wood and torches.*

Dido. Iarbas, talk not of Æneas, let him go:
Lay to thy hands, and help me make a fire,
That shall consume all that this stranger left;
For I intend a private sacrifice,
To cure my mind, that melts for unkind love.
Iar. But, afterwards, will Dido grant me love?
Dido. Ay, ay, Iarbas; after this is done,
None in the world shall have my love but thou. 290

> [*They make a fire.*

So, leave me now; let none approach this place.

> [*Exeunt* Iarbas *and* Attendants.

Now, Dido, with these relics burn thyself,
And make Æneas famous through the world
For perjury and slaughter of a queen.
Here lie the sword that in the darksome cave
He drew, and swore by, to be true to me;
Thou shalt burn first; thy crime is worse than his.
Here lie the garment which I cloth'd him in
When first he came on shore: perish thou too.
These letters, lines, and perjur'd papers, all 300
Shall burn to cinders in this precious flame.
And now, ye gods, that guide the starry frame,
And order all things at your high dispose,
Grant, though the traitors land in Italy,
They may be still tormented with unrest;

And from mine ashes let a conqueror rise,
That may revenge this treason to a queen
By ploughing up his countries with the sword!
Betwixt this land and that be never league;
Litora litoribus contraria, fluctibus undas   310
Imprecor, arma armis; pugnent ipsique nepotes!
Live, false Æneas! truest Dido dies;
Sic, sic juvat ire sub umbras.

[*Throws herself into the flames.*

Re-enter Anna.

Anna. Oh help, Iarbas! Dido in these flames
Hath burnt herself! ay me, unhappy me!

Re-enter Iarbas, *running.*

Iar. Cursed Iarbas, die to expiate
The grief that tires upon thine inward soul!
Dido, I come to thee.—Ay me, Æneas!

[*Stabs himself, and dies.*

Anna. What can my tears or cries prevail me now?
Dido is dead, Iarbas slain, Iarbas my dear love!   320
O sweet Iarbas, Anna's sole delight!
What fatal Destiny envies me thus,
To see my sweet Iarbas slay himself?
But Anna now shall honour thee in death,
And mix her blood with thine; this shall I do,
That gods and men may pity this my death,
And rue our ends, senseless of life or breath:
Now, sweet Iarbas, stay! I come to thee.

[*Stabs herself, and dies.*

310–11 *Litora . . . nepotes!*] I invoke coast against coast, waves
against waves, weapons against weapons; may they and their
children's children be at war!
313 *Sic . . . umbras*] Thus, **thus**, it rejoices me to die!

SET IN
GREAT BRITAIN
AT THE
UNIVERSITY PRESS
OXFORD
AND PRINTED BY
THE GARDEN CITY PRESS LTD.
LETCHWORTH